The Christian's Guide To Harry Potter

Leslie Barnhart

This guide is not endorsed or supported by J.K. Rowling, her affiliates, or Warner Brothers Entertainment, Inc. Harry Potter is a registered trademark of Warner Brothers Entertainment. This guide is not affiliated in any way with Warner Brothers or J.K. Rowling.

ISBN: 1477575081
ISBN-13: 978-1477575086

DEDICATION

I dedicate this book to all of my readers. May this book enlighten you to new possibilities and encourage you on your own journey.

CONTENTS

	Acknowledgments	i
1	The Harry Potter Crucible	1
2	Harry Potter "Magic" vs. Secular Magic	13
3	The Characters and their Christian Alchemy	31
4	The Guide to *HP and The Philosopher's Stone*	61
5	The Guide to *HP and The Chamber of Secrets*	92
6	The Guide to *HP and The Prisoner of Azkaban*	118
7	The Guide to *HP and The Goblet of Fire*	141
8	The Guide to *HP and The Order of the Phoenix*	177
9	The Guide to *HP and The Half-Blood Prince*	216
10	The Guide to *HP and the Deathly Hallows*	253
	Appendix: Misunderstood Christianity	330
	Works Cited	344

ACKNOWLEDGMENTS

I would like to thank Greg, Katheryn and Matthew for their support and patience through this project. My gratitude to Marjorie for her proofreading and corrections throughout the project, without which I would have missed some of the more subtle differences within Christianity. Lastly, I would like to thank Lisa, John Granger, and the countless others at Holy Comforter who encouraged me to write my own book about the connections between Harry Potter, Alchemy, and Christianity.

Chapter ONE

The Harry Potter Crucible*

In 1997, J. K. Rowling's first book, *Harry Potter and the Philosopher's Stone*, went out to the public and the debate began – is it a work of Satanic or Christian fiction? As a mother of pre-schoolers at the time, I was worried about what I saw – young children putting jinxes on each other and other mean things, and I told my children they may never read the books.

However, in 2009, my son asked me for permission to read the first book, and I agreed as long as I could read it with him so I could show him why Christians shouldn't read it. After reading the entire series over ten days, I was surprised that rather than finding arguments against the series, I was inspired by the small glimpse of Christian elements that I saw through the resurrection at the end of the story. I was inspired to find other elements that might create a valuable experiential Christian Summer Camp based on the series. In an effort to find other Christian elements, I discovered first the works of John Granger from which I learned about the basics of alchemy and the Christian tenets he discovered, then the myriad of authors who have already defended Ms. Rowling's work as Christian (for my own defense of Ms. Rowling's Christian opus, see the Appendix). With that basis, I continued my search for other pieces I could use or modify for younger students, and the more I searched the more I discovered that the Harry Potter series seemed to be a modern day Pilgrim's Progress that incorporated not only allegorical Christian elements but also historical, traditional, and Biblical Christian elements that helped deepen my faith in Christ and God from a Christian perspective.

I have often been asked whether Ms. Rowling intended for all of these intricate details when she planned the storyline. A second question that quickly follows is why she hasn't come right out and told everyone what she meant by writing the story. To these questions, there are answers both within the storyline and in her interviews. In *Deathly Hallows,* Hermione discusses the purpose of a quest with Harry, and asks why Professor Dumbledore didn't give them more explicit instructions for what he meant them to do. Harry replies that there are some things that you just have to discover for yourself, and Hermione reiterates by stating that there are clues for us to follow and find things out for ourselves (Chapter 20 "Xenophilius Lovegood"). This same question has been asked within Christianity – why didn't Jesus give us more details rather than a vague "Go out and make disciples, baptizing in the name of the Father, Son, and Holy Spirit?" (Matthew 28:19) From this discussion between Harry and Hermione, we see that Ms. Rowling feels she has given us plenty of clues and left it to us to discover them for ourselves.

In her interviews, Ms. Rowling admits that she purposely didn't give away too many pieces before the last book was out because she felt that admitting a Christian premise would give away the ending.[1] Beyond the fact that not giving a black and white explanation of what was intended or not allows for more discussion of the material, what was intended or not really has no bearing on what exists in the story. If someone discovers something within the work that was not intended,

---

[1] Adler, Shawn, 2007, "J.K. Rowling Opens Up about Books' Christian Imagery," retrieved from http://www.mtv.com/news/articles/1572107/jk-rowling-talks-about-christian-imagery.jhtml.

does it change its existence or meaning? Many books after they are written take on a life of their own, going far beyond the author's original intent so that the original intent becomes trivial.

Knowing that the quest exists, it still helps to have a map or at least a flashlight showing the general direction of a clue to discover new things. There are many websites, blogs, and books out about Harry Potter covering a variety of different topics from the alchemy within it to the literary aspects and structures to more spiritual pieces, each a worthy opus on its own. For myself, I saw how incorporating the Christian pieces I found within her work into an experiential Christian medium for younger students turned not only the students' hearts to God, but also the adults' that came to help bring the concepts of Hogwarts alive. Not to deny anyone else their own quest, I now offer the pieces that I discovered throughout the series here in this literary analysis, where they are laid out book by book, chapter by chapter, in the order created by Ms. Rowling so as to shed a bit of light on your own quest and help you find your own path toward God.

My Main Premises to Understanding the Harry Potter Series

Before I get into the details for each book in the Harry Potter series in chapters four through ten, let me set the stage for the interpretations I have offered here about Harry Potter. For the overall scheme of the series, there are some undercurrents that help pull the series together and help give some structure to the storyline. Without these, the stories could almost stand alone with no connections to each other, much like other many sequential books written by the same author. I have found that in trying to explain the details of each book to someone who's just finished the story and not understood any of the Christianity within it, I often get confused looks and admissions that they did not read the book with any intent to read beyond the black and white plot. However, once they understood the overall framework of the series, each story then took on additional meaning, and the small details found a purpose rather than produce clutter. Whether you have already read the series completely or partially, I hope that this framework gives you both a glimpse of Ms. Rowling's mastery as well as a desire to reread the series as an illuminated reader.

First and foremost, I see the series as a modern day *Pilgrim's Progress*, in which we follow Harry Potter through his discovery of his inclusion into a faithful community, his enlightenment and faithful training, and his development of a relationship with Dumbledore while constantly fighting off the everyday temptations and evil intended to take him off of his faithful journey's path. Just as the original *Pilgrim's Progress* used symbolism and allegory to depict the pilgrim's perilous journey, the Harry Potter series seems to contain these same elements throughout the series beginning with a coming to faith and ending with the triumph over death.

As part of the *Pilgrim's Progress* allegory, I also see Ms. Rowling's story as an allegorical parallel of Christians in a secular society reminiscent of the early Christian years. Primarily, the wizarding world has had to go into hiding so that the muggles, or non-magical folk, do not persecute them for their strange ways just as the early Christians were constantly on alert for being discovered, and the multiple persecutions during the early centuries of the Roman Empire. The wizards wear robes rather than the normal pants or skirts worn in England, and have a much more vibrant choice of colors than the typical shades of grey found in most downtown areas. Next, because they have magic, the wizards have no need for technology, and most of their world seems stuck in the 1700s: no electricity, cars, TVs, or modern communication systems. Rather, the wizarding world uses candles, travels through fireplaces or disapparates (disappear from their current location to reappear somewhere else) to where they want to go, and uses owls to deliver their mail. Nowadays, anytime a person goes to an old church, they might feel as if they had travelled back in time, a feeling similar to what people might feel when they enter into the magical community. Many other similarities will come forward as we go through the books, but this gives you an idea of how similar the modern wizarding world depicted here is to the Early Christian world.

Although I will go into more details about the magic element in the next chapter, the magic within the Harry Potter world is very much akin to the "magic" we see throughout the Bible, through God and His people. For those people in the Bible who did not have a personal relationship with God, the events that occur in the Bible could easily appear to be magic. Those who pray in full faith that God will answer their prayers seem to have a connection to a supernatural power that could easily be construed as magical when what they pray for occurs. For others with faith in God, this is easily explained and understood from the verse in Luke: "If you have faith as small as a mustard seed, you can say to this mulberry tree, 'Be uprooted and planted in the sea,' and it will obey you." (Luke 17:6, NIV). However, for others, this activity could be considered suspicious. For some reason, we seem to be happier believing that people really do not have any power or ability through God, and people have generally downplayed any answered prayers they've said for fear that others might look at them askance or think dark powers might be at work. Even Jesus was suspected of using dark forces after he removed evil spirits from a man (Matthew 12:22-24). Throughout this series, we see actual faith in practice in the magical world, just as the Early Christians practiced their faith, healing others and accomplishing feats otherwise impossible.

Another curiosity I noticed as I read about J.K. Rowling was how similar her self-declared faith walk followed Harry Potter's family situation. Although raised in England where most citizens are members of the Church of England, she did not go to church until she was about twelve.[2] Her discovery of who God was on a personal level most likely led to her feelings of not connecting with her immediate family that

---

[2] Klimek, D, 2010, Ministry Values, "J.K. Rowling: "I believe in God, not Magic" and the Unknown Faith of the Famous," retrieved from http://ministryvalues.com/index.php?option=com_content&task =view&id=1203&Itemid=318.

continued not to have a faith, and possibly her later estrangement with her father, much as Harry's connection to the magical world is not tolerated by the aunt and uncle that he lives with, the Dursleys. (For more details, see Chapter 4).[3] Her concept of true faith seems to show itself through the wands as well. In her series, the wand chooses the wizard, and wizards are born, not made, possibly indicating that true faith is an unavoidable direction in life. Through these similarities, we again see a parallel between the magical world and Christianity, a world in which non-believers persecute believers for their belief, echoing the past.

One last tenant I propose that helps us understand the parallels that exist within the series is the concept of the Great Shepherd. Ultimately, Hogwarts is the place of Christian formation and education, but more than that, it is the sheepfold for God's sheep. In this connection, the Biblical gatekeeper is also the one who helps collect lost sheep, and this role is clearly held by Rubeus Hagrid, the Gameskeeper of Hogwarts who goes to the apparent "ends of the earth" to collect Harry from the muggles who are trying to keep him away from his proper place. In juxtaposition to the Great Shepherd, Albus Dumbledore's brother, Aberforth, tends the goats, referring to the scripture from Matthew about the separation of the sheep and the goats (Matthew 25: 31-46) and reinforcing the concept of sheep existing at Hogwarts. Lastly, Albus Dumbledore, as the Headmaster at Hogwarts, is then the Great Shepherd who takes care of his sheep.

As the Great Shepherd, Albus Dumbledore represents the Christ figure that takes care of God's sheep, protecting them from all harm through all means possible, and ultimately giving his life for his sheep. Although Ms. Rowling has told the masses that she did not create Albus Dumbledore to be the Christ figure,[4] in the following chapters I will

---

[3] Rowling, J, Mugglenet, "J.K. Rowling Q&A," retrieved from http://www.mugglenet.com/jkr-royalalbert.shtml.

[4] Granger, J, 2009, *Hogwarts Professor*, "Dumbledore a Christ Figure in Half-Blood Prince?," retrieved from http://www.hogwartsprofessor.com/is-

present the various pieces throughout the series that create the argument that he must be the Christ figure. For the main points, however, his initials AD hint at the phrase "anno domini", Latin for "the year of our Lord", he is the great teacher who knows more than others even at a young age, his symbol is the Phoenix, a symbol of resurrection (and Christ), and he actively collects friends who agree to work with him against evil just as Christ did. Although it might not have been intentional, there are too many indications to the contrary to not allow for Albus Dumbledore to be the Christ figure in the series.

Re-forging a New Element from Alchemy and Christian Thought

J. K. Rowling's brilliant story and allegory doesn't end with the story line. Most of her unforgettable characters play a secondary role in some way, especially in the alchemical domain. In traditional alchemy, an alchemist uses a base metal, usually lead, and through various chemical reactions with the four physical elements of earth, water, air, then fire, transforms the lead into a type of gold called the "Philosopher's Stone." Through the physical transformation, the alchemist experiences a spiritual transformation as well, as he first undergoes renunciation of anything un-pure in his life (black stage), then undergoes illumination where he learns everything about the different elements and how they work together, and finally undergoes purification/ unification, the red stage, in which his soul pulls together in a new, purer form that is ready for the final stage toward immortality (for details about alchemy there are many websites, but www.alcehmylab.com has a dictionary for terms that is helpful).

There are three types of transformations that occur overall in alchemy. In the first conquest, the alchemist has to show mastery over the four base elements (earth, water, air, and fire in that order), by using each element in turn to transform the base metal into gold as it reacts to each one. In the second set of processes, during each

---

dumbledore-a-christ-figure-in-half-blood-prince/.

element's reactions with lead, the alchemist also bathes the lead in sulfur and mercury. Sulfur and mercury are both dangerous individually, but when working together, they tend to cancel out the other's dangerous effects. Third, as the lead reacts with the four elements and the sulfur and mercury, the lead has three stages noted by the color of the lead: 1) black (nigredo, or renunciation), white (albedo, or illumination), and red (rubedo, or reunification/ purification). After all of these processes are completed, the "Philosopher's Stone" can produce the Elixir of Life, a red substance which will give the drinker eternal life. It is a difficult process that takes perseverance, and many alchemists become philosophers and accept their own natural death before completing the philosopher's stone.

Although interesting, the alchemy did not grab my attention until I was listening to a gospel reading in church from the book of John. The reading was about how Nicodemus, a member of the Sanhedrin, came in the night to meet with Jesus and ask him how he might achieve eternal life. Jesus answered him that he would need to be born again, a statement which confused Nicodemus because he had already been born of his mother once, so he walked away. Afterwards, Jesus explained that a person needs to be born of water in order to be saved. The word "water" reminded me of the four physical elements of Alchemy, and I began my search in John for other references to alchemical elements. Remembering that the numbers 1, 3, and 7, the colors red, white, and black, and the four elements were important, I began to see these pieces as parts of alchemy in John's gospel. Not only is our creation in a womb our "birth through earth", but the other Christian rites all have connections to the physical elements as well: baptism represents a renewing/ birth through water, confirmation represents a renewal/ birth through air (which is combined with spirit, breath, and time in the Hebrew word *ruah)*, and our renewal birth through fire comes at the end of our lives as the chaff is burned from our lives when we enter heaven (Matthew 3:12). More searching led me to other alchemy sites, where I learned that the proper order for alchemical mastery was earth, water, air, and finally fire[5] – the exact same order that the Christians used for their progression through their sacramental rites.

Once I began to see how Christianity had hidden alchemy within it, I began to see these new applications within the Harry Potter series. From a purely alchemical perspective, the first book is about Harry mastering earth, as he battles first the troll then Professor Quirrell/ Lord Voldemort to prevent their obtaining the Philosopher's Stone to give them eternal life. In the second book, we see Harry and his friends master water (by creating the Polyjuice Potion), and Harry masters his Parseltongue (his ability to speak to snakes) to defeat the monster of the water, the basilisk. If someone is fluent in a language, then they are "fluid" in that language, meaning their use of the language flows like water over their tongue.

In *Prisoner of Azkaban,* we see the next progression of mastery – air, in all of its interpretations: air, spirit, and time. On his path to mastering air, we see Harry master riding the Hippogriff, gain a new broomstick that is faster than all others (the Firebolt), learns about animagi, people who can transfigure themselves into animals, masters the Expecto Patronus charm which allows him to defeat the dementors, and he and Hermione use time to defeat both the dementors and rescue Sirius and the hippogriff, Buckbeak. In the fourth book, *Goblet of Fire*, Harry "masters" fire by winning the Triwizard Tournament which is governed by the goblet of fire. Up until now, Harry has only had to master physical elements.

The fifth book brings together two different alchemical aspects – the fifth element, the astral plane, and the first stage of transformation – the black stage. In this fifth book, *The Order of the Phoenix,* we see Harry mastering the difference between dreams and reality, while he feels separated from everything he knows and loves. Once Harry learns the difference between the dreams he's been sent from Lord Voldemort

[5] Miller, S, 2008, "Master Thesis: Spirit Alchemy," Retrieved from http://elements.spiritalchemy.com/t3-Ch3.html.

and reality, he is reunited to Albus Dumbledore, the headmaster at Hogwarts, and everything he holds dear. *Harry Potter and the Half-Blood Prince* works through Harry's white stage of illumination where he learns many things about Lord Voldemort, his eternal enemy. Finally, *Deathly Hallows* concludes the series with the red stage, where Harry and his friends "purify" Lord Voldemort's soul by eliminating the pieces he left hidden around the wizarding world and reuniting the magical world in the final Battle of Hogwarts. In its conclusion, Harry shows his alchemical transformation to gold by returning from the dead to destroy Lord Voldemort.

This sequential mastery of the elements and stages of transformation within the Harry Potter series also seem to carry a Christian parallel to the seven weeks between Ash Wednesday and Easter. *Philosopher's Stone* is about Harry mastering earth, and the first readings of Lent (Ash Wednesday) are about the ashes God used to create Adam. Harry, as the pilgrim in *Pilgrim's Progress* similarly discovers that he was created to be part of a community with a relationship with an "unknown power", the invisible force and power of God. In *Chamber of Secrets* we see Harry mastering water, and the second readings from Lent bring in Noah's mastery of water and a new covenant with God. At the end of *Chamber of Secrets*, Harry renews his relationship with Dumbledore who confirms his mastery of water. The third readings of Lent are about Abraham and God's covenant with him about the future, an intangible element of air. Similarly, Harry masters air in the third book, *Prisoner of Azkaban*, forging a new understanding of the future and the elements within air after his discussion with Dumbledore at the end of the story where Harry learns more about how the decisions made that year might have repercussions in the future. Lent's fourth set of readings revolve around Moses, who was introduced to God through the burning bush, forming a convenient through fire. Harry in *Goblet of Fire* also similarly renewed through fire by conquering the Goblet of Fire, the instrument that called him into the tournament against great odds and against his mortal enemy, Lord Voldemort. After defeating Lord Voldemort, Harry and Dumbledore's subsequent discussion helps Harry sort out what has happened, and establishes Harry's mastery of the final physical element, fire.

On a more spiritual level, the three remaining weeks of Lent point to a more spiritual transformation within the church and the books. The fifth set of readings in Lent are from the time of the Israelites' exile, a time in which they felt separated from God, and similarly Harry is separated from Dumbledore throughout the book. At the end of *Order of the Phoenix*, Harry and Professor Dumbledore are reunited, just as the Israelites return to Israel after time.

As the sixth book opens, we see Dumbledore and Harry depicted as "the chosen one", and their titles fully restored as the wizarding community looks to them to lead them into battle against Lord Voldemort. However, the book ends with the death of Albus Dumbledore while Harry watches, unable to help. Similarly, the sixth week of Lent is Palm Sunday, in which the liturgical churches celebrate first the triumphant entry of Jesus into Jerusalem, as if he were the leader for the revolt against Rome. However, shortly thereafter in the service, the readings begin the Passion of Christ, ending with his death and laying into the tomb (exactly the ending in *Half-Blood Prince*, Chapter 30: "The White Tomb").

The seventh week, which concludes the seven weeks of readings is Easter, in which Christians celebrate the fact that Christ rose from the dead and that through their belief in Christ, they share in that resurrection at least spiritually. In *Deathly Hallows*, Harry seems to die, but being the Pilgrim, representing the everyday Christian on the faithful journey, he is "resurrected" after meeting with Dumbledore. Also, just as the Early Christians allowed other races to join them in their faith in Christ and the eternal life beyond, the wizards join together with the other magical creatures in their mutual fight against Lord Voldemort and his forces of evil.

By using the two elements — alchemy and Christian thought —Ms. Rowling seems to have created two reflective pieces that merge into one new element I would call "Christian Alchemy". In more recent centuries, science and Christianity have dueled each other for the proper explanation of how things occur in nature, scientists wanting answers from the physical realm alone, and Christian or religious leaders allowing for answers from the spiritual realm. However, alchemy historically had both physical and spiritual aspects to it, which seem to have separated during the Scientific Revolution.

Ms. Rowling, writing the series, seems to have recombined the physical elements of alchemy with the spiritual elements of Christianity. Like the alchemists of the past, the physical aspects push forward new ideas and connections that reach out towards the spiritual aspects and the spiritual aspects lead us to new understandings of God and Christ. This new understanding leads us to a deeper understanding of the Christian faith's Biblical and traditional foundations, and a renewal in our own faith and relationship with Christ.

Conclusions

In no way is the Harry Potter series a substitute for the Bible, but as a story of a pilgrim on his journey towards eternal life, it contains many references to Biblical events, historical elements of early Christianity, and examples of Christian service from mind, body, and soul. John Granger pointed out that Harry, Ron, and Hermione form the Christian trio – the body, will, and mind of Christ,[6] and from their actions, we see many modern day applications of how to be the body of Christ, the will of Christ, and the mind of Christ. Harry is always foregoing the rules to save someone from harm, Hermione is always using her knowledge to help others get past obstacles, and Ron is the emotional one that holds people together. As you read the rest of this book, you will find the alchemical and Biblical representations of many of the characters in chapter three: "Christian Alchemy", and the historical references, theological concepts, and Biblical verses that support the storyline in

---

[6] Charlton, B, 2011, "Heart, Mind and Body - Harry, Hermione and Ron," retrieved from http://charltonteaching.blogspot.com/2011/03/heart-mind-and-body-harry-hermione-and.html.

the remaining chapters. My hope is that you find a new depth to your relationship with God, and a renewal of your faith in God and His people.

Chapter TWO

Harry Potter "Magic" vs. Secular Magic

What is Magic?

One of the biggest concerns for Christians who think about Harry Potter is J.K. Rowling's use of magic. For the largest part of the argument, God clearly forbids using magic in the Bible through the first and third commandments which are explained in more detail in other books of the Bible: "Thou shall have no other god before me... thou shall not bow down or serve any other gods." (Exodus 20: 3, 5, KJV). Using magic conveys the concept that God is not sufficient for our needs and thus we require another "god" to give us what we want, which is in direct violation of these commandments. Secondly, since most of sorcery and witchcraft relies on the individual power of the sorcerer or witch as well as spirits from another realm to do their bidding, those who practice these things are also guilty of trying to become gods themselves. Furthermore, the practice of conjuring the spirits from those already deceased is not only defined in the Bible as being offensive to God (Leviticus 20:6 — And the person who turns after mediums and familiar spirits ("***wizards***" — ASV, KJV), to prostitute himself with them, I will set My face against that person and cut him off from his people. (NKJV)), but also puts the sorcerers and magicians into a deity position by trying to reverse the natural order of life, something reserved for God Himself. Lastly, since sorcerers and magicians attempt to create the illusion that they themselves are making events happen with their own power, they are guilty of turning others away from God to worship themselves as the source, as seen in the book of Exodus when Moses challenged the priests of their temples (Exodus 7:11,22; 8:7). For all these reasons, Christians and Jews rightly forbid the use of magic in their communities.

Understandably, since J.K. Rowling's characters are mostly "magical" – wizards, witches, giants, and fairies - and the first book was published differently in the United States to include the words "Sorcerer's Stone" versus "Philosopher's Stone", this series would seem to be an obvious example of the magic that God does not want us to use. Let us take a look at how others have viewed the followers of God or Christ historically, where we have examples of people performing miracles who were then martyred for having supposed magical powers. Martyrs, such as Saints Perpetua and Felicitas, were feared by their jailers for their "powers", since all of their prayers were answered, they seemed to be able to control the events around them, and they didn't fear death.[7] Furthermore, throughout the Bible we have demonstrations of challenges to determine which god is the true God through displays of apparent magic, such as Moses' competition with the Pharaoh's priests of the temple (Exodus 7:8-11) or Elijah's challenge to the priests of Baal to see whose god would burn a sacrifice (1 Kings 18:22-39). For someone outside the Christian or Judaic faith, it might be difficult to see the difference between these acts that Christians and Jews have performed in the name of God and those claimed by sorcerers or witches since both have apparent results not easily explained by natural events.

For an atheist, "miracles" attributed to God could easily have been the result of another causal element yet unknown. Atheists will claim that

---

[7] Mursurillo, H, Frontline, Apr 28, 1998, "The Martyrdom of Saints Perpetua and Felicitas," Retrieved from http://www.pbs.org/wgbh/pages/frontline/shows/religion/maps/primary/perpetua.html on 10 November 2011.

throughout history, people have tended to suggest God as the cause of anything we just cannot explain yet, such as the rising of the sun, the emergence of new deadly bacteria or plague, or the sudden disappearance of a species. As time moves on, we are able to explain more about how things occur scientifically which takes much of the mystery out of how God created the world and universe even without the creation versus evolution debate. Through science, we now know that the earth is round, revolving around the sun in the middle of the Milky Way Galaxy in one part of the universe. As we identify every part of the skies around us, we have moved from the definite idea that heaven was directly above the earth and hell directly below it to the mystery of where heaven and hell might be. With the knowledge that there is no place for heaven to exist, we could conclude that it must not exist. These types of challenges to the monotheistic traditions require a new spiritual approach in evangelism and faith instruction that does not abandon God's power and mystery and still connects to others meaningfully to capture their hearts and imaginations for God, a challenge J.K. Rowling heartily accepted and attempted through her story of Harry Potter.

From the Bible, we see historical records of various tribes of people who each worship different deities, all claiming that their deity was responsible for whatever supernatural event had occurred. Many times, the god that the people followed was not a matter of faith or belief, but rather what was told to them by the ruler of the time – those who did not worship the ruler's god were usually put to death. With this attitude of the fly-by-night deities explaining the various events in their lives, it is no wonder that many came to see God as just another magical force that controlled events, an idea that still holds true today. If many outsiders believe that God is an element used to explain everything we cannot explain scientifically, how do we help these same people understand that God does exist, and also explain the difference between the one True God and the false gods? In the Old Testament, the prophet Elijah summoned the prophets of Baal (a universal name given to the multiple false gods of Canaan) to a challenge in the first book of Kings, Chapter 18. The first group to have their god rain down fire and consume the raw meat of a sacrificial bull would be declared the new God of Israel. Elijah won, but for the fickle hearted Israelites of the time, it was always a matter of which set of prophets provided them what they needed – only a few stayed true to God regardless of what happened to them. With their unsure hearts, it is easy to see how sorcerers and magicians demonstrating false or evil powers were able to gain a foothold in their communities, making the challenge to show who the one true God is that much more difficult even today. This fickleness of character and willingness of the masses to follow power rather than love is a key theme within the Harry Potter series, as many characters are drawn to the powerful (but evil) Lord Voldemort and many of them desert Harry despite his purity of intent and purpose.

Unfortunately, although Elijah demonstrated God's supernatural power, many who were constantly subjected to such demonstrations of power might have easily attributed it to magic or sorcery. In the New Testament, Peter and John ran into this misperception of who God is and His Power when they ran into Simon the Magician in Samaria who was performing "evil magic" (Acts 8:9-25). Simon is convinced that the Holy Spirit is something a great magician could conjure, just as they might conjure any other spirit from another world and asks the two apostles for this knowledge, thinking it is a more powerful form of sorcery. The magical element for Simon is that the Holy Spirit is a spirit that does not turn evil upon entering this world, but leads its followers into good works. This was the true miracle that Simon saw and the knowledge he wished to possess. Despite Simon's inclusion in the Christian community for a time, Simon still did not truly understand who God was, because Simon still saw the apostles just as other men with conjuring abilities. He never quite understood the love of God or the indwelling of the Holy Spirit as anything but an illusion and earthly power despite all the demonstrations of God's power. In this same way, J. K. Rowling has presented a new insight about the nature of God, but many people have missed her purpose. Many only see the story as an interesting litany of magical spells when it really demonstrates the supernatural power of God as a magical quality.

To end this discussion about whether or not J.K. Rowling uses the magic condemned by the Bible, we turn to the evidence throughout the Bible itself. It is people's experience of God that helps people remember who God is, not just knowledge of God's existence. From a Christian viewpoint, it is extremely important that their hearts are also warmed by the Holy Spirit and their paths illuminated by Christ to accompany that knowledge of God. As we see with Simon the sorcerer, knowledge alone does not help someone understand God's majesty, mystery, power, and love. These personal experiences must be with the presence of the one true God, and not with any other false deity. In general, any emotional experience will override any physical knowledge they have, and false experiences can lead them to committing other acts that lead them further away from God.

The disciples discussed this very topic with Jesus when others were abolishing demons in Jesus' name although they weren't part of their disciple group. Jesus answers in Mark 9:40 that "anyone who is not against us is for us." Wasn't Jesus himself accused of being a head demon when He drove the demons out of a man into a heard of swine and then off a cliff? The Pharisees were convinced that only a devil could control other demonic spirits, but Jesus was able to demonstrate his own power over all things, regardless of their source (Matthew 12: 22-28).

Overall, when analyzing any work around us that uses "magic", we have to determine three things: 1) whether they are purposely leading us away from the one true God, 2) whether the characters are acting as gods themselves, and 3) whether they are acting against God or His people. If the answer is in the negative to all of these statements, then perhaps the group is working for God. This difference defines the distinction between the lies within witchcraft and sorcery, and the "magic" found within Harry Potter. Whereas witchcraft and sorcery attempt to take people away from the one true God, the "magic" found within Harry Potter is the Christian "Magic" of resurrection, sacrificial love for others, and a loving community.

What is Sorcery and Wizardry?

When it comes to literature, the one universal truth is that although each author creates a new world, each book still seems to abide by the internal logic that generally rules that genre. For instance, in the world of fairy tales, regardless of where the princess is, everyone knows that the princess will be in danger from an unsuspecting person, and is then rescued by her true love. There may be multiple variations on that theme, but if the theme changes too much, then it ceases to be a fairly tale. Likewise, magic and fantasy books have their own themes and rules that define that genre. These books tend to focus on how a young person obtains his/her magical abilities, the nature of a quest, the magical creatures that assist the magician/sorcerer on his/her quest, and how the magic is used, channeled, or sourced. Most fantasy books deny any references to a one true God and describe worlds devoid of morals or true consequence. However, Christian writers such as C. S. Lewis, J.R.R Tolkien, and J.K. Rowling have used the magical realm symbolically to represent the Christian themes, much in the way that stories used to be taught through stained glass windows. Although these Christian writers do use fantastical creatures and the element of magic exists, the overall question remains, is their purpose to draw people to God or take them away from God? Answering the three questions defined above, we can determine J.K. Rowling's purpose and affect on her audience: 1) J.K. Rowling has stated multiple times that she is not trying to lead anyone away from God, and Wicca, A modern Pagan religion with spiritual roots in the earliest expressions of reverence for nature,[8] has stated to the press that none of their followers have come to them because they read the series; 2) none of the characters are acting as God Himself, as a creator or judge of the universe; and 3) none of the characters within the Harry Potter series act out against God, Christ, or anyone that follows Christian values.

---

[8] "Definition of Wicca, Pagan, and Witchcraft," *The Celtic Connection,* n.d., retrieved 4 Jun 2012, http://wicca.com/celtic/wicca/definitions.htm.

"Well, that's all fine and good, but is there really a difference between this Christian Magic and witchcraft and sorcery?" you might ask. Good question! In response, I offer five generalities that we find in the secular fantasy/ magic books and their counters in J.K. Rowling's Harry Potter series: 1) the use of spells versus incantations; 2) the languages used by the magicians or wizards; 3) the source of the person's strength; 4) the determination of worthiness of being part of that world; and 5) the use of symbols throughout the rituals or story. Each of these differences might seem slight at first, but each difference points to a separate conclusion, making their purposes significant.

Secular Fantasy Magic Rule 1: In secular fantasies, the spells used by the magician or sorcerer seem to be always part of a poem, said in rhyme, or used to call on other spirits to perform the action. Such actions are definitely in violation of the first and third commandments, since the actions make the user equal to a god with creator and judgment abilities. However, in the Harry Potter world, Ms. Rowling gives a definite opinion of traditional witches' spells through Hermione in the first book, *Harry Potter and the Philosopher's Stone*: Ron says a rhyming spell to turn his rat yellow, and it doesn't work at all. Conversely, Hermione uses a simple, single Latin word and is able to correct Harry's broken glasses without any problem (*Harry Potter and the Philosopher's Stone,* Chapter 6: "The Journey from Platform 9 ¾, p. 105). Furthermore, throughout the stories, spells that involve more than one or two words and take on the secular magical flow of verse are consistently bungled, as in Seamus' attempts the turn his water into rum or other such spells ("Harry Potter and the Sorcerer's Stone" movie only). Also, since Christians are not trying to capture spirits or bring evil into the world, there is no need for complicated binding.spells – a single word or two and a pure intent are all that is needed for doing the work of God. Lastly, John Granger (author of *Finding God in Harry Potter)* distinguishes the two types of "magic" by calling Harry Potter's magic "incantational," meaning that it sings with God's design, and calling the secular magical world "invocational" magic,[9]

[9] Granger, J, 2008, *How Harry Cast His Spell*, p. 6.

since it usually involves calling on other spirits to do the wizard's bidding. Secondly, since God is the designer of the universe, God is the singer and his creations only sing parts of the overall song, not entire songs themselves. In this view, the use of only one word is more in keeping with God's more masterful musical work. By using much longer complicated verse, the sorcerers have tried to control the power of creation themselves, not acknowledging that there is a higher power. Within this difference, we see a subtler but significant distinction between these two elements – by using long verses in obsolete languages and invoking other spirits, the secular fantasies create the illusion that they do not need God, and have substituted other elements or themselves for God. In Harry Potter, it is faith in God and the proper use and direction of one's faith (through the wand) that brings about transformational change in the world around them.

Secular Fantasy Magic Rule 2: The languages used in the fantasy world always seem to be either very ancient languages (pretending to be elfin, dwarfish, or some other race's language) or obscure modern languages with complicated grammar rules. Part of the process of becoming a sorcerer is mastering the language, a demonstration of ability by itself since the languages' complicated grammar and multiple word meanings will easily lead lesser people to destroy themselves. To further the competition between sorcerers, in most fantasy tales the power of the sorcerer is limited by his vocabulary – the more descriptive the vocabulary, the more binding the spell they cast. Hence, in order to create binding spells, these secular magicians use long, complicated verses to ensure that they have covered every conceivable understanding and make themselves very clear in their purpose. This is especially important when invoking other spirits, since spirits do not like to be controlled, and thus they fight the binding spell every which way they can. J.K. Rowling distinctly uses the rhymes found in witchcraft to show that they are truly worthless in the "Magical" world of Christianity through the examples of Ron's rat-turning-yellow failure and Hermione's 1-Latin-word success. The success of the spells or charms spoken in the Harry Potter series is due to the fact that the language is Latin - the age-old language of the Church that infuses the power of God within its words. The simplicity of the Latin grammar and the fact that it is well known also demonstrate Ms. Rowling's conviction that God is tangible to everyone – anyone can use Latin words well, and as Christ said "If you have faith as small as a mustard seed, you can say to this mulberry tree, 'Be uprooted and planted in the sea,' and it will obey you." (Luke 17:6, NIV). With faith, the characters in Harry Potter eventually are even able to do spells with their thoughts without saying anything, as long as they have faith and a pure intent. J.K. Rowling uses this clear difference between the accessibility of the languages and the complex use of the languages to show how Latin itself, as the language of the Church, a true arm of God, is very powerful and thus does not need many words to clarify its meaning.

Secular Fantasy Magic Rule 3: The source of the spell's strength and power depends upon the total energy available to the magician or sorcerer, which includes the strength of the magician's mind and body as well as the living energy of any surrounding life forms (animals, plants, and sometimes earth). For instance, in another young adult magic series by Christopher Paolini, the main character, Eragon, has to train for many months to develop his physical and mental prowess in order to increase the magical abilities he has and be able to connect with the energy offered by the surrounding environment. In most of the fantasy literature, using magic without knowing your limits can result in death, since the magic uses your own energy until the magic is finished. In other secular magical books, the magician must always be very careful that the spirit he conjures is not stronger than he is. Otherwise, the conjured spirit might overtake him, making the magician no longer a true master of himself. Conversely, in the Harry Potter stories, the magic used has nothing to do with the physical or mental prowess of the wizard. Rather, the source of the power in J.K Rowling's wizards is from the wand, not the wizard him- or herself. Ms. Rowling makes a point of this throughout the series: Harry discovers that his wand can do things he doesn't even know how to do as if the wand could think for itself (*Harry Potter and the Deathly Hallows,* Chapter 4 "The Seven Potters"), and although there are many wizards who only have a faint glimmer of magical ability, they are still considered an equal part of the wizarding community.

Contrary to secular magic's power being from the sorcerer's total energies, the characters within Harry Potter's world understand that their wands are the only source of the magic's power. The wizards in Harry Potter are forbidden to use their own internal magic once they obtain their wands, hinting that although they are blessed with the ability to channel magic, they defer their abilities to that of the wand. In Christian terms, we can infer that the wand represents the power of God from John 15:5, which tells us "I am the vine, you are the branches." These are Jesus' words to his disciples that explain to them how they are a continuation of his ministry to the world. In J.K. Rowling's wizarding world, the wand is a branch of the vine of Christ, infused with the power of God. Just as Christians who pray to God for healing are not in any way drained physically in fulfilling the request since the source of healing is from God Himself. Similarly, the wizards in Harry Potter's world are not physically drained in any way when they use their wands. Furthermore, Harry understands that it is the wand alone that is responsible for saving his life many times and gives credit to his wand for these acts, just as God protects His people without their asking. Most notably, in his encounter with Lord Voldemort in the graveyard, Harry's wand connects with Lord Voldemort's wand, resulting in magic no one knew of and allowing Harry to escape. In another instance, while Harry and his friends attempt an escape from the Dursley's house in *Deathly Hallows,* Harry's wand turned in his hand and performed unknown magic against Lord Voldemort without any conscious effort on Harry's part. Also, there is no indication anywhere in the series that the power comes from anything but the wands – the wands symbolize everything. On a more theological point, Ollivander, the wand maker, explains to Harry in their first encounter that the wand chooses the wizard, just as God chooses us to do His work. Once the wand chooses the wizard it will work with, the wizard then works with the wand and other wizards to further his instruction and live his life according to magical standards. In the same way, once we are chosen by God, we work with other Christians to do His bidding, becoming a channel of His design and live according to Christian standards. Lastly, in Christianity, Christians do not claim any part of the actual healing or miracles they are near - it is always God who acts – and the healing does not depend on the strength of the Christian's mind, body, or environment – just faith. Again, J.K. Rowling has used the background of magic more as an analogy to the power of God than as a guidebook for magical instruction.

Secular Fantasy Magic Rule 4: The magician or sorcerer must show that he/she is worthy of being a magical person or be identified as worthy in some way by an outsider before being allowed to achieve status as a sorcerer. In the secular fantasy stories, the sorcerer or magician must undergo many trials to prove his/her worth, usually involving at least one dangerous task of enslaving a black magic object or spirit. By showing their strength and willingness to forego all morality and dependence on their fellow man, the sorcerer or magician is dubbed "worthy" to continue with their training. This willingness to betray, injure, or kill others with impunity leads them on a path towards believing themselves to be a deity of their own making. In many plots, the magician at some point in training has a stirring of conscience, which sets the scene for the conflict in the series. There is usually a moral point by the end of the tale as the trainee realizes that he cannot forego all his morality to continue down the dark path of magic. Unfortunately, secular magicians are either part of the group or not, there isn't a half-way, so the result of quitting the pursuit is death.

On the other hand, within the Harry Potter series, one's magical worth is not determined by one's inherent power or what abilities he or she can prove to a superior magician. These wizards within the Harry Potter series are born not made, just as we are born into a Christian family. As such, being born into a wizarding family or showing any trace of magic at all (if the parents aren't magical) is enough to grant that wizard entrance into Hogwarts. Just as God writes us into His Book of Life as soon as we are His, the wizards' names in the series are written in the admissions book for Hogwarts as soon as they are born. Even if a wizard turns out to not have magical qualities, the wizard is still invited to Hogwarts although the parents tend not to send their child to save him or her the embarrassment and help him or her learn the muggle life.[10] In direct contrast to the secular fantasies, none of the wizards ever have to pass a test to get into Hogwarts - anyone with any inkling of magical ability or hope may attend, just as God accepts all that turn their lives to Him. Lastly, just as God gave us free will to decide whether to follow Him or not, not every wizard has to go to a school to learn how to be a wizard, but many do, and without any threat of any retaliation or impending doom.

Secular Fantasy Magic Rule 5: Secular magicians and sorcerers use symbols and ritual to control other spirits or confine magical power. Usually within the secular fantasy text, the sorcerers or magicians of the story draw mathematical symbols (pentagrams, triangles, or circles) in combination with fire in some fashion, and then stand in a special place to say or read a complicated verse to create the magic or conjure the spirit into the confines of the designated space. If there is any opening in the circle, triangle, or pentagram, then the spirit conjured can be released into the world and is not bound to the conjurer. (Incidentally, this was the beginnings of mathematics in Egypt – trying to determine the angles and such to create these binding shapes for the spirits and gods that they worshipped.) Thankfully, this is not the case in Harry Potter. There are no written symbols involved with their "spells" or used anywhere to assist in magical acts. Rather, the animals and objects are themselves representational symbols of ideas. For instance, Albus Dumbledore's phoenix, Fawkes, is the symbol for Christ and resurrection. Harry Potter's patronus (a type of mist that protects the wizard against evil) is a Stag, another symbol of Christ. Other symbols found within the text are as follows: the wands represent the power of God; the Invisibility Cloak represents the Holy Spirit; the owls represent the wisdom of God; Hagrid represents the Gatekeeper of Christ's sheepfold; and Harry Potter represents the everyday man in search of Christ. In many ways, J.K.

---

[10] Rowling, J., 2007, *Harry Potter and the Deathly Hallows*, Chapter 8.

Rowling's work is a modern *Pilgrim's Progress* – it represents the common Christian in search of truth, and tells the story of his trials and challenges along the way to a meeting with Christ Himself in heaven, and nowhere in the Harry Potter series do symbols try to contain or confine magic or spirits as they do in secular witchcraft and sorcery. Through the representational symbolism, J.K. Rowling has invited Christian concepts to the storyline, bringing her readers more in harmony with God and not in any way taking her readers away from God. Thus, by using traditional Christian symbols within her series, Ms. Rowling captures both the imagination and the heart for God.

What is Witchcraft?

The last element within the Harry Potter series that causes frustration and angst is the use of the word "witch(es)", and the classes for brewing potions and studying herbology, both having strong connections with witchcraft. I wish that J.K. Rowling had used the word wizard alone and not in combination with witches, since other than the word itself, there is very little similarity between traditional witchcraft and the potions and herbology practiced at Hogwarts. Again, I refer back to the history of potions and herbology. God the Creator was the source of all that we have, and entrusted it all to Adam (and Eve) to use carefully as he saw fit (Genesis 1:26-30). Even when Adam and Eve were expelled from the Garden of Eden in Genesis 3, God told Adam that he would work hard in the fields tilling the soil to produce plants to sustain his family. In this, God gave us the plants of the world to harvest and use with the intelligence He gave us to find cures for maladies and diseases. However, as Christianity pushed further into Europe, old pockets of druidism and other cult traditions found their way into Christian communities with their strong bond to worshipping mother earth rather than God; in essence, worshipping the created rather than the creator. To establish a clearer line for the Christian communities, using herbs and having knowledge of earthly elements was linked to witchcraft and anyone that used herbs to heal others was considered a witch, regardless of their true faith. With the end of alchemy in the late 1500s, the church had an easier time of dividing the witchy herbs from the scientific chemicals, and pharmacies flourished.

For those who are still wary of their use at all, we have to ask the purpose of the inclusion of these elements just as we did with sorcery: did J.K. Rowling include these elements as a way to instruct others in the ways of witchcraft? To answer that question, we need to look into the differences between true witchcraft and the witchcraft found in the Harry Potter series and attempt to answer these questions:

1) Is the focus of the activity or power on God the Creator or on the created earth?

2) Is the intent of the potion or herb to help the user act as a deity or to help others?

3) Does the activity lead others towards worship of the earth or the Creator?

As we look at the elements of the Harry Potter story with these three questions in mind, we will attempt to come to a decisive conclusion one way or the other.

In response to the first question, whether the focus of the activity in the Harry Potter series is a worship of the earth or the Creator, we should first define "focus of worship." In true witchcraft, the focus of worship is the actual trees, herbs, or earthly elements themselves – the witches are instructed to only collect herbs at certain times of the year or moon phase or day, giving substance to a varying spiritual property within each herb or plant. Although this worship is not a physical bowing down to someone or something, the fact that they acknowledge certain powers that change according to another earthly element indicates that the two are connected spiritually. In Christianity, it would not matter when the herb was picked, although standard gardeners would tell anyone to wait until there is enough herb to take some without destroying the plant itself. Within the Harry Potter series, the students are not directed to collect herbs, sap, blooms, or other parts of plants in herbology class according to a certain time of year or day – it is all about whether the plant is mature enough to move or pick. Secondly, since there are no chants or other words said as they collect the plant samples, there is no mention or assumption of anything spiritual within the plants – only the plant's God given ability to heal a malady. As such, we can see that J.K. Rowling has not endorsed the worship of anything but the Creator Himself.

Within the Harry Potter series, we do see the wizards using herbs and learning about their abilities in both herbology and potions class. However, in all of the classes in which they learn about the herbs, the professors are giving the students instruction in how to help not harm others, and they do not instruct the students to use the herbs for their own spiritual enhancement or new- found abilities. For instance, in *Chamber of Secrets*, Professor Sprout teaches the students about the Mandrake plant, and although in folklore mandrake is used for other purposes, it is only used to help bring people back from being "petrified" (a state of frozen animation from an encounter with a deadly evil).

Outside of class, the remedies mentioned in the series are used in very similar ways to their pharmaceutical uses in the Middle Ages and Renaissance periods, keeping J.K. Rowling's connection to the older times of the high church. Most notably, Hermione learns from Madame Pomfrey (the nurse at Hogwarts) that Essence of Dittany, an herb, is helpful in accelerating healing. Essence of Dittany becomes a "must-have" in later books, as the students end up in more battles and situations requiring healing. Lastly, in Potions class, Professor Snape instructs the students in how to brew potions, similar to how a teacher would instruct students in chemistry class. The potions concocted do have very odd ingredients such as "lacewing flies", but they are not brewed at a special time of day or with malice in mind towards anyone. At the end of each class, the potions are collected and graded on their authenticity, but not used for any other purpose. Also, the more sinister potion recipes are stored in a restricted section on a need-to-know basis only, indicating a general understanding that they are not to be used lightly or every day. Since none of the herbs or potions are used for malevolent purposes and are not used to bestow supernatural abilities on the users, we can see that the answer to this second question is "no": J.K. Rowling did not intend for the users to become deities through the use of herbs or potions.

Having answered the first two questions in the negative, is there still a possibility that the herbs and potions used in Harry Potter could lead readers to believe that they should become creators in their own right and turn to witchcraft? This is a very difficult question to answer, similar to whether the creator of dynamite had intended for it to ever be used for ill purposes. There is the object, and then the use of that object, determined by the person using it. Unfortunately, most people do not consult the inventor when using something – they use it in whatever way they feel they should use it and give very little consideration to the inventor's intent. In the case of dynamite, Professor Nobel created the dynamite to help in mining excavations, never dreaming that it would be used to destroy people. However, dynamite has been used for this very purpose, so should it be outlawed? The same could be said of many everyday items – they are only good or evil depending on who uses them.

In the instance of Harry Potter, it is clear that J.K. Rowling did not intend for any of her material to be considered an instructional manual or directional toward witchcraft, but she does say repeatedly throughout the series that "people will see what they want to see." For those who might be drawn toward witchcraft already, the goodness within Harry Potter might be seen as an encouragement for other witches. However, Wicca has not acknowledged the Harry Potter series as having helped them in any way, and J.K. Rowling has told her audiences that she does not keep any letters from Wiccans, she throws them away. Through these actions, we can see that the intent of the series is not to encourage anyone to become involved in witchcraft and sorcery, and the last question is then answered also in the negative.

What About Satanism?

Although I will explain about the characters in more depth in the next chapter, I will tell you that there is Satanism portrayed in the book through Lord Voldemort and his followers. Lord Voldemort, the Satan figure of the story, is the embodiment of all that is evil, and he believes himself to be equal to the Christ figure of the story, Albus Dumbledore. His followers, the Death Eaters, are those who believe similarly that they are as good as God himself. Everything they do is in black attire, and they all believe themselves to be in control of the life or death of everything around them, as if they were gods themselves. This is the main tenant of Satanism – that we are all gods ourselves and thus do not need God himself[11]. However, since humans are either male or female and not androgenous as God is, there has to be a union of male and female to create that ultimate power. Hence, Satanic rites heavily involve sexual intercourse to create this union.[12] Although this type of interaction never occurs in the storyline itself, the female counterpart to Lord Voldemort is Bellatrix LaStrange, who adores Lord Voldemort, worships who he is, abhors Albus Dumbledore, and indicates that her place next to Lord Voldemort is established by allowing him to keep his Horcruxes (fragments of his soul) in her bank vault.

J.K. Rowling masterfully depicts Satanism as something to abhor, and readers never seem to come away wanting to be one of the Death Eaters. Throughout the series, these dark characters are portrayed as being cold, heartless, and deceitful, and their devotion is more from fear of retribution from Lord Voldemort than loyalty to the cause. The Death Eaters' joy in watching others suffer is never commended by any of the protagonists, and ultimately Harry's love for everyone and faith in Dumbledore defeats Lord Voldemort in Biblical fashion. In summary, Ms. Rowling has not endorsed Satanism through her storyline but has

---

[11] "LaVeyan Satanism," Wikipedia, 2012, retrieved from http://en.wikipedia.org/wiki/LaVeyan_Satanism on June 4th, 2012.

[12] "Ritualized Sexual Magic," Globusz Publishing, 2012, retrieved from http://www.globusz.com/ebooks/Satanism/00000014.htm on June 4th, 2012.

accomplished the opposite feat – helping young people understand the dangers of Satanism and the love and forgiveness of God for everyone.

Conclusions

With this understanding and illumination of magic and Satanism, is it then a stretch to put Christianity within the realm of magic? In the book of Acts, Simon goes to Peter and wants to know his secret for healing others. Peter says that it isn't magic, but faith, and if he would learn to believe in Christ, he would be able to heal others as well. Simon does follow the disciples, and becomes a very good Christian, but it eventually falls out that Simon was still trying to find out where the hidden ropes and lines were. The point here is that even from a short distance, the faith in God that Christians have enables them to channel God's love and healing to others resembles magic to many people. Perhaps we should call it "God's Magic" with a capital M versus the smaller m for the secular version, just as we do with God versus god? Regardless, the fact that after someone prayed about a limb or body needing healing and the broken suddenly becomes whole again is definitely "Magical" in the sense that it defies all the natural laws of science and there is no other explanation.

I believe that J.K. Rowling had this type of "Magic" in mind when she embarked on the Harry Potter series, and the simplest way of seeing it is to imagine the early Christian (or in the near future!) where the Christians have had to go into hiding. Not allowed to show who they were, they hid their miracles from common eyes, and they tended to band together into groups to live together in peace away from the more secular society. In general, children that grow up in a Christian household will become Christians, and those who are raised without faith grow up without God, creating an obvious division between the two worlds. If the atheists are convinced that God does not exist and they move to strike those who would defend God, it is very easy to imagine a world within another world - either a magical world within a muggle world, or a Christian world within a secular one. With this understanding, we can begin to understand the extent of the parallels that J.K. Rowling draws between the two worlds:

there are two Prime Ministers – one for the non-magical Muggles (the English Prime Minister), and a Minister of Magic (like the Pope or Archbishop of Canterbury); there are different traditions within the magical community than from the secular one (age of majority is 17 versus 18, and there are different types of money (shillings, pounds, and pence for the Muggles, and sickles, knuts, and galleons for the wizards). This allegory of Christian life only helps to draw in its Christian readers, since the similarities connect with what they have been taught in church, again bringing people towards God, and not pushing them against God.

In conclusion, there are many elements of God that seem to define true "Magic" which are brought to light in the Harry Potter series. With instruction, people can see that the "Magic" within the series draws many Biblical parallels and employs many Christian traditions or beliefs and that J.K. Rowling uses these "Magic" elements differently than how others use or perform secular magic and witchcraft. Furthermore, with this bit of instruction, J.K. Rowling's work should not stand in the way of God, but rather help to point the way to Christ for those who may be further away from the path than others.

Chapter THREE

The Characters and Their Christian Alchemy

Colossians 2:8 "See to it that no one takes you captive through philosophy and empty deception, according to the tradition of men, according to the elementary principles of the world, rather than according to Christ."(NIV)

In Chapter One, I explained the main basics of alchemy and how J. K. Rowling weaves the alchemy and Christianity into the storyline. Although this book is not meant to be a foundational course in the alchemy of Christianity, let me explain a little bit of the historical conflict between alchemy and Christianity so that you might understand the significance of Ms. Rowling reuniting these two concepts. Despite alchemy's beginnings as a largely spiritually secular practice amongst the oldest empires in the world, it was seen as a secular means of searching for God.[13] Over time, alchemy migrated around the empires and various people added their knowledge to the practice.

[13] Cockren, A, "History of Alchemy from Ancient Egypt to Modern Times," retrieved from http://www.alchemylab.com/history_of_alchemy.htm.

From the verse at the beginning of this chapter, I suggest that there must have been enough dissention right after Christ's time about the purpose of alchemy (the elemental principles of the world) that Paul has to remind people that the philosophy of the time (alchemy) is not about the physical four elements of earth, water, air, and fire, but that they center about Christ. After a couple more centuries, the attraction of physical gold again became a distraction, so Emperor Diocletian banned all alchemical work, burning many of the historical documents.[14]

After another resurgence of alchemy in Europe during the early Middle Ages, the ability to physically create gold from a base metal again lured many people in that saw alchemy as a "get rich quick" scheme. Rather than devote one's life to the study of philosophy to further understand Christ to be The Philosopher's Stone and learn the complicated physical formulas and processes, many of these people resorted to bribery, threats, and burglary to achieve their aims.[15] In 1404, the number of burglaries and lack of morals that followed alchemy created a panic that ended with Henry IV's "Act Against Multipliers" that among other similar restrictions on the continent essentially halted alchemy for more than 250 years.[16]

In the later centuries, philosophers were able to reinstate the allowance for alchemy, and many insisted on its philosophical principles of searching for a purity of soul or returning to God what He created.[17] Unfortunately, over the centuries of misinterpretation and destruction of many written works about the philosophy of alchemy, much has been lost and there are only fragments of written works connecting alchemy in any way to Christianity.

---

[14] Ibid.

[15] Ibid.

[16]Baes, J, "Puzzle 17," retrieved from http://math.ucr.edu/home/baez/puzzles/17.html.

[17] Cockren, A, "History of Alchemy from Ancient Egypt to Modern Times," retrieved from http://www.alchemylab.com/history_of_alchemy.htm.

Despite the destruction of most of the written connections, certain connections seem imbedded in the churches' infrastructure. Alchemy might have begun with gentiles many centuries before Christ appeared, but the concept of a spiritual transformation in order to overcome the physical draw of this world has been written into the Old Testament along with a progression of covenants with God that seem to mirror mastering the physical alchemical elements. Just as Harry first masters earth, then water, air, and fire, God creates covenants with given patriarchs that progress through the elements in the same order.

With Adam (and Eve), we see the covenant of creation and earth – God created them from dust and gave them the Garden of Eden. Betraying His trust, Adam and Eve ate from the Tree of Knowledge of Good and Evil and they were banished (Genesis 3:1-24). We next have the covenant of water between God and Noah, which again first isolates Noah and his family from the world, but ends with his being reintroduced to the world after the flood (Genesis 6:9-8:22). Abram and Sarai are renamed to Abraham and Sarah and promised many future generations through their covenant of air, which incorporates the concepts of spirit, time, and breath (Genesis 17:1-15). The last of the covenants before Israel becomes its own nation is Moses, who enters into a relationship with God through the burning bush, representing fire (Exodus 3:1-22). Do these sound familiar? Yes – they are the same readings from the Old Testament between Ash Wednesday and Lent that J. K. Rowling seems to use for her first four books.

There are many more stories and structures within the Bible that seem to indicate a head bob toward the four elements, and Ms. Rowling incorporates many of those pieces in her Harry Potter series. For instance, Moses and Elijah were the only two prophets shown to have mastered the four elements through their works, and thus they appear at Jesus' transfiguration, giving us pause about the meaning of Hogwart's Professor McGonagall's "Transfiguration" class. Throughout the series, we see that Transfiguration class is about the application of life to inanimate objects, or vice versa, as they convert slippers back into rabbits, or rats into glasses. Bringing objects closer to the nature of God, or something with an animate soul, seems to be the purpose of the Transfiguration class, as we are reminded from the Biblical reference.

Foundationally, I would suggest that "Christian Alchemy" is the spiritual transformation of a person from an organic being born of Original Sin into a Christian being with an immortal soul through these same alchemical processes. The four elements in Christian terms are these: 1) earth (birth); 2) water (baptism), 3) air (the Word and the Spirit, acknowledged through confirmation), and 4) fire (the "burning of the chaff" before entrance to heaven). In the end, it is Christ who has brought us through the physical transformation process to immortality by showing us the way, but there are other transformations that must also exist in order to ensure that the being has converted his heart to God. Through the series, we see Harry as he first learns of his connection to the magical world (earthly birth connection), then his initial baptism through water as he conquers the basilisk and is washed in the sewers; he confirms his belief in a love greater than for himself as he dispels dementors, and his protection from his mother is burned off, purifying Harry for the final journey to purification. There is a similar series of "baptisms" through *Deathly Hallows*: the trio emerges from the Ministry (baptism of earth) with the locket, Harry is baptized by Ron and they destroy the locket Horcrux, Harry, Ron, and Hermione fly out of Gringotts on the wings of a dragon after being buried in the gems but emerge with the cup Horcrux, then they emerge from the Fiendfyre with the remnants of the tiara Horcrux. Again, not only do we see the alchemy, but we see the Christian stamp of overcoming evil through the sequential baptisms that symbolize a progression of the depth of love and relationship Harry has with Dumbledore, the Christ figure of the saga.

The three transformational color stages, the next set of transformations that occur, are evident in the Christian formational rites, especially in the rites of Baptism. The renunciation, a key element of the black stage, is evident in the first set of three questions asked of a Christian candidate. During this phase, they renounce works of evil, evil forces, and Satan.[18] Traditionally, when baptismal candidates were older and it took a couple of years to complete the process, this was their time to turn away from worshipping other gods, lying, cheating, stealing - isolating themselves from their old ways of life. After withdrawal from all things against God, there is a conversion, literally a "turning", in which the candidate's path is illuminated towards God and the candidate declares openly his or her decision to follow Christ. This is the white stage of training and learning about Christ. In the reunification/ purification stage, the newly baptized Christian is then asked three questions of faith as outlined by the Apostle's Creed – accepting God the Father, God the Son, and God the Holy Spirit, and symbolically they have been reunified with God the Creator through Christ.

Although there is only one true Philosopher's Stone, Christ, it is a Philosopher's Stone that shares itself with all who believe in Him, willingly. Thus, Christians drink the Elixir of Life every week or month – the "blood" of Christ in the Communion Cup. Ultimately, as long as the Christian believes in Christ and drinks of the cup, that person will have life within him (John 6:53-56). Rather than the Philosopher's Stone being a physical, inanimate object that transforms other physical, inanimate objects from one entity to another, the Christian Philosopher's Stone is a person that transforms other people. Beyond the multiple methods of physical transformation that we see throughout the series – Polyjuice Potions that help someone take another's appearance, animagi wizards that can transform into an animal at will, and werewolves – we also see transformation in the characters themselves, mostly as a result of interaction with Professor Dumbledore or the trio Harry, Ron, and Hermione. It is this transformational idea that Ms. Rowling carries into her literature –people transforming others in a perpetual chain of transformation towards perfection. (For more information on this concept, see Chapters Four through Ten.)

---

[18] The Catholic Community of Northwest Wyoming, 2012, "History of Christian Initiation of Adults," retrieved from http://www.stanthonycody.org/rcia-history.html.

Nowadays, the "spiritual" change of a substance in alchemy is defined as a chemical property or change, but in the Middle Ages, every known substance's properties were written as being similar to an animal or other descriptive object.[19] Jesus uses similar analogies in the New Testament, calling his disciples the "salt of the earth", and indicating that he himself is the "bread of heaven" broken for the world. In a similar manner, J.K. Rowling uses traditional alchemical animal characteristics as well as "Christian Alchemy" and symbolism in the characters themselves to help her readers understand her interpretation of the events within the story. These alchemical identities of each character tells more about their interaction with others and helps the readers understand why the plot unfolds as it does. For those who are not familiar with the characters, here is the complete list with descriptions to help you understand their symbolism and purpose. For those who are very familiar with them, I have added bits of information that might help give more depth to the characters as you understand them now. I have grouped most of them into the three main groups they fall into in the fifth book, so as to help explain who's on which side, but within each group, they are listed in the order of centrality to the main story line.

Dumbledore's Army:

Although twenty-five students signed their name on the parchment labeled "Dumbledore's Army", those who were not named or were only mentioned in the book without any significant contributions to the story line and are not mentioned here. Other important characters that were not part of Dumbledore's Army are listed and described in a separate section.

Harry James Potter: Born to James and Lily (Evans) Potter, Harry's parents died when he was a year old because Lord Voldemort thought Harry would be the wizard prophesized to conquer him through some

---

[19] The Alchemy Dictionary, retrieved from http://www.alchemylab.com/dictionary.htm.

unknown power (love). The name Harry means "king", a reference to the future Arthurian part he plays with Guinevere and the Sword of Gryffindor. Recalling Arthur to mind, we are reminded of the one "perfect" king from English history whose life became consumed by trying to locate the Holy Grail (essentially the Elixir of Life from the true Philosopher's Stone).[20] The last name, Potter, is a reference to Jeremiah 18:4-6, where God uses the potter symbolically to display His power over Israel. Just as God transforms clay into a useable vessel, we are transformed with Harry through the story of Harry Potter. With both parts of the main character's name referring to high historical standards, we know right from the beginning that it is both a Christian tale of formation and a spiritual quest for Christ.

Harry lives with his uncle Vernon, his aunt Petunia, and his cousin Dudley who treat Harry like the live-in servant, lucky to be allowed to live with them. The most famous characteristic of Harry Potter is his scar – a lightning bolt on his forehead that he received when Lord Voldemort tried to kill him. This lightning bolt traces the pattern made by the musical cross in the middle ages. In baptism, Christians are anointed with oil in the sign of a cross on the forehead and the blessing states that we are "marked as God's own forever", although invisibly. For Harry, this mark becomes visible when Lord Voldemort's evil strikes Harry, just as lemon juice writing is invisible until stricken with a light. Harry himself also represents the typical Christian person on his journey, a modern *Pilgrim's Progress*. Also, Harry, Ron, and Hermione play the close-knit trio of Peter, James, and John (Harry is St John – more on this in Chapter Nine), acting as Christ's closest disciples as they carry on Professor Dumbledore's quest.

On his 11th birthday, a stranger named Rubeus Hagrid tells Harry that he is a wizard and is given a placement at a strange magical school named Hogwarts. Harry also discovers that his parents died protecting him from Lord Voldemort, and they left him an inheritance in wizard's

---

[20] "Holy Grail and King Arthur," retrieved from http://www.legendofkingarthur.co.uk/holy-grail.htm.

money. He learns more about his parents throughout the series as the past unfolds, and eventually connects with his parents' closest friends as they all fight against Lord Voldemort. A natural in the air, Harry is recruited to be the seeker on the Gryffindor's Quidditch team his first year at Hogwarts, and helps Gryffindor win the Quidditch Cup three years in a row.

One key piece of the wizarding world's puzzle is the Invisibility Cloak given mysteriously to Harry for Christmas his first year at Hogwarts. Having once belonged to his father, the cloak allows Harry to commit multiple infractions of the rules unseen, although his misdemeanors are usually in an effort to help others. With the gift of invisibility, Harry tends to suffer from a "people-saving thing",[21] meaning that he feels empowered to do anything he can morally to save a friend, including breaking the rules (a trait he shared with his father). Overall, his strongest asset is his ability to love others, despite his cruel upbringing, and it is his faith and love of others that protects him from Lord Voldemort's grasp.

Alchemically, the celestial trio refers to the three elements that always coexist: mercury, sulfur, and salt,[22] just as Hermione, Ron, and Harry are always together. From Matthew 5:13, we get the words from Jesus "You are the salt of the earth", which explains Harry's part of the trio. Harry also represents the purity of salt. Additionally, Harry is the lead substance that we connect to as he undergoes the slow transformation throughout the series from lead to gold, struggling with his faith in God, himself, and others until his faith guides his resurrection at the end of the series and he becomes like gold. Lastly, Harry represents the "body" of Christ in the "heart, mind, and body" trio of Christian formation. As such, he is the one who physically has to fight evil in all the books and breaks the rules to help others.

---

[21] Rowling, *Order of the Phoenix*, "Out of the fire," Chapter 32.

[22] Magical Path, 2011, "A Brief Introduction to Alchemy," retrieved from http://magicalpath.net/a-brief-introduction-to-alchemy/.

Hermione Jean Granger: Hermione is one of Harry's two best friends and a fellow Gryffindor in the same grade. They meet on the train to Hogwarts, and their friendship is solidified during the first year at Hogwarts during their battle against a troll in the bathroom on their first Halloween at Hogwarts. Hermione was born of non-magical parents, but has a remarkable mind and knack for magic. Of the three, she is the thinker who expects the library to have all the answers and is always willing to share her knowledge to help others. As such, Hermione represents the mind of Christ and throughout the series, she demonstrates how we can use our minds to help others in need.

Alchemically, Hermione is named after the female name for Hermes, the messenger, healer, and wisdom of the group.[23] The Roman name for Hermes, mercury, has the chemical symbol Hg, just like her initials.[24] Mercury is one of the celestial three elements and one of the two elements that alchemically help transform lead to gold in alchemy. Mercury itself can be deadly by penetrating the skin, and in the chemistry lab, a mercury spill is tempered with sulfur to deaden the effects of the mercury vapors. Similarly, throughout the series, Hermione is very bright, and her keenness in studies and astute observations provide penetrating insights that keep the three friends ahead of their peers. Although off-putting at first, she becomes closer friends with Ron (who represents sulfur) as the series progresses, and with his influence, she grows to understand that sometimes there are other factors beyond the rules to consider.

Ronald Bilius Weasley: Ronald Weasley is Harry Potter's best friend and fellow Gryffindor throughout the series, and was one of the first wizards to meet Harry Potter on the train to Hogwarts. He is the sixth child of Arthur and Molly Weasley, and is constantly worried about living up to the reputations of his five older brothers who all earned distinctions

---

[23] Granger, *The Deathly Hallows Lectures,* pp. 61-63.

[24]Ibid.

throughout Hogwarts. His father does not have a high paying job, limiting the resources available for the family, so Ronald gets mostly hand-me-down clothing, brooms, wands, and pets, which he endures very patiently. As Harry's best friend, Ronald is Harry's sounding board, almost always supporting Harry throughout Harry's trials, despite a couple of arguments.

The Weasley family all have red hair, red being one of the colors of sulfur. Additionally, Ron's middle name, Bilius, is the yellowish color of bile, another color of sulfur. Sulfur is one of the three celestial elements in alchemy that symbolizes the eternal hope of enlightenment[25] and tempers lead by deactivating the mercurial vapors. These two agents theoretically dissolve then re-congeal the lead continually until the metal forms into gold. Also, the name Ronald means "counselor", and as the name implies, Ronald is the emotional one of the three friends – the "will" of Christ. As such, Ronald is usually moody, but in the end, he begins to lead the trio and they begin to "follow the heart", and his constantly maroon/ red wardrobe points to the Christian color representing passion. Ronald and Hermione fight constantly throughout the stories, but by the end, they have resolved their differences, and eventually end up in love and married.

Neville Longbottom: Neville has lived with his paternal grandmother since he was about a year old, and is exactly the same age as Harry Potter.[26] Neville's parents were tortured by Bellatrix LaStrange to find the whereabouts of Lord Voldemort when Harry's parents died because they thought Neville's parents were hiding Lord Voldemort somewhere. Their torture left them mentally insane, and they live at St. Mungo's Hospital for the duration of the story. Neville is a timid, bumbling fellow

---

[25] Venefica, A, 2011, "Elemental alchemy symbols," retrieved from http://www.whats-your-sign.com/elemental-alchemy-symbols.html.
[26] Harry Potter Wiki, "Neville Longbottom," retrieved from http://harrypotter.wikia.com/wiki/Neville_Longbottom.

Gryffindor with Harry, Hermione, and Ron, who tends to forget everything but is a fabulous herbology student. Throughout the series, he is in the background gaining strength and confidence, converting from a student who is hardly able to keep up with others to the student leading the revolt from within Hogwarts against Lord Voldemort in the seventh year.

Ginerva Weasley: "Ginny" is the youngest of seven children (including Fred, George, and Ron), and the only girl for the past seven generations.[27] In alchemy, this magical seven of seven makes for a very powerful wizard, and Ginny is no exception – all of her wand work causes strong reactions. She is possessed by a fragment of Lord Voldemort's soul in *Chamber of Secrets*, but is saved by Harry and is forever in love with Harry. She becomes a strong member of Dumbledore's Army, and begins a relationship with Harry in Half-Blood Prince that ends in marriage despite a few bumps in the road. Her name is a reference to the Arthurian legend, as the mate for Harry the king, but without the legendary treason.

Luna Lovegood: A Ravenclaw student a year behind Harry, Luna "Loony" Lovegood has very unique beliefs about many things others believe do not exist. Because of this, others make fun of her, and tease her by taking away her shoes and clothing until she has to walk around barefoot at school. Luna, meaning moon, is representative of the astral plane - that place between heaven and earth, represented by dreaminess and ruled by the moon since our minds leave the physical realm at night. Despite her dreaminess, Luna is very bright and helps Harry through many difficult logistical problems throughout the last four books. She also helps connect her friends to her father's newspaper, "The Quibbler." As one of the key members in the fifth book who helps Harry and the

---

[27] Harry Potter Wiki, "Ginerva Weasley," retrieved from http://harrypotter.wikia.com/wiki/Ginevra_Weasley.

Army fight the Death Eaters at the Ministry of Magic in *Order of the Phoenix,* she also tells Harry about the Diadem of Ravenclaw, an important element for the end of the series.

Fred and George Weasley: Fred and George are twins that are two years ahead of Harry, Ron, and Hermione, and are Ron's older brothers. They are well known for their rule breaking and sense of humor and eventually begin a very successful joke shop in Diagon Alley, sponsored by Harry Potter's Triwizard Tournament's winnings. Both play"beaters" for the Gryffindor Quidditch team, and are part of the seven duplicate Harrys that help Harry escape from Privet Drive when Harry comes of age, breaking the protective charm around that house. George is reminiscent of both "Saint George", especially once he loses his ear and becomes "holey", and the servant who loses his ear from Saint Peter's blade at the Mount of Olives. Fred's death at the end of the series marks the beginning of the end of the red alchemical stage of purification / reunification, and shows that he is the representative martyr for Christ.

Seamus Finnegan and Dean Thomas: Seamus and Dean are Harry's roommates that mostly support Harry and are part of Dumbledore's Army. Seamus is named after the patron saint of Ireland, and his mother was a "witch", making him a half-blood. From Seamus, we hear directly what the wizarding world's opinions are about Harry as they fluctuate throughout the series. Dean's mother was a muggle and since his father died when he was young, they never knew whether his father was a wizard or not making his blood status a worry later in the series. Dean thus goes into hiding until his capture in the last book when only half-blood or pure-blood wizards are allowed to return to Hogwarts, but both Seamus and Dean return for the final Battle of Hogwarts in book seven.

Colin and Dennis Creavy: These two brothers are both muggle born Gryffindors, and are both younger than Harry. Colin is an insufferable cameraman, and one of Harry's great fans who is petrified/ frozen by the basilisk in *Chamber of Secrets*. Dennis, upon entering Hogwarts, fell into the lake and was rescued by the giant squid. Both boys are very dedicated members of Dumbledore's Army, and although they are not part of the core that went to the Ministry of Magic, they snuck back into Hogwarts to fight and died in the Battle of Hogwarts at the end of the book.

Cho Chang, Michael Corner, and Terry Boot: Cho, Michael, and Terry are Ravenclaw students at Hogwarts concurrently with Harry at Hogwarts. Cho Chang becomes a love interest of Harry's during his fifth year at Hogwarts, while Michael Corner is Ginny Weasley's first boyfriend. Terry Boot is a member of Dumbledore's Army, but not much else is known about his career at Hogwarts. All three students return to Hogwarts for the final Battle of Hogwarts.

Susan Bones, Ernie MacMillan, Justin Finch-Fletchley, and Hannah Abbott: Susan, Ernie, Justin, and Hannah are four Hufflepuff students at Hogwarts that become part of Dumbledore's Army. Susan Bones' aunt, Amelia Bones, who works for the Ministry of Magic, was killed by Lord Voldemort in the sixth book. Hannah's mother also worked for the Ministry of Magic until she was killed by Lord Voldemort while Hannah was at Hogwarts. Although Hannah did not return to Hogwarts after her mother's death that year, she did return to Hogwarts and fought in the Battle of Hogwarts at the end of the seventh book. Ernie Macmillan, a pure-blood, and Justin Flinch-Fletchley, a muggle-born, were both strong supporters of Dumbledore's Army, making a decisive attitude change in support of Harry after Justin was petrified by the basilisk in the second book. Ernie returns to Hogwarts his seventh year, and defends their right to fight rather than flee, but as a muggle-born, the Justin was not allowed to return to Hogwarts that last year and nothing is mentioned of him in the seventh book.

Order of the Phoenix:

This group of adult wizards represents the twelve disciples – the twelve most integral members of the adult opposition to Lord Voldemort. Since Albus Dumbledore's symbol/ patronus is the Phoenix, the Order of the Phoenix is his twelve closest friends working with him to fight evil. There are many parallels between the disciples and the order – both groups are for the most part "misfits" of society that do not recruit until after their leader has died/ left this world, and they all understand the mission of love over all else, doing whatever they can to support each other, regardless of the cost. Furthermore, their headquarters is Sirius Black's house, 12 Grimmauld Place (again, the number 12), a magically hidden place that is converted from a staunch purist lineage to the safe house for the Order of the Phoenix. Lastly, at the close of the series, five of the twelve members die, leaving seven members to carry on the mission, the alchemically perfect number.

Albus Dumbledore: Although Albus Dumbledore is not a member of the Order of the Phoenix per se, he is listed here as the character around which the order is created. The name Albus means white in Latin, and his initials, AD, stand for Anno Domini, "the year of our Lord." From these, we begin to understand that Albus Dumbledore represents the Christ figure in this saga. His office is at the top of the highest turret, with a griffin door knocker - the griffin being the symbol of the Kingdom of Heaven on earth. The stairs that bring people to his door are representative of Jacob's Ladder, with people moving up and down between heaven and earth.

As the Headmaster at the Hogwarts School, Albus Dumbledore chooses who comes and who does not come to the school. For the most part, he allows anyone with any magical talent to come to Hogwarts, regardless of their pedigree of pureblood or not, echoing Matthew 11:28: "come, all who labor and find rest; come, all you who thirst, and find drink, come." In this way, he is very much the good shepherd tending his sheep, and he places protection around the school so that no one may enter except through the gate (echoing John 10:9: "I am the gate; whoever enters through me will be saved." (NIV)) Dumbledore believes and finds the good in everyone, regardless of what their choices have been in the past. Also, his symbol is the phoenix, a resurrection symbol, and his pet Phoenix, Fawkes, flies to Harry many times to save Harry's life. After winning the Elder Wand from the tyrannical dark wizard Grindelwald in a wizarding duel, Albus Dumbledore decided to change the fate of the wand to bring about only good, and not destruction and evil.[28] Dumbledore is also known for discovering the 12 uses of dragon's blood.[29] Since Dragon's Blood is a name for the elixir of life from the Philosopher's Stone, it is also known as the blood from the Eucharist, again an element introduced to us by Jesus. Lastly, Dumbledore possesses a 12 handed watch in which each hand depicts the status and whereabouts of his 12 closest friends - his twelve disciples. J.K. Rowling has stated that Dumbledore is not Jesus in her interviews, and thus Dumbledore does not rise again from his death. However, the other similarities parallel Christ too well to not consider them.

Rubeus Hagrid: Hagrid is the half-giant gatekeeper at Hogwarts, a position he obtained when he was wrongfully expelled from Hogwarts in his third year of schooling (*Chamber of Secrets*, Chapters 13 and 15). As Dumbledore's trusted assistant, Hagrid develops a very close relationship to Harry through the years. Hagrid first rescued Harry from his parents' house after their untimely deaths, and rescues him again from his aunt and uncle on Harry's eleventh birthday to introduce him to Hogwarts and

---

[28] Rowling, *Harry Potter and the Deathly Hallows,* p. 720.

[29] Rowling, *Harry Potter and the Sorcerer's Stone,* p. 103.

his magical community. For the majority of the story, Hagrid is Harry's subtle guide. In Harry's third year, Hagrid becomes the Care of Magical Creatures Professor, and introduces the students to many magical creatures and the Book of Monsters (an allegory to the Bible). As Harry's essential zoological guide, Hagrid introduces Harry to the animals that are critical to his success in mastering the elements of earth, water, air, and fire in the first four books. By showing Harry how to care for each animal until Harry can work with each animal by himself, Harry obtains confidence and knowledge about the elements each animal represents helping Harry become master of that element. Overall, Hagrid has a very androgynous personality – while he is thick-skinned with giant's blood, he also enjoys cooking and mothering animals. Hagrid and Dumbledore share the opinion that all people or animals have goodness in them, and kindness will win over evil in the end. With this opinion in mind, Hagrid harbors a secret desire to raise dragons, and enjoys working with animals regardless of their ferocity.

Minerva McGonagall: Professor Minerva McGonagall is named after the Roman goddess of wisdom, but she represents the disciple Martha from the Bible, the sister of Mary and Lazarus. Her name both begins and ends with the same letters as well: *M*, and *a*. For instance, in the first chapter of *Harry Potter and the Philosopher's Stone*, she sits all day long waiting for Professor Dumbledore to arrive rather than celebrating the end of Lord Voldemort's Reign of Terror. As the Head of Gryffindor house, she teaches Transfiguration at Hogwarts – the embodiment of alchemical Fire since nothing can be touched by fire without being transformed. Transfiguration, in a truly Biblical sense, is the transformation of something or someone into something more God-like, or from one state that is more God-like to one that is less so. In this instance, being more like God means having life and His spirit, and all of her transfigurations involve either animating objects to life, converting a given object back to its original state (as in slippers back into rabbits), or transforming animals into a less animate form. Professor McGonagall follows in Headmaster Dumbledore's footsteps, as he was the Transfiguration professor before her, a fact also depicted in their garments. In the world of wizardry, the head wizard always wears a purple or a very purplish blue robe (a reference to the royalty of the position), and the apprentice always wears a green robe, as these two professors do. She is the Head of Gryffindor house, and places Harry on the Quidditch team as their seeker after seeing him catch a small object in midair on his first broomstick flight. She is very strict, but fair to all students, and although she will never grant leniency towards her own house students, she does support Harry in all of his responsibilities and dreams and protect him from unfair treatment.

Sirius Black: Sirius Black is Harry Potter's godfather and was James Potter's best friend. He and James were the rule breakers and top students during their time at Hogwarts. During that time, they also befriended Remus Lupin and Peter Pettigrew. Due to Remus' werewolf condition, the other three became animagi (meaning they could transform into animals at will) to keep Remus company during the full moon and keep him from harming others. The four of them created the Marauder's Map, a map that shows everyone's location in Hogwarts, but is only blank parchment unless the correct words are spoken. Sirius is named after the main star in the constellation *Canis Major*, reflecting his animagus' shape, a large black dog, and his death begins the end of the black stage of the series in book #5. His initials, SB, are the chemical symbol for antimony, an element that was also used in small amounts to transform the lead to gold and is nowadays used as a flame retardant. Some alchemists say that antimony is an element that tends to stay on the periphery, and has animal characteristics[30] – just like Sirius' existence in Harry's life through the series. Sirius was framed for Peter Pettigrew's death, and spent twelve years in Azkaban Prison (the wizard's prison)

---

[30] Visual Elements, 2005, "A visual interpretation of the Table of Elements," retrieved from http://www.rsc.org/chemsoc/visualelements/pages/alchemist/alc_antimony.html.

until he realized that Peter Pettigrew was still alive. He then escaped from the prison, but is forced into hiding when Peter Pettigrew escapes. For the three years Sirius appears in the series, he can only help Harry, Ron, and Hermione from the periphery, many times assuming the form of a dog, Snuffles.

Severus Snape: Professor Snape teaches Potions class at Hogwarts from the time of Lord Voldemort's downfall until Harry's sixth year, when Dumbledore switches him to teaching Defense Against the Dark Arts. As the Head of Slytherin House, he represents alchemical water, which is why he teaches Potions. He then becomes the Headmaster when Professor Dumbledore dies at the end of the sixth book. He is one of the most pivotal and controversial characters of the series, since he had loved Lily Evans for most of his life, but was mortal enemies with James Potter throughout their time together at Hogwarts. As soon as he graduated from Hogwarts, Severus Snape joined the Death Eaters and followed Lord Voldemort, becoming a very strong member of that group. Unbeknownst to all except for Professor Dumbledore, Severus turned against Lord Voldemort when Lord Voldemort killed Lily and James, feeling true remorse for having turned to the Death Eaters at all and dedicating his life to protecting Harry while keeping the appearance of being a true follower of Lord Voldemort. He is one of the few true Occlumens (having the ability to read others' minds and protect his mind from others) in the story line, making his position as a spy even more singular but also making him privy to many thoughts and insights he would not normally have access to.

Remus Lupin: Remus is named after one of the wolves that nurtured the founders of Rome, and Lupin is the Latin term for Wolf. No surprise, Lupin is a werewolf, bitten as a child by a vindictive werewolf named Fenrir Greyback in punishment for his father's refusal to join Lord Voldemort.[31] There aren't any alchemy symbols with Lupin, just flashes back to his name sake's symbolism – Lupin is a strong guide to Harry's generation, helping them understand the dark arts and bolstering their fight against Lord Voldemort, just as the mythological Remus nurtured the founders of Rome. As a werewolf, he is not trusted in society and is banned from many jobs, which makes him an undesirable. Professor Dumbledore hires Remus to teach Defense Against the Dark Arts during Harry's third year at Hogwarts. During his year at Hogwarts, Remus is instrumental in helping Harry understand his parents' time at Hogwarts and produce a patronus, a large protective light that chases away evil in the form of Dementors.

Arthur and Molly Weasley: This couple is the parents of Bill, Charlie, Percy, Fred, George, Ronald, and Ginerva Weasley, and they all live in "the Burrow", the name given to a house of weasels. True to burrow form, their house is a rambling collection of rooms with no particular order. They are consistently called "blood traitors", a term never truly explained, but considering JK Rowling's' Scottish background and the fact that the Weasley's all have red hair, we can suppose that she is referring to a resemblance to Elizabeth I. Elizabeth I was the only red-haired monarch, and considered to be a blood traitor to her family when she imprisoned her own cousin, Mary Queen of Scots, for almost nineteen years before executing her.[32] Arthur is fascinated with Muggles, works unceasingly to help ensure that muggle artifacts are safe from magical interference, and suffers a snake attack while on duty guarding the Hall of Prophecy in book five.

Molly Weasley represents Mary, Martha and Lazarus's sister and good friend of Jesus, and her name also begins and ends with the same letters as Mary, *M* and *y*. Whereas Martha (Minerva McGonagall) works

---

[31] Rowling, J, *Harry Potter and the Half-Blood Prince*, "A Very Frosty Christmas," Chapter 16.

[32] Trueman, C, 2011, "Mary Queen of Scots," retrieved from http://www.historylearningsite.co.uk /mary_queen_of_scots.htm.

all the time and tends to worry more about the work involved than the fun and enjoyment of life, Molly tries to preserve the innocence of the teenagers, cooks all of the meals at every gathering of the Order of the Phoenix, and ensures that everyone, regardless of parentage, has what they need for school. Everything for her is about community and pulling people together, always willing to listen to everyone just as Mary did.

Alastor "Mad-Eye" Moody: Alastor Moody was a great friend of Dumbledore's for many years, and worked as an auror for the Ministry of Magic. Alastor is a reference to a white compound called alabaster, making Alastor Moody another symbol of the white stage of alchemy. His nick-name "Mad Eye" was in reference to the magic all-seeing swiveling eye that replaced an eye lost during one of his pursuits of a dark wizard. In book four, Moody accepted the job of Defense Against the Dark Arts professor as a favor for Dumbledore. However, it was an imposter who actually took the position, keeping Alastor in the bottom of a seven compartmented trunk. He is the most able wizard in the Order of the Phoenix, and leads Order members through both escapes from Privet Drive. His death at the beginning of book seven is one of the three "white" deaths that signal the end of the white stage of Harry's transformation from lead to gold.

Kingsley Shacklebolt: A key member of the Order, Kingsley Shacklebolt is the most able and undercover member within the Ministry of Magic. A very capable, likeable fellow, he is placed in key positions within the Ministry of Magic and wins the trust of the Minister himself as his aide de camp. His name, a hidden reference to "The Shackled King", is referencing his eventual rise to the top, the Minister of Magic, once Lord Voldemort had been vanquished.

Nymphadora Tonks: "Tonks" is a metamorphmagus, meaning she can change her appearance at will, and is one of the few members not associated with Hogwarts in some way during the series. She is also Sirius Black's cousin. She was recruited to the Order by her fellow auror, Mad-Eye Moody, and is instrumental in helping Harry through difficult situations and battles throughout the series. (An auror is similar to a secret police network.)

Bill Weasley: The second oldest child of Molly and Arthur Weasley, Bill works for Gringotts, the wizards' bank run by goblins. He is one of the first members to join the Order of the Phoenix, and gets attacked by Fenrir Greyback, the werewolf, while at Hogwarts fighting the Death Eaters when Dumbledore dies. John Granger suggests that Bill's marriage to Fleur is an alchemical wedding of the red king to the white queen, which sets up the golden age at the beginning of the seventh book.[33]

Mundungus Fletcher: Mundungus is the Judas of the group, always thinking of how to make money and not very loyal to anyone within the Order. He is a bit more extreme than Judas, since Mundungus is an actual known thief, only concerned with saving his own life and not worried about the how his actions might affect others. JK Rowling gives her opinion of his behavior through her loving nickname for him, "Dung", and his last work with the Order results in his abandoning Alastor Moody during the Escape from Privet Drive in book seven, giving Lord Voldemort an open opportunity to kill Alastor Moody.

---

[33] Granger, J, *The Deathly Hallows Lectures*, p. 52.

Death Eaters:

The Death Eaters, the Satanists of the story, are those who live by the Biblical verse "The last enemy to be vanquished is death", from 1 Corinthians 15:26. However, they misinterpret the verse to mean that they have the power of life and death within themselves over others – death for others, and life for themselves, as if they themselves were gods. This group, one of the three key groups (the 1/3 fraction of angels that was thrown out of Heaven by God in Isaiah), wears masks to hide their true identity, but also as a reference to the death masks that morticians would place on corpses in the middle ages.[34] Their belief is that the magical community should control the world since they have additional abilities and not hide their magic. All other beings, including wizards that do not have a direct wizarding line, should be under their control. The thirteen closest Death Eaters to Lord Voldemort are branded with the "Dark Mark" on their left forearm – the sign of a skull and a snake.

Lord Voldemort: Born Tom Riddle, Jr., to a love-potioned Tom Riddle and Merope Gaunt, Lord Voldemort is the last living heir of Slytherin. Merope died within an hour of the birth of her son, and her husband had abandoned her once he realized she was a witch who had put a love charm on him.[35] Through the Gaunt line, Tom was the last of the Slytherin bloodline, and he inherited the ability to speak to snakes, the language called Parseltongue. Having grown up in a muggle orphanage, Tom Riddle used his self-discovered magical abilities to dominate and terrorize the other children. Upon going to Hogwarts, Tom found a true home, and became a fabulous student, winning many awards and honors.

---

[34] WiseGEEK, 2011, "What is a Death Mask?," retrieved from http://www.wisegeek.com/what-is-a-death-mask.htm.

[35] Rowling, *Harry Potter and the Half-Blood Prince,* p. 212-214.

Despite Professor Dumbledore's watchful eyes, he began his work on how to immortalize himself and began his group of Death Eaters, a group of almost one-third of the magical community that began to work on plans to promote the magical community's place over all other creatures. As he sank more into hatred, self-worship, and obsession with death, he took on the name Lord Voldemort – the "flee-er of death", an anagram for his given name Tom Marvolo Riddle (as "I Am Lord Voldemort").[36]

In order to secure life for himself, he split his soul into seven pieces and placed each into a different object, called a Horcrux. Thus, when he tried to kill Harry and the spell rebounded, Lord Voldemort didn't die, but he didn't really inhabit space either. Over time, he was able to gain strength and come back to lead his followers against the world and especially Harry. Lord Voldemort's life parallels that of Lucifer, the archangel of God that led one-third of the angels in a revolt against God, believing he could be as powerful as God Himself (Isaiah 12:12-14, Revelations 12:4, 9). Just as God abolished Lucifer from Heaven, Professor Dumbledore would not allow Tom Riddle to return to Hogwarts once he graduated from Hogwarts. There is no real alchemy symbol for Lord Voldemort, since he is the representation of all that is evil, and is the Satan figure of the story.

Peter Pettigrew: Peter Pettigrew's nickname is "Wormtail," so named because of his animagus form of the rat when he would join James Potter, Remus Lupin, and Sirius Black on their monthly romps. The nickname is a reference to "Wormwood," literally "Bitterness," the star that causes the poisoning of 1/3 of the water of the world and causes the annihilation of many people in Revelations. (Revelation 8:10 and is used in the Bible multiple times concerning the destruction of people in response to their disloyalty to God.) In the Harry Potter series, Peter Pettigrew was good friends with James Potter, Sirius Black, and Remus Lupin, but was drawn to Lord Voldemort's power and betrayed the

---

[36] Rowling, *Harry Potter and the Chamber of Secrets,* p. 314.

Potter family's location to Lord Voldemort, causing the death of James and Lily Potter. After the betrayal, Pettigrew staged his own death and framed Sirius Black for the muggle deaths that occurred with the explosion. He transformed himself into a rat named Scabbers, and lived with the Weasleys for twelve years before being found out. He then sought out Lord Voldemort and was instrumental in returning Lord Voldemort to a physical body to rise up against the Order of the Phoenix and Harry Potter. More Death Eaters join the new Lord Voldemort, resulting in the loss of 1/3 of the wizarding community because of "Wormwood."

Bellatrix LaStrange: the most faithful and loyal of the Death Eaters, Bellatrix is also related to many of the Order of the Phoenix (most directly to Sirius Black and Nymphadora Tonks). As the lieutenant Death Eater, Bellatrix also plays the very satanic role of the female element that is joined with Lord Voldemort. As Lord Voldemort's most adoring servant, she and her husband searched frantically for Lord Voldemort when he first was thought dead after his encounter with the Potters, and tortured Neville Longbottom's parents into insanity in order to gain information. She is responsible for Sirius's death, and her bank vault provides Lord Voldemort a hiding place for his Horcruxes (again a reference to her being a vessel for Lord Voldemort). Her name means "the strange beautiful tricks", and she acts as Lord Voldemort's deputy, taking charge whenever he is out of the immediate area.

Lucius Malfoy: Although part of the house of "Bad faith", Lucius also undergoes a partial transformation through the series. At first, he is cruel to everyone, working tirelessly to continue Lord Voldemort's works of purifying the magical world. However, after his loss to Harry at the Ministry of Magic in the fifth book and his subsequent sentence in Azkaban, Lucius realizes that there is no forgiveness with Lord Voldemort, and begins to question the workings of the Death Eaters. He allows his house to be the new Headquarters for the Death Eaters, but he is obviously disgusted with his new permanent house guests: Lord Voldemort and Bellatrix LaStrange. By the conclusion of the series, he walks away from the Death Eaters.

Barty Crouch, Jr.: Barty Junior is a Death Eater who does not appear in more than one book, but he was instrumental in Lord Voldemort's rebirth. Posing as Alastor Moody the new Defense Against the Dark Arts professor in the fourth book, Barty is able to win Harry Potter's trust and get him to the graveyard for Lord Voldemort's rebirthing ceremony. He was essentially destroyed after Dumbledore, McGonagall, and Snape discovered the truth about him, since the Dementors did not wait for the questioning and took his soul early.

Amycus and Alecto Carrow: This brother and sister pair are professors during the seventh book, and they enjoy torturing students. They are defeated before the final Battle of Hogwarts.

Walden MacNair, Crabbe, Goyle, Rookwood, Dolohov, and Nott: These are other Death Eaters that are mentioned and in action occasionally, but there is nothing else really known about them.

Severus Snape: Severus Snape is the only character that plays on both sides convincingly, and although branded with the Dark Mark, is not one of the true twelve Death Eaters. True to his name, Severus cuts himself off from both groups, acting as a spy for Dumbledore within the Death Eaters' group, but not trusted by the others in the Order. As an accomplished Occlumens and Legilmens, Severus Snape is able to keep his thoughts that concern Dumbledore and the Order of the Phoenix from Lord Voldemort, although Snape has no concerns about Dumbledore knowing what is happening in the Death Eaters' camp. Dumbledore and Lord Voldemort are also both great Occlumens and Legilmens, reading pertinent thoughts of those around them, and thus being able to keep track of what Harry knows and does. In the fifth book, Snape is told to instruct Harry in how to block his mind from Lord Voldemort, but he uses the time to discover what Harry already knows about Lord Voldemort instead. After Snape kills Dumbledore at the end of book six, people are convinced that Snape is Lord Voldemort's right hand man.

Miscellaneous Characters:

Here are other important characters that were not defined by the above three groups but still played significant roles in the series.

Filius Flitwick: As the head of Ravenclaw house at Hogwarts, Professor Flitwick was best known as the professor for Charms class. Since Charms are more ethereal, working with controlling the object in space and time, the Charms teacher is always the Head of Ravenclaw, the alchemical representation of Air. Professor Flitwick is half-human and of very short stature. Although he does everything he can to support Professor Dumbledore and the Order of the Phoenix, he is never an actual member of the Order.

Pomona Sprout: Professor Sprout, as her name implies, was the head of the Hufflepuff House at Hogwarts. As the embodiment of the alchemical representation of Earth, Professor Sprout taught Herbology, where she taught the students about soil, plants, and how best to interact with the earthly elements around them. She is always supportive of Professor

Dumbledore, even though she is never a member of the Order of the Phoenix.

Draco Malfoy: Harry's nemesis at school, Draco's name means "the dragon of bad faith."[37] The Malfoy family has pureblood status and believes that magical people should only marry other magical people and have nothing to do with muggle people, even if they show any magical abilities (and thus genetics). This is from Paul's letter to the Corinthians (2 Corinthians 6:14)– "Do not be unequally yoked with unbelievers," but the Malfoys incorrectly translate this to mean marrying only those with proven status and the law has no room for converts. Throughout the series, the Malfoys support Lord Voldemort, but once Lord Voldemort begins to punish them for their failures, they decide they would rather side with Harry and convert at the end to being better people and save Harry's life and the wizarding world. Draco has a transformational event himself during the last two books of the series, in which Harry helps convert him from someone willing to do anything to harm others to someone incapable of harming others. After this transformation, Draco becomes an allegorical Judas in the series. Having been tasked with killing Dumbledore, he shows remorse and concession instead, accepting Dumbledore's mercy for his actions right as the Death Eaters arrive. Draco never again does anything to hurt Harry or anyone related to the Order of the Phoenix.

Vincent Crabbe and Gregory Goyle: These two students are Draco Malfoy's best friends, and the three of them are rarely seen apart. They act as Draco's bodyguards, always willing to get into a fight but not bright enough to speak intelligently about anything. Magically, these two characters acts as golems, clay creations without the ability to do anything but what is written and placed in their mouths. The name

[37] Wikipedia, 2011, "Draco Malfoy," retrieved from http://en.wikipedia.org/wiki/Draco_Malfoy#cite_note-3.

Vincent Crabbe brings to mind the pinchers from the word "vince" as well as the name of Crabbe, and he also represents the alchemical color red. Gregory Goyle is a modification of the word gargoyle, and represents the alchemical color black. As a trio, they represent the three stages of red, black, and white (Draco with his white hair). Other than being the oppositional characters to Harry, Hermione, and Ron, they mainly serve to cause trouble and depict what happens when students embrace evil that they do not truly understand.

Dobby, the House elf: When we are introduced to Dobby, he is the servant possession of the Malfoy household where he is mistreated and threatened many times a day. Once we meet other house elves, we realize how different Dobby is from the others because he allows himself to do things, even if he would have to punish himself afterwards. This allowance shows that Dobby frees himself by first freeing his mind, and allowing himself to think of freedom, but is chained to the old rules of loyalty to his masters. Fighting off these chains, Dobby warns Harry of an impending disaster at Hogwarts and tries to save Harry many times. At the end, Harry wins Dobby's freedom, and Dobby is forever grateful to Harry. In this sense, Harry is Dobby's Christ figure – the mind was free, but Dobby needed Harry's true sacrificial love (taking off his sock) that would free him from the previous rules of punishment for doing as his freedom allowed. The reigning party, the Malfoys, would never have granted Dobby his freedom because they needed his magical abilities and service. This servitude parallels the story of Paul and Silas freeing the girl from demons, only to be chastised by her masters who were making money from her work (Acts 16:16-19).

Lily Evans Potter: Lily (Evans) Potter was Harry Potter's mother, and was born into a muggle household. Lily's green eyes are perhaps a flashback to Godric Gryffindor's eyes and perhaps her magical lineage and abilities were only repressed through the ages (her family still lived in Godric

Hollow, named after Godric Gryffindor). Her name, Lily, is the Christian symbol for the Virgin Mary – innocence and purity. Lily lost her life deflecting Lord Voldemort's killing curse from Harry, which is what saved Harry's life – her sacrifice was then embedded in his skin and made Harry untouchable by Lord Voldemort. Her symbol was also the doe, or the hart, also both symbols of a Christian.[38]

James Potter: James Potter was Harry's father, and a direct descendent of Ignotius Peverell (named after one of the founding fathers of Christianity) and Godric Gryffindor who were two legendary wizards in history. During his years at Hogwarts, he convinced Sirius Black to become a Gryffindor rather than a Slytherin, played seeker for the Gryffindor Quidditch team, made top grades for all of his subjects, and eventually won the heart of Lily Evans. His animagus is a stag, the symbol of Christ, giving him the nickname Prongs. Unfortunately, since he did not suggest that he would take Harry's place in death, his death was not sacrificial in nature and thus didn't protect Harry from Lord Voldemort the way Harry's mother's did. One key inheritance that James possessed and passed down to Harry was the Invisibility Cloak, handed down from father to son through Ignotius Peverell's line, just as we receive many elements of faith from our own parents.

Fleur Delacour: Fleur is a student from the Beauxbaton School of Witchcraft and Wizardry who came with her fellow students to Hogwarts for the Triwizard Tournament in *The Goblet of Fire*. She was selected to represent her school as their champion, although she did not win any of the contests. Her school was symbolic of both the French people and the element of air, and their students sat with the Ravenclaws for meals. At the end of that contest, she met Bill Weasley, and decided to stay in England to work on her English. With Veela genes, she is very beautiful

---

[38] Tucker, S., 1997, "ChristStory Bestiary," retrieved from http://ww2.netnitco.net/~legend01/stag.htm.

and fair and has undue influence over most males in her presence, but alchemically represents the White Queen in her marriage to Bill Weasley, the Red King.

Victor Krum: Victor Krum is a celebrated Quidditch seeker on the Bulgarian national team, but is also a student at Durmstrang School of Witchcraft and Wizardry in *The Goblet of Fire*. He and his fellow students travelled to Hogwarts to participate in the Triwizard Tournament, and Victor was chosen to be Durmstrang's champion. During that year, he becomes good friends with Hermione and Harry, and is invited to Bill and Fleur's wedding in the last book.

Narcissa Malfoy: The wife of Lucius Malfoy and sister to Bellatrix LaStrange, Narcissa also underwent a transformation during the seven books. Initially, Narcissa lives up to her namesake, the Greek mortal Narcissus, who thought of no one but himself and was eventually turned into a flower. However, as the story progressed, her love for Draco, her son, helped her to see the lack of love, forgiveness, and caring that drove Lord Voldemort and the other Death Eaters and she decided not to continue with the Death Eaters. Her understanding of love going beyond just one's own person gives her the courage to defy Lord Voldemort and save Harry Potter in the end.

Fenrir Greyback: The name Fenrir comes from the Old Norse "Fenris," the giant wolf. True to the name, Fenrir Greyback is a werewolf that uses his condition for personal or Lord Voldemort's gains. When he is not in his wolf form, he threatens others to do his bidding and join him. If/when they don't follow his demands, then when he is about to transform, he goes back and gets into position to bite either that person or someone that person cares for. Through this process, he creates an army of werewolves that are under his control. Throughout the series,

Fenrir is a marginal character, never truly a member of any side even though Lord Voldemort promises many things to the werewolves in return for their help. Although Fenrir is allowed to chew on any of the Death Eaters' victims, he is never allowed into the inner circle of those with the Dark Mark on their right forearm and the Death Eaters never consider the werewolves as equals.

Aberforth Dumbledore: To accent the fact that Hogwarts is essentially a Christian sheepfold with Albus Dumbledore as the shepherd, Dumbledore's brother, Aberforth Dumbledore (also an AD name) is symbolic of the goats in the Biblical story of the separation of the sheep and the goats (Matthew 25:32). Aberforth's patronus is a goat, and he was found guilty of working with goats as a youngster.[39] Although Aberforth seems never to be in agreement with his brother Albus, he runs the tavern called "The Hogs Head" near the school and keeps Albus informed of the rumors and doings at his pub. Until he meets Harry, Aberforth only concerns himself with about saving his own neck, and tells Harry not to take on Lord Voldemort and keep safe instead. However, at the final battle, Aberforth joins the fight for Harry and against Lord Voldemort.

Conclusion:

With these character descriptions, I hope that you will now be able to read a bit deeper into each story and gain a better sense of how multiple elements fit together throughout the series. Within the Harry Potter books are many levels – alchemy, Christianity, morality, e.g. – much like the holographic two-dimensional screens. From the side, each is a two dimensional flat page. However, when you look into the screen and tilt it to different angles, you begin to see the screen as a three dimensional object and forget that it is only two-dimensional. In the

[39] Rowling, J., 2007, *Harry Potter and the Deathly Hallows,* p. 25.

same way, as we first read through the Harry Potter series, we tend to remember the plot alone with some basic character information. Once we begin to look at each character in depth and the different aspects of the plot, we begin to tilt the plot and see the three dimensions within it, making it more interesting and artistically beautiful every time you read it again.

Chapter FOUR

The Guide to *The Philosopher's Stone*

Plot summary: In this first book, we are introduced to Harry Potter, a boy of eleven years old who has been raised very ungraciously by his aunt, uncle, and cousin, because Lord Voldemort killed Harry's parents. These relatives, the Dursleys, hate everything that is not normal, especially things that cannot be explained such as magic. Anytime that Harry unknowingly uses magic, the Dursleys punish Harry more than the usual neglect and malice. On his eleventh birthday, Rubeus Hagrid arrives to tell Harry about his acceptance at Hogwarts and place within the magical community, taking him to Diagon Alley to purchase his school supplies and show him the monetary legacy left to him from his parents. While at Gringotts, the wizards' bank, Hagrid also empties vault 713 by removing a small parcel to be secured at Hogwarts. Harry also meets Draco Malfoy, a pureblood wizard that belongs in Slytherin House, and receives Hedwig, the white snowy owl, as his first real birthday present.

On September first, Harry meets Ronald Weasley and Hermione Granger on the train to Hogwarts, where they are sorted into the Gryffindor house. We meet Albus Dumbledore, the Headmaster of Hogwarts, Professor McGonagall who teaches Transfigurations, Professor

Quirrell who teaches Defense Against the Dark Arts; Professor Severus Snape who teaches Potions, and Professor Binns who teaches History of Magic. Shortly after the school year begins, the first year students are taught how to fly on their broomsticks, and Harry's natural ability to fly earns him an automatic spot on the Gryffindor Quidditch team.

On October 31st, a troll shows up at Hogwarts, and Harry and Ron run to the girls' bathroom to rescue Hermione while the other students are being ushered back to their common rooms. However, the troll is in that same bathroom, and Harry, Ron, and Hermione defeat the troll, cementing their friendship. They later discover where the package that Hagrid picked up from Gringotts is being protected at Hogwarts, and Lord Voldemort is somehow trying to get it. On Christmas, Harry receives his first real presents in his life- from his friends Ron and Hermione, and the Invisibility Cloak from Dumbledore, who had held it for Harry's father.

By the end of the school year, Harry, Hermione, and Ron learn enough about the package and how to get around the first of seven protections that they attempt to retrieve the package themselves to thwart Lord Voldemort. Harry ends up face to face with Professor Quirrell, who has been possessed by Lord Voldemort, trying to get the Philosopher's Stone. Harry discovers that he is protected by his skin – as Lord Voldemort touches Harry, Lord Voldemort's skin burns, due to the protection of sacrificial love Lily Potter left that is in Harry's skin and blood. Lord Voldemort leaves, which kills Professor Quirrell, and Harry survives. At the conclusion, Headmaster Dumbledore destroys the Philosopher's Stone, Gryffindor wins the House Cup for the year, and the students return home via the Hogwarts Express train with many promises to keep in touch over the summer.

Chapter One: The Boy Who Lived

In this first chapter, it is obvious that something extraordinary has happened – there are owls flying everywhere, fireworks, and odd people in robes all over the city. However, we see how blind the Dursley family is to everything as Vernon Dursley decides to ignore everything throughout his day. While there are multiple displays of celebration, the Dursleys choose not to see anything that's not "normal" and thus miss the bigger picture and only think that the world is going crazy. In many ways, this is similar to the ongoing debate about the existence of God – although religious communities see evidence of God's existence everywhere around us, there are many who chose to see nothing, declaring that there is nothing around that proves His existence.

From the radio announcement about the bonfire celebrations being a week early, we notice that it is November first, All Saints Day. It is interesting to note that Harry's parents were killed on Halloween, which helps us understand that the series is not part of Witchcraft. For witchcraft, great wonderful things would happen on Halloween, not horrible things like a double murder. All Saints Day, or November 1st, is a day celebrated in different ways in different countries, but honors the lives of those who have gone before us in defiance of evil as they trusted in God through their deaths. In actuality, the reference to the bonfire is about Guy Fawkes Night, a common celebration in England on November fifth commemorating the failed attempt to destroy James I and the House of Lords in 1705. Again, we see the muggle community focusing on the secular celebrations and not acknowledging the religious holidays.

One of the ironies in this chapter is Vernon Dursley's conviction that Harry Potter's first name is a very common name. In the book of names, "Harry" means "king", which means that although it might be used to name people quite often, the royal quality it infers is NOT very common. Alternately, Petunia, Lily's sister, is named after a very common garden flower, and Vernon has always prided himself on being completely normal so as not to stand out in any way.

However, things change with the introduction of Albus Dumbledore arriving at Privet Drive. Using his "Deluminator", we get our first glimpse at the man who acts as the Christ figure in most of the saga. Christ is the "light of the world", and Albus Dumbledore has mastery over the light, being able to hide it and relight things as he chooses. The Deluminator is a device of Dumbledore's making and is the only one in existence.[40] As such, Dumbledore can illumine those he wishes to, and keep in darkness those who will not see the truth, an attribute we see many times in the Bible, as God hardens people's hearts or opens them to hear God's word and receive the light of Christ.

As we meet Harry, we are introduced to his most identifying characteristic – his lighting shaped scar on his forehead. Interestingly, this shaped scar tells us right away that Harry is a Christian. In the Baroque Period, composers such as J.S. Bach would create a "musical cross" in their music using the notes to highlight important words or concepts in the lyrics. The notes, if we used them as connect-the-dots, would form a lightning bolt on the music staff. This same mark left on Harry's forehead is a reminder of our own mark given to us through our baptism: "You are sealed with the Holy Spirit and marked as God's own forever" (Book of Common Prayer, p. 308). Although the crosses we received at our baptism don't become scars, the effect is somewhat like lemon juice on paper – it remains invisible until the right light turns the lemon juice brown. Similarly, Harry's baptismal mark is hidden until the evil of Lord Voldemort rebounds on it, illuminating it for all to see.

Chapter Two: The Vanishing Glass

Through this chapter, we get a better sense of Harry's relationship to the Dursley's – they treat him a bit like Frances Hodgson Burnett's Sara Crewe: an orphan with a mysterious past that should be grateful for any scrap of clothing, food, or lodging given to him and consider them to be kindness. We do learn of Harry's rather peculiar and newfound ability to

---

[40] Rowling, J, *Harry Potter and the Deathly Hallows*, "The Will of Albus Dumbledore," Chapter 6.

talk to snakes here, and we see through his everyday conversation with the snake that he has no fear of snakes. Harry's lack of fear shows his depth of compassion for all living creatures since he sees a creature imprisoned, not a dangerous creature, but symbolically it shows his lack of fear of evil. We have seen how Harry responds to the negligence and malice bestowed on him through the Dursleys and Dudley's friends, so perhaps Harry is immune to fear from unkindness and evil now. Most importantly, we see that despite Harry's upbringing, he is not a "victim." Not only does Harry keep his self-confidence and self-worth intact, he is able to find little ways to assert himself in defiance of his treatment and stand up to those who would bully him.

Chapter Three: The Letters From No One

For the first time, Harry sees mail intended for him, and the Dursley's won't let him read it. Beyond the obvious human rights violation, there is the question about what Hogwarts is – they are trying to get a message to Harry, and know about him almost omnisciently. These letters are the truth that will tell Harry who he is, and give him guidance to the path he will follow the rest of his life, just like a tract gives the basics about what it is to be a Christian. The Dursleys travel to unimaginable places to avoid hearing the truth and letting Harry know the truth about who he is – a member of the wizarding world! If a Christian were born and baptized, then adopted out to an atheistic family and the child was then invited to attend Sunday School classes, the response would probably be the same. They would do anything to try and keep the child from knowing that he was part of a larger community of faith they didn't share. The chapter ends with that very familiar Bible passage – someone not to be ignored knocking on the door to come in with the truth. ("Behold, I stand at the door and knock." Rev 3:20)

Chapter Four: The Keeper of the Keys

Connecting to the events that closed the last chapter, we are introduced to Hagrid, the gatekeeper at Hogwarts. In Christian terms, Hagrid is actually a gatekeeper for Hogwarts the sheepfold, and goes to the ends of the earth to find and return the lost lamb, Harry. This concept is based on the Biblical verse John 10:3: "to Him, the gatekeeper opens the gate and the sheep hear His voice. In many ways, Hogwarts is that sheepfold where sheep are taught to love and serve the Lord. To further this analogy, Albus Dumbledore is the Great Shepherd, who protects his sheep in the sheepfold. The Dursleys, representing those who try to deny the truth of God, try to find the most isolated place so that the truth can't find them, but nothing can prevent the gatekeeper from finding the lost lamb Harry.

As Hagrid begins to explain to Harry his true wizarding nature, Hagrid finally gets to reclaim Harry into the wizarding world. By shedding light on his past, Harry finds that what Hagrid says makes sense of everything and he sees the truth. Hagrid also shows the first bit of true kindness to Harry since his time with the Dursleys, by giving him a hand-made birthday cake. Acting as the shepherd taking care of his Lord's sheep, Hagrid also gives Harry his warm jacket to sleep under for the night, and protects Harry from further interference from the Dursleys by keeping watch over him.

The last point in this chapter comes from something that Hagrid mentions. While discussing Hogwarts and Harry's destiny to be part of that school, Hagrid mentions that Harry's name has been down in the book for Hogwarts ever since he was born. This is a clear reference to God's people being chosen from the beginning, not having to prove that they are worthy of Christ before being accepted and put into the "Book of Life" (Revelations 3), but also Psalms 139:13 "Before you were born, I knew you.." This is a continuation of the Hogwarts/ sheepfold of Christian formation analogy, and further indication that Albus Dumbledore is the Christ figure as the Great Shepherd.

Chapter Five: Diagon Alley

In this chapter, Hagrid introduces Harry to the physical wizarding world, and their main shopping market in London, called Diagon Alley. Although it would be easy to think that Diagon was a stand-in for Dragon, it is not. Diagon Alley is actually the world "diagonally" made into a street name. Why the word "diagonally"? This is a reference to the alchemy of her book, but also in chemistry, elements diagonal from each other share very similar properties and are considered to have a diagonal relationship. Elements with a diagonal relationship can have many similar physical properties such as the melting point, boiling point, or reactivity. From this viewpoint, "Diagon Alley" refers to the fact that the wizards have very similar properties to the muggle world – they are both human with human emotions and lives. However, the wizarding world is in a universe of its own, apparently invisible to the muggle society despite their similarities.

In the movie, Hollywood does a very good job depicting the magical world as a Christian one, although from a European perspective. In the United States, all the churches are very new, with whitewashed walls, few stained windows, and no bombing history or centuries of candle smoke and incense darkening their walls. In Europe, the large churches were built as architecture expanded, so many have small high windows that don't let in a lot of light. Their purpose was to provide a large place for worship, so it began with thick walls with few windows and thinner walls with buttresses as the architecture developed. The architecture, in combination with the longstanding traditions of the churches, contributes to a very old, dark feeling when entering these Christian domains. Many churches have new lights, but candles are still prevalent, and upon entering you feel as if you've returned to a world three hundred years earlier. This is the magical world J. K. Rowling portrays – the European Christian church world, where people still do things the old fashioned way with candles, handwritten parchments, quills, herbs for healing (a Christian practice until modern medicine arrived in the late 1800s!), and symbolism to help connect us with the past and each other.

Another element at Diagon Alley redefines who Harry is within the wizarding world in direct opposition to his place in the muggle world. Although in the muggle world Harry is a poor orphan with no friends, in the wizarding world, Harry is rich and the whole wizarding world wants to befriend Harry. When Harry realizes that he will need money to purchase his school supplies, Hagrid explains to him about Gringotts, the Wizard's Bank, and tells Harry that his needs are taken care of. This is from Philippians 4:19-20: "And my God shall supply all your need according to His riches in glory by Christ Jesus." Also, the concept that the wizarding world would have a different form of money than the muggle world is direct from the Bible as well. In Biblical times, there was Temple money from which people gave to the synagogue, and Roman or other local currency, which was given to pay taxes to Rome. The exchange rates between galleons, sickles, and knuts make fun of the odd exchange rates of past centuries, where it was not metric in fashion but rather based on the value of the metal in the coins used.

At the bank, we are also introduced to the first non-human creatures in the story (other than Hagrid who is half-giant) – the goblins and dragons at Gringotts bank. Goblins are magical creatures known for their metallurgical abilities, but also for their cunning and trickery, while dragons are known for their hoarding and viciousness. It is quite fitting that these creatures control the bank and money, since their love of money portrays greed and the "root of all evil." (1 Timothy 6:10.) Although the goblins do not seem to have any other magical abilities, their instinctive, protective hoarding complements the dragons' traditional caste of honoring money/ metal above all else. It is also the beginning of the alchemical process of the story – Harry goes into the bank, the collection of most base metals, beginning the alchemical and transformational storyline while the dragon represents the outcome of alchemy – immortality after mastery. Harry and the Philosopher's Stone come out together from the bank with Hagrid because one must be destroyed to allow the other to take its place.

In the underground of the bank, Harry discovers the wealth of treasure left to him by his parents, and begins to feel loved and a sense of belonging. In the other vault that they visit, number 713, we see another suggestion of alchemy at work in the number itself. First of all, we know there is something special in the vault since Dumbledore himself asked Hagrid to bring its contents to Hogwarts. Secondly, the vault's number combines the two magical numbers in alchemy: 7, and 13. 7 is the number of perfection, and 13 is the number of completion. These are also numbers in Christianity – the seven is mentioned numerous times in the Bible, including the days of the week, how many times you must forgive someone, the number of days it takes to set up Jesus' ministry in the book of John, and multiple other references in Revelation and John. The number thirteen is understandably debatable about being a good number, since there were thirteen in the group of disciples if you count Christ as part of that group. However, there were actually 13 tribes of Israel – 11 tribes were named after the children of Jacob, but Joseph was never a tribe to himself – his honor was to have two tribes named for his own two children, making 13. (Since the Levites were never given any land for themselves, there were only 12 tribal lands given out, but there were thirteen groups.) Lastly, although the law says that you have to forgive someone seven times (the number of perfection); Jesus augments this by saying that you have to forgive 7 times 7 times: 7 times 7 = 49, 4+9 = 13, the number of completion.

Another place Hagrid takes Harry to visit in Diagon Alley is Ollivander's Wand Shoppe, a key element of Christianity within the wizarding world. From the first sight of the shop, we see the sign over the door that says it's been in operation since 382 BC. Although nothing significant occurred in 382 B.C. (other than the unification of Macedonia shortly before Alexander the Great), the numbers add to 13, the alchemical number of completion. Combined with B.C., this turns to "thirteen before Christ", another Christian reference to the thirteen main prophets before Christ (Samuel, Jonah, Elijah, Elisha, Isaiah, Jeremiah, Amos, Micah, Daniel, Zephaniah, Hosea, Ezekiel, and John the Baptist). Secondly, the name "Ollivander's" itself is a reference to the olive wood, the wood of Christ's time and cross, possibly (many different woods lay claim to being the wood of the cross). With these two elements together, we see how J. K. Rowling has connected the Alchemical with the Christian elements to create a new intellectual twist for Christianity.

Inside Ollivander's shop, we are introduced to the many wands created for future wizards of the wizarding world. From John 15:5, we have the verse "I am the vine, you are the branches", from which the wands are created and hint at their true nature – that of the power of God. In truth, in the Harry Potter series, the wands represent God's work, especially since the wizards are not to do things through their own persons after they receive their wands. Similarly, Christians never lay claim to having done the actual act of healing themselves – they are always careful to put the glory in God's work, not their own. Furthermore, as Ollivander explains to Harry, "the wand chooses the wizard, Harry. No one is exactly clear why." This is an exact take from the Bible, John 15:16 "You did not choose me, but I chose you and appointed you to go and bear fruit--fruit that will last. Then the Father will give you whatever you ask in my name" (NIV). The wand that eventually chooses Harry is a combination of the holly wood and the phoenix feather, also showing how wands are a Christian symbol. In general, the holly wood represents "holy wood", and all of its symbolism of Christ – the white lily of Mary, the red berry for His shed blood, and the sharp thorns that circled his head on the cross. For all of the wands, Ollivander only uses three elements for the cores of his wands – phoenix feather, dragon heartstring, and unicorn hair, all of which are also Christian symbols. The Phoenix represents Christ's resurrection; the unicorn represents Christ's purity and innocence, and the dragon heartstring represents His mastery over the four alchemical elements and immortality. In Harry's case, the combination of the Holly and the Phoenix is a double reference to Christ, and a signal that Harry is definitely a disciple of Christ, even if he does not understand everything yet.

At the end of the chapter, Harry also receives his first real birthday present from Hagrid – his snowy owl, Hedwig. Hedwig means "contention, strife,"[41] but she serves as Harry's only true connection to the magical world when at Privet Drive with the Dursleys. Owls

---

[41] 2011, "Hedwig meaning and name origin," *Think Baby Names,* retrieved from http://www.thinkbabynames.com/meaning/0/Hedwig.

themselves are a symbol of God's wisdom, and act as a connection between the earthly and heavenly worlds, just as Hedwig acts as Harry's connection in the muggle world to the magical one.

Chapter Six: The Journey from Platform 9 ¾

As the Dursleys drop Harry off at King's Cross, they sneer at Harry since they know that Harry is looking for something that doesn't exist – Platform 9 ¾, just as many sneered at Jesus as he hung upon the cross knowing that he would rise from the dead, a concept completely impossible to any unbelieving onlookers. At the train station, we see the switch from the muggle world to the magical world completed at King's Cross, symbolic in two ways: a) a cross is where two paths meet and continue on in different directions as we see here with the muggle and the wizarding world, and b) Christ the King's Cross is where the transformation from being a slave to death to be redeemed to life begins. The barrier between the muggle to the magical platforms takes faith to overcome, as Harry discovers from the Weasley family who guide him and show him the way to the truth behind the barrier. Although Harry discovered that they were magical because they had an owl like his own, the muggle world around them is oblivious to the magical platforms' existence. Again we see that despite the multiple clues all around them, the muggle world turns a blind eye to those who have the faith to cross through the barrier to the magical world on the other side of the wall, not even noticing that they have disappeared from view.

As Harry meets the rest of the Weasley family, he becomes good friends with Ronald, the sixth boy of the family. In direct contrast to the Dursleys, the Weasleys are welcoming and friendly. They also guide Harry through the dividers to the magical world without first asking who he is, helping him first get to the platform then getting his luggage loaded onto the train. Even once the Weasleys discover who he is, they only treat him as a loved equal, without any reservation. As it says in Matthew 25:40 "As you did for the least of my brethren, you did for me," another example of the Biblical concepts embedded throughout the series.

Once on the train, Harry learns from Ron that he's not going to be too far behind anyone else in what they are already expected to know. As it turns out, many people weren't aware that they were chosen much earlier than Harry was. Also, at Hogwarts they teach beyond the usual things people learn at home. Similarly, people who come to faith later in life are given the same reward as those who have been Christians their entire lives, and both are given the same gift of the Holy Spirit. In this, being born into the faith does not entitle anyone to greater rewards; it just means that they have lived within the loving Christian community longer.

Amongst other facts obtained on the train, we learn more about who Albus Dumbledore is through Harry. When Harry buys the Chocolate Frogs from the trolley cart, he learns that the packages include information cards about famous wizards. Harry happens to get Dumbledore's card, and learns that he and Nicholas Flamel created the Philosopher's Stone and that Dumbledore discovered the twelve uses of Dragon's Blood. The Philosopher's Stone is the gold transformed from lead that gives a red elixir of life, hence its red color. This red colored elixir is also called dragon's blood, which when drunk regularly (about once a month) will give the drinker eternal life.[42] Dumbledore's "discovery" of the twelve uses for the dragon's blood is for the salvation of each of the twelve sons of Israel or the twelve disciples. The wine becomes the "blood of Christ" despite it holding the same qualities of wine, in the same way that lead becomes gold – it is a "spiritual" transformation of the solid, not a physical one per se. Finally, Nicolas Flamel could never have completed the Philosopher's Stone without Professor Dumbledore's assistance – no one can achieve immortality without a relationship with Christ and His redemption.

Chapter Seven: The Sorting Hat

As the students approach the Hogwarts station, Hermione reminds Harry and Ron that all the students have to put on their black robes as

---

[42] Granger, J, 2007, *Unlocking Harry Potter,* p. 63-64.

they go to Hogwarts. Again, these robes could be seen as the robes of warlocks or witches, but there are many differences. First of all, these robes do not have hoods, and resemble the academic gowns worn by all students until the late 1800s in advanced academic institutions such as Harvard. Indeed, in the movies, they do a great job of doing everything they can to NOT make the students' robes look like witches' robes – the students' hats look more like dunce caps, and although Professor McGonagall wears a tall black hat, it is bent in half so as not to look like a straight, conical witch's hat. All the other staff members wear other types of hats, none of them black, and the robes they wear are of all different colors. The student robes are black to show their novitiate status, just as they would wear going into a monastery or nunnery to learn more about God through a relationship with Christ.

In continuation of the sheepfold theme, Hagrid leads the new students into Hogwarts in the boats across the lake. Furthermore, people may only enter Hogwarts through the gate, a continuation of John chapter 10, verse 1. "I tell you the truth, the man who does not enter the sheep pen by the gate, but climbs in by some other way, is a thief and a robber." Hagrid is careful not to lose a single student as they cross the water (a reminder of a Christian's baptism into the faith) into Hogwarts itself and are handed over to the care of the Assistant Headmaster, Professor McGonagall.

As we meet Professor McGonagall, we see that she is dressed in green emerald robes, just as her letter to Harry was written in emerald green ink. The significance of the green is that it is the liturgical color of "ordinary time" and learning, but more specifically, that of magical apprenticeship of the Lord. The master always wears purple, which we see is Professor Dumbledore's attire with gold markings, the purple and gold representing his kingship and dominion over Magic and the Christian world. Another set of characters that we meet at Hogwarts are the ghosts. These ghosts represent those Christians from the Church Triumphant, or those martyrs and saints that we might still communicate with through prayer. Even within the wizarding world, they are only found at Hogwarts, another hint that Hogwarts is the sheepfold of the Great Shepherd akin to a heaven on earth. At least, there are no mentions of ghosts lurking anywhere else in the magical world, either because they cannot exist outside of Hogwarts or they are collected at Hogwarts if they do not choose to move on when they die.

One special oddity we are introduced to at the Great Hall is the Sorting Hat. This talking hat, given enough intelligence by the Founding Fathers to be able to communicate with new students, sorts all new students into the appropriate house depending on what the Sorting Hat sees in the students' mind and soul. As another link to alchemy, the four houses the students are sorted into represent the four basic elements from alchemy: earth, water, air, and fire. Gryffindor represents fire with the red and gold coloring and the bravery requirement. Ravenclaw, with the colors of blue and bronze and students with their brilliant minds in the clouds all the time, represents air. Hufflepuff, with their steadfastness and friendships, represents earth. Lastly, Slytherin, with the colors of green and silver and the symbol of the snake, represents water.[43] Although the students are divided into four separate houses, it will only be when all four houses work together that Hogwarts will achieve its conquest of true harmony within the wizarding world.

As Dumbledore gives his four words of grace before the students can eat, he says four nonsense words that mean very little to those around him: "Nitwit, blubber, oddball, tweak." However, in many ways this is exactly what happens in many houses before a meal - people say words that are meaningless to them before meals as a grace, either because they are thinking about something else and are not truly thankful for what is given to them, or they do not understand why they are saying thank you before a meal. In another interpretation, John Granger suggests that these words are cue words for the four houses.[44]

---

[43] Harry Potter Wiki, "Houses of Hogwarts," retrieved from http://harrypotter.wikia.com/wiki /The_four_houses_of_Hogwarts.
[44] Harry Potter Wiki, "Houses of Hogwarts," retrieved from http://harrypotter.wikia.com/wiki /The_four_houses_of_Hogwarts.

While the new students eat their first meal at Hogwarts, Professor Severus Snape is introduced here as a key questionable character. Always dressed in black, never eating or communing with others, and never happy, Professor Snape seems forever in a dour mood. Hollywood reinforces the evil stereotype by casting Alan Rickman, who has played many sinister characters in other movies, and in the book, Harry's scar burns when he first sees Professor Snape, suggesting that this Professor must have some evil link to Harry's scar.

At the end of this chapter, Harry encounters Lord Voldemort for the first time in many years through his dream, which gives a foreshadowing of the reality to come: Lord Voldemort, in Professor Quirrell's turban, tells Harry that he should be in Slytherin, perhaps in an effort to be closer to Harry and bind the two of them together within the dark arts. For better or worse, Harry forgets this dream and is not aware of Lord Voldemort's near presence throughout much of the book.

Chapter Eight: The Potions Master

As the first week of classes starts and Harry has to figure out how to get to each class, we learn more about how Hogwarts is situated. There are 142 staircases (1+4+2 = 7), and many staircases that shift while you're on them or with tricky steps that you have to jump, etc. In many ways, this parallels any Christian path set by someone else – what works for one person may cause pitfalls for others, and there are many written documents that are supposed to help people get to some goal, but actually take them somewhere else. Also, anything can be misconstrued, causing people to fall rather than climb towards their goal unfortunately. It is wise to always be mindful of the big picture destination, and keep an eye out for anything that might change that direction. Sometimes, pitted paths are best left alone and ignored, as Harry discovers which paths are unavoidable and which can be avoided altogether.

In one of Harry's first classes, we learn a little about transfiguration. The transfiguration class, taught by Professor McGonagall, is about switching between an animated form and an associated unanimated form of all objects, just as the transfigurations in the Bible involve bringing people closer to a Godly form. Since God is the ultimate source of life, transfiguration is about bringing out animation, or life/spirit to otherwise inanimate objects, either in a form that was used to create it or a related one. This is not about being a creative spirit; it is about helping other objects find their life within or leading them to the light of God. In another way, transfiguration is the opposite of transubstantiation – transfiguration is the physical change of something but maintaining the same spiritual qualities, whereas transubstantiation is the spiritual change of a substance without a physical change.

In each class, the students either learn how to channel their faith to use their wand, or they learn that wands are not needed for the task at hand. For instance, although it takes faith to bring things closer to God in transfiguration class or create miracles in charms class, it does not take faith to create potions or learn about the herbs God provided us to use for healing. The wands used in the wizarding world also represent the student's faith, and a stronger faith usually brings on stronger magic from the wand. As long as the wand has chosen the wizard and the wizard has faith in his/her wand, the wand will perform the required work at hand: Luke 17:6 "If you have faith like a mustard seed, you would say to this mulberry tree 'be uprooted and plant yourself in the sea' and it would obey you."

As Harry takes his first potions class, we get another glimpse into Professor Snape's apparent hatred of Harry Potter as the professor ridicules him in front of the class. However, knowing that Harry's mother was fantastic at potions, Professor Snape might have been testing Harry to see if he had any innate knowledge of potions. Another interesting note is that Professor Snape spends a lot of time staring into Harry's eyes, unlike anyone else, perhaps for two reasons: 1) Snape is a great Legilmens and can read minds, and 2) Harry's eyes look just like his mother's and Snape loved his mother. By looking into Harry's eyes, Snape reminds himself of Harry's mother whenever he seems to lose hope or forgets why he is doing the task given to him to complete.

Chapter Nine: The Midnight Duel

This chapter begins with an insight into the mechanics of broomstick flying, and shows us the only class that Hermione doesn't excel at – flying. However, Harry is able to show his innate physical and mental abilities in his flying duel against Draco Malfoy, and thus wins his place as the youngest seeker in a century on the Gryffindor Quidditch team. This begins the long parallel of Harry's life to St. John the Evangelist's life. St John was also the youngest disciple to seek Christ, paralleling the position of seeker on the Quidditch team (more on this in the next couple of chapters). Professor McGonagall introduces Harry to Oliver Wood, a clear reference to Olive Wood (just as Ollivander's was a reference to the olive wood) both references to Christ's cross of wood. It is fitting that Oliver Wood is the one to teach Harry the rules of how Quidditch game is played, since the symbolism is that the olive wood of the cross teaches everyone where to find the truth of Christ.

As another link to the concept of the hereafter, we also meet the monstrous dog with three heads behind the locked door on the third floor, the one Dumbledore warned the students of in his opening speech. The three headed dog, Cerebus, is known in Greek and Roman mythology to guard the Underworld for Hades, preventing anyone from escaping death. At the end of the chapter, Harry figures out that the little package from vault 713 must be what is being guarded by the three headed dog, an allegory to the three headed dog guarding the representative of alchemical perfection (since 7 and 13 are perfect numbers). It is imperative that the alchemical representative of immortality not escape into the mortal world, since in order to obtain immortality, one has to die to self first.

After the escape from the three headed dog, we discover that the Gryffindor Tower is on the seventh floor. Again, this shows the alchemy of the series since seven is the perfect number in alchemy, Judaism, and Christianity. Ravenclaw's dormitories are also in a tower, since it represents air, and as a side note, Hufflepuff's common room is located down by the kitchens and Slytherin's is located underneath the lake.[45]

Each common room is placed according to their alchemical representation.

Near the end of the chapter, Hermione gives us an interesting thought to ponder: "we could all have been killed – or worse, expelled." (p. 162). Ron returns with a comment about Hermione needing to get her priorities straight, but the truth is that in medieval churches, being excommunicated (expelled) WAS worse than being killed. At least if you were killed, you knew that you would still go to heaven. If you were expelled, you had no hopes of Heaven[46] until you were reconciled by the bishop (sources vary on this point). Overall, this chapter further defines many Christian concepts of the afterlife, and subtly sets the pivot point of mortality first.

Chapter Ten: Halloween

For most of the books, the conflict between Harry and Lord Voldemort begins on Halloween and is concluded by an ambiguous Pentecost time. Although J. K. Rowling does not give exact dates other than Halloween and Christmas, we can infer the other dates since Easter, Ascension, and Pentecost are floating holidays depending on when the moon is full that spring. At the beginning of book one, we see Harry's parents killed on Halloween, setting up the entire series' conflict for resolution by the end of the seventh book on Pentecost, and here at Halloween we begin the conflict for the first year of Harry's schooling – the troll sent by an unknown someone. That someone, ultimately Lord Voldemort, will be the source of the conflict throughout the book.

Before Halloween, Oliver Wood teaches us how Magical Quidditch is played, and as an aside, it is of course all about the symbolism of numbers. There is one Golden Snitch, which alchemically represents truth and the ultimate desire of all perfection, which is the goal of all seekers.

---

[45] Harry Potter Wiki, "Hogwarts Houses," retrieved from http://harrypotter.wikia.com/wiki/ The_four_houses_of_Hogwarts.

[46] Alchin, L., *The Middle Ages*, "Middle Ages Religion," retrieved from http://www.middle-ages.org.uk/middle-ages-religion.htm.

The game logically ends when the seeker catches the snitch. There is only one goalkeeper per team, representative of keeping the ideas in bounds; the two beaters represent the two testaments, constantly throwing in ideas in new directions and the three chasers represent the heavenly trinities, focused on sending the baffling ideas (represented by the Quaffle – an English Frenchism perhaps of "what a baffle") out of bounds. Together, there are seven players, each with a particular purpose on the pitch.

In this chapter, we see more details of their Charms class. In Charms, we see further proof that the Harry Potter series is set in the church setting, since the charms are all spoken in Latin, and are not rhyming verse spells from witch lore. However, the pronunciation, as always, is important in giving the correct meaning and is a kick-back to the days of reciting the correct lilt of each world or conjugation in Latin or Greek class. However, at the end of the class, Ron is rather unkind to Hermione, and Hermione runs to the bathroom crying, where she remains for the remainder of the day.

Towards the end of the chapter, we see all the wizards at the Halloween dinner, when Professor Quirrell arrives to announce that there is a troll in the dungeons. Although all the students are instructed to go to their common rooms, Harry again breaks the rules by ignoring the order that all students go to their common rooms. At the last minute, Harry remembers that Hermione is in the bathroom and ignorant of the troll, and thus he sets out with Ron to save her. Thankfully, with Harry and Ron's help, Hermione is rescued from certain death. Dumbledore does not criticize Harry for his misconduct – rather, he smiles, as would Christ, since by defying the social etiquette laws, Harry was able to save someone from a horrible death.

As a side note, a troll is a very earthly creature. From the multiple stories from various cultures, trolls are depicted as selfish, childish, nightly creatures that capture children that stay out at night, but will turn to stone when caught in daylight.[47] In the first of the seven books of this series, Harry's challenge is to master earth, the first of the four alchemical elements in the alchemy scheme. Thus, Harry's defeat of the troll is the beginning of his mastery of the element of earth, setting him on the alchemy path towards Christ.

From this chapter on, we have the trio set – Harry, Ron, and Hermione. These three represent the trio of the church of Christ – body, soul, and mind. Harry is always the doer of Christ's will, Ron is always the emotional one who is a true friend and counselor to all, and Hermione is the mind of the trio, bringing in her wisdom and research diligence to the task at hand. Throughout the series, we see that when the three are working together, they are able to conquer the task at hand, but if willingly separated, they do not move forward.

Chapter Eleven: Quidditch

Most of this chapter is dedicated to the details of the first Quidditch match, Gryffindor versus Slytherin. During the match, Professor Snape seems to try to curse Harry off of his broom, and Hermione comes to the rescue. Hagrid explains to them later that Professor Snape is trying to protect something, but gives away another clue – Nicholas Flamel is involved. In reality, Nicholas Flamel was born in 1330 and before his death in 1418, was a well known alchemist who bestowed much upon the old city of Paris – hospitals, almshouses, and refurbishing cemeteries and is acknowledged as having created a Philosopher's Stone.[48] As a book seller, he mysteriously came into contact with The Codex, a book supposedly written by the philosopher Abraham the Jew, and the book gives instructions on how to create the Philosopher's Stone.[49] In creating the Philosopher's Stone, the alchemist's soul transforms from being solidly connected to the tangible world to one looking beyond the

---

[47] Troll Collectors Center, 2010, "The History of the Nyform Troll," retrieved from http://www.trollshop.net/trolls/history.htm.

[48] Merton, R, "A Detailed Biography of Nicholas Flamel," Flamel College, retrieved from http://www.flamelcollege.org/flamel.htm.

[49] Merton, R, "A Detailed Biography of Nicholas Flamel," Flamel College, retrieved from http://www.flamelcollege.org/flamel.htm.

tangible, to an immortal spiritual one. There were many rumors from gravediggers that Nicholas Flamel's body was not found in his grave, and combined with various sightings of Nicholas Flamel in the 1700s, this gave rise to the concept that he discovered the Elixir of Life that kept him alive beyond the grave. The information that the small object being guarded is for Nicholas Flamel will give the trio enough to work on for the next while.

Chapter Twelve: The Mirror of Erised

This chapter begins with Christmas morning, where Harry receives his first set of true Christmas presents, and within them, an invisibility cloak from an unknown sender. The cloak, a representation of the Holy Spirit, is given to him by Dumbledore, the Christ figure, as one's faith is also inherited from one's parents: John 14:26 "But the Counselor, the Holy Spirit, whom the Father will send in my name, will teach you all things and will remind you of everything I have said to you" (NIV). Although the only instructions that come with the cloak are "Use it well", Harry does use the cloak as intended in the Bible – he uses it to discover and learn things within Hogwarts for himself. Harry is then able to use the cloak to help others, explore areas that others can't, and come to new understandings that helped piece together the path to Lord Voldemort in each book for the climax of Harry versus Lord Voldemort at the end of each book. In another Christian parallel, many Christians are confirmed at the age of 11 or 12 and symbolically receive the Holy Spirit with the laying on of hands at the confirmation rite, the exact age that Harry is at the time that he receives his cloak. As with many other things, we don't always really understand the full greatness of what we've been given until we have had a chance to explore its limits and use it.

As Harry is running away from Mr. Filch because of his illegal use of the restricted section of the library, Harry discovers an enchanted object in an empty classroom – the Mirror of Erised. The writing on the mirror, "*Erised stra ehru oyt ube cafru oyt on wohsi*" is not some strange language, curse, or spell – since it's on a mirror, the inscription is written backwards so that it reads correctly when read through a mirror, although the spaces are not in the right places. Backwards, it reads "I show not your face, but your heart's desire." This gives a significant insight into each person's heart. For Harry, his heart's desire is to have a family and belong to a loving community. Looking in the mirror gives him a sense of connection with all those green eyes, again a reference and symbolism of the apprentice and seeker of truth.

After a few days of noticing that Harry has lost his appetite for food and life in general, lost in his hope and dreams of a family, Dumbledore finally steps in to help Harry find life again. How Dumbledore always seem to know what Harry is doing and what Harry is up to, regardless of where Harry is or how little is spoken is perhaps a spell that Dumbledore placed on Harry when he was left on the Dursley's doorstep; but more than likely, it is a characteristic of Dumbledore as the Christ figure. As such, Dumbledore would have the power of omniscience, and since Harry is a disciple, there is a special connection between the two as they begin Harry's alchemical journey together towards immortality. One of the key elements that we learn from Professor Dumbledore as he speaks to Harry is how unique Harry's heart is, especially given his ill-treatment from the Dursleys. Whereas Harry's friend Ron sees how great he could be, Harry only sees the result of love – family, and community. It is this love, and not Harry's quest for greatness, that protects Harry from Lord Voldemort and keeps him from evil.

Chapter Thirteen: Nicholas Flamel

In the Anglican tradition, there are three axes of Christian formation – love the Lord with all your heart, mind, and body. There are not too many examples of using one's mind to show others your love for God other than teaching except for Elijah's clever challenge to the priests of Baal, but the three friends represent these three elements and provide additional examples of how to use these three to help others: Harry represents the body of Christ, Ron the will/ spirit of Christ, and Hermione the mind of Christ.[50] Harry's memory makes the connection between Nicholas Flamel and the Philosopher's Stone and Dumbledore's significance in that

[50] Granger, John; 2002, *The Hidden Key to Harry Potter;* p. 117.

connection. Hermione then explains to the two friends the importance of the Philosopher's Stone in the world by explaining the basis of alchemy – the transformation of any metal (usually lead) into gold using the Philosopher's Stone.

The Stone, which is not said to be a solid substance, also produces the Elixir of Life, which transforms our mortal souls to immortal souls able to live with Christ, taken from lines from the Bible: "In the same way, after the supper he took the cup, saying, 'This cup is the new covenant in my blood, which is poured out for you' " (Luke 22:20). With her explanation, the trio finally understands how important the Stone's secrecy is, and the necessity to keep it from those who are not true owners of the stone. With the Philosopher's Stone, once the elixir of life is produced, anyone who believes in the Philosopher's Stone can drink of it and have immortal life without regard to that person's worthiness or efforts to obtain the transformation of soul that is required to create it in the first place. In Christianity, we see a very similar aspect – Christ did not wait for people to be worthy of his love, and knew that others could not be as pure as they needed to be to achieve their own philosopher's stone, so Christ became the Philosopher's Stone for the rest of us to have the Elixir of Life despite our unworthiness.

Another element that shows that Nicholas Flamel is not in any way part of a satanic group is that he is 665 years old, one number less that the devil's address. This perhaps suggests that Flamel is limited by the devil's instigated original division between God and Man, which no one but Christ can overcome, even though it was Dumbledore that helped him create the stone. Furthermore, within alchemical circles, there can only be one stone in existence at a time, so Flamel will have to destroy the stone in order for the new stone to emerge. It is somewhat preordained that the satanic number will not be a magical number for a Christian alchemist, since with the help of Christ, Flamel could pass through the curse and death unharmed.

One other key element in this series comes through in this chapter - we see that Harry is getting the sense that Professor Snape can read minds, an accurate assessment. Professor Snape is following Harry, trying to protect him as promised, although for his own edification, Professor Snape makes these encounters as horrible as possible. With their recent knowledge of the Stone and its location, Professor Snape is probably mind reading to check on their progress. At the Quidditch game, especially with Professor Dumbledore in attendance, Professor Snape, Hermione, and Ron are perhaps expecting trouble, although from different sources, but no one attempts anything with Harry's spectacularly quick win.

Chapter Fourteen: Norbert, the Norwegian Ridgeback

Worried that Professor Snape is trying to take the Philosopher's Stone for himself, the trio goes to talk to Hagrid. As the trio meets up with Hagrid, he tells them the number of professors that are protecting the stone – seven, the most powerful alchemical number - and each with a different type of enchantment. Although seven different enchantments or challenges should be sufficient protection for a stone, especially one in the middle of Hogwarts, there is a wolf in sheep's clothing at Hogwarts: Matthew 7:15 "Watch out for false prophets. They come to you in sheep's clothing, but inwardly they are ferocious wolves" (NIV). It is interesting that none of the other professors are suspected of wanting the stone. With seven enchantments, that means there are five professors (in addition to the headmaster and the gamekeeper) that know about the stone, and one of them is a new teacher – Professor Quirrell. This suggests that each professor asked to guard the stone was chosen more for their subject matter and type of protection, rather than for their individual traits or loyalties, and might be considered a huge matter of questionable trust on Professor Dumbledore's part.

One interesting side note in this chapter comes with Hagrid's discussion of dragons with the trio. With the reminder of Hagrid's interest in dragons, Harry, Ron, and Hermione are outraged at the danger Hagrid seems oblivious to. Hagrid's desire to own a dragon is also symbolic, as Hagrid is the gatekeeper to Hogwarts and dragons are symbols of immortality: dragons are masters of all four alchemical elements: they breathe fire, they fly, they swim, and they walk the earth.

In many ways, dragons are also symbols of heavenly creatures – since they have mastery over all four elements, they have immortality, as do the angels. Hagrid's preoccupation with the dragons being misunderstood but beautiful creatures attests to this heavenly understanding, especially since heavenly beings/ creatures are always portrayed as being too beautiful to be seen or touched without permanent damage, and their abilities can destroy cities (i.e. Sodom and Gomorrah) or create victories (e.g. Joshua and the Battle of Jericho). A dragon would be punished by losing its wings and limbs, reducing the dragon to a snake, a truly cursed creature that loses everything and represents evil as seen in Genesis.

Chapter Fifteen: The Forbidden Forest

In the forbidden forest, there exist many types of mythical creatures – unicorns, centaurs, werewolves, and other unnamed creatures. I propose that the forbidden forest is so named because it both warns us of these myths and legends and pokes fun of our own anxieties about mythological creatures and their symbolism. The unicorns are symbols of Christ's purity and innocence, and its blood is said to bring someone back to life, even if they were on the brink of death, just like the Elixir of Life can grant eternal life. However, the difference is that the unicorn's blood can only be obtained by killing the animal and bringing on a cursed life, whereas nothing is harmed by creating a Philosopher's Stone and drinking its Elixir of Life. The same is said in the Bible, although under slightly different circumstances. 1 Corinthians 10:28: "'This has been offered in sacrifice,' then do not eat it," and also 11:29: "For anyone who eats and drinks without recognizing the body of the Lord eats and drinks judgment on himself." Thus, no one should have anything to do with a sacrificed animal, and especially a sacrificed unicorn, representative of Christ's body and blood, since the act of sacrificing the animal itself would make the person unworthy to partake in the elements. Furthermore, we hear the most important requirement that determines worthiness to drink the Elixir of Life, whether it is the unicorn's representational blood of Christ or the dragon's blood of the Philosopher's Stone – the drinker must not be the one who sacrificed the animal, but also must recognize it as the blood of Christ in order to achieve the eternal life it promises.

Another set of creatures we meet in the Forbidden Forest are the centaurs. As with many of the magical creatures, the centaurs are very neutral creatures, neither siding with humans or against them. They are obsessed with astrology and the big picture, seeing everything as part of the plans set in motion long ago, much like the Deists of the 1700s and 1800s. In their view, we are given very vague clues about what is to happen, but it is all a script set in motion in the beginning, and we are not supposed to do anything but go along with what is pre-ordained to occur. Their constant vigilance to the skies demonstrates a bit of J.K. Rowling's mistrust of astrology, and the overall belief in God's unpredictability. ("No one knows about that day or hour, not even the angels in heaven, nor the Son, but only the Father", Matthew 24:36.) At a deeper level, this also denounces the pre-determined events since they oppose the free will of human kind to choose Christ and interfere with evil rather than accept fate and condone whatever evil exists. Again, this demonstration points to a firmer Christian foundation of the series, where Christians can choose to put their faith in Christ and not rely on the stars to dictate their fates.

Chapter Sixteen: Through the Trapdoor

After Harry's revelation that Hagrid has given away the first clue for the enemy to steal the stone, they also discover that Dumbledore is gone. Doggedly, Harry decides that he needs to save everyone else and fight the enemy himself, but Ron and Hermione loyally tell Harry that they are there to help him and will not leave him to suffer alone. Here again, we see first that the trio must stay together to survive – heart, mind, and body – since the trio has all three elements in balance, but also the strength and value of community over self. With Dumbledore away on a fool's errand, Lord Voldemort can go after the stone unchallenged, especially since Lord Voldemort does not count anyone but Professor Dumbledore as a challenge to his abilities.

As the trio arrives at the start of the seven challenges to get to the stone, we begin Harry's final journey to achieve his mastery over earth, the first of the four elements in Harry's transformational process. In the first challenge, we see that getting past the three-headed dog is just another of the earthly creatures that Harry has to overcome to achieve mastery of earth. The three previous ones that Harry helped master were the troll in the bathroom, baby Norbert, the dragon, and the centaurs/ unicorns of the forest: 1) Harry, Ron, and Hermione worked together to defeat the troll; 2) the trio helped Hagrid learn how to raise baby Norbert with Harry's insistence on trying to tame the dragon until the dragon began to master the other three elements (flying, swimming, and fire-breathing); and 3) Firenze the centaur allowed Harry to ride on his back, a true submission to Harry's existence, showing that Harry had mastered or won loyalty from these representations of earth. There is one element left that Harry must master to achieve mastery over earth, and that is the final earth "monster" protecting and connected to Lord Voldemort.

In the second task, the trio encounters the herbologist's work to protect the stone. With the "Devil's Snare" plant, there are multiple Christian connections. First, just like many small things in life that seem benign at first but then grow into malevolent traps, the Devil's Snare has snakelike tendrils that tighten without your notice until it has a death vice on you. Secondly, it likes the dark and damp, the exact opposite of what Christ represents – warmth and light. Thirdly, in the movie, they add a cute descriptive jingle: "Devil's snare, Devil's snare, it's deadly fun, but sulks in the sun!" This jingle speaks the truth about the multiple "snares of the Devil": things that might be fun at first, but since they are ultimately about doing things against one of the Ten Commandments, these unsure people do not like the Light of Christ or His truth shining light on the darkness. Shining the light on what they are doing shows them how wrong they are, and losing their strength of conviction, they sulk. Thus, Hermione's solution of shedding light (of Christ) on the plant is the only true solution to defeat a snare of the Devil.

The third task, the charmed keys, again shows the trio working together to ensure that they use the correct key element to help their progress through their seven challenges. Following the challenge of the keys, the fourth task, the troll, is not an issue in this set of challenges since the person already ahead of them was able to dispose of him, but since the trio has already shown their ability to overcome a troll, this task wasn't necessary again.

The fifth task, the chess game, tells us a little bit more of how J.K. Rowling sees the story line played out – in the fight between good and evil, each side will have sacrifices. The biggest difference though, as Ron shows, is that on the side of goodness, the pieces themselves willingly sacrifice themselves to protect each other out of love; whereas on the side of evil, the master sacrifices others to protect himself out of selfishness and fear. Thus, there will be good people that die to ensure the ultimate victory of life over death. Ron, as the will of Christ, demonstrates here his willingness to sacrifice himself to help his friends so that they may go on to defeat Lord Voldemort.

Leaving Ron after the chess game, the sixth challenge is one of courage and logic. Within the seven potion bottles we have a mystery in rhyme, riddle, and logic. We also see that Harry is slowly, unwillingly being singled out as his friends leave so he can complete his mission – Ron to the chess game, and Hermione safely to the potions. Harry, representing all Christians, will have to face Lord Voldemort (evil) by himself in the deep underground of Hogwarts, just as Christ battles the devil alone in the bowels of hell before he returns to his disciples on earth.

Before Harry leaves Hermione, she has a line that is fundamental to the entire series and the key to how Harry survives Lord Voldemort's continual attacks: "Books! And cleverness! There are more important things – friendship and bravery..." (p. 287) Hermione understands that cleverness is not the only piece to being a great wizard or Christian. The true test of Christianity is how much one shows love to others in need and bravery in combating the evils that surround us.

Chapter Seventeen: The Man with Two Faces

Once in the bowels of Hogwarts, Harry meets the true enemy – Lord Voldemort embodied in Professor Quirrell. Professor Quirrell believes that the Mirror of Erised itself is the key to finding the Stone, demonstrating a common misunderstanding about the Stone: that possession of eternal life is given to anyone who wants it. Understanding this, Dumbledore places a charm on the mirror so that only those who are looking for the stone, but not looking for the eternal life it promises, are able to get the stone. In essence, it is about the process of making the stone that really gives the creator eternal life and not about the elixir itself.

In fact, anyone who just drinks the elixir of life doesn't truly enjoy eternal life (Corinthians 11:27-29). In Christian terms, it is the things you do every day to help your fellow humanity and the relationship you develop with Christ that grants you eternal life, not necessarily the Eucharistic bread and drink by themselves. Through this process, the soul transforms from an organic, selfish entity to an all-loving, all-giving "stone." In the process, the person learns to accept that death is the completion of life, and the immortal life beyond with Christ is what makes life valuable. As it says in Luke 17:33: "Whoever tries to keep his life will lose it, and whoever loses his life will preserve it." (NIV) Thus, since Harry has no immediate desire for his own eternal life but understands the inevitability of death, he is able to find the Stone, and Lord Voldemort destroys Professor Quirrell for his failure to obtain the stone for him. In the end, Professor Quirrell is the earthly element of evil that Harry masters in order to achieve mastery over earth in this first part of the alchemical process.

Even with Harry's ability to get the stone, Harry can only hold off Lord Voldemort for so long without help. The fire that Professor Quirrell conjured around them reminds us of a crucible, and signifies the change of one thing into another. With the destruction of the first Stone in the fire and the certain death of its owner, Nicholas Flamel, there is room for a new alchemy drama and stone: Harry. Representing lead, Harry has already begun the process of transformation as he slowly masters the four elements, and passes through the three stages (black, white, and red) while the two friends, sulfur (Ron) and mercury (Hermione), help shape Harry into the Philosopher's Stone and achieve eternal life. As for the death of Nicolas Flamel, Dumbledore tell Harry what an alchemist's understanding of death is: "death is but the next great adventure,"[51] and not something to be feared.

In addition to the Christian theme of eternal life, Harry's three day near-death experience replicates each Christian's own death to self and resurrection with the help of Christ: Harry was rescued by Dumbledore from the worst of Lord Voldemort and slept for three days. It is Harry's love for everyone else that kept Harry focused on thwarting Lord Voldemort's attempts to possess the Stone, just as Christ's love for us overcame Death. Through the dialogue with Professor Dumbledore, we also learn that it was Lily's sacrificial death and love for Harry that also helped save Harry from Lord Voldemort's direct touch. Thus in essence, it was love that helped Harry master the final task of "earth", the physical forms of Lord Voldemort and Professor Quirrell.

Another line Professor Dumbledore uses that arises a few times in the series is this: "Always use the proper name for things. Fear of a name increases fear of the thing itself."[52] Many Christians are afraid to name elements of evil, such as hell and Satan in particular, either believing that saying their name will call them, dirty their souls in some way, or acknowledge that they actually exist. However, J.K. Rowling gives her opinion on that matter through this comment that by allowing ourselves to speak about these elements: we help gain control over them in our own minds.

At the end of this chapter, Hermione and Ron visit Harry in the infirmary after Professor Dumbledore left and discuss what happened with Lord Voldemort. Harry seems to understand that Professor

---

[51] Rowling, *Harry Potter and the Philosopher's Stone*, p. 297.

[52] Rowling, *Harry Potter and the Philosopher's Stone*, p. 298.

Dumbledore gave Harry the tools he needed, and trusted him enough to do what he could. Perhaps Professor Dumbledore was a little more relaxed since he was usually around, but when it counted, he saved Harry when Harry was in dire need. This is very much how God seems to help humankind – He has given us all the tools we need, and He gave us free will to use them the best way we can. However, we are not alone - He will step in when necessary as long as we are working within God's purpose. It is in fighting off evil for ourselves using what God gave us and giving thanks for what we have been given that we learn how strong our defenses truly are. Alchemically, this is how metals are tested before being used in battle.

Two concluding thoughts in the final pages of this book include Hagrid and the Great Feast. Hagrid's guilt about trading a Hogwart's secret for a dragon's egg shows what happens when we try to get clues about heaven that we haven't earned on our own. And finally, at the great closing feast, when it seems that Slytherin House has won the House Cup again, Professor Dumbledore surprises everyone with the awarding of additional points, resulting in Gryffindor's victory. The switch of Slytherin's hangings for Gryffindor's lion is symbolic of Harry's defeat of Lord Voldemort: the steadfastness of faith and lion's bravery overcoming the ultimate evil and snake in the wizarding world. With this conclusion, we see how the title is fitting for the story, since the old stone has now been replaced with a new stone that we will see transform throughout the series.

Chapter FIVE

The Guide to *The Chamber of Secrets*

Plot synopsis: In this second book, Harry Potter learns about a plot at Hogwarts through Dobby, the Malfoy family's house elf. At 4 Privet Drive, Harry meets Dobby in his room while the Dursley's are holding a dinner party. House elves have magic without wands, are slaves of their family, and are never allowed to wear anything except their one article of clothing that resembles an old pillow case. Since Dobby uses magic at Harry's house and the Ministry of Magic does not know about Dobby's visit, Harry is warned that more magic would get him expelled from Hogwarts. Since the magic destroyed the Dursley's dinner party, Harry is barred into his room with Mr. Dursley's threat of only bread and water for the rest of his life. He is rescued from the Dursley's house on Harry's twelfth birthday when Fred, George, and Ron Weasley use an illegally flying Ford Angelia. They take Harry to the Weasley's house, called The Burrow, and we are introduced to how a wizarding house functions. At the end of the summer, Harry, Ron and Hermione return to Hogwarts.

At Hogwarts, strange messages about an "heir of Slytherin" appear, and muggle-born students are being petrified (frozen). During the new Defense Against the Dark Arts teacher's dueling lessons, Harry learns that his gift for talking to snakes (called Parseltongue) is a rare talent usually indicative of a dark wizard such as Lord Voldemort. With this discovery, most of the Hogwarts students turn against Harry, thinking he is the cause of the strange incidents. Over the next few months, Harry learns that he has many other things in common with Lord Voldemort such as his orphaned status and his sense of Hogwarts being his only true home. As more students who are not pure-blooded wizards begin to petrify from some unknown monster from the "Chamber of Secrets", Harry and his friends, Ron and Hermione, begin to uncover clues as to the whereabouts of the Chamber and what monster might lie within. Once Hermione is petrified as well, Hagrid is sent to Azkaban for his supposed involvement with opening the Chamber of Secrets, and Professor Dumbledore is deposed as headmaster at Hogwarts.

However, such drastic actions do not affect the monster, and it takes another victim, Ginny Weasley. Right before this last victim, Harry and Ron had finally put the last pieces in place, figuring out that the monster is a basilisk and the opening to the Chamber is in a girls' bathroom. Hearing that Ginny has been taken down to the Chamber to lie there forever, Harry and Ron ask for the Defense Against the Dark Arts teacher's assistance (Mr. Lockhart) and open the Chamber using Parseltongue. A backfiring memory charm makes Professor Lockhart lose his memory, and causes a collapse of the tunnel, isolating Harry from the others. Harry must then continue on, to face the basilisk alone and free Ginny.

In the Chamber, Harry encounters Tom Riddle's memory near Ginny Weasley's near-lifeless body. Through this encounter, Harry learns that Tom Riddle became Lord Voldemort, and that it is a diary that has Tom's sixteen year old soul and memory that has possessed Ginny. Ginny then opened the Chamber and used the basilisk to petrify the other students. Tom Riddle tried to kill Harry using the basilisk, but by declaring his loyalty to Albus Dumbledore, Dumbledore's phoenix arrives with the Sorting Hat and the Sword of Gryffindor. The Phoenix blinds the basilisk, so then Harry is able to use the sword to slay the basilisk. With basilisk venom in his blood from the fight, Harry uses the basilisk fang to destroy the diary, which destroys Tom Riddle's memory and restores Ginny Weasley to life. Fawkes the Phoenix's tears heal Harry's mortal arm wound, and he then flies all of the students and Professor Lockhart out of the Chamber to the main building of Hogwarts to see Professor Dumbledore. In Professor Dumbledore's office, Lucius Malfoy arrives with Dobby asking for details about which student will be expelled for opening the Chamber of Secrets, and Professor Dumbledore explains that it was Lord Voldemort's doing. Understanding now that Dobby is the property of the Malfoy family, Harry returns the diary to Lucius Malfoy with one of his socks in the diary. As Lucius Malfoy gives the diary to Dobby, he mistakenly gives Dobby the sock as well which frees Dobby from his enslavement to the Malfoys, Dobby then saves Harry from Lucius' retaliation and devotes his life to being friends with Harry Potter. Everyone then returns to London, and Harry returns to the Dursleys for another summer.

Chapter One: The Worst Birthday

As this story begins, we are given two sides of what happens at the Dursley's house: Harry's view, and the Dursley's view. For Harry, his birthday serves as a reminder of what brought Harry to his relative's house – the death of his parents and his move into the house of the only family he has left. In direct antithesis to this raw emotion, we see the Dursleys' obsession with material elements, completely devoid of true emotion. Ignoring Harry's birthday, the Dursleys have planned a dinner party focusing on manipulating the company into accepting a new deal. Their comments highlight their focus on money and material items, while ignoring Harry and his birthday, a celebration of life.

Chapter Two: Dobby's Warning

In this chapter, we are introduced to Dobby, a house elf. Although house-elves have magic, and magic without the same rules or bounds of the human wizards, they are not allowed wands. If wands represent a Christian's faith in God, and other magical creatures are not allowed to possess wands, this depiction seems to be an indication that other beings/ cultures/ religions might have a relationship with God as well, but Christians are too afraid to allow them an official status or acknowledgement of having the same relationship with God. Furthermore, since other wizards can't track other magical creatures (or rather they don't count other magical creatures as worthy of acknowledgement), Harry takes the blame for Dobby's actions, just as others might take the consequences for unknown sources of trouble.

Worried that Harry was having trouble, Ron goes with his brothers to check in on Harry. At the end of the chapter, Harry's dream is a faint prayer for help. The reality of Ron's appearance at Harry's barred window shows again that God will assist us when in need, knows our needs even before we do, and answers prayer. It also depicts Ron's concern for Harry and his ability to connect emotionally with others which drives him to help others in need as the will of Christ.

Chapter Three: The Burrow

As Harry recognizes the Weasley boys, we learn more about Ron, Fred, and George. In many ways, Fred and George are saints, saving others through their wit and ability to think through unique solutions. In this scenario, Fred and George have come to rescue Harry from starvation, and have thought of every angle of the problem. Not only do they just happen to have a rope and hairpin with them that they use to assist in obtaining the trunk and pulling the bars from the windows, but they also figure out how to drive a muggle car and did some fancy car maneuvering without using any magic.

After the Weasleys rescue Harry and introduce him to a wizarding house, we learn about how wizards track time versus the traditional muggle methods. Mrs. Weasley's clock pokes fun at a traditional clock, which only makes sense of there is something of meaning attached to each of the hours. However, the reality is that it doesn't matter what the actual hour of time is, but what is supposed to happen at that time, such as "time to feed the chickens" or the "time to go to Church." In the movie, they only show the Weasley's other clock, one that has one hand for each member of the family. With this system, rather than numbers, there are locations such as "travelling", "at home", "in mortal peril", etc, which is a much more useful clock for knowing what others are doing at that "time."

Harry is thrilled to be at The Burrow, despite or because of its odd appearance. There is a definite contrast between Privet Drive and The Burrow, as indicated by the names. A privet is a plant that is always nicely manicured and cut, and everything prim and proper. This is somewhat reminiscent of a "high mass" affair where everything occurs when cued and no one sings a false note lest the congregation be starved (physically and spiritually). The Burrow, on the opposite end, is very much the "low mass", where the occupants tend to make do with what they can, there is lots of individualism expressed, and as long as in the end everyone is physically and spiritually fed, it is counted as a success.

On a somewhat obscure note, J.K. Rowling has had a bit of fun with the Weasley family. Here, she names the Weasley's house The Burrow as a pointer to the similarity between the name Weasley and the weasel. A Weasel's house is called a burrow, and is generally a random collection of tunnels that move in many directions with many rooms. Similarly, The Burrow is a rather haphazard collection of rooms connected to each other built above ground and the Weasley family acts like a family of weasels – they are all very close and love each other dearly. After years of neglect, this warmth is exactly what Harry craves and thrives on.

Chapter Four: At Flourish and Blotts

As we get to know more about the Weasley family, we learn about Mr. Weasley's fascination with the non-magical world and their creations to make up for their lack of magic. However, Mr. Weasley's fascination with the muggle world is what other wizards don't like about him – he's not being "true" to his magical blood since most other wizards feel the non-magical world is not worth noting. In his discussions with Harry, Mr. Weasley shows his surprise and amazement at how well muggles have gotten along without magic, a surprise many find when we run into people who have lived their whole lives without Christ or a relationship with God. However, as Mr. Weasley notes, the contraptions and scientific things that have come to replace magic are fascinating.

Among the Weasleys, Harry learns what true acceptance of magic is and how magic plays out in a wizarding household. For instance, in The Burrow, the Weasleys are not surprised that Professor Dumbledore knows that Harry is with them. They acknowledge Dumbledore's awareness as par for the course and in direct contrast to the Dursleys' house, where information is only obtained by spying on one another. Here, Dumbledore's awareness is another indication of Professor Dumbledore's omniscience and similarity to Christ.

As the Weasleys help Harry get to Diagon Alley to get his books for the year, Harry misspeaks and ends up in a store called "Borgin and Burkes." This shop sells very old magical artifacts, very similar to the multiple shops that sell ancient relics such as bones of past saints, jewelry worn by certain famous popes, or furniture that was handed down from Jerusalem that someone sat in that always exist around historical Christian sites. However, just as the magic in old relics is supposed to be powerful, some of that power over the years is perhaps tainted by heresies around that person in the same way that the objects here carry dark curses. The difference would be that old relics should not affect or curse anyone who touched it now.

Once Harry is able to get out of the shop and starts wandering to find Diagon Alley, Hagrid comes to the rescue and tells Harry where he is - Knock Turn Alley. With this introduction, we finally realize why there are dark arts sold on this street. "Knock Turn Alley" is a reworking of the word "nocturnally", meaning "of the night" or dark, where the darker magic is sold. It is also a reminder that Harry is in the black stage of his alchemical transformation in the series.

As Harry emerges from Knock Turn Alley, he is reunited with his friends Ron and Hermione. Hermione's parents are at the money-changer's counter, changing their muggle money to wizard money at odd rates. In the Bible, we see this same exchange taking place in the temple courts. The money changers in the temple courtyard would exchange roman coin for Temple tax coins, the only acceptable money within the temple walls.

Goaded by Hermione's parents' appearance, we also get a purist view of the hierarchy of wizards and muggles. One of the key "pureblood" families in the series is the Malfoy family, and Lucius Malfoy speaks openly about how disgraceful he feels the Weasley family is, indicated by their sneaky weasel-ly surname. Lucius Malfoy indicates that Mr. Weasley's interest in muggles has tainted his family forever, and looks with disdain on Hermione, who comes from muggle parents despite her obvious magical ability. There is some thought that Christians should only interact with other Christians and not with those who are not seeking God or chosen by God, from the Biblical verse direction: 1 John 2:15 "Do not love the world or anything in the world. If anyone loves the world, the love of the Father is not in him", and 2 Corinthians 6:14 "Do not be unequally yoked with unbelievers" (ESV). The "purebloods", such as Malfoy, translate these statements to mean that Christians are not to have any dealings with those who are not in the Christian realm, since that will keep the Christian faith pure. This is also a belief carried by many other religions, although some soften it to mean shunning only those who have no faith. However, if someone comes to faith from a family that does not have any faith, are we to shun them? What about a family that is rich in faith, but they have a child who despises their faith and does not receive the gift of a relationship with God? Do we shun them as well? Professor Dumbledore, as the Headmaster of Hogwarts, the Christian training ground and sheepfold, accepts all people who have an inkling of faith, regardless of their parentage, and will hold out hope for any child of a faithful family that has not yet shown a proclivity towards magic.

Chapter Five: The Whomping Willow

With the platform to Hogwarts mysteriously closed to Harry and Ron, Ron gets the idea to use the Ford Anglia, which flies them to Hogwarts, then leaves once the job is complete. The Ford Anglia in this case is another name for an angel – those heavenly creatures that assist when needed. Professor Snape's concern is mostly that they were seen by muggles, since anything involving magic is to be hidden from them. As Ms. Rowling has mentioned a few times, the muggles will think of anything except the truth to explain what they've seen anyway, but the magical community encourages the muggles to think of the ordinary rather than the supernatural when extraordinary things occur.

Ron and Harry arrive at Hogwarts just as the car is running out of gas and energy. Miraculously, the car manages to get past the gates to Hogwarts, but runs into The Whomping Willow. This tree itself acts as the Tree of Life – it was planted by Professor Dumbledore, in order to help defend a special student against any intruders, not allowing anyone who didn't know the secret past the tree. The actual Tree of Life, planted in the Garden of Eden, is a rather unknown entity in the Bible. Adam and Eve are told not to eat from the Tree of the Knowledge of Good and Evil, and were told they could eat of any other tree in the Garden, so they could eat from the Tree of Life. However, after Adam and Eve ate from the Tree of Knowledge, the Tree of Life was banned from them: "He must not be allowed to reach out his hand and take also from the tree of life and eat, and live forever." .... [24] After God drove Adam and Eve out, he placed on the east side of the Garden of Eden cherubim and a flaming sword flashing back and forth to guard the way to the tree of life. (Genesis 3: 22, 24, NIV)). The Whomping Willow's arms act as the swords flashing back and forth guarding the way to the tree, but the tree did provide life to those around it, since it was the holding cell for an uncontrollable animal (more about this in a later chapter).

Chapter Six: Gilderoy Lockhart

Beginning with this book, J.K. Rowling begins to explain more about the various herbs and potions at Hogwarts and how they might be used. In this first herbology class of the year, we hear about a questionable magical element – the explanation of the mandrake. Although J. K. Rowling perpetuates the mandrake as a shrieking plant, she digresses from the usual magical collection of the plant by showing the students how to collect it without dying from the cries – by using earmuffs to protect them. Also, even though the mandrake is poisonous and historically used to induce sleep or even death,[53] J.K. Rowling uses the mandrake later in the complete opposite fashion as is traditionally used in witchcraft magic, further showing that J.K. Rowling is not interested in witchcraft, but in Christianity.

Later in this chapter, we begin to see one of the themes of this book – the question of nature versus nurture within any particular community. Colin Creevey, a muggle-born wizard, asks about the basics of wizarding genetics. In the discussion that follows, we hear that there is no guarantee that wizards marrying wizards will have magical children. However, given the environment and encouragement, these children

---

[53] Morgenstern, K, 2002, Sacred Earth, "Mandrake," retrieved from http://www.sacredearth.com/ethnobotany /plantprofiles/mandrake.php.

would have a better chance of understanding and accepting magic than those not born with magical parents. There was some speculation in 2004 about whether or not spirituality was a genetic factor [54] which seems to have similar patterns to the wizarding inheritance patterns. The wizarding gene could skip generations to show up in an apparent muggle family, or not exist in a child of pure wizarding descent. We see evidence that within the wizarding world magic could develop within someone over time and manifest itself as late as ten years of age.[55] Similarly, the question of genetics in our world could be changeable over time -perhaps since a person that has a spiritual experience feels changed forever, this change becomes permanently marked in the genes.

Chapter Seven: Mudbloods and Murmurs

Draco's placement on the Slytherin Quidditch team as a seeker shows an interesting development at Hogwarts. As a seeker, Draco is suggested to be someone who searches for truth. However, the reality is that his position was purchased by his father. Throughout history, there have been many wealthy families who placed some of their second or third sons in monasteries in response to generous donations to the church. Their placement was not due to any spiritual pining of the son. Rather, the son would serve as a political pawn within the church, earning "grace" and power for the family. Within Hogwarts, Draco's placement on the Slytherin team as their seeker gives the Malfoy family a higher social status within the school and magical community.

As the Slytherin and Gryffindor Quidditch teams debate their rights to the training field, Draco resorts to calling Hermione a mudblood. Subsequently, we hear an explanation of the terms "mudblood", "half-blood", and "pureblood." From Ron and Hagrid, we learn that a "mudblood" is a derogatory term for someone born of muggles, half

[54] Dulle, J, "The God-Gene: Is Religious Faith and Experience a Biological Misunderstanding?" retrieved from http://www.onenesspentecostal.com/godgene.htm.

[55] Harry Potter Wiki, "Neville Longbottom," http://harrypotter.wikia.com/wiki/Neville_Longbottom.

bloods are from one muggle and one magical parentage, and purebloods are from full wizarding stock. However, the terms are used rather loosely, and not by exact percentage of pure wizarding blood either. The Slytherins pride themselves on being "purebloods", but there are many wizards in Slytherin that were only half-blood, most notably Lord Voldemort himself and Professor Severus Snape. However, since it was important to those wizards to appear to be purebloods, they were allowed into Slytherin. Since the Sorting Hat evaluates the frame of mind rather than their blood status, someone who chooses the ideals of ethnic purity will be placed in Slytherin. In Christianity, there are some who have the same concerns – those who are recent converts to a particular faith and those who marry outside the faith/ denomination are many times regarded as "lower class citizens", many times not given the same rights or privileges. Their children are not welcomed as cordially as those who come from parents who married within the faith, many times given "waitlist" status for Christian formation classes, choirs, or any other place in the church.

At the end of the chapter, we get another clue about this year's mystery at Hogwarts – a disembodied, menacing voice that only Harry can hear. With some speculation about why Professor Lockhart couldn't hear the voice, the various pieces of the mystery start to come into view.

Chapter Eight: Deathday Party

Harry has a chance discussion with Nearly Headless Nick after Quidditch practice as this chapter opens, and we learn more about how Sir Nicholas de Mimsy-Porpington died. When the trio attends the Deathday Party, we learn that he was a victim on Halloween, showing that he was not a part of witchcraft, but a Christian. Furthermore, the celebration of those who have died in the faith before us was the original meaning of Halloween – "All Hallows Eve", where people celebrated the lives of those in faith who had died as martyrs in older days and sometimes even dressed as their favorite martyr in their honor. Even in pagan rituals, the end of October was the celebration of the harvest, not a celebration of evil spirits.[56]

Also within this discussion, Sir Nick explains more about what the Headless Hunt is about. The Headless Hunt is very similar to the quest for sainthood – there are very particular requirements that have to be met, and only exacting matches qualify. Nearly Headless Nick's request for Harry to put in a good word for him is much in standing with how sainthood or martyrdom status is achieved – someone well known to the departed has to give testament to the church authorities that the departed did indeed perform something miraculous.

Once Harry and his friends realize that the Deathday party is very somber without refreshments, they are not as keen to stay. Harry's dilemma between staying at the Deathday Party and attending the Halloween celebrations upstairs is the same dilemma that many face every year – attending the All Hallows Eve celebration at church with its somberness and pageantry, or dressing up and getting candy from neighbors. Although the Deathday party is more significant, the celebration is more fun and thus more attractive to younger generations.

True to the form of the books, the enemy makes its presence known on Halloween. Harry, having heard the strange voice before is reassured about hearing it again, but his friends are bewildered. Harry, Ron, and Hermione are on a more solid trail to discover the details and clues required to solve the mystery and save the school from its evil.

Chapter Nine: The Writing on the Wall

Argus Filch's status of "Squib" means that he is a non-magical person born to magical parents. Usually, a squib would be given every opportunity to show magical ability and still be part of the magical community. However, in the rare cases that the child didn't display any abilities by the age of ten, the child would be sent to muggle schools to learn how to be a muggle and live without magic. The hope overall is that

---

[56] Bry-Back Manor, "Harvest Festivals," retrieved from http://www.bry-backmanor.org/holidayfun/harvestinfo.html.

the magical gene, suppressed for some reason in this one particular person, will return in a future generation.

From Harry's previous encounters and intuitions with Professors Snape and Dumbledore, we get the sense that they are both able to read minds. By paying attention to Harry's thoughts, both are probably aware of Harry's hearing voices in the walls. They do not press the issue here, perhaps because they do not want others aware that they can read minds or that they also aren't sure why Harry hears voices and the others don't and need to figure out the puzzle as well.

As the year progresses, Ms. Rowling gives us a glimpse of another class taught at Hogwarts – the History of Magic. This class is not presented in any way in the movies, but in the book we meet Professor Binns and learn that he is extremely boring as he describes the various historical conventions and battles. Although J.K. Rowling could be admonishing dry lecturers throughout the school system, she could also be giving her opinion of the battles between Christian sects or other religious groups and the legislation that seems to follow as unnecessary details that detract from the big picture of God's love for humanity.

With the horror of a Chamber of Secrets fresh in the students' minds, they are able to get Professor Binns to deviate from his usual history lectures, and discuss something they find interesting and pertinent. As Professor Binns launches into an explanation of the Chamber of Secrets, he also gives us readers a short history of Hogwarts. The names of the four founders give an insight into their history and/or characteristics they cherished, not only being the four alchemical representations but also the four representations of Christ as presented or foretold in Isaiah:

- Godric Gryffindor, with the name of God in his first name, also has a last name named after the "golden griffin", the symbol of heaven on earth. The lion symbol represents the characteristics Gryffindor cherished in his students – leadership and bravery. With these traits, these students aren't afraid to speak out against misdeeds, atrocities, or injustice. In this way, the Gryffindors represent the warring leader and sacrificial Servant of the fourth song from Isaiah (Is 52:13-53:12), since it takes great bravery and leadership to sacrifice oneself to take on new life for all peoples.

- Helga Hufflepuff, with her name reminiscent of "huff and puff", and tenacity, is symbolized by the badger. Her preference was for students who were not afraid to stay with their friends, regardless of the difficulty, nurturing others without resignation. This representation from Isaiah is the first servant song that describes Christ: .." a bruised reed he shall not break, and a smoldering wick he will not snuff out" (Isaiah 42:2-3). Salazar
- Slytherin, the name itself sounding like the snake of his emblem, chooses only the faithful and pure of spirit amongst all those that claim wizarding status. As such, he is reminiscent of the second song of Isaiah (Is 49:1-7), where we see the collection of "purebloods" (those Israelites that did not mix with the gentiles) to be "a light to the nations." These people call to themselves all the scattered remnants of Israel or in this case, the scattered pureblood wizards of England. Additionally, the snake represents a fallen being, such as a dragon (representing a heavenly creature with immortality) without limbs or wings, since it has fallen from grace just as the Israelites did as they turned away from God and were scattered.
- Rowena Ravenclaw, with the raven mascot, cherishes those who draw upon the academic side of Christianity. With the raven's symbolism of prophecy and discernment, the Ravenclaw house represents the servant from the third song of Isaiah, Isaiah 50: 4-9. In this servant song, God gives the servant constant instruction, in which the servant finds solace when harassed and scorned by others.

As for the Chamber of Secrets itself, the Chamber is like the vaults every ancient church has underneath their main sanctuary. Many old churches were built over historical sites or ancient burial grounds, which tend to have their own ghost stories. To keep the sacredness of the burial grounds, many churches covered the openings to protect people from getting lost in the vaults. However, the monster that lies within the Chamber of Secrets is not a ghost, although it is of an ancient nature.

Chapter Ten: The Rogue Bludger

After the rogue bludger broke Harry's arm on the Quidditch pitch, Harry is placed in the infirmary until his arm bones mend. In the infirmary, Dobby visits him and explains to Harry the history of the Chamber as well as the magical abilities that house-elves have beyond those of ordinary wizards. For instance, Dobby can apparate into and disapparate out of Hogwarts, even though there are charms around it that wizards cannot get around. It is implied that within the magical community, many charms are only intended for wizards since wizards don't expect other magical creatures to be a threat. In general, wizards underestimate the other magical races' abilities, an oversight that Harry and his friends exploit through the series.

While Dobby visits Harry, Dobby again pleads for Harry to save himself from the horrors that will come at Hogwarts and go home. Potter's response is "I'm not going anywhere!", giving us more insight into J. K. Rowling's concept of what it means to be Christian in light of upcoming adversity: 1) to help one's friends and ensure their safety; and 2) to face the end times bravely without running away so as to assist those who need help. Again, we are reminded that with Harry's background of abuse, his devotion to loving and helping others at his own peril is very rare.

Chapter Eleven: The Dueling Club

As the trio visits Hagrid, we learn that Hermione has figured out how to create travelling flames to help keep them warm and light their path. Since Hermione is named after Hermes, the god of travelers, Hermione's ability to conjure up travelling flames is part of her "genetic make-up."

As the trio decides to create the Polyjuice Potion, they realize they can only obtain some ingredients from Professor Snape's stores. Harry's likens mayhem as a distraction in Potions class being like poking a sleeping dragon in the eye. Although an odd phrase, this is a rephrasing of the school's motto of "never tickle a sleeping dragon." Whether the sleeping dragon referred to is Professor Snape or the entire wizarding community is unsure. Either way, the reference points to a monstrous immortal power that chooses to stay aloof or unaware of dangers lurking nearby, but will be a determining force once awakened.

During Harry's duel with Draco, Professor Snape apparently whispers instructions on creating a snake for the duel. Is this a test for Harry, or is Professor Snape trying to get back at Harry for creating mayhem in his Potions class? If it's a test, perhaps Professor Snape wants to see what powers Harry might have and if any have passed to him from Lord Voldemort? Since we know that Professors Snape and Dumbledore are both Legilmens, whose idea is it? Regardless, we know that Professor Snape will be reporting Harry's Parseltongue abilities to Professor Dumbledore, who might be able to make sense of any connections to previous events this year at Hogwarts.

After Harry is able to speak to the snake during the wizard duel, Ron explains to Harry that his ability to speak to snakes makes him a "Parselmouth" like Salazar Slytherin. This Parselmouth connection between Harry and Salazar Slytherin is a loose one, since it requires a direct inheritance from one's parents and neither one of Harry's parents had the ability to speak to snakes. However, any true heir of Slytherin could speak Parseltongue (the language used to speak to snakes), and there is an unintended connection through Harry's scar that will come forward in a later chapter.

After the second attack and the school turning against Harry's supposed connection to the Chamber of Secrets, Harry is marched up to Dumbledore's office. This stairwell, described as a moving staircase between the ground floor and the highest tower is representative of Jacob's Ladder, which in Genesis 28:12 is described as a stairwell resting on the earth and reaching heaven, with angels moving along the ladder. In continuation of the concept that Dumbledore's office is representative of heaven, Harry instantly knows he's at Professor Dumbledore's office as soon as he see the griffin doorknocker – it is the doorway to Heaven, with the griffin, the symbol of Heaven on Earth, announcing everyone's approach.

Chapter Twelve: Polyjuice Potion

In Professor Dumbledore's office, we get to meet Fawkes, Professor Dumbledore's pet Phoenix. Fawkes is named after Guy Fawkes, who was arrested before the explosive assassination attempt on King James' life in 1605. In celebration of the failure, Britain's bonfires provide a perfect reference for a phoenix. The Phoenix is the symbol for resurrection and thus of Christ, again, evidence that Professor Dumbledore is the Christ figure. Professor Dumbledore makes further comments about faith in the resurrection when he discusses the beauties of the Phoenix – they can carry heavy loads (Matthew 11:28-29 "Come to me, all you who are weary and burdened, and I will give you rest...and you will find rest for your souls."), they have tears of healing powers (Christ has a healing touch for everyone), and they are extremely loyal, indicating that remaining with Christ is a matter of faith. (Romans 10:10 "For it is with your heart that you believe and are justified, and it is with your mouth that you profess your faith and are saved." (NIV)

The phoenix's red and gold plumage represents the magnificence of heaven, and all the red and gold art in Dumbledore's office further indicates both the magnificence of heaven and the alchemical gold and dragon's blood/ Elixir of Life. In medieval art, many early portraits were painted with gold leaf for the background, but the gold leaf required a red clay base to help the gold leaf adhere to the picture. In iconography, this now represents the transformation of man from the clay of Adam's creation to the gold of Christ and heaven.[57]

As Professor Dumbledore speaks with Harry about Harry's concerns, he uses a phrase "Is there anything you'd like to tell me?" Psychologically, this brings to mind exactly the thought that a person feels most guilty

---

[57] Porter, B. (2011), "Gilding, Gold Leaf over Red Bole," Art and Iconography. Retrieved from http://www.betsyporter.com/gilding.html.

about. For mind-readers, this is the easiest way to find out what they need to know. In this way, Harry has not said anything about the voices he hears, but Professor Dumbledore is assured that Harry has nothing to do with the incident. Lastly, the Professor's assurance of his innocence before asking Harry anything is another indicator of his Christ-like omniscience.

Within the series, there are very few potion concoctions described or used by the students. The Polyjuice Potion produced here is the first potion the trio creates to help them solve the mystery about who might be opening the Chamber of Secrets. In one sense, creating the Polyjuice Potion is another element of Harry's mastery over water sine they are transforming water into a potion and using it to help them solve the mystery of who the Heir of Slytherin is. It is called Polyjuice, since it takes on multiple flavors, depending on the person it is impersonating. For instance, Gregory Goyle tastes like overcooked cabbage - he belongs to the green Slytherin house, and they are representative of water, hence the overcooking. Vincent Crabbe is also a creature from the water, making his potion of "essence of Crabbe" just as appealing.

Chapter Thirteen: The Very Secret Diary

Although the diary Harry finds in the bathroom seems to be a muggle diary, the diary is another member of those that are more than what they seem. Knowing that Tom Riddle is a wizard and probably did not have access to muggle money, there must be more to the diary than a collection of blank pages.

As Harry begins a dialogue with the diary, we subconsciously feel that people should beware of items that can think for themselves. Beyond the simple dialogue of a thinking, inanimate object, even more worrisome is a book that draws you in physically, especially if it's a "memory." Harry is on the alert, although he is still very trusting of everything around him, Regardless, anyone's memory only gives the one point of view, with the agenda that carries with it. Trusting has he is, Harry forgets that it is always important to hear both sides of any story and not trust a singular memory.

Despite the powerfully dark magic that takes Harry to a memory of past events, the trip into the diary provides us with key information to solving the current mystery as well as historical evidence of the ages of some of the main characters: Hagrid was 13 fifty years ago, so he is now 63, and Tom Riddle is 66. The memory, is addition to Dobby's warning that events at Hogwarts were about to repeat themselves, is also a foreshadowing of what's to come.

Chapter Fourteen: Cornelius Fudge

As the year progresses, the mandrake plants have matured and are ready for Madame Sprout to make a concoction to revive the petrified students. Although in witchcraft mandrakes are used to cause death or a death-type stupor and the Bible depicts women using mandrakes to increase their fertility, J.K. Rowling chooses to use the mandrake to revive people, transforming the normally witchy potion into a potion used to restore life.

Harry, Ron, and Hermione go to Hagrid to discuss what they know about the Chamber of Secrets, but are stopped by the appearance of important wizards in the wizarding community. This is the first time that we have heard anything about a regulatory body within the magical community and who the key members are. Ronald introduces us here to Cornelius Fudge, the Minister of Magic. In the Christian domain, this is akin to the Archbishop of Canterbury (since it is only the local jurisdiction of the United Kingdom). As such, he is always seeking Professor Dumbledore's advice, since Professor Dumbledore is the Christ figure of the saga.

Hagrid's removal to Azkaban is a dangerous move, since it is removing the gatekeeper and gameskeeper of Hogwarts. Without the gatekeeper, anyone can come in through the gate as we see here with Lucius Malfoy's arrival. Malfoy's announcement that Professor Dumbledore has been suspended from Hogwarts shows that without the gatekeeper, the wolves can remove the shepherd. As for the timing during the year, Dumbledore's leaving Hogwarts also coincides with the Ascension, when Christ rose leaving his disciples behind. Before Jesus left, he said that he would send a paraclete that would guide them (Matthew 28:20 "And surely I am with you always, to the very end of the age" and John 16:15 "That is why I said the Spirit will take from what is mine and make it known to you." (NIV), and to keep the faith. In this parallel, Professor Dumbledore gives a short speech to no one in particular guaranteeing that he will always be there to help those who ask for it (Matthew 7:7: "Ask and it will be given to you" (NIV)).

Hagrid's fear of Azkaban prison is well founded. Azkaban is the wizard's prison, a fortified prison in the sea that is surrounded by Dementors - horrid, soul-less wisps of creatures that feed on despair, meaning that the wizards sent there are without hope or the joy of Christ within them, much like the hell described in the Bible.

Chapter Fifteen: Aragog

Harry's fear about the loss of Dumbledore echoes the disciples' fears when Christ ascended into heaven – what will happen now that He is gone? Just as the disciples carried on as best they could trying to discern meaning of everything they know about their mission, Harry and Ron carry on with the mystery trying to figure out what they can about the monster, the Chamber of Secrets, and who is providing access to those horrors.

Draco Malfoy's comment about knowing his father would be the one to get rid of Albus Dumbledore because Dumbledore does not understand things the same way as the rest of the wizarding community rings of the Pharisees' in the Sanhedrin's problems. They too were hoping to have a Messiah that would "clean house", reunite Israel, and march on Rome. However, they were keen to get rid of Jesus once they realized that he was not going to be the Messiah they thought he would be. It was one key player in the Sanhedrin, Caiaphas, who led the remaining Sanhedrin against Jesus, just as Lucius Malfoy has led the other governors against Albus Dumbledore.

Draco's comment that he is hoping the next victim actually dies from the monster shows a common attitude within a selective group towards those who are not part of it. Many times, the negative attitude is increased when the non-selected are marginally accepted into the group as we see with wizards who are muggle-born. Ron's reaction to Draco's uncaring comment wishing Hermione had died shows that Ron and Hermione are starting to get along and need each other. Alchemically, as the two elements that transform leaden Harry the most, sulfur and mercury, they are bound to fight and get along in alternating patterns until their union at the end of the transformation process.

When Harry and Ron decide to follow Hagrid's advice to "follow the spiders", they are led into the Forbidden Forest and the land of mythical and symbolic creatures. Within the forest, we hear the story of Aragog, an acromantula that lives with its descendants deep within the Forbidden Forest. Tolkien uses spiders in his *Lord of the Rings* series, in a similar conceptual means of showing people trapped by someone else's cunning. Here, Tom Riddle has used cunning to make them think that Hagrid was the one who loosed a monster from the Chamber of Secrets, when indeed it was someone else.

Chapter Sixteen: The Chamber of Secrets

In the transfiguration class, the students are transfiguring slippers into rabbits. This is an example of transfiguration being the oscillation between an animate and an inanimate form of an object. In this instance, the oscillation is between rabbits and slippers, a typical product from rabbit fur in the middle ages.

Once Harry and Ron figure out that the monster is a Basilisk from Hermione's torn piece of paper and that Ginny Weasley has been taken into the Chamber of Secrets, they have a mission to save Ginny. In ancient times, the Basilisk looked like a large rooster with a long snake tail, and the myth ran that only a weasel's stench could kill a basilisk, but the weasel would die in the process. True to the myth, Ginny, representing the weasels, is taken down to the Chamber of Secrets to die with the Basilisk as the Heir of Slytherin takes over Hogwarts.

Within the alchemy process, Harry is mastering the second element in this second book, the element of water. Mastering water will require Harry's conquest of the monsters in the water as well as using water to save him from death. The basilisk moving through the pipes and the connection with the bathroom highlights the monster that Harry has to master in order to master water.

As Harry reads through the description, he is slightly puzzled by the reference to the crowing roosters and why they might be fatal to a basilisk. In Christianity, a crowing rooster was the victory of Christ – the rooster crows in the morning, just as Christ rose Easter morning, which is thus fatal to the Basilisk with its snake-like connection to evil.

At the end of this chapter, we again see Harry by himself (not of his own choosing) facing an unknown enemy in the bowels (the sewers) of Hogwarts. This set-up is echoed in the first book, but it is also a reminder of Christ's descent to the dead to destroy that death then rise again after a time. As further reminders, Harry and Ron run into many bones of previous victims in the sewers – they are certainly in the realm of the dead.

Chapter Seventeen: The Heir of Slytherin

We can sense that there is something evil in Tom Riddle for many reasons if the diary itself didn't make anyone think evil of Tom already. First, he fuels himself through fears and secrets, using them as things that he doesn't share to comfort others but to use against them to empower himself. Furthermore, Tom shows his strong magical abilities in that he is a memory that is able to gain strength, flesh, and spirit from those he interacts with as he slowly possesses them. Both of these aspects remind us that Satan would slowly possess anyone that spends enough time pouring out his/her soul to him, and Satan would not hesitate to use our own fears against us.

As the discussion between Tom Riddle and Harry unfolds, we hear about Professor Dumbledore being the Transfiguration teacher before Professor McGonagall. This indicates that the Headmaster is first very accomplished in the animation of life, and that the Transfiguration teacher is also the apprentice to the Headmaster. In a way, we could see the past Headmasters as being those past prophets who led the people as a shepherd does, protecting his sheep as long as possible until the next shepherd is called to take care of the sheep.

One of the more complicated word games, anagrams are a well-encoded sequence of words that rearrange to form another set of words or phrase. Here, Tom declares his desire for immortality through his new name, Lord Voldemort. Lord means "master," so Vol-de-mort translates then to "fleer of death."[58]

Through the discourse, we gain a lot of history of who Tom Riddle was. We begin to see Lord Voldemort trying to match himself up to Professor Dumbledore, just as Lucifer tried to match himself up to God. Both Lucifer and Lord Voldemort thought they were as capable and powerful as the God or Professor Dumbledore, and both developed plans to establish their immortality if their bodies were destroyed.

Despite his predicament in the sewers, Harry in his despair shows his faith and loyalty to Dumbledore. In response, Fawkes comes to Harry's rescue bringing the Sorting Hat. This is symbolic in two ways: 1) Fawkes is Professor Dumbledore's spiritual side coming to Harry's aid as promised; and 2) faith in Christ brings the resurrection with the Word of God. The Phoenix represents the resurrection, and the Sorting Hat is symbolic of the Word of God – it sorts students into which Song of Isaiah servant it sees, and continues the words of the Four Founders (the four gospels)

---

[58]Harry Potter Lexicon, 2011, "Lord Voldemort: Data," retrieved from http://www.hp-lexicon.org/wizards/voldemort.html.

into the present day. Both the resurrection and the Word of God come to give Harry the weapons he needs to fight death.

In an effort to win Harry over, Lord Voldemort is trying to get Harry to see their similarities – they are both orphans, muggle-raised, and Parselmouths. However, Harry and Lord Voldemort couldn't be more different. Harry has friendships and community, and loves others enough to be willing to sacrifice himself for them. On the other hand, Lord Voldemort is alone, trying to possess others in a desperate attempt to cling to life for himself at the sacrifice of others.

To Tom Riddle's surprise, the Phoenix is very helpful in Harry's fight against the Basilisk, blinding the monster so that Harry can fight with all of his senses. Without an obvious weapon, Harry despairs and cries for help and the Sorting Hat presents him with the Sword of Gryffindor. In essence, the duel Word of God/ Helmet of Salvation comes to Harry's rescue, and gives him the Sword of the Spirit to defend himself and defeat the enemy. (Eph. 6:11-18)

Properly armed, Harry defeats the Basilisk, the monster of the water, and Fawkes' tears (water) heal and save Harry from death from the Basilisk's venom. Furthermore, as Harry turns the Basilisk venom against its master, Lord Voldemort by destroying the diary with the Basilisk fang, Harry comes out the ultimate victor after three grueling hours in the sewer. The water is also the symbol of Slytherin, so in defeating Tom Riddle in the sewer, we see Christ's Resurrection again as Harry completes his mastery over all things related to alchemical water. At the conclusion of the drama in the Chamber of Secrets, we see the Phoenix in action, carrying the loads of those who put their trust in him and completing the resurrection story.

Chapter Eighteen: Dobby's Reward

Back in Professor Dumbledore office, Dumbledore smiles at Harry because Harry is doing exactly what he should be doing – helping others even though it meant breaking the rules (not going to the common rooms but fighting evil, and being willing to sacrifice himself at all costs for the life of another.) One of the things that Harry does throughout this series is not wait for others to do the work for him – he steps forward to do what he can, even if there might be others that generally take care of those people.

Ginny is very remorseful for what she had done, even though she wasn't conscious of having done wrong and was easily drawn in to Lord Voldemort's scheme. Professor Dumbledore restores her with his words of assurance, just as Christ restores people's health by forgiving their sins with his words. One of the themes of the later books is that remorse is what heals a broken soul, and with Ginny's return after only a short jaunt down the wrong direction, she is easily restored.

Through the discussion between Harry and Professor Dumbledore, we learn a little bit more about why Harry is so much like Lord Voldemort – some of the powers were transferred to Harry when he received the scar. In many ways, we are more able to defeat an evil if we know a bit more about it rather than just guessing about how that evil works. This is actually Taoism, from the book *The Art of War*: "know thine enemy."[59] Although not entirely clear yet, we can begin to see that Harry is better suited to defeat Lord Voldemort than anyone else, since he can understand Lord Voldemort through their abilities and the scar connection.

Now that Harry realizes how similar his background is to Lord Voldemort's, he is even more wary of becoming exactly the person he despises the most – Lord Voldemort. In answer, Professor Dumbledore explains one of the main themes to Harry: "It is our choices, Harry, that show what we truly are, far more than our abilities." Through this, J.K. Rowling is telling us that nothing is set in stone from birth. We can have very similar lives and circumstances to others, but through our choices,

---

[59] Tzu, Sun, "Sun Tzu Quotes (Author of "The Art of War"), Goodreads, 2012. Retrieved from http://www.goodreads.com/author/quotes/1771.Sun_Tzu.

we live a very different life, especially if we choose to do good in the world.

As a conclusion, Dobby obtains his freedom through the sacrificial sock from Harry, even if it isn't that great of a sacrifice. Dobby's mind was free, thinking beyond just obeying his masters' every whim as all the other house-elves do, but he was still bound by the old magic that required punishment for his freedom of thought. Similarly, the Jews were bound by laws of punishment for various law infractions and unable to get free from their enslavement to the law. However, with the coming of Christ, we were freed by his sacrifice and those laws were broken.

Chapter SIX

The Guide to *The Prisoner of Azkaban*

Plot summary: As the story begins, Mr. Dursley's sister, Aunt Marge, comes to stay for three weeks. Aunt Marge has no compassion for anyone not directly related to her. Mirroring the common industrial age attitude towards orphans, Aunt Marge constantly berates Harry for how ungrateful he is for having a roof over his head and food on his plate, since she herself would have left him to an orphanage. Since he is so ungrateful, her continued insults about how horrible Harry's parents must have been finally solicit a reaction from Harry, and he accidentally makes Aunt Marge expand like a balloon. Worried about an expulsion from Hogwarts for this bit of magic, Harry runs away from the Dursleys. As he begins to wonder where he should go, he sees a large black dog watching him and pulls out his wand. Instantly the Knight Bus arrives, which takes Harry to the Leaky Cauldron. At the Leaky Cauldron, Harry meets the Prime Minister, who assures Harry that all is right with the Dursleys, Hogwarts, and Harry has a room at the Leaky Cauldron until he needs to leave for Hogwarts. The one requirement is that Harry stay out of the muggle world since Sirius Black, an escapee from the wizarding prison, Azkaban, is in London. Shortly before leaving for Hogwarts, Mr. Weasley tells Harry that Sirius Black was Lord Voldemort's main supporter who has escaped Azkaban to find and destroy Harry.

As the students travel on the Hogwarts Express, some of the Dementors that guard Azkaban are searching for Sirius Black. To protect the students at Hogwarts, they travel north but are drawn to the train en route and specifically Harry's memories of his dark past. The Dementors enter the train causing wide-spread gloom and despair and attack Harry, who begins to relive his moments before his mother's death. Their new Defense Against the Dark Arts teacher, Professor Remus Lupin, is travelling in their compartment on the train and dispels the Dementors with an unknown spell. Throughout the year, the Dementors patrol Hogwarts and Hogsmeade, the local town near Hogwarts, for Sirius Black, but they attack Harry during a Quidditch match causing him to fall many feet from the sky and destroying his broom.

Throughout the year, his new classes prove to give him new insights about the magical world. In the Care of Magical Creatures classes, Hagrid teaches Harry's year group how to control their Books of Monsters and how to handle the Hippogriff, Buckbeak, which is a mix of a horse and an eagle. Unfortunately, Draco tests the validity of Hagrid's safety instructions and gets bitten by the Hippogriff, causing an investigation and subsequent execution sentence for Buckbeak. In their Divinations class, Professor Trewlaney tells Harry constantly that he is doomed to die soon, and the constant reports of Sirius Black getting closer to Hogwarts and into Gryffindor tower cause him much stress. Unable to go to Hogsmeade with the other students, Harry befriends Professor Lupin, who teaches him how to master the Dementors using the "*expecto patronum*" spell. Through Lupin, Harry also learns more about his parents who were Lupin's good friends until they died. For the second trip to Hogsmeade, Fred and George Weasley feel sorry for Harry and give him the Marauder's Map, a secret map that shows all hidden entrances to Hogwarts and everyone's locations. With the map and the cloak, Harry is able to explore everywhere within Hogwarts without detection, and one evening he goes out to find a spot on his map named "Peter Pettigrew," since Peter

Pettigrew is supposedly dead. Mid-search, Professor Lupin confiscates the map when he encounters Harry in the hallway, worried that if the map fell into Sirius Black's hands, he would be able to find Harry. Meanwhile, Ron's rat, Scabbers, is supposedly eaten by Hermione's new cat, Crookshanks, and the two of them argue constantly about Crookshanks' behavior. At the end of the year, the trio goes to Hagrid's hut to comfort Hagrid before Buckbeak's execution, and Hagrid shows Ron that Scabbers is actually alive and well.

Upon leaving Hagrid's hut, the trio head towards Hogwarts, but watch Buckbeak's executioner from a distance, and Harry and Hermione watch as Ron is dragged off by the large black dog Harry has seen a few times around campus hanging out with Crookshanks. The dog takes Ron down the Whomping Willow hole, where Harry and Hermione follow and find it leads to the Shrieking Shack. They are quickly joined by Professor Lupin, and the truth comes out that Scabbers the rat is really Peter Pettigrew in animagus form – the particular animal a person can transfigure to. Furthermore, Pettigrew betrayed Harry's parents to Lord Voldemort, and Sirius, Harry's godfather, had gone to confront Pettigrew when Pettigrew staged his own death, framing Sirius. As they leave to return to Hogwarts, Professor Lupin becomes a werewolf with the arrival of the full moon, Pettigrew transforms back to a rat and escapes, and Sirius and Harry are almost killed by the Dementors down by the lake. Luckily, they are miraculously saved by an unknown wizard's patronus from the opposite shore. Back at Hogwarts, Ron is hospitalized for his broken leg, and Sirius is locked up for escaping Azkaban, since no one credible is available to tell the truth. At Professor Dumbledore's suggestion, Harry and Hermione go back in time using a time-turner. Knowing the order of events, they are able to rescue Buckbeak and Harry is able to save himself and Sirius using his stag patronus. With Buckbeak, they free Sirius from the tower, which allows Sirius a means of escape. With the posting of exam scores, the term is over and they then return home via Hogwarts Express with promises to free Harry as soon as possible from the Dursley's house.

Chapter One: Owl Post

Throughout the series, Harry discovers many things that are not what they appear to be as the pocket sneakoscope shows here – Ron tells Harry in his letter about how the sneakoscope lights up when someone untrustworthy is around. Since the sneakoscope keeps lighting up, Ron dismisses the scope as a fake. However, J.K. Rowling is showing us here how much of both her writing and literature in general is deeper than just what the words show or what people appear to be, hinting at the amount of symbolism she has put into her work and inviting her readers to discover those for themselves.

Chapter Two: Aunt Marge's Big Mistake

As Aunt Petunia returns to her ever watchful state at the window, we are reminded of how some can be so watchful and know everything that is going on around them and miss what is happening in their own families (such as Harry's birthday). This is also reminiscent of J.K. Rowling's favorite book, *Emma,* in which Emma acts as if she knows everything about everyone and tries to match up her friends with those she feels would make a good match but ends up missing what everyone else sees. Emma also lived in Surrey, where the Dursley's live according to the movie *Chamber of Secrets*.

As further reflection on Petunia, it is interesting to compare her to her sister, Lily. As different as they were – muggle versus wizard, we see the difference between the two through the symbolism in their names as well – whereas Lily is the symbol of purity and innocence, Petunia is symbolic of anger and resentment,[60] and both of them lived up to their names.

As J.K. Rowling introduces Aunt Marge to her readers, she presents a person with such prejudices about social class that she can't find any compassion for those around her. In a way, she is the extreme of the

---

[60] FlowerDot Ltd, 2010, "Flower Meanings," retrieved from http://www.clareflorist.co.uk/meanings.asp.

Dursleys' attitudes – always knowing what would be best for everyone else, and convinced that their attitudes should be the national attitudes.

Chapter Three: The Knight Bus

Frightened from the large black dog, Harry pulls out his wand and is saved from his misery by a mysterious bus, called "The Knight Bus." The bus itself is akin to the Knights of Columbus, an organization dedicated to helping those in need. As the bus suddenly appears in the minutes of Harry's need to get somewhere safe, we are reminded of God's providence for our needs sometimes through others.

Stan Shunpike, the conductor on the Knight Bus, explains the ways of the Knight Bus to Harry, and as Harry wonders about why the muggles don't see the bus coming, Stan explains that the muggles don't see anything. This is a continuation of one of J.K. Rowling's themes – people will see what they want to see, and if people do not want to see anything Christian, their minds will create any probable reality that will answer what they saw rather than the truth. Furthermore, it is her conviction that there is evidence of God working in the world all around us and there are many who are unwilling to acknowledge it.

While on the Knight Bus, Stan Shunpike explains to Harry who Sirius Black is, and gives him the newspaper. In the article that Harry reads about Sirius Black's escape, it mentions that thirteen people died in the explosion that he created, including one wizard, Peter Pettigrew. The scene itself shows us the completion of that war against Lord Voldemort since thirteen is the number of completion and the battles between Lord Voldemort's followers and Professor Dumbledore's followers came to a peace thereafter.

J.K. Rowling's description of the sky lightening as Harry looks out of the window of his new room for the summer shows us all the alchemical stages – an almost black sky to a lighter sky, to rose, then a hint of gold. Harry has just finished at Privet Drive with a small transformation of his own in the minds of the Dursleys, and everything is good at the moment as he leaves the muggle world for his own world.

Chapter Four: The Leaky Cauldron

Although Harry learned about the dangers of the Book of Monsters on his birthday, readers learn more about how the books act in the bookstore as the bookkeeper prepares for battle getting books out for the students. John Granger suggests that the Book of Monsters represents the Bible, since many people are afraid of their Bible, and act as if it would bite them if they ever touched it.[61] At this stage in the book, the only way to control the Book of Monsters is to lock it away so as no one gets hurt. In many ways, this is what many religious authorities do - when they sense that people are seeing more than what is there, they remind people of the dangers of the Bible and forbid its use. However, it is more important to learn how to tame the Bible in order to handle its information properly, being both a history and instruction manual.

As Ron and Harry meet with manager of the Magical Menagerie, we learn more about Ron's rat, Scabbers. Here we get another clue that the rat is more than what he appears to be, since a common rat usually only lives three years. Scabbers has no magical abilities, but he has lived much longer than the three years. In addition to this, Ron brings a rat to school when the school list specifically says that the students may only bring a cat, toad, or owl. Lastly, we are reminded of the phrase "to smell a rat", meaning that something is amiss, a very true foreshadowing of events to come.

Chapter Five: The Dementor

As Harry, Hermione, and Ron occupy the train car with Remus Lupin already in it, we have some clues presented to us. Hollywood does what it can to tell the audience much about the character by casting David Thewliss as Remus Lupin. Thewliss generally plays a questionable

---

[61] Granger,J, Nov 5th, 2010, Lecture notes: "Unlocking Potter-Mania: The Christian Content Behind the World's Best Selling Books," Vienna, VA.

supporting character with a dark past, leading the viewers to suspect his intentions right from the beginning.

When the Hogwarts Express is stopped mid-ride, we are introduced to the Dementors. The name Dementor is both a take-off of the Latin word *dementia* meaning "madness" or out of one's mind, and a modified form of the word "demon." As such, Dementors are more than mindless cruelty – they are also without souls, representatives of the living undead. Although the substance of a soul is still unknown, many medieval philosophers thought the soul was what gave a body form.[62] Without a soul, a body feels a void and seeks out form for itself. This is why the Dementors are magnetically drawn towards people with emotional substance, and the larger the accompanying soul, the larger the attraction. Lastly, as dark, floating creatures, the Dementors tend to resemble multiple Grim Reapers with their skeletal figures, lack of facial features, black cloaks, and attraction to the living.

John Granger suggests that J. K. Rowling uses the climate to hint about how things are going for Harry. For instance, if it's hot and dry (the characteristics of alchemical fire), then everything is going well for Harry.[63] On the flip side, whenever the weather turns cold and wet, Lord Voldemort's characteristics (cold and wet) are in control and Harry is in trouble. Here, we see the Dementors create an atmosphere of ice and darkness, signaling to the readers that evil is about to appear and Harry is no longer safe.

Although the rest of the students in the compartment with Harry didn't faint or react physically when the Dementors came through, Hermione mentions that Ginny shook. Ginny's reaction shows the strength of her soul since the dementor is able to affect her from a distance, and hints at her very powerful magical core. Alchemically, this

---

[62] MacDonald, S, and Kretzman, N, *Routledge Encyclopedia of Philopshy,* "Medieval philosophy," retrieved from http://www.rep.routledge.com/article/B078.

[63] Granger, J., 2010, Lecture Notes "Unlocking Potter Mania," Vienna, VA.

again hints that Ginny is a key person in the story, since she is the seventh child of the family and the first girl in the past seven generations.[64]

At the Great Feast, there is some display of animosity between Professor Snape and Professor Lupin. The animosity that exists between Professors Snape and Lupin has been suggested to be the natural enemy relationship between a vampire and a werewolf, since Professor Snape is described many times as being "bat-like", always roaming around at night, and never eating with anyone else. Professor Lupin, as his name suggests, is a werewolf, although he is one of the few that does what he can to fit into normal society.

Chapter Six: Talons and Tea Leaves

With Harry's third year, Harry, Ron, and Hermione have some new, additional classes. As J.K. Rowling introduces her readers to the new class of Divination, she is hinting at the ethereal element of air, since thought is not a physical substance. However, she also portrays the class as being beyond both reason and substance, and thus nearly impossible to study.

Psychologists have proved the strength of the power of suggestion, and given the suggestion that two concepts are related, people will create those connections. In the Divinations class, Professor Trelawney tells Harry that he has the Grim, the dog-like symbol that indicates a sure and sudden death soon. In response, Harry suddenly connects everything he's seen with the dour Grim prediction and begins to make connections in his mind where there are none. Again, the power of suggestion is a factor of the mind, created in air, the element that Harry will unknowingly attempt to master through this book on his path of transformation.

Now a professor, Hagrid has a better opportunity to introduce Harry to the creature he will have to understand to help him master the element air. Here, the creature is the hippogriff, a combination horse and eagle similar to the griffin, which is the symbol of the kingdom of heaven

---

[64] Harry Potter Lexicon, 2011, "Ginerva "Ginny" Weasley," retrieved from http://www.hp-lexicon.org/wizards/ginny.html.

on earth. Secondly, Hagrid brings out a dozen hippogriffs, further indication that they are related to a Christian concept. Through his introduction in class, Harry gets the basics on how to handle the hippogriff and will have to learn to master the hippogriff to fully master the element of air.

Chapter Seven: The Boggart in the Wardrobe

As their first true Defense Against the Dark Arts teacher, Professor Lupin teaches the students about boggarts. In the magical realm, boggarts are water creatures that will capture people and drag them to the bottom of their bog until the person drowns. As an evil representative of our fears, they symbolize those fears that will drown someone until they can no longer function. To get rid of a boggart, Lupin explains that it is better to go with companions, since that confuses it and gives the companions more power. In many ways, this also speaks of the power of many over evil. Furthermore, as a single entity, evil personified in persons such as Lord Voldemort have no true power except that which others allow the person to have over them since as a whole, they could overcome the "leader."

Chapter Eight: Flight of the Fat Lady

While in Professor Trelawney's class, Harry constantly senses that there is hidden knowledge that he just can't access. This is typical of the class since there is nothing tangible to work with, and again points to thoughts as an element of air and another piece that Harry will have to master to gain mastery over air. In many ways, this is also reflective of the Gnosticism in the early church – a sect of early Christianity that spoke of hidden knowledge that went beyond what was in the letters and written accounts of Christ's life at the time.

As Halloween arrives, Harry has a horrible day, reiterating that the Harry Potter series is not a witchcraft series. First, he's not allowed into Hogsmeade, then he runs into many people he doesn't want to spend time with. However, by the end of the evening, the arrival of Sirius Black, the supposed supporter of Lord Voldemort, follows the format that Harry's adversary announces himself in some form on Halloween, setting up the challenge and mystery for the current book.

Chapter Nine: Grim Defeat

How Sirius gets into the castle is the mystery of that year, but it also alludes to the fact that he can get in and out of solid buildings as if by air. Incidentally, both Azkaban and Hogwarts are protected by either air-like creatures (the dementors) or protective aerial charms, indicating that Sirius Black has mastery over the air element and all its aspects. Since the Hebrew word for air is also the same word for breath and spirit, having a spirit that changes form is similar to moving as if by air, again a piece of the air mastery puzzle for Harry to solve.

Professor Lupin's ailment that keeps him from teaching class gives Professor Snape some license about what to teach the students. For the first substituted class, Professor Snape gives a big clue about Professor Lupin being a werewolf by teaching them how to recognize the difference between an animagus and a werewolf. Although the two are similar in that they involve the same spirit but different forms, the larger contrast is about the choice: animagi can change their shape at will, whereas werewolves have no choice. Secondly, whereas an animagus is only a physical change stemming from one's own will, an element of alchemical air, a werewolf transforms both physically and spiritually, a bodily transformation representative of elemental earth. Lastly, whereas animagi are seen as positive elements and completely in control of their spirits and actions, both the werewolf and the vampire are evil, and have no control over their faculties being driven by their fleshy desires and hunger, the law of nature. (Galatians 5:18 "But if you are led by the Spirit, you are not under law." NIV)

At the Quidditch match, Harry faints under the influence of the dementors and loses his broom. This is the lowest point of the year for Harry, where we see his bottoming out on his control over alchemical air. Again, as air represents spirit as well as breath and air, Harry's inability to control his own breathing and consciousness under the influence of ethereal spirits causes him the loss of his broom, the one piece he usually controlled very well in the air. However, this also points out that sometimes we have to destroy what we have in order to build a better one later, just as Jesus had to destroy his own temple to rebuild a better one in three days.

Back with Professor Lupin as the instructor for the Defense Against the Dark Arts class, the students learn about the Hinkypunk, a false light that misleads travelers and causes their deaths. There are many such things in this world that will lead pilgrims looking for the path to Christ astray. Christians usually call them "anti-Christ", since they act like the light of Christ but lead people away from Christ.

Chapter Ten: The Marauder's Map

As the chapter opens, we see that the dementors are still staying away from Hogwarts, afraid of Professor Dumbledore's anger. This shows the strength of Professor Dumbledore's persona, since not only can he tell the dementors what to do, but he does not require a patronus to keep his mind free when they are around. The fact that the dementors do not affect him shows that he feels forgiven for his own sins, and is free from sin in his mind.

Fred and George have pity on Harry, and present him with The Marauder's Map. The four purveyors that created the map for others to follow represent the four gospel writers who wrote the gospel to light the way for other followers of Christ. Interestingly, no one knows how the two Weasley brothers discovered how to work the map, but since they represent the saints and martyrs of the Church, it is not impossible that they are gifted enough with some knowledge to discover the secrets of the map. In keeping with the alchemical air element, the map can sense the spirits of everyone in Hogwarts and depict their physical locations. There are also seven known entrances or exits to Hogwarts, like holes in the sheepfold's fencing, seven being the perfect alchemical number. However, over time, many have fallen into disrepair eliminating opportunities for travelling outside the protection of the great shepherd. In many ways, this elimination of passages shows the progressive lack of freedoms as Christian regions have slowly eroded away.

In Hogsmeade, the trio hears more about Sirius Black from Minister Fudge's description of Sirius on his last visit. Most wizards sent to Azkaban go mad as they relive their sins from their lives, but the dementors don't seem to affect Sirius. Sirius' ability to withstand the soul magnetism of the dementors without a wand for protection (the strong power of God) shows both his inner strength and the fact that he didn't have anything to be sorry for. In many ways, Azkaban seems like Purgatory or the Jewish *Sheol*, where you have to live with your own sins until your chaff is burned away and you are sent to heaven or hell.

In the movie portrayal of the book, Hollywood casts Gary Oldman as Sirius Black, an actor that traditionally plays the key psychotic antagonist in films. This stereotype helps mislead viewers into thinking that Sirius Black must be a servant of Lord Voldemort, or in some more menacing way connected to Lord Voldemort. Although the "physical" manifestation of Lord Voldemort himself would be in keeping with what we have seen in the past two books, this third book is about air and the various forms of transformation that occur so we can be on the watch for a trick surrounding Sirius Black's character.

Chapter Eleven: The Firebolt

As Hagrid brings in the twelve Christmas trees, we are reminded again of the importance of the number twelve. Each tree represents a tribe of Israel, and the golden stars show the perfection of the number and beauty of Christmas. Also, since Christmas is the day that the light came into the darkness, we know that Harry is about to turn a corner from where everything seems to be against Harry to a new phase where he begins to gain strength.

While the trio is in the boys' dorm room, Harry hears the sneakoscope alarm going off again meaning that something isn't what it appears to be.

Since it is only Harry, Ron, Hermione, Scabbers, and Crookshanks in the room, Harry's assumption that everything is as it appears to be makes him doubt the validity of the sneakoscope. However, it is another clue that one of them isn't what it appears to be and that spiritual matter can have different forms.

True to form, J.K. Rowling begins Harry's white stage of illumination for the book at Christmas time. With the mysterious gift of the Firebolt, Harry begins his illuminated ascension towards mastery of the elemental air. Secondly, the mystery of who sent him the Firebolt will help Harry discover the truth about the past and those around him.

As the students and staff all sit down to Christmas dinner, there are twelve people total. With the arrival of Professor Trelawney, there are thirteen, the alchemical number of completion. The black stage of Harry's school year is thus completed. Additionally, with the thirteen people at the historical dinner, we can also see the last supper. At the Last Supper, Jesus shows that not everything is as it appears to be and tells the disciples that the bread (matzah) is his body, broken for them and introduces the fourth cup of wine as his blood shed for them. At the dinner at Hogwarts, Professor Dumbledore similarly shows everyone that things are not what they appear to be with the crackers – when they pop open - there are many different hats that appear alluding to the different personalities that each person can have, another aspect of spirit and alchemical air.

Chapter Twelve: The Patronus

When Professor Lupin's recurring absences is absent due to a recurring illness, Hermione begins to speak but changes her mind. Since Hermione was the only one that actually completed the werewolf essay as assigned, she has figured out that Professor Lupin has a secret around the full moon, but understanding the danger of the situation and trusting Professor Dumbledore, she is keeping quiet and chooses not to tell anyone.

Now in the stage of learning how to master the aspects of air, Harry is able to take lessons from Professor Lupin about how to defend himself against the monster of the air – the dementors. Professor Lupin describes the concept of the patronus to Harry as a means of defeating the negative energy of a dementor. In essence, a patronus is a complex creation generated by one's happy thoughts. The name patronus comes from the concept of a Patron Saint – someone who would watch over you and protect you, although the charm itself is not calling another entity to your protection. The fact that a wizard uses an incantation rather than an invocation shows again how the wizardry of Harry Potter is singing with God rather than invoking spirits. Rather, since the dementors are devoid of soul matter, the sudden strength of hope and happiness focused in one spot repels the darkness, just as a light dispels darkness (John 1:5 – "The light shines in the darkness, and the darkness has not overcome it." (NIV))

As Harry goes through the process of finding the right type of happy memory or hope that will guard him against the dementors, he finds that focusing on events that were all about things he did were not strong enough. However, when he finally discovers that it is only the happiness that comes with Christ and belonging to a Christian community, he has the strength to battle both the dementors and the death they represent.

In Oliver Wood's discussion with Professor McGonagall about Harry's new Firebolt, Oliver mentions that he doesn't care too much about whether a broomstick is safe or not as long as Harry catches the snitch first, to which Harry agreed. This sounds a bit reckless, but for some, finding the truth about Christ is more important than one's personal safety since it is better to die with Christ than be ousted out of the Christian community and have to live without Christ. Since the snitch is the representation of the truth, Oliver Wood, namesake of the wood of the Cross, would, of course, choose to seek the snitch rather than play it safe.

As Professor Lupin explains about the Dementor's Kiss, J.K. Rowling shows us what she understands the soul to be – a person's identity, sense of self, and memories. It is interesting that the dementors, which have no soul of their own, are not able to keep the soul that they take, as it would be if they were true Grim Reapers of sorts. However, there is also the question of whether a person would ever deserve to lose his or her soul on command from anyone other than God. Since losing a soul does not constitute a true "death", it also raises the question of when the soul begins its existence if a person could theoretically exist without one. Does the soul begin before birth or upon conception, and are there other ways to lose one's soul (as hinted at by Goethe's *Faust*)? Lastly, although wizards are the only people who can see Dementors, all people can sense the cold and despair dementors cause, meaning that the ability to see a dementor is not related to the existence of a soul in the body.

After the build-up and natural relationship between a cat and a rat, Scabbers' disappearance leaves little to the imagination about what happened to him. With blood traces on the sheets, the accusations are strong between Ron and Hermione, just as a person's reason and emotions would alternately excuse and mourn for the loss. However, the disappearance is an echo of Peter Pettigrew's earlier disappearance, and a foreshadowing of the truth to come.

Chapter Thirteen: Gryffindor versus Ravenclaw

With the argument over the cause of Scabbers' death, Ron and Hermione's friendship looks like it has come to an end, and we see the first time that the trio has separated willingly. Alchemically, sulfur and mercury are stronger separately and more able to wear on Harry, the lead, accelerating his true transformation. Lead is a very solid metal and resistant to corrosion, so it will take time even as separated elements to help convert this lead to gold.

Although the early Christians used passwords and symbols to show membership to their group, they also needed face recognition to help identify who was allowed into the meetings. As Sirius Black was able to obtain the passwords to the Gryffindor tower and the Fat Lady allowed him entrance, this reinforces the need for face recognition. The biggest clue that Sirius is not after Harry Potter is that he went to Ron's bed instead, and we also see that he is not a cold blooded killer, since Sirius did not harm anyone before his disappearance "into thin air."

Chapter Fourteen: Snape's Grudge

With the return of the Fat Lady and the additional guards she requested for her protection, the references here remind us of icons. Icons are prayerfully created to provide a window to the saints in heaven. As such, the icons can act either as reminders of stories in the past, or as pictorial protection as well, a connection to God.

J.K. Rowling here places another clue for the very sub plot of Professor Lupin's antagonism for Professor Snape, as Professor Lupin has his class write an essay about vampires in return for the essay on werewolves. For the readers, this shows that both professors have a connection to the dark possessive side of evil. Although neither of them are willing elements of that darkness, they do everything they can to keep a positive outlook and do whatever is necessary to protect themselves or others despite their touches of darkness. For Snape, this is his occlumency – his ability to shield others from reading his mind, and for Professor Lupin, it means drinking his assigned tonic so that he does no harm to others during his wolf phase.

Chapter Fifteen: The Quidditch Final

In this chapter, we see Harry finally coming to the crux of his journey toward mastery over air. First, he is introduced to the crystal ball, a simplified form of scrying. Scrying is the magical art of seeing something or someone from afar either in space or time. Since the object viewed is not tangible, it is an element of air, and Harry never does seem to fully understand these balls. Second, Harry finally is able to produce a patronus (outside of his tutoring sessions) on the Quidditch field, showing his emerging mastery over the demons of the air, the dementors. Third, Harry finally gets to use his new broomstick and demonstrate his mastery over the physical air with his excellent flying skills that lead to Gryffindor winning the Quidditch Cup. Through the chapter, Harry shows progress in his relationship with air, thus concluding the white stage of the book and moving toward the red stage of resolution.

Chapter Sixteen: Professor Trelawney's Prediction

It is interesting that divination is on the seventh floor's tower, indicating a nature of perfection. As we discover however, the seventh floor is also the same floor as many other things that tend to change with the day, as if by the whim of a thought. In this way, this is another reference to the aspects of alchemical air. An addition J.K. Rowling makes in this book to alchemical air is the connection between time and air. Throughout the book, there is the mystery of how Hermione is able to take so many classes at once. Even with her ability to do so many things, Hermione states that divination is a waste of time. This is both a resignation on Hermione's part to recognize anything beyond the physical realm and a demoting of the whole concept of divination since Hermione has a time-turner and all the time she wants.

Returning to the Divinations classroom, Harry witnesses Professor Trelawney's transformation into a true seer. As we hear Professor Trelawney's prediction, we find out first that she does have an ability to predict the future and second that Harry's mastery of air involves divination only in the sense of owning and possibly causing predictions. Prophecy is an aspect found mostly in the Old Testament, the only true test recorded being that the predictions come true. Many times, the prophets were called by God to speak only a few times in their lives – very few actually have more than a few messages for the people. Regardless, once they have the ability to prophecy for God, they are kept in the sheepfold and protected from roaming wolves that might prey on them.

Chapter Seventeen: Cat, Rat, and Dog

The animal trio of the cat, rat, and dog are related to the three friends, creating an animalistic trio and a continuation of the theme that the air or spirit of something stays the same regardless of what shape it takes. In a way, the three animals are a new rendering of the actual trio.

Crookshanks is the bright one associated with Hermione, Snuffles is the action figure associated with Harry, and Scabbers is the dear friend that is almost a sidekick, associated with Ron.

As Harry and Hermione descend to help Ron as he disappears into the Whomping Willow, again we see Harry and his friends descending to a low place to fight off an element of Lord Voldemort. However, this scene is more about the conclusion of Harry's stage of illumination – the last piece of the puzzle that will help him succeed in defeating the creatures of the air that will demonstrate his true mastery over air.

Chapter Eighteen: Moony, Wormtail, Padfoot, and Prongs

With Professor Lupin's accusation that Scabbers, the rat, is in fact Peter Pettigrew, Harry reminds us that Sirius Black was imprisoned for Peter's death twelve years ago, twelve being the perfect number for redemption in both Judaism and Christianity. With this reminder, we know that a wrong will be righted and there will be some form of closure for a past deed.

The discussion of animagi between the trio and Sirius and Professor Lupin tells us that an animagus has the same spirit as the person that transformed. This is a critical key to transubstantiation: whereas in an animagus the spirit is the same but the substance is different, in transubstantiation, the substance is the same, but the spirit is different. In the context of air, Harry's understanding of animagi help him master alchemical air. Similarly, the four gospels in the New Testament are represented not by people but by animals that show their characteristics symbolically. 1) Harry's father James, represented by the stag, Prongs, is a seeker who has found the truth of Christ and embodied it; 2) Sirius, a shaggy dog, is alchemically the antimony – someone very supportive of those who seek Christ, nearby but not really in the action themselves. 3) Moony, as a cursed creature that does everything to avoid his curse, still follows Christ with the thorn in his side; and 4) Peter Pettigrew, represented by the rat that began as a true follower but was quickly lured off course and seeks to save his own hide, is named Wormtail, who will eventually cause the destruction of one-third of God's people.

As Professor Lupin tells his story of how his three best friends became Animagi, he is haunted by the memory since it was what led to the Potter family's downfall. It was Peter's ability to transform that allowed him to sneak out to see Lord Voldemort and betray his friends. The admission of his betrayal of Dumbledore's trust makes Professor Lupin afraid of Professor Dumbledore since he knows that he deserves expulsion for not reporting his friends' abilities to illegally transform. However, Professor Dumbledore's occlumency would have kept him informed. Nonetheless, Professor Dumbledore would also probably forgive Remus Lupin in his remorse, following Christ's example of forgiveness whenever we disobey and have true remorse for our actions.

Chapter Nineteen: The Servant of Voldemort

As Peter Pettigrew tries to defend his actions to Sirius and Remus, J.K. Rowling poses an important philosophical question through Peter Pettigrew's confession – if evil is taking over, what good is there in refusing it? Sirius' answer of "only innocent lives" are saved is an important answer, as well as his retort that death is better than betraying friends or giving in to evil. Again, this is a reminder of Hermione's statement that it would be better to die than be expelled from Hogwarts, and a recurrence of the theme of how many things are worse than death. Biblically, this comes from Christ's message through the book of Matthew:"It is better for you to enter life maimed or crippled than to have two hands or two feet and be thrown into eternal fire" (Matthew 18:8) as well as The Golden Rule: "Do to others as you would have them do to you." (Luke 6:31.)

Harry's defense of Peter Pettigrew, which includes a request for justice through the proper system and subsequent Dementor's Kiss, shows both Harry's ability to forgive others and show mercy despite what's happened to him. It also shows a growth in his understanding of the larger picture in that there are worse things than death for those that are afraid of death. Peter Pettigrew, understanding the mercy he's been given, now owes his life to Harry, even though he has sold his soul to Lord Voldemort.

Chapter Twenty: The Dementor's Kiss

As the dementors move in on Sirius at the lake, we again see Harry fighting off evil and death as his friends leave him one by one, although not by choice. Harry does what he can to think of something that will give him hope and happiness, but the amount of death and negativity around him overwhelms his ability to transform his love for Sirius to hope and send them away. His inability to produce a patronus also shows that thinking about events or just happy occurrences isn't enough to dispel evil or death. However, a symbol of Christ, the stag patronus, again comes to save Harry and his friends from eminent death, driving away the dementors. In essence, the light of Christ dispels the darkness of death (John 1:5).

Chapter Twenty-One: Hermione's Secret

In the hospital wing, Professor Dumbledore tells us a little bit about Madame Pomfrey by using her first name – Poppy. Poppies are the source of opium and the symbol of remembrance for the dead. As a clinic's healer in this world, she would use opium to help patients through physical pain and memories. As a wizard's healer, her name is more indicative of her position than of the actual substances she might use.

Hermione, Harry, and Ron try desperately to save Sirius, and plead to Professor Dumbledore for help. Professor Dumbledore reiterates the moral from the parable about the rich man and Lazarus in his statement "I have no power to make other men see the truth," realizing that if people don't want to see the truth, nothing he does will make any difference. Again, J. K. Rowling reiterates her theme that people will see what they want to see, and believe what they want to believe, regardless of what is actually there. Ultimately, it is man's own free will that decides what he sees.

By suggesting that Hermione use time to solve the problem, J.K. Rowling is again connecting the concept of time to air. As people travel through time, they move through space or air as well. By expanding time, Hermione will lead Harry to his opportunities to show his mastery both of the creatures that are representing air – the hippogriff and the dementors.

J.K. Rowling shows Sirius' importance in the series through the numbers used to indicate where Sirius is – seventh floor, and thirteenth window from the right. This seven- thirteen connection again shows another alchemical completion and perfection in Sirius, another key metal in the transformation to gold and the subsequent Philosopher's Stone.

From the alternate point of view as they relive the events, we see that Harry's final victory over air coincides with his victory over death again with a symbolic number of three – three hours, reflective of the three days for Christ's victory over death. As Hermione points out, managing the feat at all is a miracle.

Furthermore, from the new point of view, J. K. Rowling gives a clue about the evilness of Buckbeak's execution – the timing of the execution for June 6th (6/6) at 6 PM, the numbers of the address for Satan. By saving Buckbeak, Harry and Hermione are saving another soul from a foul death and Harry shows his mastery of the hippogriff, an animal of the air, or at least his ability to work with Buckbeak without fear.

True to the story format, Harry is again alone having left Ron in the hospital and Hermione in the hut. Harry is in duplication on both sides of the lake, to fight off the alchemical representation of death for alchemical air. In a clear detour from the victim that Harry usually plays during the scene, Harry is now able to play the savior figure, showing his mastery over the air by using a figment of both air and Christ, the stag patronus, to overshadow and dispel the representations of evil and air – the dementors. (The White Stag became a symbol for Christ after a legend about a hungry Roman centurion who prayed, then followed a white stag with a cross in its antlers to safety.)[65] It was the strength of his belief and love for his father that created the stag patronus, the stag that was his father's animagus form. It is the true love for a person that brings us protection from evil and the patronus shows a form of that person. Again, we see that it isn't how much a person knows that saves him, it is his love for others and for God.

With the expansion of time, Harry has made another transformation – one from victim that needs saving to the hero that saves others. As he and Hermione save Sirius using the hippogriff that they also rescued, Harry shows his mastery over all three elements of the air – time, wind, and spirit.

Chapter Twenty-Two: Owl Post Again

Professor Snape's response to his disappointment that Sirius Black was saved shows a common trap of many people – wanting justice for what seems just from their point of view, without seeing the whole picture or another side of the truth. Just as Jesus protected the woman who was going to be stoned as an adulterer, Professor Dumbledore protects Sirius and provides for his safety. Professor Snape, on the other hand, is very disappointed that he was denied justice. Similarly, Jonah suffered the same disappointment when God rescued Nineveh when the people repented and changed their ways. God eventually reminded Jonah that His decision to save Nineveh was His own choice, given from His own compassion for His people and has no impact on Jonah. Although nothing is known about whether Jonah ever repents of his anger, there is still hope for Professor Snape to recant his anger and become a positive servant of Professor Dumbledore's.

After Professor Lupin resigns, he and Harry have a good concluding conversation. During this conversation, Professor Lupin explains to Harry that his father would have been disappointed if Harry had not discovered the secret passages to the castle. Why would a disciple of Christ want to

---

[65]Jones, T, 2012, "The Golden Legend: The Story of St. Eustace," retrieved from http://www.catholic-forum.com/saints/golden298.htm.

lead his son out of the safety of the sheepfold of Christ? I am suggesting that Harry's father wanted Harry to know that he had a choice to be part of the sheepfold or not, but also to know that there was to freedom to go in and out of it like a true owner of the sheepfold.

Professor Dumbledore in his final discussion with Harry mentions a deeper magic that is impenetrable, that involves mercy, sacrifice, and life debts to others. Perhaps the impenetrable magic is not very clearly understood, or was lost as newer rules overtook the older ones. Regardless, in many ways, this is the same magic spoken of in the Chronicles of Narnia's *The Lion, the Witch, and the Wardrobe*, which requires payment and imprisonment for false deeds.

Chapter SEVEN

The Guide to *The Goblet of Fire*

Plot summary: As the story opens, the Weasleys do everything they can to connect with the Dursleys via muggle post and telephone to invite Harry to the World Quidditch Cup. The planned rescue from the Dursley's house ends up a bungle, as the Weasleys arrive by floo powder to the Dursley's blocked up fireplace. Eventually, Harry and Hermione end up at the Weasley's house in time to attend the Quidditch World Cup. At the World Cup, Harry loses his wand, but doesn't realize it until Death Eaters are harassing muggles and setting the camp on fire. Shortly thereafter, the Dark Mark appears over a portion of the forest nearby where the trio are hiding, and they are accused of setting the Dark Mark. They are absolved, and return to The Burrow to wait til the school year begins.

Upon arrival at Hogwarts, the students learn that things will be a little different this year. First of all, there are no Quidditch games planned. In its place, there is to be a Triwizard Tournament, which involves students from the other two main schools: Beauxbatons, and Durmstrang. Select students from these two schools would be studying at Hogwarts this year during the year-long tournament. In order to be considered by the Goblet of Fire to participate, participants must be seventeen years of age, and only one student per school will be chosen by the Goblet. By some quirk, Harry ends up included in the selected participants, making the number four rather than the normal three: Fleur Delacour (Beauxbatons), Victor Krum (Durmstrang), and Cedric Diggory (Hufflepuff).

Over the year, the class that attracts attention is the Defense Against the Dark Arts class with its new professor, Professor Alastor Moody. Through Professor Moody, a somewhat unorthodox teacher, we learn about the three unforgivable curses that will land any user into Azkaban, and that it is important to learn counter curses or how to defeat curses on your own. Another aspect of Harry's training is subtle coaching from Professor Moody, Hermione, and Ron that help him through the three tasks of taking the golden egg from a dragon, swimming an hour through the lake to rescue a best friend, and getting through a life-size maze to the winning cup. Lastly, Rita Skeeter, a reporter for the Daily Prophet, makes her mark as she appears everywhere reporting the multitude of events that occur during the year regardless of the facts or privacy of the subjects.

At the end of the third task, Harry and Cedric get to the cup at the same time, and the cup transports them to an old graveyard. Upon arrival, they see Peter Pettigrew coming towards them carrying a bundle, and Harry's scar burns as Pettigrew kills Cedric with the Killing Curse. Harry is unwillingly part of the rebirthing ceremony for Lord Voldemort, and duels the newly risen Lord Voldemort. Somehow, their wands connect which brings forth the last few people Lord Voldemort has killed, including his parents. These ghosts are able to hold Lord Voldemort off long enough to let Harry escape with Cedric's body and return to Hogwarts.

Back at Hogwarts, they discover that Barty Crouch, Jr., pretending to be Alastor Moody through a Polyjuice potion, created the portkey that put Harry in the graveyard. In Professor Moody's office, we discover that Barty Crouch Jr. killed his own father and kept the real Alastor Moody captive in a trunk. The Minister of Magic called the dementors to collect

Barty, Jr., but the dementors destroyed Crouch Jr. using the Dementor's Kiss. However, Professors Dumbledore, Snape, Hagrid, and McGonagall know the truth. Headmaster Dumbledore exposes Sirius Black's alternate form of the shaggy dog, and the six of them (including the real Alastor Moody) begin the next Order of the Phoenix. The students mourn the death of Cedric Diggory, and return home via the Hogwarts Express. On the train, Harry hears about Fred and George Weasley's hopes to create a joke shop, and he gives them his Triwizard Cup winnings to begin their new endeavor.

Chapter One: The Riddle House

John Granger's Ring theory states that this middle book in the series is a turning point in the series, where there are mirror images to the first and last book.[66] To that end, this book and the first book don't start at Privet Drive or with Harry Potter. Also, both of these beginnings speak of a murder of a family – two parents and a son in each case, although in the first book, Harry Potter lives and in this fourth book, Tom Riddle, Senior, dies.

Unfortunately, the family gardener was framed for the murders of the Riddles. Knowing that Lord Voldemort was their murderer, the gardener ends up as the scapegoat of the evidence presented. Despite the lack of evidence, the accusation alone is enough to sway the public opinion against him. There is another theme throughout the series that comes to light in this chapter – the fact that even when inconclusive evidence is presented, people can be judged in various ways, depending on what people choose to see.

Within this first chapter, we return to the alchemy straight away. The first alchemy number shows up with Frank the gardener's age. At 77 years old, he has reached two numbers showing perfection - almost a certain death sentence. Secondly, Lord Voldemort has waited 13 years to try his hand against Harry Potter again. Thirteen being the number of completion, it is a predictable time for the story to change directions. With both of these numbers in the first chapter, we are reminded of the alchemy of the series and sense that this will be a turning point.

Biblically, we see Lord Voldemort's "kindness" in allowing Wormtail to exist so that he might perform some small sacrificial service to him. This is actually a bit of foreshadowing, since Wormtail's sacrifice for Lord Voldemort is literal – it will cost Wormtail his right hand, and his life, in the end.

---

[66] Granger, J, Lecture notes, Vienna Virginia, Nov 3rd, 2010

Chapter Two: The Scar

As Harry wakes up from his nightmare with pain from his scar, Harry remembers Sirius Black, his closest parental stand-in. True to his antimony and dog-like nature, Sirius Black is not easily accessible but he does what he can to stay involved and help Harry whenever possible. Continuing the alchemy, J. K. Rowling mentions gold many times in describing Harry's bedroom. Gold being the perfection of all things, it shows the end of Harry's loneliness and the true beginning of his having a "family."

Chapter Three: The Invitation

As Harry's birthday arrives and Harry's friends all send him sweets to hold him through the summer, we find out that Hermione's parents are dentists since they sent along sugar-free sweets. This is Ms. Rowling's means of subtly emphasizing that Hermione represents alchemical mercury since dentists are one of the few professions that work with mercury (although not so much anymore).[67]

Chapter Four: Back to the Burrow

Vernon Dursley's comment about how the wizards dress in strange ways reflects many people's attitudes towards religious expectations or requirements to wear robes. However, there are many cultures that wear robes and not pants for many non-religious reasons, and Ms. Rowling is showing how the Dursleys extreme prejudice and very limited point of view is both extremely superficial as well as transferring from their hatred of Harry to all things he represents.

As a continuation of the cultural clash, we have the two cultures represented by Mr. Dursley and Mr. Weasley that are divided by a common language (even though they are both living in England!) as Mr. Weasley tries to explain how he will fix the mess his family has made in the Dursley's house. As awkward as the situation would be without the

---

[67] Granger, J., 2007, *Unlocking Harry Potter,* p. 62.

Dursley's lack of social skills and compassion, with the Dursleys not trying to understand or acknowledge the Weasley's existence, there is no hope. In many ways, the two families are exact opposites, beginning with the number of children, and continuing with their names. Whereas D for Dursley is the fourth letter from the beginning of the alphabet, W for Weasley is the fourth from the end of the alphabet. The Weasley's have seven children, but the Dursleys only had one. The Dursley's are just at the beginning of their understanding or journey, and the Weasley's completely understand their journey and where they need to go.

We see this same cultural division many times in churches, even if the church is operating within the same denomination and language. While at a church service, the visitor can feel completely lost with the change of the cultural use of the language even within the same format and the local flavor of music that adds dimension to the service. The Catholic Church did what they could to help their universality by requiring Latin as the language in all churches, but people needed their own language to understand what was happening. Eventually Vatican II allowed for local language use in their Sunday services. As their last difference, the Dursleys devote their entire time and talents on their son, Dudley, while the Weasleys work together to raise their seven children. Both numbers are alchemical numbers, 1 and 7, but although the Dursleys show no affection for anyone outside themselves while the Weasleys care for more than their own without worry about the additional cost, who would be watching, or any other limitations.

Chapter Five: Weasley's Wizard Wheezes

In this chapter, J.K. Rowling gives a very succinct explanation of the different types of jobs available to wizards upon graduation from Hogwarts and the parental expectations of their children. Fred and George's hopes of beginning a joke shop is not taken seriously, since everyone is supposed to take life seriously, especially in the church. However, there is much to be said for seeing the lighter side of things, with many medical professionals in agreement that laughter can cure some diseases or promote faster recoveries. (Proverbs 17:22: "A cheerful heart is good medicine, but a crushed spirit dries up the bones.")

Chapter Six: The Portkey

Even though we are in the fourth book, the portkey is the last air piece for Harry's mastery of air that he began in the last chapter. The portkey is an object that has been charmed to move through the air at a specific moment either of time or event and transports people to a predetermined location. The actual order of mastery, according to the alchemy books, is earth, water, air, then fire, and after salvation and mastery through each element, there is a bonus piece given to help with the mastery. This portkey is the bonus piece for Harry for having mastered alchemical air so well in the previous school year.

Chapter Seven: Bagman and Crouch

As the Weasleys lead Hermione and Harry through the security created for the Quidditch Cub and introduce them to many of the key characters in the book, Harry and Hermione are able to contribute their muggle knowledge about fire to the camping adventure. As they light the campfire for food, we are introduced to Harry's journey through alchemical fire. The fire theme continues throughout the book, showing us that the fourth book is Harry's mastery over fire.

Chapter Eight: The Quidditch World Cup

As the Quidditch World Cup begins, the description of the teams and the top box that Harry and everyone ends up in are a foreshadowing of events at the end of the book. First, the Irish are in green and the Bulgarians are in red – the color opposites that correspond to Slytherin and Gryffindor as well as their representatives, Lord Voldemort and Harry. The Irish have many plays that put Bulgaria at a true disadvantage, and from the start, it looks as if the Irish will win. However, the Bulgarian seeker, Victor Krum, is able to make a couple of plays that not only keep the Bulgarians from losing badly, but ends the game on Krum's terms in a way that makes the score very close in the end. In the same way, Lord Voldemort has everything set up to defeat Harry, but in the end, even though Harry is hurt, he is able to come back on his own terms and survive the encounter.

In *Chamber of Secrets,* we learned much about how the house-elves were a trodden on race. However, whereas Dobby gave us insights into the punishment of house-elves and their obligations, Winky gives us insight into how strong their requirement of their obedience is to do as they are told, without pay despite their own magic or fears. As Harry and his friends attend the Quidditch Cup in the announcer's box, they meet Winky, Barty Crouch's house elf. Despite her fear of heights, Winky is an extremely loyal house-elf and is very proud of the wizard she works for. The attitudes between the two elves differ most likely from their treatment by their masters, but also by how much is entrusted to them by the wizards. Whereas Dobby was always treated like a slave only worthy of punishment, Winky was treated more as an equal, entrusted with important tasks and secrets.

As the Quidditch Cup continues, we see many details within the descriptions of the tournament. For instance, it is the 422nd World Cup – since 4+2+2 = 8, we are now past perfection to a new beginning of something. The number eight is the number the Jews associate with a new beginning: King David was the 8th son of Jesse, circumcision occurs on the eighth day, the eighth day begins the new week, etc.[68] Applying this to the knowledge that Wormtail has returned to Lord Voldemort, we know that this book will produce a stronger enemy than Harry has had to fight before, beginning a new dimension to the good versus evil element.

---

[68] McGough, R., 2009, Bible Wheel Forum, "Spoke 8 – Symbolic meaning of the number 8," retrieved from http://www.biblewheel.com/wheel/spokes/chet_eight.asp.

Chapter Nine: The Dark Mark

As the Quidditch Cup's celebrations continue into the night, we also see another element of the alchemy within the books. In alchemy, there is a black stage of isolation, a white stage of illumination, and a red stage of purification or reunification. John Granger suggests that each of J.K. Rowling's books follow this pattern within each book as well,[69] but it is not as obvious in the first three as it is in the second half of the series.

In this chapter, we begin to see that Harry's black stage has begun in earnest – while it is night time, there are fires burning at the camps, the Death Eaters walk around with black hoods, and we begin to see the beginnings of a true separation of the Death Eaters from the rest of the wizarding community. Continuing with the black stage theme, the muggles are being separated out from the wizards, and Harry and his friends are separated from others. Furthermore, after Harry's had a wand for three years, he realizes that his wand is lost. Suddenly, not having it makes him feel vulnerable and alone, as it has become representative of his faith and connection to his wizarding community. All of these situations act to show Harry's descent into isolation from others as the beginning of the book sets the stage for the conflict in the story.

Even though Harry loses his wand, he thankfully discovers that with his friends around him providing protection with their own wands, he is still safe. More significantly, when we or a friend has lost faith or sense of community, it is even more important for the community and friends to provide that protection and community until they have found their own faith again.

At the conclusion of this chapter, we see that there were 13 glorious years without Lord Voldemort, even if there were a couple of small events at Hogwarts. However, with the apparition of the Dark Mark, Lord Voldemort's followers have come back in force, ending the peaceful years without Lord Voldemort. The Dark Mark itself, a green skull with a snake

---

[69] Granger, J, 2007, *Unlocking Harry Potter,* p. 141.

issuing forth from its mouth, is particular to the Harry Potter series and not found anywhere else. However, the symbols individually both represent either evil or death, and together could be a variation on the skull-and-crossbones of piracy fame meaning no quarter would be given to any from the opposing side.[70]

Chapter Ten: Mayhem at the Ministry

As the Weasleys, Harry, and Hermione return to the Burrow, Molly Weasley gives us the first reference to the well-known clock at the Burrow – the clock with a hand for each person in the family, spun to show each person's location. Although this is the first description of the clock, Professor Dumbledore has a very similar watch, with twelve hands on it (mentioned in the first chapter of *Philosopher's Stone*.) There are seven locations on the clock, again the perfect number of places someone could be, and mortal peril is at the twelve o'clock position. This shows that the clock is an astrological clock, not necessarily a Christian one, since twelve is where misfortune lies in divination studies.[71]

After the hype of the dangers of the Quidditch Cup, the inhabitants in the Burrow settle down, looking toward the new school year and the secrets in store for them this year. One hint at what is to come is Mrs. Weasley making a balaclava for Charlie. A balaclava is a large ski-type mask that covers the face and shoulders. Since Charlie is the wizard who works with dragons, a fireproof version would be very useful against dragon fire, another reference to Harry's journey to master fire. Furthermore, the mention of Harry's Firebolt while he's packing provides a transitional air-fire item, since he didn't use the broom until after he mastered air, and the name introduces the element fire.

Lastly, as the dress robes arrive, we are reminded of the significance of the colors within the series. Harry's dress robes are green, an

---

[70] Raeside, R, 2012, Pirates, "An Overview of Pirate's Flags," retrieved from http://www.crwflags.com/fotw/flags/pirates.html#overview.

[71] Buckwalter, E, 2000, "The Twelfth House," retrieved from http://www.astrologyclub.org/articles/planets_signs_houses/pisces/twelfth.htm.

indication that he is now a full wizarding apprentice of Professor Dumbledore's, as all apprentices are green. Ron's maroon robes are maroon again, (the color of everything else his mother gets for him) representing passion, and another pointer to Ron's representation of the "will" in the Christian trio of body-mind-will of Christ.

Chapter Eleven: Aboard the Hogwarts Express

As the students get ready to leave for Hogwarts, we can see how things are turning against Harry now, a continuation of the black stage of the book as more pieces desert him. This year, there aren't any Ministry cars available, although in the previous year they were trying to protect Harry from Sirius Black and could give him one. The black stage doesn't only apply to Harry – others are also "in the dark", not understanding or responding correctly to Sirius Black's escape from Azkaban. While most of the Ministry is still looking for Sirius Black as the instigator for the incident at the Quidditch Cup, they are not seeing the other pieces that connect together to form a different picture of who the enemy truly is. Individually, we tend to do this as well - we get too focused on a small detail and explore that detail to the detriment of understanding the larger blot expanding next to it that is more important.

Chapter Twelve: The Triwizard Tournament

From the different reports about the incident at Professor Moody's house, we hear that he is well known for his highly suspicious nature, never trusting anything given to him or around him. Ironically, as suspicious as he is, no one is suspicious of him, despite his enhanced abilities with his magical eye. With the introduction of Professor Moody and his magical eye, J.K. Rowling brings in a new element of knowledge – seeing that which is physically invisible, within sight of Professor Moody as opposed to Professors Dumbledore and Snape who can read minds and "see" that which is mentally invisible.

During the Opening Feast, Professor Dumbledore explains about the Triwizard Tournament. During his explanation, the number 700 comes up

– again, the perfect number of centuries. Combined with the alchemical number three, we see more references to Christianity in the description of the three champions, pointing to the number of the trinity and the three-legged stool. The three legged stool is a very important concept in Christianity (especially the Anglican tradition) since no matter how long or short any of the legs are in a three-legged stool, it will not rock. No other number of stool legs will give that stability.

Another element J.K. Rowling brings in during Professor Dumbledore's speech is age. This is a more subtle theme presented here for the first time that recurs many times in the rest of the series – that of the significance of age. Here, it's the age restriction – no one younger than seventeen is allowed to participate in the tournament, even though Harry has already proven himself a few times against tremendous odds when he wasn't seventeen yet. The concept that someone has to be "old enough" to actually do something significant is a misconception that J.K. Rowling is trying to redirect, helping the youth of today see that they can do something significant for the world already.

Chapter Thirteen: "Mad-Eye" Moody

In this second year of Professor Hagrid's teaching the Care of Magical Creatures class, Professor Hagrid introduces Harry to the fire monsters that he will have to master in order to master the alchemical element he's mastering this year. One of the fiery creatures that Harry has to master we meet in this first lesson where Hagrid can teach Harry how to determine what care an animal needs- the blast-ended skrewts, just one of the fire monsters Harry will face in the months to come.

Later on in the chapter, we see Draco trying to put a hex on Harry as Harry turns away from his taunts. In Harry's defense, Professor Moody uses Malfoy to demonstrate his attitude towards those who decide to be dishonest and hide their true intentions by transfiguring Draco Malfoy. The fact that he turns Malfoy into a ferret shows how closely linked Ron Weasley and Draco Malfoy really are, since the weasel and the ferret are from the same family. Although a definitely unintended connection from either viewpoint, this family tree is the wizarding tree where all pureblood wizards are related somehow. Secondly, although Professor Moody states that he distrusts anyone who sneaks around behind others' backs, he is again being hypocritical in his remarks, doing exactly what he says he detests.

Chapter Fourteen: The Unforgiveable Curses

Although we don't normally see the interaction between staff members, Professor Snape usually shows antagonism against the staff member that will become the critical character in solving the mystery of the story. In the antagonism that begins to build here between Professors Snape and Moody, we have the all seeing eye of Moody versus the all seeing mental eye of Severus Snape, and almost a show-down of which is more powerful. Although Professor Snape knows that Professor Moody is an auror, and highly suspicious by nature, perhaps Professor Snape can sense something strange about Professor Moody that makes him uneasy, either because of Professor Snape's past, or because of Professor Moody's current situation. Likewise, Professor Moody is suspicious of Professor Snape's hidden marks that identify him as part of the Death Eaters although he teaches at Hogwarts as if he were one of Professor Dumbledore's supporters.

Harry, Ron, and Hermione give us another glimpse of who Professor Moody is through his teaching methods in their first Defense Against the Dark Arts class. As Professor Moody introduces the three unforgiveable curses, we understand that he is not afraid of these curses and feels that in order to truly conquer these curses, wizards have to test themselves against them and fight off the temptations they encourage. Their names given here also give their description – *imperio* sounding like "imperial", a royal command that cannot be ignored; *crucio* – reminding us of the crucifixion of Christ, and *Avada Kadavra,* meaning "before the cadaver", referring to a dead body. It is interesting to note that the three curses are the three parts of Christ's passion – he was handed over to the imperial government, he was then tortured, and killed on the cross. The death from the Killing Curse leaves no mark (as in the unblemished lamb led to slaughter), and the rush of wind is the spirit being taken away.

In this second year of Divinations class, Harry has a different viewpoint on the class based on his experiences from the previous year. Although Professor Trelawney gave an accurate prediction at the end of the year, the rest of the class was very hazy and subject to much interpretation. Throughout the Divination class, where they are supposedly trying to predict what God will do, J. K. Rowling gives her opinions about its usefulness and misdirection: Professor Trelawney's insistence on misery in her outcomes directly counters God's message of love and compassion for his people. As a second indication of a lack of confidence in prophecying on one's own accord rather than waiting for God to tell you what to prophecy, Harry just makes something up to give an answer to the request. Even so, Harry's comment about Venus being in the twelfth house is curious, since Christians and Jews alike think of twelve as a perfect number. However, in astrology, the twelfth house is where misfortune lies,[72] hence the predicted misery on that day.

Chapter Fifteen: Beauxbatons and Durmstrang

A phrase used in this fourth book that comes up repeatedly is Dumbledore wanting a character to do something that otherwise seems questionable. For instance, in Professor Moody's Defense Against the Dark Arts class, he indicates that although the three curses are banned, Professor Dumbledore thinks they should learn them and practice fighting off the imperious curse. We tend to be very trusting people, and if someone tells us that Professor Dumbledore wants us to do something, then we believe we should do it. In actuality, this is a use of the imperious curse – using someone else's authority rather than your own to control someone (manipulation techniques). Knowing that Professor Moody might not be who he says he is (as have been all the other Defense Against the Dark Arts teachers), we have to wonder why he requires the

---

[72] Buckwalter, E, 2000, "The Twelfth House," retrieved from http://www.astrologyclub.org/articles/planets_signs_houses/pisces/twelfth.htm.

students to experience the imperious curse and try to fight it off. This is perhaps a test to see whom he can control and whom he can't for whatever purposes he might need followers in the future.

In the other classes this year, there are a couple of symbolic indicators. First, in Divinations class, the name "Trewlaney" is a play on the word "trawling", where fishermen scrape the bottom looking for anything edible. Similarly, throughout Divinations class, we see Professor Trewlaney scraping for any hint that might be prophecy. Secondly, in Transfiguration class, Professor McGonagall has the students transfigure a pincushion into a hedgehog. Since the two resemble each other, it is easier to see the connection between what the transfigured form of something is to its un-transfigured form – the transfigured form has a spiritual element as well as a physical element, showing that it is closer to God in this form.

With the excitement of the arrival of the other schools, the trio discusses the various methods that the students from the other schools could possible arrive and Hermione has another opportunity to remind all of us that all newcomers have to enter through the gate. Regardless of an invitation or not, all wizards cannot just suddenly appear in Hogwarts. This is again a reiteration of John 10:3, that no one may enter the sheepfold except through the gate, and reinforcement of the analogy that Hogwarts is the sheepfold of Christian formation.

As it turns out, the all girls' school, Beauxbatons, arrives by air, and the all boys' school, Durmstrang, arrives by water. If you consider that the Hogwarts students' arrival by train represents alchemical earth, all three elements that Harry has mastered are now represented: earth, water, and air. Since there are four alchemical elements, we know that something is going to happen to fill in that fourth element, and that the addition will challenge Harry in his efforts to master alchemical fire.

Chapter Sixteen: The Goblet of Fire

As the three schools sit together in the Great Hall, there are many understandings and interpretations of this triangle. John Granger suggests that the three schools working together duplicate the Allies (French, England, and Russia),[73] with America's representative, a littler fellow from England, arriving late to the scene but saving everyone else at one time or another. From the alchemical point of view, we see Durmstrang sitting with the Slytherins since they are both representatives of water. The Beauxbaton girls sit with Ravenclaw, since they both represent air. Cedric Diggory is chosen from Hufflepuff, which represents earth, and as Harry is chosen, we see that he completes the quartet by representing fire.

From Christianity, we see another symbol hidden within the Goblet of Fire – the "Holy Grail," the cup that Jesus used to show the connection between the Passover and the Easter event, also known as the Eucharist in Christianity. More explicitly, the Goblet of Fire itself is reminiscent of the Holy Grail in many ways: 1) it is wooden, encrusted with jewels (a later addition to the Holy Grail's concept), and very old;[74] 2) it is only accessible by those who are worthy (the age line), 3) it grants fame and honor to the winner, and thus 4) grants immortality of sorts. Once the winner is declared, there are other requirements of the Holy Grail that will come forward. Lastly, the Goblet of Fire also shows us what Harry has to overcome to win mastery over fire – somehow, he will have to win the Triwizard Tournament, even if his fellow students don't think him worthy to do so.

In keeping with the traditions within the series, Harry's task and enemy makes a move against Harry at Halloween and Harry gets his first taste of what mastery over that element will mean. Here, Harry is at the receiving end of the power of the Goblet of Fire, and Harry is now aware of an "enemy" at work against him. Regardless of the overarching danger,

---

[73] Granger, J, *Unlocking Harry Potter,* p. 226.

[74] Colbert, D., 2002, *The Magical Worlds of Harry Potter,* p. 85-86.

Harry doesn't have enough information to know who the enemy is, so for the moment it only looks like he has to master the dangers within the Triwizard Tournament.

Chapter Seventeen: The Four Champions

With extreme angst, the staff of Hogwarts and their guests meet to discuss the anomaly of Harry's unorthodox entrance into the tournament. However, with the ministry's insistence on following rules and the unwavering magical restrictions beyond wizarding control, we are reminded of the Jewish laws. In the Pentateuch, it is clear that these 613 laws may not be broken. Also, the overarching rabbinic thought suggests that although we do not understand God's will at all times, all things will work themselves out in the end and we will see God's will in the end. Coincidently, this is exactly what Professor Snape suggests – that they allow things to play out and see if anything becomes clearer.

As Harry returns to his common room for some friendly support after his ordeal with the tournament selection, he finds that Ron has chosen not to believe his innocence. With Ron's disbelief, Ron is now out of the picture for the next little while, which allows Hermione and her mercury to work on Harry without interruption. Again, this is a continuation of the black stage of the book as another person or entity distances himself from Harry.

Chapter Eighteen: The Weighing of the Wands

Sirius' response to Harry's concerned letter suggests that Hedwig should not deliver letters to him anymore, which antagonizes Hedwig. With Hedwig now not speaking to Harry, we can see how far the black stage has progressed. After Harry was admitted to the tournament, most of Hogwarts and the other two schools rose against him. Without Ron and Hedwig's friendship, there are only a few loyal people left to support Harry and help him understand what he has to do to succeed.

Despite all the glares, Harry still has to continue doing what is expected of him for the tournament. As we are reacquainted with Mr. Ollivander, we are reminded of the importance of the wands and we learn more about each character from their wands. Fleur's wand, made of rosewood and vela hair, brings her back to her native France, where the rose is a symbol for Mary's child, Christ, and the Holy Grail. The veela hair shows a bit of whimsy, perhaps to show that the connection to the Holy Grail is not real. Cedric Diggory's wand of ash says that he is tenacious and well connected to heaven and earth[75] whereas his unicorn hair connects his purpose with Christ's intentions. Victor Krum's wand, hornbeam, is also known as ironwood, shows his perseverance and determination[76] while his connection with Dragon Heartstring serves two purposes: 1) the create the full complement of the wand cores present in the tournament; and 2) to show his connection to a more cerebral, perhaps dark, side of Christ, since most of the thinkers or Death Eaters at Hogwarts have dragon heartstring wand cores. However, the dragon heartstring is also a symbol of Christ, since dragons have immortality, and the dragon's blood is the name given to the Eucharistic drink, which is also Christ's blood. Harry's wand, a combination of phoenix feather and holly wood is a double representation of Christ – the Holly from the "holy" wood, and the Phoenix feather for Christ's sacrifice and resurrection.

In response to Harry's letter, Sirius decides to take a risk and talk to Harry through the use of someone else's fireplace. Through their conversation, Harry learns more about the Death Eaters and the people at Hogwarts, but he also learns about how floo powder can transport not only your whole body, but part of it so that you don't completely change location. Here again, we see the use of fire in Harry's alchemical formation through this educational piece of magic. On another level, Harry is also enjoying the fact that Sirius cares and treats him like a son, something Harry has never had for his very own. This part of Harry's

---

[75] Trees for Life, 2011, "Mythology and Folklore of the Ash," retrieved from http://www.treesforlife.org.uk/forest/mythfolk/ash.html.

[76] Tree Divination, 2011, "Hornbeam- Yoke," retrieved from http://www.treedivination.com/hornbeam.htm.

transformation - his acceptance into Sirius' life as Sirius somewhat adopts Harry as his own - is another piece of the alchemy that will become more apparent later in the series, as we learn more about Sirius's family and the roles they have played in magical history.

Chapter Nineteen: The Hungarian Horntail

With the first task close at hand, Hagrid invites Harry to come visit him, and shows Harry the dragons they will be using for the first task. As Hagrid points out repeatedly, dragons are very misunderstood creatures. While dragons are an omen of fortune in Oriental folklore, they represent evil in most European folklore as seen in Revelations 12:9 (The great dragon was hurled down—that ancient serpent called the devil, or Satan, who leads the whole world astray. He was hurled to the earth, and his angels with him). Perhaps this confused image is also because they are unpredictable. Dragons, representing heavenly creatures, can cause either death/destruction or blessings, depending on what God has in store for that city. The "serpent" in Genesis that spoke to Adam and Eve was acting on its own devices. After God discovered what had been done, the "serpent" was punished by losing its limbs and crawling on its belly, meaning that it had to have had those elements before. A snake with limbs that doesn't have to crawl is a dragon! However, the dragons here represent the four elements in their four colors (red - fire, green-water, blue-air, and black-earth), and more importantly represent Harry's first true test of mastering fire.

Sirius's surprise visit and conversation with Harry through the fireplace shows another side to the Harry/ Sirius relationship. Throughout the conversation, Sirius has a prophetic, monastic outlook that at least guides Harry in the right direction, but it also points more to his alchemical property as the representative of Antimony – his distance from the main storyline. As an outlaw, Sirius is required to stay away from main areas of civilization, just as monks would.

Chapter Twenty: The First Task

After seeing the dragons, Harry decides that the others need to know about the danger, even if it means that he comes in last place. This shows his true compassion for others, since he is more concerned with others than his success or failure in the task itself, and we have another example of Harry breaking the "rules" again to help a fellow student. Although students aren't supposed to help each other or receive any help from others, Harry tells Cedric about the dragons so that he's a little prepared for the task.

After seeing Harry's display of regard for Cedric rather than his own placement in the tournament, Professor Moody takes Harry aside for a talk. In Professor Moody's office, we see the secrecy sensor that is trying to tell ever-trusting Harry that there's a liar in the room, but Professor Moody is able to cover it up using the students' lies as a decoy. However, all of the previous Defense Against the Dark Arts teachers have all had a secret, so why would this one be any different? Secondly, after the sneakoscope last year proved to be correct about someone they weren't suspecting, Harry should have been more suspicious about Professor Moody after this conversation in his room. However, although Harry's unwavering trust of everyone around him is what brings his enemies close to him, his attitude fulfills Jesus' requirement that we are to have the faith of a child, and trust those around us implicitly. (Luke 18:17: Truly, I say to you, whoever does not receive the kingdom of God like a child shall not enter it;" as well as Matthew 10:16: "I am sending you out like sheep among wolves. Therefore be as shrewd as snakes and as innocent as doves.")

As Harry completes the first task, we see that his work with Hermione has granted his some mastery over fire by using his broom – the Firebolt, a representative of fire to help Harry conquer another monster of fire, the dragon. At the end of the task, Harry gets the golden egg, showing the completion of the first task and symbolically the end of the renunciation stage of the book.

Chapter Twenty-one: The House-elf Liberation Front

Now that Harry has Ron back, the school is supporting him again, and there's a golden egg to show that he's completed something. This shows that Harry is now moving into the white stage of the book, where he's learning more about how to control fire (Rather than just discovering all the pieces of the fire element) while making connections with everything around him. With his community back to its normal attitudes that support him, Harry feels invincible. This shows how important community is to every believer.

As part of the celebrations, the Weasley twins show Harry, Ron, and Hermione the secrets of the kitchen at Hogwarts. In the kitchen, we see positive wizard-house elf relationships, but we also see things from the house-elf perspective. It seems that as long as the house-elves receive respect and gratitude, they are happy to work for others. They show what it means to be a truly happy servant of God, knowing that everything they do helps others, and in return, they receive sincere gratitude and happiness. When offered freedom, they respond suspiciously and shun any conversation or offers from that person in the future.

More specifically, although Dobby is a very happy free house-elf, other house-elves, like Winky, seem lost without a "master" or someone to dote on, someone to give them direction, or someone to live for. From a Christian perspective, Jesus begins this servant relationship in the book of John, saying that anyone who wants to follow him must first be a servant of all (John 13: 15-17: "I have set you an example that you should do as I have done for you. Very truly I tell you, no servant is greater than his master, nor is a messenger greater than the one who sent him. Now that you know these things, you will be blessed if you do them. NIV) From this, we can understand why the house elves are suspicious of Hermione, who thinks that only free will can give someone happiness.

Chapter Twenty-three: The Yule Ball

The Yule Ball itself raises an interesting connection to the secular magical world. Although the neo-pagans have reintroduced the Yule as their holiday of the winter solstice, the Anglophones have used the word Yule to indicate Christmastide for centuries, having converted the original pagan holiday into a Christian one.[77] With Ms. Rowling's Scottish heritage, her use of the word Yule here is a reference to Christmas on the 25th of December, not to the 21st day of December, the shortest day of the year and the "Yule" for neo-pagans.

In addition to learning how to dance and ask a girl out to a dance, Harry continues his illumination in this book by learning all about giants from the wizards' perspective. Through his conversation with Ron after overhearing Hagrid's confession to Madame Maxine, Harry finally begins to understand why giants are not a revered race and have not been granted any sort of magical status in the wizarding community. Another illumination here comes as Cedric tells Harry the secret to understanding the egg. Lastly, Harry begins to see how Ron and Hermione might have something more romantic blooming between them as their strong animosity is ignited mostly by their awkwardness around each other as they work together to help Harry.

Chapter Twenty-four: Rita Skeeter's Scoop

After the word gets out about Hagrid's status as half-giant, Hagrid's sulking brings Professor Dumbledore to his counsel. This is the only time we see Professor Dumbledore really give Hagrid a talking to, letting Hagrid know his expectations. As the shepherd, Professor Dumbledore isn't letting his gate keeper go and is ensuring that Hagrid knows his worth. This is also the first time that we hear mention of Professor Dumbledore's family, and that his brother has a thing for goats. This furthers the Christ-figure parallel – there are sheep, and there are goats, and whereas Albus

[77] Broome, F, 2008, "Yule history – Pagan and early Christianity," retrieved from http://celticarthistory.com/yule-history-pagan/.

shepherds the sheep, Aberforth tends the goats and the two hardly acknowledge one another. (Matthew 25:31-46)

Chapter Twenty-five: The Egg and the Eye

Whereas with the first task Harry had to use his mastery over air to master the dragon and fire, Harry uses water to help him master the knowledge needed for the second task. Again, as Harry goes to the prefect's bathroom and learns about the secrets of the egg, this furthers his illumination into how to master another element of water, using the water to decipher a new clue on his way to mastering the tournament and thus mastering fire (the fire of the Goblet).

Upon his departure from the prefect's bathroom, Harry's good luck barely holds out. Although he lost his egg, he didn't get caught by Professor Snape who could have made his life miserable. Rather, he ends up with another counseling session with Professor Moody. This is the second time that Harry has given over his map to a teacher, and both times the professor was able to make better connections and use of it than Harry was himself, being the trusting person that he is. Professor Moody wants to use the map, yes, but probably more so he can continue his false motives than to keep a lookout for Harry.

Chapter Twenty-six: The Second Task

After his night visit to the prefect's bathroom, Harry reports to Hermione and Ron that Professor Moody is acting on Dumbledore's orders to search other offices. Surprisingly, no one questions him about it so Professor Moody is able to do to others what he keeps warning others not to do – never trust anyone's word for what someone else said and always get information first hand. Despite Professor Snape's ability to read minds, Professor Moody is able to take advantage of him by telling him that Professor Dumbledore gave him permission to search his office. Although we saw that Professor Snape was very suspicious of Professor Moody's actions, it could be that he is taking notes on the behavior before saying anything about how Professor Moody's mind feels different than it used to be.

Despite the suspicions about Professor Moody, Professor Hagrid is as solid a character as ever and begins to show the students more alchemical animals, again a demonstration of Harry moving forward with his studies learning how to master the elements. As Hagrid explains about the growth of unicorns, he explains that they begin as gold skinned animals, representing purity and perfection. A second display of the unicorn's symbolism of purity and perfection is also mentioned here – they become mature at the age of seven, the number of perfection. Although Harry is not at the golden stage of his alchemy yet, this fourth book is the turning point in the series and in Christianity, half-way through a season they remind themselves of the purpose of the season by taking a look at the bigger picture. Here, the bigger picture is that it is an alchemical work with pure gold as the ultimate goal of the series, giving us a reprieve from the gloom that begins to settle in during book four. Lastly, as Harry is beginning to learn how to master the last of the four elements, the new challenge is to learn how to master combinations of the elements.

Finally, Harry has decoded the ear-splitting clue from the golden egg, but he is now frustrated by how to combine two different elements – the ability to breathe (air) with the ability to stay underwater (water). As his two best friends are led away, Harry exhausts himself seeking a solution, asking questions of the books around him. Dobby comes to Harry's rescue, first waking him for the task then providing him with a solution, again a demonstration of the fact that help is always there for those who ask for it or need it. This is a statement made by Dumbledore a few times throughout the series – that "help will always come to those who ask for it" at Hogwarts.

Thankfully, Dobby's solution of gillyweed provides Harry with the solution he needs, and is the only solution that combines three elements: using an earthly element to provide a transfiguration that will provide air in water. The other three champions use either a partial transfiguration to a shark (using only the water element), or the bubble-head charm (which uses only the element of air). Once his problem is solved and Harry realizes that people he cares for are involved, he gets worried. Here again, at the bottom of the lake, with a limited amount of air, Harry breaks the rules and waits to make sure that everyone's safe and won't suffer, risking everything for everyone else. Thus, when Harry emerges from the lake, glad to be able to breathe normal air and not be on the bottom of the lake, Professor Dumbledore is beaming at Harry. Professor Dumbledore knows what Harry's done and why, just as Christ smiles down on us when we go out of our way to help others.

Throughout the book, we have seen a reference to a beetle many times. Here we hear about the beetle again as Hermione talks to Victor after her rescue. In alchemy, a "beetle" is always a bard, someone who writes things down. Here, the constant appearance of the beetle right before a big story shows up gives us another clue that everything is not what it appears to be, a main theme in Ms Rowling's work. For starters, how many beetles hang out at a freezing cold lake in Scotland in the middle of February? (J.K. Rowling uses this thought again, when she creates the *Tales of Beedle the Bard,* a clear nod to the alchemical writings of a beetle.)

Chapter Twenty-seven: Padfoot Returns

As further illumination about what is truly going on around him, Harry gets a chance to meet with Sirius at Hogsmeade. Harry learns that Sirius can survive pretty well as a dog on the periphery and still be nearby enough to keep track of what is going on. While meeting with Sirius in the cave, the trio gets a quick history lesson of which wizards are former/current Death Eaters, and it brings us up to speed on the question of what might have happened that made Albus Dumbledore trust Severus Snape. As the trio leaves the cave, Ron's comment about how much Sirius Black must love Harry to live out in a cave and have to eat rats is reminiscent of John the Baptist's love for God. John lives on the periphery of society in a deserted area eating locusts and honey, the plentiful food of that area. This is a continuation of Sirius Black's monastic life, where Sirius sleeps on bare stone floors without any heat in the middle of

Scotland and tries to comfort Harry from his fears. Behind the scenes, Sirius is doing everything he can to find out what is going on: keeping up with the current news, paying attention to the news around town, and listening to news from Professor Dumbledore; always ready to protect Harry as soon as he knows of possible danger.

Chapter Twenty-eight: The Madness of Mr. Crouch

After Harry's completion of the second task, the Daily Prophet gives an expose' on the private discussions between Hermione and Victor Krum. Harry's suggestion that Rita Skeeter might be using technology results in Hermione's explanation of why everything in the magical community is old-fashioned (candles, etc) – the magic makes the technology go haywire. Again, although this point could have been made in book one, our turning point in the series is refocusing us on the bigger picture and answering questions that we forgot to ask in the first book. A second element of this explanation from a Christian perspective is that many people might ask why we don't use technology to find God and prove his existence. If we were to use technology to find heaven, for instance, the suggestion here is that the technology would probably fail us and go haywire.

One of the most interesting aspects of the meeting Harry has with Mr. Crouch is behind the scene. How did Barty Crouch even get to Hogwarts in his condition? Did he disapparate (move through time and space in an instant), or walk the whole way? If he did disapparate, was it during one of his saner moments to a spot close to Hogwarts? We know that people can't disapparate onto the grounds of Hogwarts, so perhaps he was able to disapparate to somewhere close by and walk the rest of the way. However, the first question is more about why he would go to Dumbledore in the first place rather than the Minister of Magic or someone that could help undo the wrong that he had done? In its presentation, this scene plays out as an end-of-life confession. Barty Crouch knows that what he did was wrong, but he didn't realize the implications until things got difficult. With this understanding, he has gone to find Dumbledore, the Christ-figure, who will absolve him of his sins. Since he feels "unclean", he doesn't feel he can go into Hogwarts itself, so he asks Harry to bring Dumbledore to him to confess his sins to him, and Dumbledore will then invite him into Hogwarts. Unfortunately, since Mr. Crouch disappears before Dumbledore finds him, he is not forgiven for his sins.

All of the people involved with Barty Crouch's reappearance and disappearance meet in Professor Dumbledore's office, and although they do not discover anything, Professor Dumbledore tells Harry to wait until tomorrow to send any owls. Since Harry doesn't know that Professor Dumbledore is in communication with Sirius, this is even more an example of the omniscience or legilmens abilities of Professor Dumbledore. Also, the professor's strong caution to stay in the tower is also an acknowledgement that he senses the danger that might still be lurking around the grounds at Hogwarts.

Chapter Twenty-nine – The Dream

One of the very sidebar threads through the series is the vampire and werewolf conflict. As the friends continue to discuss the disappearance of Barty Crouch, Harry makes a fleeting comment to his friends that Snape couldn't have beaten him to the forest unless he could turn himself into a bat or something. This subtle nod at Severus Snape being a vampire is just one more indication that there is more to the characters than what meets the eye.

After news of the disappearance dwindled to a simmering storyline, the ministry decides to go ahead with the third task in June. This third task is the last task, since there are three defining tasks to prove one's worthiness of obtaining the Holy Grail: the first task is determination (such as how much are you willing to risk to obtain the golden egg) balanced by lack of greed; the second is of destination (knowing where you are going and which goal is your own), and the third is of deliberation – slowly and carefully making choices that will lead you in the right direction towards the goal. (Coincidentally, these are also the three D's that J.K. Rowling uses when teaching the students about apparition /

disapparation – the ability to transport one's self to another place in an instant.) Of course, there are also three tasks because there are three elements of God, and the Holy Grail brings you closer to God himself.

Chapter Thirty: The Pensieve

Worried about the dreams that he keeps having that connect his mind to some unknown evil, Harry goes to see Professor Dumbledore. In his office, Harry discovers a pensieve, a magical container for thoughts. It is very likely that this pensieve is based on a book put together based on the writings of Blaise Pascal, called *Pensees*. Pascal was an extremely bright mathematician, theologian, and philosopher of the 1600s who devoted his free time to trying to bring his well-educated friends to Christ. In this pursuit, he would have random flashes of thought, which he wrote down on any scrap piece of paper he could find at the time, supposedly to write a book for his friends. However, Pascal died before the book was ever completed, leaving us only with his notes. Upon his death, the notes were discovered, and many people have tried to recreate the patterns and thought direction with varying results.[78] Professor Dumbledore's Pensieve, a collection of random thoughts through which he tries to find connections and patterns is a copy of this exact process.

Chapter Thirty-one: The Third Task

As the third task begins, Harry keeps feeling like someone is watching him. Physically this can be attributed to Professor Moody's magical eye seeing everything from outside the maze, but there is another reason why the eye theme appears in the pivotal book in the series and continues until the end. Up through now, we have mostly seen only suggestions that either Professor Dumbledore or Snape is able to read Harry's thoughts and actions no matter where Harry is. Throughout the series, Professors Dumbledore and Snape have confessed that they don't need cloaks to be invisible, and one of them always seems to appear whenever

---

[78] Perrine, T, 2011, Christian Classics Ethereal Library, "Pensees," retrieved from http://www.ccel.org/p/pascal/pensees/.

Harry seems to be in the wrong place at the wrong time. From now on, this increasing watchful eye theme is because the ultimate goal of Christian alchemy is to become like Christ and join Christ in Heaven. With John Granger's ring theory in mind, the fourth book now changes the focus of the series back toward the end goal – sacrifice and victory with Christ. Thus, from now through the end of the series, many different versions of the eye appear, perhaps as a nod to the famous "God's eye." This, in turn, points to God himself, Harry's ultimate destination as he continues his pursuit of elemental mastery and completion of the three stages.

Harry's completion of this final task is a test to see whether Harry can make the right decisions consistently. Throughout the maze, Harry runs into elements that he has mastered already – air (the dementors), water (upside down fog), and earth (sphinx), and for the most part, he handles them easily enough despite the distractions from his competitors. In addition, we see Harry beginning to master fire as he completes the maze by fighting off the blast-ended skrewts (the magical creature introduced by Hagrid). However, as the two boys have to work together to defeat the spider, symbolic in itself that animals of cunning need combinations of material to defeat it, we see Hufflepuff in its glory. Cedric is fantastic in helping save Harry, and perhaps this display shows us what extraordinary people they both are. After everything they have endured, and having completed all three tasks required, both are worthy of the Goblet of Fire/ Holy Grail and hence "masters of fire."

Chapter Thirty-two: Flesh, Blood, and Bone

Back to the theme that nothing is as it appears to be, the Triwizard cup is a portkey. Also, rather than travel to a glorious place where they are applauded for their victory, they are brought to a graveyard – the antithesis of human victory. In this deserted graveyard, there is a hint of what's to come – there is a yew tree planted in the yard. The yew tree, with its ability to withstand rot and it strength, has long been thought to be able to repel death. As such, the English tend to plant a yew tree in graveyards, to protect the dead. Fittingly, Lord Voldemort's wand is also made of yew, which appeals to his wanting protection from death.

As Harry tries to make sense of what he is seeing, we are reminded again of the watchful eye. Harry's feeling of being watched, again, is also an opening of the connection he has with Lord Voldemort through his scar. Whereas before the scar pain was only if Lord Voldemort was nearby, with the increase in Lord Voldemort's strength, there is now a deeper connection. Many people have a sense that God is watching them all the time and can feel a heavenly presence everywhere they go, similar to Harry's feeling of both evil and good watching over him.

Unfortunately, all who reach the Holy Grail are not "worthy" of the Grail, and thus Cedric is killed after obtaining the Grail. In Grail folklore, those who arrive at the Grail but are not deemed worthy are not allowed to touch it.[79] This is very similar to the verse from 1 Corinthians 11:29, in which those who do not truly believe are cursed for having drunk the Cup of Christ. Although well familiar with Lord Voldemort's cruelty, this is the first book in which we see that Lord Voldemort and his followers use their abilities as wizards to act as gods, granting life or death to those they deem "worthy."

Lastly, as the rhyme directs Wormtail to reconstruct a new body for Lord Voldemort, there are three parts of the body (again with the three!) – flesh, blood, and bone, one from each generation – Tom's father, Tom's contemporary (Wormtail), and Harry from the younger generation. I propose that the three generations have to be represented to create a strong immortal bond – the past, present, and future intertwined as one, as if that person has lived forever – to ensure that the body can live as if time did not exist.

---

[79] Caldon, A, 2012, "Find The Grail," retrieved from http://www.theholygrail.org.uk/find_who_found_grail.html.

Chapter Thirty-three: Death Eaters

Once Lord Voldemort's body is regenerated, to celebrate this completion, he has Wormtail call the Death Eaters to celebrate and worship him. Thirteen is considered an unlucky number in Christianity, since there were thirteen people at the Lord's Supper. However, it can also be considered to be the number of completion. As such, the Lord's Supper was the completion of Christ's mission – to live as one among us, die, and restore us to God by destroying the power of Satan. Here, in addition to a complete body, Lord Voldemort mentions the past thirteen years, which are now finished/ completed. From here on, there is a new, larger battle to fight. Harry has mastered the four elements, and is about to enter the three stages that will bring him closer to a spiritual immortality and conflicts with Lord Voldemort.

In the monologue that follows, we hear Lord Voldemort admit that he is powerful and thus able to avoid death. This arrogance carries to the Death Eaters who are so named because they are supposed to be more powerful than death and the weakness that deserves death. Secondly, Lord Voldemort sets himself in contrast to his antithesis, Professor Dumbledore - the one who embraces those who are weaker than himself rather than trodding on them. Finally, we get the sense of how Lord Voldemort really wins followers – it's all about loyalty/servanthood to him, payment for service, and pain/death for disobedience. There is no room for friendship, love, community, or forgiveness, all the pieces of life that Professor Dumbledore and Harry embody.

As the graveyard scene plays out, we learn much about the Death Eaters and their past. Primarily, we have a listing of the loyal Death Eaters listed: Lucius Malfoy, Avery, Wormtail/ Peter Pettigrew, Bellatrix LaStrange, Mr. LaStrange, MacNair, Crabbe, Goyle, Nott, Barty Crouch, Jr., Igor Karkaroff, and Severus Snape – twelve loyal servants of Lord Voldemort, making a total number of 13 evil servants, a complete number. Lord Voldemort also reveals to Harry that he had traveled farther than any wizard has ever traveled towards immortality, a path he travels alone. Furthermore, Lord Voldemort considers the horcurxes to be experiments, as if the deaths and horribleness of the magic involved meant nothing to him. Through this, we see that although Lord Voldemort understands that he has a soul, it means nothing to him since he is willing to squander it away, experimentally, attaching all meaning to a physical form, regardless of its appearance. J.K. Rowling continues a theme here of the soul versus the physical body – the dementors representing soulless forms, and the dementor's kiss representing an existence worse than death, when the soul is removed.

Regarding the more current events that led to Lord Voldemort's current body and health, Lord Voldemort explains the potion that Wormtail had to create to help Lord Voldemort exist, which is a mixture of unicorn's blood (which looks and acts like mercury) and snake venom (a yellowish substance looking like sulfur). Lord Voldemort knows that a soul, fed/ nurtured by mercury and sulfur, will help transform that soul into immortality, but doesn't understand that it also requires the mastery of the four elements and the three stages to make the transformation complete. Because of this lack of understanding, although the concoction keeps Lord Voldemort "alive", the small fragment of soul he has left and his resistance to change makes a continual supply a requirement for survival. To end this continual requirement of unicorn's blood and snake venom, Lord Voldemort feels that the immortal body he created with the verse should be able to live without further feedings, and since Harry's blood seems to have some protection in it, the immortal body would be stronger if it carried Harry's blood in it.

Now that Lord Voldemort and Harry share the same blood, they develop a strange bond that no one can truly figure out, and although it is not a Christian concept, I will attempt to explain the connection here. By taking Harry's blood to create his own body, Lord Voldemort is now doubly connected to Harry. Harry has part of Lord Voldemort's soul inside him through the scar, and Lord Voldemort has part of Harry inside himself through the blood, the blood that keeps Harry alive through his mother's sacrifice. Since Lord Voldemort unknowingly took on Harry's mother's sacrifice, Harry is now protected from death through his link to Lord Voldemort.

At the end of the monologue, Lord Voldemort's sidebar discussion with Wormtail shows what Lord Voldemort defines as faith. According to Lord Voldemort, faith means living to do things for that person. Sacrifices and service for someone else given out of fear do not count as faith. This brings up an interesting point – does someone have faith if they do something out of fear of retribution, or sacrifice in order to gain reward? Essentially, this is a remake of 1 Corinthians 13, in which St. Paul explains that powers do not matter without love. Lord Voldemort has corrupted this to be "sacrifice and service mean nothing if you have fear." After all of these revelations, Ms. Rowling concludes Harry's illumination stage of the book, since he now has more knowledge about what is going on than anyone else.

Chapter Thirty-four: Priori Incantatem

With the end of the white stage of the book, we know a battle is coming between Harry and Lord Voldemort, as it is in each storyline. Even though Harry and Cedric were already reluctantly taken from their families and friends when they entered the maze, they were even further separated from them when they were transported to the graveyard. With the loss of Cedric, Harry is once again alone in a place that symbolizes death in some form (here, the graveyard) to face Lord Voldemort; although this time, Lord Voldemort is not alone.

Although we have seen that Peter Pettigrew probably has some remorse for Harry, we have more reason to suspect that he is very reluctant to hurt Harry. As Dumbledore remarked at the end of book three, Harry's mercy that saved Peter's life has created a debt. Peter has tried to avoid using Harry as a sacrifice to Lord Voldemort, but his every effort is thwarted. Here, we can see that Wormtail is not all evil – he cannot stand to look into Harry's eyes, whose purity would weaken Wormtail's resolve and show his fondness for Harry Potter.

After the preliminaries to the true wizard's duel between Harry and Lord Voldemort, Harry faces Lord Voldemort and attempts to expel Lord Voldemort's wand. When the two wands connect on their own accord, their opposition is even color coded – red and green being color opposites, and the two together form gold, the sign of completion. Harry has finally completed his mastery of the four elements and is now moving on to the black stage of the whole series, where he begins his larger scale descent into loneliness and the acknowledgement, debunking, and recanting of all that is evil. As the golden connection generates a world of its own, it surrounds them by the golden orb, and the phoenix song (the spirit of resurrection and hope) revitalizes Harry, filling him with hope to continue on.[80]

In their golden orb that separates them from the other Death Eaters, the two wands vie for mastery over the connection, each one trying to force the other to confess what it's done. With the bolstering from the phoenix song, Harry's connection with his wand overrides the other. As Lord Voldemort's wand recounts the past actions he has done, we are reminded of the book that writes down all of our own sins, read back to us at the end of time unless we have asked for forgiveness, which erases those sins. In this case, Lord Voldemort has never asked for forgiveness, has no remorse, and fears death, so for him, the recounting of his past crimes and murders is truly horrifying especially when the ghosts appear to have substance. Finally, as Harry's parents and others who would do anything to stop Lord Voldemort emerge from the wand and devise a way to keep Lord Voldemort occupied, we see again how the martyrs of the past, now members of the church triumphant, are able to help those in need when called upon.

Chapter Thirty-five: Veratiserum

With the beginning of the black stage, we begin to see those around Harry renounce Harry or separate themselves from him in some way, beginning immediately. Professor Moody, feigning concern for Harry,

---

[80] Granger, J, *Unlocking Harry Potter*, p. 275.

takes Harry back to his office to talk. However, as Professor Moody calls Lord Voldemort "The Dark Lord", we begin to see that Professor Moody is a servant of Lord Voldemort's, the first slip of many. Professor Moody is the first person that Harry thought was on his side to show that he is actually against Harry, having helped plan his demise all along.

One of the interesting objects in Professor Moody's office that we finally get to learn more about is the trunk. This magical trunk, with its seven locks, is rich with symbolism. First, the seven locks indicate that someone would need seven keys to understanding each level. Each level suggests a different level of understanding of the elements covering who the true person is inside. Thus, the spells, quills, and invisibility cloaks are all used to help create the illusion, but underneath all of the lies is the true Professor Moody, deep in the seventh chest. Next, once through the different levels, whatever is behind the seventh lock, within the seventh level, is being held by more than physical means, and the one who has the seven keys is truly the master of what is inside. Essentially, no matter what we try to hide, eventually the seven locks will find keys and the truth must be revealed to someone.

Chapter Thirty-six: The Parting of the Ways

As Harry tells Professor Dumbledore what happened in the graveyard, Dumbledore smiles in apparent triumph as Harry tells the story of how Lord Voldemort took Harry's blood for his own in the graveyard. Although this seems to be a very strange thing to smile about or seem victorious about when the ultimate Dark wizard has returned, Professor Dumbledore seems to know, suspect, or hope that the blood will form a bond between the two wizards that will keep Harry alive as long as Lord Voldemort is alive as well. Thankfully, being the omniscient mind-reader that Professor Dumbledore is, he was able to read the remaining story from Harry's mind and can make further connections and explanations from other knowledge he has. Ms. Rowling's mention of Fawkes during the silence reminds us of the small resurrection of sorts from the dead – the resurrection of those who had been killed by Voldemort, but brought back to life as an echo. Although they are not permanently returned to this earth, they are still able to rescue Harry from Lord Voldemort's hand.

Before the Minister leaves Hogwarts, Professor Dumbledore defines his position against Lord Voldemort and invites the Minister of Magic to do the same. In his invitation, Professor Dumbledore uses a Biblical passage – Luke 9:50 – "he who is not against me, is for me" to help create some solidarity. However, since it is the black stage, it is not too much a surprise that Cornelius Fudge, previously a huge supporter of Harry Potter who protected him from Sirius Black, suddenly turns from complete support to complete denial of everything Harry stands for. In his denial of the return of Lord Voldemort, the Minister leaves to control any damage done at Hogwarts to public opinion and begins his crusade against Harry Potter and the truth he stands for. With this departure, we see Harry's beginning descent into isolation.

In a true reversal of roles, Professor Snape actually supports Harry and Professor Dumbledore by giving his testimony of Lord Voldemort's return to the Minister with hard evidence. With the Minister's denial of the obvious truth, we are reminded of Jesus' explanation in John 9:39 – "I came so that the blind may see, and those that see might be blinded." As a further insight and illumination to everyone, Professor Dumbledore has Sirius reveal his true form to the others. While they all agree to be friends or at least halt hostilities, we are reminded of the first disciples - just as the tax collectors and fishermen were not good friends, they were able to work together towards a common end.

Chapter Thirty-seven: The Beginning

On the return to London, Hermione is finally able to tell her friends about Rita Skeeter being an animagus beetle. Although J.K. Rowling hinted at this all along with the beetle flying around and the alchemical beetle being a bard, we finally have the mystery solved about who the beetle is. On a more symbolic note, as the students at Hogwarts return to Kings Cross, we are reminded by the title of the chapter that everything begins and ends at the Cross of Christ, just as the numbers three and seven (Chapter 3-7) reference the trinity and perfection of God's mission on the cross . Here is where Harry will begin a new life against Lord Voldemort in both the muggle and magical communities and we begin our return trip on the ring towards the end of the series with a new focus.

Chapter EIGHT

The Guide to *The Order of the Phoenix*

Plot summary: At the Dursley's, Harry and his cousin Dudley are attacked by dementors when walking around the town, setting into motion his escape from Privet Drive and a court hearing regarding his use of magic to fend off the dementors. Shortly after the dementor attack, Alastor Moody and six others go to Privet Drive, help Harry pack, and take him to the new headquarters of the Order of the Phoenix, an unplottable secret location located at 12 Grimmauld Place, Sirius Black's house. At Headquarters, Harry learns that there are twelve members of the Order of the Phoenix, an order dedicated to alerting the world as to the rebirth of Lord Voldemort and stopping the Death Eaters from their plot of ruling the wizarding world and subjecting all others to Lord Voldemort's whims. Also, for some reason, Professor Dumbledore won't meet Harry's eyes, and the wizarding world is convinced that Harry made up the rebirthing story to gain more notoriety despite a new link that Harry seems to have with Lord Voldemort through his dreams. Lastly, Harry learns about a weapon that Lord Voldemort is after, one that they didn't have before, and it is hidden in the Ministry of Magic.

Although he is cleared of his charges in court, the Ministry of Magic begins to interfere at Hogwarts, first by providing the next Defense Against the Dark Arts teacher, Professor Delores Umbridge, then by requiring all teachers to use Ministry approved curriculum. Over the year, Delores Umbridge slowly takes over Hogwarts, the Ministry's instrument to quell any mention of Lord Voldemort. In defiance, Harry, Hermione, and Ron create a student group whose purpose is to learn how to defend themselves against Lord Voldemort and the Death Eaters. They call themselves "Dumbledore's Army", and practice in a very obscure place in Hogwarts called "The Room of Requirement."

As Umbridge takes over Hogwarts, eventually becoming the Headmaster of Hogwarts, Lord Voldemort gets closer to obtaining "the weapon" and Harry sees more of Lord Voldemort's thoughts and actions in his dreams. Eventually, Lord Voldemort, aware of the connection, uses it to plant a vision of Sirius Black being tortured in the Ministry's Department of Mysteries. Using thestrals (black horses invisible to those who have never seen death), Harry, Ron, Hermione, Neville, Luna, and Ginny fly to London to rescue Sirius, only to discover the hoax and that the "weapon" is actually a prophecy about Lord Voldemort and Harry Potter. Death Eaters fight with Harry's friends, who are then joined by Order of the Phoenix members, climaxing into Lord Voldemort fighting Albus Dumbledore in the basement of the Ministry.

At the end of the skirmish, Lord Voldemort tries to possess Harry to get Dumbledore to destroy Harry, but Harry fends Lord Voldemort off when he remembers how much he loved all the people who have died for him. Lord Voldemort leaves Harry, and right before he disappears, the Minister of Magic returns and acknowledges that Lord Voldemort has indeed returned. The minister is forced to step down, Delores Umbridge is taken from Hogwarts, and now the wizarding world looks to Professor Dumbledore for guidance and Harry to lead them in the battle to defend the wizarding world against Lord Voldemort.

Chapter One: Dudley Demented

As the book opens, we are reintroduced to the heat of the summer and the dryness which is even stronger this year than in years past. John Granger suggests that whenever the conditions are hot and dry, Harry is safe and in control of what is around him. The dry heat is indicative of the element of fire, Harry's house element. As we have seen with the dementors, whenever the conditions become cold and wet we know that Harry has problems – foretelling us that something will happen at the end of the chapter with the Dementors or some evil force.[81]

Hiding so that he can listen to the news, Harry's "unnatural" interest in the news causes suspicion among the Dursleys. Primarily this is another recurrence of the age theme that strengthens as the series continues - there is an assumption that teenagers have no concept of how the world works and are therefore excused for anything they do. We see this in the Dursley's house as they harass Harry about listening to the news since people his age shouldn't be interested in the news and the world's interactions. On a lesser point, the lack of media coverage continues Harry's despair that he has heard nothing of significance from anyone – from the muggle or wizarding world. With the cryptic messages Harry gets from his friends and the lack of information, we see Harry's continued descent into the black stage. Cut off from information and the world around him, Harry feels deserted on many angles.

This interest in the news points out two of the differences highlighted in this first chapter. The Dursleys point out that Dudley has no clue about what is going on, but perhaps this is because there is no expectation for him to be interested. Harry, on the other hand, has been rudely thrust into the middle of world events through his curiosity and the fact that the evilest man to ever exist is planning on killing Harry, putting Harry on the defensive. The second point of contrast between the two boys comes through the elder Dursleys' hypocrisy. Whereas they are proud of Dudley and twist all neighborhood reports of miscreant behavior as

---

[81]Granger, J, 2007, *Unlocking Harry Potter,* p. 82.

misunderstandings of Dudley's true nature, they twist everything positive that Harry does into something evil. Knowing that everything with the Dursleys is about appearances, more than likely because they worry about what they themselves think other people think of them, they have to create their own reality to live with what they see.

As Harry saves himself and Dudley from the Dementors and realizes that Mrs. Figg is a squib, we get the feeling that this is a bit like a nightmare or dream state. Although this fifth book is mostly about Harry's descent into isolation from everything he holds dear, it is also about Harry mastering the fifth element, quintessence. Quintessence is between the two worlds of reality and dreams, a place we visit upon waking or just falling asleep.

Chapter Two: A Peck of Owls

As the chapter opens, we learn a little bit more about the squibs in Harry's life. Mrs. Figg, the neighbor that would watch Harry when he wasn't invited on outings with the Dursleys, turns out to be a Dumbledore informer. Interestingly, she has a cat named Mr. Tibbles, who has special abilities and was able to help Mrs. Figg. Similarly, Mr. Argus Filch has a cat named Mrs. Norris, another cat who has some intuitive abilities and possibly some telepathic connection with Mr. Filch. It's interesting how the squibs all have an animal that helps them, as a guide or protector, since they do not have a wand or other abilities of their own.

The owls' arrivals bring a whirlwind of emotions, beginning with utter dejection and ending in a mystery. The first owl declares Harry's expulsion from Hogwarts, a declaration that paralyzes Harry. This is a continuation of the black stage as he is now losing everything he held dear – his wand and his place at Hogwarts the only place he feels is home. Thankfully, the next two owls relieve the pain by renouncing the expulsion and assuring Harry that everything will work out. The last owl is a mystery. Here is the only time that the Dursleys themselves get an owl message with a warning, and it's not signed. Very similarly, in the Bible (the Book of Daniel), there are times that handwriting appears on the wall meant as messages to other nations that interact with the Israelites, and it is only by heeding those messages that all are protected from destruction.

Chapter Three: The Advance Guard

Out of the blue, Harry is again rescued from Privet Drive. Rather than the Weasleys this time, it is Professor Moody with Professor Lupin and seven other wizards Harry has never met before. Nine is a curious number that isn't really used anywhere else in the series, but it is three groups of three, using three as the solid base for a foundation. Although only four of them are part of the Order of the Phoenix, we are introduced to other wizards sympathetic to the cause who are willing to help Harry get to a safe house. These are akin to the multitudes of disciples that followed Jesus in his day in addition to the twelve that were Jesus' closest friends.

Chapter Four: Number Twelve, Grimmauld Place

With the Advance Guard, Harry is able to enter the safe house where he meets many of his closest friends. John Granger suggests that "Grimmauld Place" is fanciful for "grim old place", where everything is dark.[82] I further propose that the number 12 is again a reference to the twelve true disciples of Christ that go in and out of the house on a regular basis. Further Biblical references include the twisted serpent on the door. Although clearly a display of pride in their Slytherin ancestry, this is also a more obscure reference to the incident in the desert with Moses, when the Israelites complained and were then plagued by snakes that bit them. The Israelites repented, and Moses was instructed to put a bronze snake on a pole, so that anyone who is bitten by a live snake can look to the pole and live (Number 21:8-9). The wizards that seek refuge at 12 Grimmauld Place in support of Harry or Professor Dumbledore are being saved from

---

[82] Harry Potter Wiki, "12 Grimmauld Place," retrieved from http://harrypotter.wikia.com/wiki/12_Grimmauld_Place.

Lord Voldemort, the Heir of Slytherin, and the embodiment of the symbol of evil, the snake.

Finally reunited with his friends, Harry finally gets some answers. Ron explains what the Order of the Phoenix is – a collection of adults dedicated to helping Professor Dumbledore in his mission to fight against Lord Voldemort. The name "Order of the Phoenix" represents the twelve disciples of Christ – with Professor Dumbledore being the Christ figure, the Order is then those who follow Christ. As such, there are many disciples, but only twelve that are named and considered his closest friends, listed here if they are named as going in and out of 12 Grimmauld Place: Severus Snape, Bill Weasley, Arthur and Molly Weasley, Nymphadora Tonks, Kingsley Shacklebolt, Minerva McGonagall, Rubeus Hagrid, Remus Lupin, Sirius Black, Mundungus Fletcher, and Alastor Moody.

With George's report that the Minister of Magic has declared that anyone who works with Professor Dumbledore is thrown out of the Ministry, we see a replay of the Sanhedrin's declaration to Peter and John that they are not to declare Jesus Christ as the awaited for savior(Acts 4:18-20.) .Just as Peter and John go about healing the sick and declaring the good works of Jesus anyway, we see the members of the Order of the Phoenix declaring what they can where they can, knowing that they will suffer public humiliation and work sanctions if they do. To help ease Harry's pain as he realizes the extent of his isolation, his friends explain that Professor Dumbledore's character is also besmirched because he speaks of an eminent evil. This descent is parallel to Christ's descent as well – first honored as a teacher that is wise beyond his years at a young age, the people then turn on him as he begins speaking about spiritual matters and showing command over them.

Although we had a hint of the anger Harry feels at the beginning when he was being left out of the planning, the anger we keep seeing in Harry now is very uncharacteristic for him, especially his current loathing of Albus Dumbledore. This sudden change in emotional status indicates that the connection he now shares with Lord Voldemort goes beyond the physical pain in the scar to a more emotional connection since he and Lord Voldemort now share the same blood, symbolic of passion and emotions.

Chapter Five: The Order of the Phoenix

Through the dinner discussion, we see a contemporary version of the events during Jesus' time after Jesus has begun his ministry in earnest. Up until now, we have heard reports that Professor Dumbledore was asked many times to be the Minister of Magic, but he refused the position choosing rather to be part of the education system for new wizards. During Jesus' day, many wanted Jesus to rise up and take over their kingdom, leading them against the Romans and freeing them from oppression. In contrast, Jesus chooses to be a rabbi and teach the people about love, compassion, and forgiveness. Cornelius Fudge plays the contemporary figure of King Herod or the Sanhedrin that moves against Jesus' ministry once they realize that he might be the Messiah as he preaches more intently against the evils of the world (Lord Voldemort). Afraid that any news of Lord Voldemort will only make the people demand that Professor Dumbledore take the Minister position and oust Fudge from his position, Fudge turns against Dumbledore and does everything he can to belittle his claims, helping persuade the public to ignore anything he says.

More worried about truth and souls than power and public opinion, Professor Dumbledore, as the Christ figure, has called his initial set of disciples and asked them to recruit anyone they can (proclaim the gospel) to see the truth. However, through Remus Lupin's explanation of how they are getting the word out, this is not as easily done as said. In explanation, we need to take a closer look at the members of the Order of the Phoenix, where we see more similarities between them and the original twelve disciples: they are both collections of outcasts. The original twelve disciples are fishermen, tax collectors, thieves, prostitutes, women, etc, none of whom anyone within Judaism would pay any attention to. Similarly, the Order of the Phoenix is a collection of werewolves, blood-traitors, escaped Prisoner, half-blooded metamorphagi, half-giants, and very suspicious aurors, none of whom have good standing within the magical community. Since both groups are marginal elements of society, no matter how hard they try to recruit, we see that it is up to Christ / Dumbledore to try to get the community to listen with limited results, mostly additional marginal members of society since the mainstream believes what they are told by the Ministry of Magic authorities.

Chapter Six: The Noble and Most Ancient House of Black

As part of the multiple new elements at the House of Black, we meet yet another house-elf, Kreacher, so named as to be "a creature of God." Acting like many other creatures of God, Kreacher is as God made all creatures – loving those who are kind to them, and hating those who are cruel to them regardless of the person's moral standing. As the only one who does not choose to be there, Kreacher makes the point that all of the Order members are outcasts of society, even though he confesses that the great Professor Dumbledore and Harry welcome them as friends. This is a reference to John 15:15, where Jesus says "I no longer call you servants, because a servant does not know his master's business. Instead, I have called you friends, for everything that I learned from my Father I have made known to you. We see this throughout the series – Harry tells Ron and Hermione everything that he learns from Professor Dumbledore and others, and Professor Dumbledore tells the Order of the Phoenix almost everything they should know (save for a few things that are reserved for Harry alone regarding Lord Voldemort). Kreacher, as a servant, does not know everything going on, but he knows enough to be dangerous to the Order if he fell into the wrong hands. Although a point not all of them quite understand, they need to be friendly to him to win his loyalty (a point that is only somewhat successful).

In an effort to rid the house of everything that relates to Lord Voldemort and the Death Eater mindset, Sirius and Harry go to look at the tapestry of the Black lineage. In Sirius' family tree, the first member, Phineas Nigellus is representational of the original lead. The symbol for lead is Pb, Phineas Black, although Nigellus is just a disguised name for black by using a small derivative of the Latin *"niger."* As the original transformational person and the motto *"toujours pur"*, the lead never transformed, but stayed pure lead, ready for Harry (adopted by Sirius) to take up the charge and continue the transformation to gold.

Other elements we see as Sirius explains the family wizarding tree to Harry are the complications and pride some people show in their heritage, always tracing their lineage back to a noble family. In a way, the nobility of the Black family is very similar to the noble house of David, where we have the lineage preserved that connects King David to Christ. Even in the lineage of David, there are many branches cut-off from God, as that descendent chose to abandon God. Harry's connection to Sirius somewhat puts him on the tapestry, as in ancient times an adoption was as true an inheritance as pure blood relations, although I suspect that J.K. Rowling is trying to suggest that lineage doesn't matter as much as what you do with what you have.

Chapter Seven: The Ministry of Magic

After Harry and Mr. Weasley enter the Ministry of Magic through the visitor's entrance, Harry describes the Ministry of Magic as decorated in peacock blue and gold, the colors traditionally symbolic of heaven. This suggests that the Ministry imagines itself to be more a representation of heaven on earth, a subliminal suggestion that everyone should do as they say. Secondly, the seven levels at the Ministry again point to a representation of perfection, another subliminal message that the Ministry knows best for the wizarding community.

Chapter Eight: The Hearing

As a continuation of Harry's black stage, we sense that Harry has lost Professor Dumbledore's support as well at Harry's hearing. Although the professor is willing to testify for Harry, the professor won't look Harry's way. John Granger suggests that the professor suspects that the scar allows Lord Voldemort to use Harry as his "eyes", and so he avoids looking at and speaking to Harry so that Lord Voldemort won't be able to read Professor Dumbledore's mind and know what the Order is up to.[83]

Chapter Nine: The Woes of Mrs. Weasley

When Ron and Hermione get their prefect badges, Harry feels even more deserted by the magical community. Between Alastor Moody's discussion with Harry about the past Order of the Phoenix members, and Mrs. Weasley's fears of a death in the family, Harry sees the bigger picture of what's really important. From the Bible, we see this same perspective with Job, just as Job finally saw the bigger picture when God asked him why he thought he could question why things happened the way they did.

Chapter Ten: Luna Lovegood

Now that Lord Voldemort's back, anytime that someone is supposed to be somewhere and doesn't show up, we have to worry that something happened to that person. Here, Sturgis Podmore is mysteriously absent, and as in Roman times we know that whenever someone is missing, it is better to pretend nothing has happened, so as to escape suspicion. Despite the delay and missing person, they do manage to ensure that there are three people (for a fundamental protection triangle) to guard Harry as he gets to the station to Hogwarts.

Being separated from Ron and Hermione as they go to the Prefect's Cabin, Harry gets to learn more about Ginny, who sees people for who they truly are. In many ways, she's just like Harry's mother – she has green eyes and red hair, is also in Gryffindor house, and sees the best part of people when others can't see it. In their cabin, Ginny introduces Harry to Luna Lovegood, a girl who tends to believe in anything as long as there isn't any proof of it. However, Luna's presence represents more in the alchemical realm of this work, of course. Luna means moon in Latin, and represents the more ethereal/ intuitive way of understanding the world around us and the path that leads us to believe that which is not seen or tangible. Luna's introduction is not an accident – she also shows us more

---

[83] Granger, J., 2007, *Unlocking Harry Potter*, p. 250.

substantially that Harry's task is now to master the fifth element, the astral plane (the quintessential element), which is ruled more by emotion than by logic. With Harry's emotional connection to Lord Voldemort, this element will be a more difficult challenge than the past four which were more a physical challenge than a mental/ emotional one.

As we learn more about Luna, we hear that Luna is a member of Ravenclaw. Although this seems a bit odd, since she seems to lack evidence for clear thought, there are many people who are book smart without any common sense. It is also another reminder that the Sorting Hat takes someone's preferences into account when making the final decision, and perhaps Luna sees herself as a very intelligent person. As Ron and Hermione join them in the train car, we see the true core of Harry's friends in one place for the first time – Harry, Hermione, Ron, Ginny, Neville, and Luna. Although all of them are labeled as misfits, they seem also bound to each other for that very reason, making a strong lasting friendship among them.

After disembarking from the train, Harry gets another shock when he sees the thestrals. This is again more evidence of his black stage – black horses that only he and Luna can see, setting them apart from the rest of the magical community. The hint of the reptilian, either symbolizing death or evil, clues us about why Harry can see them and others can't. We are also introduced to the idea that we are now seeing Harry working with the fifth alchemical element by the name "thestral", a play on "the astral" plane. In ancient times, this was an element thought to be composed of plasma which was neither physical nor mental.[84] This plane is only accessible after near death experiences, and is the plane in which angels exist.

Harry's incredulity that Ron and Hermione can't see the "horses" is only slightly tempered by Luna's telling him that she can see them too, saying that he's just as sane as she is. Sanity, of course, is relative I

---

[84] Wikipedia, "astral plane," retrieved from http://en.wikipedia.org/wiki/Astral_plane.

suppose, but it does bring to mind the multiple stories of paralytics suddenly being able to walk and blind people able to see. After Jesus healed one blind man, the Pharisees expressed their doubts that the blind man was ever really blind to begin with, and even brought in the parents to verify the fact. Regardless of the answers they received, the Pharisees questioned the blind man's sanity, and accused him of many things (John 9: 1-41).

Chapter Eleven: The Sorting Hat's New Song

Even though Hermione is the only one to truly understand both the Sorting Hat's new song and Delores Umbridge's speech, the students do understand that things have changed for this year. As the Sorting Hat sings its new song about the founders and warns about staying united against external dangers, the Sorting Hat gives a good introduction to qualities of the four elements and how they must work together to create harmony. Now that Harry has mastered the four elements individually, he must now continue to work with the elements together to complete the transformation to gold.

Now that we finally have an insight into Delores Umbridge's persona, we have to wonder if Dolores Umbridge represents the Queen of England, with her plethora of cute little hats. Following Ms. Rowling's tradition of names being more than they appear, we can also see more about who Ms. Umbridge is from her name: "taking umbridge" means to take the high ground and not retaliate, *delores* is the Latin word for sad, and abbreviated, her names becomes D. Umb. Together, we get the picture that Ms. Umbridge is a misguided witch who only understands basic orders, cannot move beyond the simplistic ideas of purity, and assumes that "high ground" means not getting involved with those "beneath" her in status.

Chapter Twelve: Professor Umbridge

Since there was not a lot of time for discussion at the end of the past school year, the ministry has had all summer to convince parents that all is well and Harry Potter and Professor Dumbledore are liars. In response, Harry hears many stories of students who were not going to be allowed to return to Hogwarts because of him. Furthermore, as Harry goes about his school day, he sees more and more past supporters of his avoiding him – taking Harry further into the black stage of both this book and the series.

As Harry goes through his classes, we finally discover the name of the Astronomy professor, Professor Sinistra. "*Sinistra*" is Latin for "left hand", and the use of the name here either gives Ms. Rowling's opinion of Astronomy class, or is further indication of the dream/ astral plane since supposedly when we are in a mirror state things are opposite of reality. Another interesting name we hear in this chapter is in Trelawney's Divinations class. During class, she offers them the book of dream interpretations by Inigo Imago, a name that means "un-noteable images", a true description of what J.K. Rowling probably thinks of trying to read into dreams. Lastly, as a teacher, it's been my experience that teachers, such as Professor Umbridge, who need their title and name repeated after every student's statement are the least competent and most insecure teachers.

Chapter Thirteen: Detention with Delores

Harry's torturous detentions with Professor Umbridge are reminiscent of the Beatitudes: "Blessed are those who are persecuted because of righteousness, for theirs is the kingdom of heaven." (Matthew 5:10) Professor Umbridge's accusations against Harry and the subsequent blood drawn are similar to the lesser daily tortures the early Christians might have endured, but they endured them more happily again because of the last line of the Beatitudes, Matthew 5:11-12 – "Blessed are you when people insult you, persecute you and falsely say all kinds of evil against you because of me. [12] Rejoice and be glad, because great is your reward in heaven, for in the same way they persecuted the prophets who were before you."

Harry gains some strength from the fact that Professor Dumbledore also is under attack, but since they are not looking at each other, there isn't any camaraderie for support, isolating Harry even further. Harry's unwillingness to go see Professor Dumbledore because the professor won't look at Harry is a very common response many people have: if the other person won't come to us, then we won't go to them. We tend to take this same road with Christ, though – thinking that Christ might not respond the way we want him to in a situation, we decide not to take any situation to him, not allowing for Christ to give us another solution that we hadn't thought of before as a plausible option.

Chapter Fourteen: Percy and Padfoot

The newspaper article about Sirius Black's history reminds us that right after Harry's parents died, Sirius and Wormtail met and thirteen people were killed. With thirteen being the number of completion, these deaths signaled the end of the former Order of the Phoenix group, allowing for a new Order of the Phoenix to be established. This is also symbolic of the bird itself, since a new one rises out of the ashes of the former one, with Alastor Moody, Rubeus Hagrid, Remus Lupin, and Sirius Black as the cornerstones.

In a surprise piece of correspondence, Percy writes to Ron to warn him of things to come. We know for sure now that Percy has been blinded by the ministry to the truth, as he chooses to understand the happenings in light of the ways before Lord Voldemort regenerated. Although Percy does not play the part of St. Paul, we see a little of the same elements here. Percy's letter to Ron, intended to save him from falling into the wrong and dangerous teachings of Professor Dumbledore and Harry Potter shows more how the Ministry of Magic mirrors the Sanhedrin of Christ's time. With Professor Dumbledore's solid evidence of Lord Voldemort's doings, the Ministry has to work overtime to discredit any followers so as the keep their control over everyone.

In addition to trying to control the wizarding community, the Ministry of Magic is also trying to ensure that the wizards don't rally behind Dumbledore and rise up against them. Sirius' explanation to the trio that the Ministry is afraid that Professor Dumbledore is creating an army is exactly what the Sanhedrin and King Herod was afraid Jesus would do, especially given his abilities. The Messiah was to come and vanquish the enemy, which they all thought meant creating a huge army that would rise up against the Roman Empire with Jesus at the lead. However, they were against Jesus more because Jesus didn't agree with them and was not under their control, but also because they never understood it to be a spiritual battle, rather than a purely physical one.

Sirius Black explains this exact phenomenon between Professor Dumbledore and the Ministry – Hogwarts is not under Ministry control while Professor Dumbledore is headmaster. To rectify this, Professor Umbridge keeps working to gain more control over any element she can, real or artificial, and asserts repeatedly that Defense Against the Dark Arts is a theoretical subject and not a practical one. In essence, this means that the spiritual element is not something "real", again a reference to the astral plane and the quintessential element Harry has yet to master.

Chapter Fifteen: The Hogwarts High Inquisitor

As Professor Umbridge discredits Hermione for disagreeing with the approved text, we are reminded of the many people who do not believe that we should question anything, especially if it is written in the Bible. There are others, very similar in attitude to Professor Umbridge, who feel that studying the theory of anything is enough and if we study it enough, we will not have to actually do anything about it. There are many churches that have studied how to be more welcoming, how to pray, how to study the Bible (without looking at a Bible), or how to grow a church, but after months of study, they do not implement anything that they've studied. Rather, they get a new idea and decide to study something else or more of the same. This is a defining point for Hermione, who usually embraces the study of anything, but here we see that Hermione appreciates the study of things only so much as they can help her be pro-active in the world.

The Minister of Magic, believing only what Professor Umbridge tells him about Hogwarts, decides to allow their representative to become the

High Inquisitor and evaluate the other professors at Hogwarts. During Professor Umbridge's evaluation of Professor McGonagall's teaching ability, we find out that Professor McGonagall has been teaching for 39 years, which is 3 sets of thirteen, a full completion cycle, since it is the number completion grounded in the number three, the number for a firm, stable foundation.

In response to Professor Umbridge's assertion that theory is all that is required to learn how to repel evil, Hermione and Ron convince Harry that they need him to help them begin a group that will actually practice what they are learning. Since the current Defense Against the Dark Arts class is just knowledge based, this practical aspect will help Harry and his friends master the quintessential element by bringing thought into the physical plane. Through their discussion of what Harry has done in the past, we see that Harry's secret weapon (that he denies he has) is love for those around him. His love for others compels him not to fear death or pain himself as long as he can save others, something he cannot admit to himself.

Chapter Sixteen: In the Hog's Head

The trio decides to hold their meeting in the Hog's Head tavern so as to avoid suspicion. As the trio looks at the sign for the Hog's Head, the description reminds us of the severed head of John the Baptist served to Herod's daughter on a platter. John, a relation/ cousin of Christ, helped Christ's mission by preaching about repentance. Coincidently, the Hog's Head's barman, Aberforth Dumbledore, is Albus Dumbledore's brother and helps him on many occasions in a similar manner. There the similarity ends, since Aberforth keeps his head at the end of the series.

During the discussion of how to practice Defense Against the Dark Arts, Harry gets upset about the number of people who want to hear the story about Cedric's death from him personally, and not from someone else, even if it was the correct version. Although many people do not like to relive their worst memories, Harry's frustration is more about wanting to let the past speak for itself, just as the Law speaks for God in the Old

Testament. In the Bible, there is a story about Lazarus, a poor beggar, and the rich man. When they died, the rich man wanted to return to his brothers and warn them of the hell that awaited them if they didn't mend their ways and begin caring for others. In response, Christ tells them that if they won't listen to the prophets that went ahead of him, then they wouldn't listen to him even if he were to rise from the dead. (Luke 16: 19-31) Harry wants to move on and act on Lord Voldemort's threat rather than debate the past.

After understanding that they were not going to get any more out of Harry about the past, the meeting continues and many are convinced to join their group and begin translating the theoretical into action. Signing the parchment to be part of their dubbed "Dumbledore's Army" is similar to people signing their names to the baptistery list in the church. They are now bound magically to a group dedicated towards defeating Lord Voldemort and anything other than the truth, something we do not emphasize in the Christian traditions nowadays.

Chapter Seventeen: Educational Decree Twenty Four

In this chapter, we see the ministry trying to control even more elements at Hogwarts as they renounce any groups from meeting and require special signatures to allow a group to continue. This tactic is used many times in military *coup d'états*, emphasizing the rigidity of how the Ministry is hoping to keep all connections between Hogwarts and the outside closed. Again, this is another step descending into the black stage for Harry although Sirius' comment bolsters their hopes, "... better expelled and able to defend yourselves than sitting safely in school without a clue." An educated public is exactly what the Ministry does not want in these times of unrest.

Chapter Eighteen: Dumbledore's Army

While in Charms class, Ron has difficulty with his silencing charm, because he isn't focused on what he is doing. Essentially, charms are like prayers and the whole concept is to learn how to use and focus the faith we are given for God's purposes. If a person is not focused or thinking about what is being said in the prayer or the person for which the prayer is said, the prayer will only get a"no". Through practice, we learn how to focus our faith and mind on the matter at hand, and gain confidence and faith in God's answering prayer.

Now that Dumbledore's Army is more than an idea, Dobby helps them find a special room to work in. As with all things at Hogwarts," help always comes to those at Hogwarts who ask for it", and the Room of Requirement is no different. You have to ask three times (the number of assurance), and it will respond, giving you exactly what you need: "Ask, and it shall be given to you" (Matthew 7:7). Also, we finally hear how many names are on the list for Dumbledore's Army – 25. These 25 names on the Dumbledore's Army list represent the two numbers of completion: 12 + 13. 12 is the end number for time, and 13 is the number of completion in alchemy.

Chapter Nineteen: The Lion and the Serpent

In this chapter, we see multiple opposites played one after the other. The over arching battle is between Gryffindor and Slytherin, the Lion and the Serpent of course, but smaller skirmishes spring up both during the game and at the end of the game between the two teams. There's the battle between the Weasleys and Malfoy, Harry and Draco, more obviously elements of the two oppositional symbols, fire and water. A lesser known "skirmish" also between a lion and a serpent is Professor McGonagall up against Professor Umbridge, Professor McGonagall as the head of Gryffindor house and Professor Umbridge representing those against Professor Dumbledore, and hence the Slytherin house with Lord Voldemort. With Professor Umbridge claiming her ministry rights to ban Harry, Fred, and George from Quidditch, we see the historical persecution fn Christianity before the fourth century. Since Harry represents the everyday Christian, Fred represents the martyrs, and George represents the saints of God, their ban from Quidditch is meant to stop Christians from continuing to seek truth. Alchemically, this ban from the one thing Harry does very well is another notch down for Harry in the black stage, making the astral plane more attractive than the physical realm for now.

Chapter Twenty: Hagrid's Tale

Finally, Hagrid returns and we get a sense that everything has to get better now that everyone is where they should be. In Hagrid's story, we get a déjà vu about the scouts from the Old Testament that went from the desert to Canaan to see what they were up against. The giants that Hagrid talks about are very similar to the Canaanites – although there used to be many tribes of them in Moses' time, by Christ's time, there weren't so many left. Also, when the Israelites were on the move from Egypt to Canaan, they were told that giants lived there and to be careful.[85] Since the giants were enemies of the Israelites in the Old Testament, it isn't a surprise that the giants don't chose to help the Order of the Phoenix and join up with Lord Voldemort instead.

Chapter Twenty-one: The Eye of the Snake

During Professor Umbridge's evaluation of Professor Hagrid's first class, Hagrid again is in a position to teach Harry about the creature that represents the current element Harry is working to master, in this case, thestrals. Since "Thestral" is a play on the word "astral", we see that Ms. Rowling is pointing us to the fifth element, plasma, the quintessential element. This element can only be accessed by alchemists once they have mastered the four physical elements, and is the element between the four physical elements and the two mental elements, mercury and sulfur.[86] In this fifth book, Harry will have to master the astral plane – his dream-

---

[85] Finney, D, "Giants of the Bible," Retrieved from http://www.greatdreams.com/reptlan/giants.htm.

[86] Wikipedia, 2011, "classical element," retrieved from http://en.wikipedia.org/wiki/Classical_element# Elements_in_Medieval_alchemy.

like mind connection to Lord Voldemort - and use the thestrals to help him define the difference between dreams and reality.

Unfortunately, Professor Umbridge's distorted view of giants and other magical creatures in combination with her authority as a representative of the ministry enable her to project whatever opinion she wants of Hagrid onto others. Most of all, Professor Umbridge's evaluation of Professor Hagrid demonstrates one of J.K. Rowling's big themes – people will see what they want to see, regardless of what the truth is.

In Harry's dream, we see that the white stage of the story has begun. Up until now, Harry has only gotten glimpses and introductions to the various parts of the quintessential element – short dreams, feelings, introduction to Luna, and the sense of unreality with the various changes made at Hogwarts, most of which have not affected Harry physically. With the dream, Harry has now begun transcendence – his mind now connects his body to actual events in other places, a very different connection than possession. This is the same process that occurs when people learn intercessory prayer – how to go beyond one's own mind, allowing the Holy Spirit to speak through that person and act in that person's stead.

This transcending mental connection between Harry and Lord Voldemort is exactly what Professor Dumbledore was afraid of, and is why the professor doesn't seem to make eye contact with Harry. Indeed, we see the anger that is not Harry's when Harry looks at Professor Dumbledore. Knowing that Professor Dumbledore and Lord Voldemort are both accomplished Occlumens (mind readers), we can understand the additional necessity of Harry not staying in eye contact with Dumbledore for the sake of everyone's safety. On a more philosophical perspective, Lord Voldemort is able to connect to everyone at some point or other, either through other people or more slowly through their minds. It's what we do when we feel that dark connection that determines who we are. In this instance, Harry uses the connection and the information he gets to save Arthur Weasley's life, showing that regardless of his feelings during an event, he will still do whatever he can to save others from pain.

Chapter Twenty-two: St Mungo's Hospital for Magical Maladies and Injuries

After the dream, Harry, Ron, and Professor McGonagall go to see Professor Dumbledore in his office, where we again get more information about his position as the shepherd of his flock and the Christ figure of the series. Professor Dumbledore uses a mysterious instrument to determine something about what Harry has told him and never explains what he finds out. All we have is the clue that it's a snake with a divided essence. Knowing that Harry and Lord Voldemort are two sides of the same coin – they both share mind, soul, and blood – they essentially have one soul but different essences. However, we should not assume a division means that only two elements now exist. From what J.K. Rowling said in her answer to this very question, we understand that the question Dumbledore asks is about how Lord Voldemort could control the snake so well. To this, the answer is that the soul is divided, so it is the same soul but divided into pieces. The sentient pieces, Harry, Lord Voldemort, and Nagini are thus one soul but in essence divided. [87] This is also an answer to the question of the Trinity – how can one soul be shared amongst three entities? If God has an infinite soul, then dividing it between the Holy Spirit and Jesus does not diminish the soul at all, and it keeps the three united although separate in space.

Another piece to the connection that Harry has finally identified as one with Lord Voldemort is that we have defined the "monster" that Harry has to conquer to master the astral plane – his connection to Lord Voldemort. Essentially, with this shared connection, Harry is moved mentally from his own physical body to other sentient bodies that share Lord Voldemort's soul. In order to conquer this monster, Harry will have to learn to control when Lord Voldemort can access his mind and in turn be able to move in and out of Lord Voldemort's mind at will. At this point in the book, Harry cannot choose whether to see what Lord Voldemort is

[87] Bodnick, M., 2009, retrieved from http://www.quora.com/In-Harry-Potter-what-does-in-essence-divided-mean.

up to or not, and each experience weakens him mentally just as the dementors weakened him physically.

The one good thing about the dream is that we see Harry finally entering the white stage of this book. People are beginning to join with him, and Harry feels more a part of the community than he did before. However, he's also becoming more aware of the anger as a foreign part of his essence, and is aware that at least a part of it is awakened by Professor Dumbledore's presence and eye contact. If the eyes are the mirror of the soul, and Lord Voldemort's soul is evil, we see here that Lord Voldemort's soul is now stronger and exists through Harry's eyes as well. When Harry meets Professor Dumbledore's eyes, the love and concern that show in Professor Dumbledore's eyes bring out the strongest alien feelings of anger within Harry, who until now has not understood that the anger is not his own.

Back at 12 Grimmauld Place, the Weasleys sit in Sirius's kitchen awaiting news. Curiously, we see a piece of parchment appear with a single golden phoenix feather, the only time that we see how Professor Dumbledore sends his messages outside of Hogwarts - using his phoenix instead of an owl. As a magical creature, the phoenix can send things anywhere with the smallest part of itself, like the feather used here to send Molly's letter to 12 Grimmauld Place assuring her family that everything's fine. This is perhaps due to the phoenix's ability to carry heavy loads, an ability that exists even in the smallest part of the bird, just as Christ's healing exists in all parts of him and is accessed just by touch (Luke 8:43-47).

Despite the confidence that Mr. Weasley will be fine thanks to Harry's timely intervention, Harry still worries about the anger that he can't seem to control. In the book, Sirius and Harry have a short dismissive conversation during which Sirius tells Harry not to worry about anything and go to bed, which is not very insightful for a brilliant wizard. The reality is that we know Sirius and Professor Dumbledore are in close communication, so Sirius probably understands a lot more than he's letting Harry know. John Granger suggests that since Harry is connected to Lord Voldemort, the Order members have to be careful of what they say and do in front of Harry so that Lord Voldemort won't know what they know.[88]

In the movie, the producers have another take on this interaction between Harry and his godfather that highlights another theme of J.K. Rowling's – the role of free will. In the scene that occurs by the tapestry, Harry describes everything that happened in the snake dream to Sirius. Harry then shares his concern that the anger rising inside him will eventually control and possess him and he will become another Lord Voldemort. Sirius answers Harry by telling him that the world is not split into good people and bad people. Everyone has dark and light within them - it's a matter of how we act on those impulses that determine who we are.[89] Through the movie sequence, we get a better understanding that J.K. Rowling does not believe in fate or destiny as much as she believes in free choice to embrace and create who you are.

Awaiting Mr. Weasley's return to health, the remaining Weasleys, Harry, and Hermione are allowed to visit him at St Mungo's Hospital. As they wait, we get a tour of what a wizarding hospital contains and learn the difference between doctors and healers. Whereas doctors cut into people, healers just heal people, much like the healings we hear about from the disciples and Christ in the New Testament. Secondly, we have another name that has a double meaning. Here, the name of "Dai Llewellyn" is again one of J. K. Rowling's creative spellings for another idea, since Dai Llewellyn is another spelling for "Daily Welling", the outpatient daily care. One last piece that occurs at St. Mungo's is Mrs. Weasley's inclusion of Harry into Mr. Weasley's room when it should be family only. Through this, J. K. Rowling hints at the fact that Harry is part of their family already, but more importantly, including Harry into the family makes it eight children in that generation, the Christian number symbolic of a new creation. This is a reminder of 2 Corinthians 5:17: "Therefore, if anyone is in Christ, then he is a new creation."

---

[88] Granger, J, 2005, *Unlocking Harry Potter,* p. 17.

[89] Warner Brothers, 2007, Order of the Phoenix.

Chapter Twenty-three: Christmas on the Closed Ward

After hearing Mad-Eye Moody's ponderings about whether or not Harry has a strange possessive connection with Lord Voldemort, Harry begins to suspect that he is the cause of everyone's problems and has an insightful conversation with Phineas Nigellus. During the conversation, Phineas explains how the Slytherin house works – they are brave, but prefer to save their own necks rather than stick it out for anything or anyone. In essence, we come to understand that the Slytherins are the law-abiding, self-serving Sanhedrin who are always more worried about appearance than reality. For Harry, this is not very attractive since he feels he has no choice – reality seems to follow him, whether he likes it or not and he has never worried about appearance, especially since that was what defined the Dursley household philosophy.

Although not attracted to becoming a Slytherin like Phineas Nigillus, Harry begins to pity himself as he reminisces about how just a day ago, things had been so perfect. Suddenly, everything has changed and he feels "dirty", or unclean (much like the lepers of the Bible.) His feelings that his friends don't want to be around him is a flashback to how things changed for Job. In the book of Job in the Bible, everything is going well, and suddenly Job loses everything – his friends, his family, and the beginnings of his health. When his friends come to question him, they turn on him as well telling him that he must have done something horrible to bring this on himself. As his wallowing continues, Harry find himself thinking as Job did, that he would have been better off without God (Dumbledore and the wizarding community) after all.

On their last visit to the hospital, Harry, Ron, and Hermione run into Neville visiting his parents at St. Mungo's. From what they learn from Neville and his grandmother, we get a better picture of who Bellatrix LaStrange is as a person: she is devoted to Lord Voldemort, devoid of compassion, and unmatched in her desire to rule over others.

Chapter Twenty-four: Occlumency

Although in theory, occlumency would be a fabulous thing for Harry to learn and master on his way towards determining reality from dreams or mental visions, the question is more about whether it is even possible. Does Harry's ability to determine the difference between what he" sees" and what is reality depend only on blocking his mind to Lord Voldemort? It seems that every time Harry gets relaxed and his mind begins to drift away from the physical world, he gets a dream from Lord Voldemort. As the dreams become more prevalent, Harry begins to share in these visions, hoping for the same things that Lord Voldemort hopes for. Trying to help Harry block Lord Voldemort's mind from touching his while he's asleep is next to impossible, even if he could accomplish it during his wakeful hours.

Regardless of the fact that occlumency would be good for Harry, the entire quest towards "occlumency" as taught by Severus Snape to Harry Potter is questionable. Although helping shield Harry's mind from Lord Voldemort is part of Severus Snape's interests, he never teaches Harry how exactly to shield his mind. Rather than tell someone to just empty his mind, it is better to tell the person what to think about so that it gives the person a direction to go. It could be that Professor Dumbledore would like to know what Harry knows from Lord Voldemort but is unable to do so directly, since any eye contact with Harry only awakens the soul fragment from Lord Voldemort within Harry. Thus, by using Severus Snape to pretend to teach Harry, both Professors Dumbledore and Snape can determine what Lord Voldemort's plans are undetected.

As Professor Snape continues to try to teach Harry how to block his mind from others, the professor continually tells Harry to "empty your mind." However, Harry's empty mind always results in a dream from Lord Voldemort. This rings of the old adage "an idle mind is a devil's play thing" – when our minds are not focused, then our minds are subject to influences that we would not normally undertake. Thus, as Harry discovers later in the series, it is by focusing on something or the love for someone that truly blocks out all evil thoughts from entering the mind.

Professor Snape never admits this fact to Harry because his focal point of peace is his one secret love and is the one thing he returns to whenever his mind is empty of all else.

From the continued conversation between Professor Snape and Harry, we see another difference between Lord Voldemort and Harry Potter: Lord Voldemort focuses on having no emotion, no love, and no attachment because he sees those things as weak. For Harry Potter, it is his strong love for others that makes him powerful against Lord Voldemort, and the love gives him immunity against legilimency and Lord Voldemort's schemes, even if Harry can't keep Lord Voldemort from connecting to him whenever he chooses to.

Chapter Twenty-five: The Beetle at Bay

Throughout this chapter, the significant events revolve around the media and the news as reported. First, we hear about Azkaban. As the magical community discovers the mass breakout from Azkaban, they begin to understand that perhaps the Ministry of Magic has not been completely truthful to them about Lord Voldemort. Soon, others begin to return to Harry and Professor Dumbledore's side. This is furthering Harry's white stage in this book, the stage of illumination, which is now not only providing Harry with information and truth, but his position within the rest of the wizarding world as well.

The second discovery in the Daily Prophet is that Broderick Bode died. Since they were at Mr. Bode's bedside when he received the dangerous plant, they feel very guilty. This changes Harry's mindset from one of looking out only for obvious attacks to looking out for more subversion around him in unexpected places as well. This is another clue that Harry picks up about how Lord Voldemort works – not always in obvious ways, but rather slowly so that no one notices. This also furthers his illumination into Lord Voldemort's mind as Harry begins to see all the various pieces add up to help him understand what Lord Voldemort is after in the Department of Mysteries and to what extent he is willing to pursue it.

The last piece of interest regarding the newspaper in this chapter is about Rita Skeeter. Although the media has never been known for its truth and honesty, the expose' here from Rita about how the newspaper is a business made to make money regardless of the truth gives us an insight into the historical church. Pressed upon by others to make money in any way it could to support itself, the church turned to many avenues to make money that were not exactly in line with pursuing the truth of Christ. As soon as making money becomes the goal, truth is always lost as people begin to ride with the public emotional tides rather than the solid rock of truth of Jesus Christ.

Chapter Twenty-six: The Seen and Unforeseen

Since Harry is not able to do the Occlumency that Professor Dumbledore told him to learn, Harry is afraid to face him and tell him what he has seen through the link that was supposed to close. Similarly, when people are being disobedient to God or others and get into trouble, they tend to try to solve the problem themselves rather than get help, since getting help would mean admitting that they did something against the rules and get them into even more trouble. However, God promises that even if we break a rule, if we are repentant about it and turn to him, He will come to our aid (Acts 3:19, Isaiah 45:22).

Unfortunately, while Harry is trying to figure out how to reach Sirius, he doesn't seem to remember the mirror that would provide him with a connection to Sirius without interference or monitoring. This is a continuation of the dream state of this book, since one common element of any dream is that the obvious solution doesn't seem to be the way to go. For whatever reason, it's always the most complicated way that we get focused on in dreams and nothing else makes any sense. In this case, the Floo powder seems to be the easiest way to talk to others quickly and is the method used the most in any communications with Sirius, so the mirror at the bottom of the trunk lays forgotten.

Chapter Twenty-seven: The Centaur and The Snake

When Firenze takes over the Divinations class after Professor Trewlaney is fired, we get a clearer understanding of what J.K. Rowling wants us to understand about people trying to tell the future – nothing is perfect, and only God truly knows the future. Mark 13:32: "But of that day and hour no one knows, ... but only the Father." (NIV) The centaur Firenze's name represents the Renaissance: Firenze is the Italian word for "Florence", the birthplace of The Renaissance. The Renaissance was all about finding the truth in art form and incorporation of old ideas into new ideas, all of which Firenze tries to put into his classes. His classes are very different from the traditional Divinations classes taught by Professor Trewlaney, since it is more about how the individual interprets the information rather than ensuring that the individual interprets the information the way the teacher expects. A bigger piece of what is taught here is that nothing is foolproof – a lesson for all those who feel that belonging to a group is enough protection from something without doing anything else.

Dumbledore Army's luck runs out, and they are finally discovered. As Harry Potter is brought to the Minister of Magic for running Dumbledore's Army, we see again an example of Christ taking on our sufferings and our punishment as Professor Dumbledore inserts himself into the situation between Harry and the Minister, taking the punishment meant for Harry. (Isaiah 53:5: "But He was pierced for our transgressions, he was crushed for our iniquities; the punishment that brought us peace was upon him, and by his wounds we are healed." (NIV). Of course, being Professor Dumbledore, the punishment expected is not the punishment given because of Dumbledore's magical abilities, and we see a fabulous exit as Fawkes transports him somewhere unknown. This parallels Jesus' many escapes from the Temple Guards, as in John 7:33-34: "Jesus said, 'I am with you for only a short time, and then I am going to the one who sent me. [34] You will look for me, but you will not find me; and where I am, you cannot come.'"

With the end of the Defense Against the Dark Arts classes for the year (in this case, the real ones taught by Harry), it's interesting that every Defense Against the Dark Arts class never seems to make it past Pentecost or Easter. Just as those two events mark God's victory over evil and vanquishes the need for learning defense, so the classes seem to end up dismantling for one reason or another before the year comes to an end.

Chapter Twenty-eight: Snape's Worst Memory

As Harry continues his Occlumency lessons, they come to an abrupt end when Harry sneaks a look into Snape's memories. In the memory, we see Gryffindor students bullying the Slytherin students, but in the present, we see the result of past bullying – a reversal of the roles. In any situation, regardless of age, people are responsible for their actions and whom they try to bully, since the repercussions can come for generations to come. As it says in Jeremiah 32:18 "...you bring the punishment for the fathers' sins into the laps of their children after them." In this case, it is now Snape who can bully Harry, especially since Harry's father isn't around now.

Chapter Twenty-nine: Career Advice

As Harry reflects on the visions of his father and his friends bullying Severus Snape as a Slytherin student, he has to come to terms with the fact that his father was not a saint in school and was rather obnoxious as a teenager. As adults, people have somewhat arrived at a more mature and understanding nature, so that younger generations have a difficult time seeing the older generations with any fallacies in their youth. This could be one of the main reasons why the generations do not understand each other – the younger generation thinks that the older generation always did the right thing because the older generation doesn't seem top make the same mistakes. However, what makes a person mature is the ability to learn from one's mistakes and not repeat them – the transformation of a person makes it impossible to see what the person was before the transformation. Hopefully, knowing that the older generation made mistakes and still managed to do good in the world should give us all hope that even if we make mistakes ourselves, we can learn from them and become better people as we get older.

While Harry is talking to Remus Lupin and Sirius Black through the fireplace about what happened when Harry's father was fifteen, we see another recurrence of the age theme. Lupin and Sirius want to disregard James's actions since they were only fifteen at the time, but Harry reminds us that he is fifteen and his decisions are significant. Again, J.K. Rowling's theme that people do not seem to expect teenagers to have any bearing on the world or a very limited effect on what they can do for the world. In another view, now that the Order of the Phoenix exists, the question about whether someone can be significant at a young age is answered in the person of St. John the Evangelist, who was a teenager when he became a disciple of Jesus, and became one of Jesus' best friends. As the story progresses, we see Harry taking on this part of the original disciples – St. John, who overcomes death many times before dying a natural death at 105 years old.

Chapter Thirty: Grawp

As the discussion about blocking out Lord Voldemort continues, Harry finally realizes that he is not able to do so, even though everyone else thinks it is possible. Part of it is that Harry finds it advantageous to know what Lord Voldemort is thinking, but since there is also a part of Lord Voldemort's soul in Harry, that link is impossible to block completely. Harry still has no control over when Lord Voldemort makes a connection, and he hasn't figured out how to initiate one to Lord Voldemort, other pieces to the mastery puzzle Harry has to solve.

Chapter Thirty-one: O.W.L.'s

As Harry is taking his transfiguration Ordinary Wizarding Level exam, he learns from the examiner that Professor Dumbledore was able to do things with his wand that advanced wizards had never seen before. As the Christ figure, this memory parallels Christ's time at the temple after he was bar Mitvah'd. Jesus astounded the rabbis at the temple, and they heard explanations of the Torah that they had never heard before. (Luke 2:46-47 "After three days they found him in the temple courts, sitting among the teachers, listening to them and asking them questions. Everyone who heard him was amazed at his understanding and his answers."

Chapter Thirty-two: Out of the Fire

As soon as the OWL exams are over, Harry has a vision of Sirius being tortured. However, he comes to the realization that all the adults he had counted on are now gone for various reasons, and he must work with his own friends or by himself. With the slow removal of all of Harry's support system, we are beginning to see the ending climax, where Harry will somehow run into Lord Voldemort by himself.

For Harry, Sirius' torture is the greatest challenge he has faced with the visions he has. His dreams are more often becoming reality and his reality is sometimes a nightmare so it is hard for Harry to tell the difference. From the beginning of the dreams in the Goblet of Fire, Professor Dumbledore told Harry not to think about his dreams as being anything other than just dreams. With this type of advice, it is hard to tell whether Professor Dumbledore suspected that Harry's mind, so intertwined with Lord Voldemort's, would become a telepathic link incapable of shutting out the other side or if he just wanted to keep Harry from worrying about what a true telepathic link might mean.

Harry's vision turns into a nightmare as he finds that every effort to save Sirius is continually thwarted by other events taking place. This is a classic dream sequence where sometimes a person feels a compulsion to save something and everything keeps that person from doing just that for various legitimate reasons. In a way, J.K. Rowling is trying to demonstrate that Harry's dreams and reality are becoming so mixed that they blend into each other. Here, it is the ultimate test for Harry to show his mastery over what is real and what is dream-state.

One of the circumstances that keeps Harry away from saving Sirius is Professor Umbridge. As Harry and his friends are detained for breaking into Professor Umbridge's office, their last hope of warning the Order is through Professor Snape. Harry does everything he can to give Snape the necessary information, but is pretty sure that Professor Snape is not going to help him, even if he is on the Order. The reality is that as Snape looks into Harry's eyes, he can read what is in Harry's mind even as he pretends not to understand what is going on. However, the question is then why Professor Snape made the occlumency lessons so painful earlier in the year. None of the other times that legilimens is used are any of the people aware that their minds were being read, but perhaps Snape used a different type of mind-reading. It does make one wonder however, if legilimens is used to obtain memories the person doesn't remember having, whereas simple mind-reading is just reading the current thoughts of the individual.

Chapter Thirty-three: Fight and Flight

As Harry, Hermione and Professor Umbridge go into the forest to find "the weapon", they run into the centaurs. Hermione was hoping that they would see how evil Professor Umbridge was and would help her and Harry get rid of the professor, but they see it as a manipulation ploy to get them to do the dirty work. Throughout the series, we see the centaurs playing the role of those who have a good relationship with Professor Dumbledore and usually with Hagrid, but are too internally focused to work with anyone else. Arrogant and proud, these creatures will help no one but themselves, regardless of how near the danger is to them. In magical stories, these creatures are usually the dwarves, and in Biblical terms, we see the Pharisees – they are interested in what is going on and watch for the moment that it might involve them, but otherwise, they stay to themselves. By never interfering with what was fated to be, they are able to keep themselves untainted by the races around them. Nowadays, there are many who feel that God will tend his own, punishing those who deserve to be punished, and rewarding those who deserve rewards as it is written without any interference on their part. Firenze is the Good Samaritan, who defies the group and joins Professor Dumbledore's cause to fight what will eventually become their problem if not stopped before hand.

Within the wizards themselves, as Neville, Luna, and Ginny come to help Ron, Hermione, and Harry, we see the next generation of Order of the Phoenix emerging, beginning as Dumbledore's Army. As in the first twelve disciples of Christ and the current Order of the Phoenix, we see another group of misfits - blood traitors, mudbloods, orphans, and believers in anything unproven – that are willing to fight for their community, friendship, and love of others.

Harry eventually gives in to letting Neville, Luna, and Ginny help him, and his fears of their inabilities, hesitations, and questionable ideas are replaced with thanksgiving for their companionship and ideas. Luna of course helps Harry remember the Thestrals, the symbol of the astral plane, while Ginny and Neville are now bold and brave in the face of danger despite their previous history, and prove to be formidable allies. This change in attitude also shows the move from the white stage to the red stage of the book, where we are now approaching reunification, purification, and battle.

Chapter Thirty-four: The Department of Mysteries

Ron, Hermione, and Ginny mount their thestrals for departure to the Ministry, and we see an instance of where even believing isn't enough to see something. From John 20:29: "Blessed are those who have not seen and yet have believed." Harry's comfort with using the thestrals shows that Harry has finally mastered a creature of the astral plane, and he is now on his way to the final battle that will help him conquer the other "monster" that will grant him mastery of the astral plane.

When Harry and the other members of Dumbledore's Army arrive at the Ministry of Magic, the fact that no one is around further leads readers to realize that the situation is a dream sequence – everything is the opposite of what it should be. Again, the evening hours is another reference to the fact that Harry is also in the Black stage of his alchemical transformation and learning to master those elements of the night, especially dreams and the astral plane.

At the Ministry's Department of Mysteries, Harry and his friends try to find the prophecy room. On the way, they accidentally run into a rectangular room with a tattered, black veil in the very center, on a dais. Harry and Luna can hear voices from the other side of the veil, which flutters in the still air. Symbolically, this is a reference to the veil that hides the connection between the physical and the ethereal realm,[90] the veil that must be crossed to fully master the astral element. Biblically, the veil is used in the temple to separate the Holy of Holies from the rest of the temple, representing again the separation of the physical realm from the spiritual realm, and only those who had been sanctified properly were allowed to enter on Yom Kippur in to the Holy of Holies to speak with God (Leviticus 2:2).

Chapter Thirty-five: Beyond the Veil

Once Harry and his friends finally get to where Sirius was supposed to be, Lucius Malfoy explains that Harry needs to hurry up and master the astral element – "learn to tell the difference between life and dreams." As the title of the chapter suggests, this will be the chapter during which Harry finally masters moving in and out of the astral plane, learning to understand the difference between dreams and reality, and controlling the connection between himself and Lord Voldemort.

When Neville's wand breaks from a curse sent at him by a Death Eater, Neville has an opportunity to redefine who he is. His wand was a hand-me-down from his father, and the wand represents the wizard's faith. As a hand-me down, or a cradle Christian, a person does not feel truly connected to God. However, in breaking his father's wand, Neville is

[90]International Alchemy Guild, 2011, "Alchemy Electronic Dictionary," retrieved from http://www.alchemylab.com /dictionary.htm#sectQ.

redefining himself as a new Christian with his own path of faith as he battles his own dark forces in the wizarding world.

True to Ms. Rowling's form, Harry is now mostly alone fighting the Death Eaters in the bowels of the Ministry of Magic, and Professor Dumbledore comes to his rescue, very Christ-like. Interestingly, Professor Dumbledore arrives immediately after the prophecy's container is destroyed, in perfect symbolism of embodying the prophecy itself. In the movie, Warner Brothers emphasizes this by having them apparate with white light, like the light of Christ, and oppositional to the black Death Eaters. The Death Eaters, even in mass numbers, are afraid of Professor Dumbledore's wand abilities, but perhaps also because they are like naughty children caught by their true master.

Unfortunately, Sirius dies from Bellatrix LaStrange's curse and passes through the veil. Now, Harry finally sees the purpose of the veil – to obscure those who are now beyond the physical realm and in the astral plane. The reality of the situation begins to wake Harry up from his real-life confusion of what is real and what is truly a vision. With the death of Sirius Black, we have the beginning of the end of the black stage of Harry's alchemy, and after the pain of the transition, Harry is ready to begin the white stage.

Chapter Thirty-six: The Only One He Ever Feared

After Professor Dumbledore constrains the Death Eaters in the veil room, he follows Harry to the main floor where he runs into Lord Voldemort. From the ensuing duel in the bowels of the Ministry, we get a more distinct view of the differences between these two key opponents' views on life and death. Despite everything that Lord Voldemort has done, the professor does not seek to kill Tom Riddle, stating that a physical death would not be enough to make up for everything he has done and that there are other things worse than a physical death or lack of existence. For Tom Riddle, there is nothing beyond existence in the physical world, even if it's only as a soul (as he did for the past thirteen years). With this understanding, he fears a physical death since it means the end of his existence on all levels. For Professor Dumbledore and those who know and believe that there is an existence after death, as we have seen with the ghosts at Hogwarts and the spirits that helped Harry at the end of Goblet of Fire, the end of the this physical realm is not the end of one's existence.

During the battle, one of Lord Voldemort's attempts to kill Professor Dumbledore is dividing his efforts between a snake and the Killing Curse. Despite the cunning move, Fawkes takes the curse while Professor Dumbledore captured the snake. Fawkes was able to resurrect himself from the curse just as Jesus did from the grave, and Professor Dumbledore is able to render the snake useless, symbolic of Christ's ultimate victory over Original Sin from the Garden of Eden. In this display, we have the cunning snake versus the resurrecting phoenix, and it shows that the resurrection will always win over cunning. It is also the embodiment of Corinthians 15:55 ", O Death, where is your sting? O grave, where is your victory?" (KJV): Fawkes fought free of the grave, and Professor Dumbledore fought free of the sting of the snake.

After failing to defeat Professor Dumbledore, Lord Voldemort decides to do what he can to defeat the combined forces of Dumbledore and Harry by trying to get Professor Dumbledore to kill Harry. As Lord Voldemort possesses Harry's body, we see the juxtaposition of opposites, Harry and Lord Voldemort, and Harry has to fight Lord Voldemort alone since no one else can help him. To clarify that it is the end of the black stage, we see the golden statues helping Harry, moving around the floor, protecting some and trapping others, and acting as a portkey back to Hogwarts. It is a quick internal battle that happens in the mind, and Harry wins the fight by thinking about Sirius. This recall reaches beyond the veil to the ethereal, which will always conquer the physical realm. As such, Lord Voldemort cannot possess the same physical substance, and leaves Harry for good. Whether by accident or not, Harry now has more control over the connection between himself and Lord Voldemort, and his love for those beyond the veil give him power and mastery over the astral element.

With the apparition of Cornelius Fudge and many other ministry officials, Lord Voldemort disapparates, leaving chaos behind. Professor Dumbledore has a discussion with Cornelius Fudge during which we again see Dumbledore with the twelve-handed watch. Since Professor Dumbledore knows about Molly Weasley's clock, it is very likely that his watch works the same way. Now that we have the Order of the Phoenix, we can guess what the twelve hands represent – the twelve members of the Order of the Phoenix, although one of them is Harry Potter. Just as the Weasley's clock indicates their position in one of the seven areas, Dumbledore's watch tells him where everyone is and how they are doing, which aides his omniscience.

Chapter Thirty-seven: The Lost Prophecy

As the chapter opens, Harry sees the dawn's beginning of a new day, symbolizing the entrance to his white stage of his alchemical transformation - illumination. In the outside world, the Ministry has seen Lord Voldemort, the wizarding world now knows he was telling the truth, and Professor Dumbledore is talking to Harry again. In fact, Professor Dumbledore is giving Harry every insight possible, to bring Harry both up to speed and help him further along his journey. Now that Harry has mastered the difference between the dream state and reality by keeping love as his shield, Professor Dumbledore has no problem telling Harry everything that he has missed the past year without worry of Lord Voldemort's intrusion. Now that the white stage has begun, Harry's education in all things regarding the Dark Arts, Lord Voldemort, and magical life takes on more meaning as he learns the inside story to everything.

One of the first things that Professor Dumbledore offers to Harry is an apology by way of an explanation. Professor Dumbledore explains that if he had told Harry about what Lord Voldemort might do and what he wanted, then Harry might not have fallen for the trap Lord Voldemort set for him. In the same way, we should tell others about the traps that are set out for them and us in general - things that will keep us away from God.

Professor Dumbledore's explanation to Harry about why he hadn't told him the prophecy earlier also explains why Lord Voldemort wanted to destroy Harry at a year old. Professor Dumbledore further explains that his love for Harry had blinded him to any dangers to all the others involved in "the plan." Although Professor Dumbledore never explains what "the plan" is, the context implies that Dumbledore has had this plan since Harry's parents died. This echoes of a similar dialogue that might have occurred between God the Father and Jesus before the Last Supper – God's love for Jesus is extreme and God doesn't want Christ to suffer, but He knows that the Son must in order to bring about the plan of salvation to all.

As further explanation, Professor Dumbledore explains to Harry that his scar is the curse that marks Harry as Lord Voldemort's equal, we see that the scar is a marking more than anything else. It rings of the baptismal vow "You are now sealed with the Holy Spirit, and marked as God's own forever", but it also rings of stories where the original marking was modified to change the direction of the original intent, even if the original intention can never be entirely erased. Thus, Lord Voldemort's curse changed God's marking on Harry, emblazing Harry with additional abilities that make Harry himself the juxtaposition of both good and evil. This significance means that Harry is the only one with the abilities to destroy Lord Voldemort, making him "The Chosen One", the marked one.

The last piece of Harry's conversation with Professor Dumbledore is a revisiting of the fate and destiny theme in the series. As Dumbledore explains to Harry that even though the fate says that one of them will destroy the other, there is a distinction between whether he goes in because he wants to, or cannot avoid it. In life, perhaps there is some prophecy for each person that tells exactly what will happen to that person, but there is a difference between looking forward to whatever fate has to offer, and regretting everything that happens to someone.

Chapter Thirty-eight: The Second War Begins

One of the pieces of the prophecy that is not very clear is the eventual fate for Harry and Lord Voldemort. Although Harry leaves Professor Dumbledore's office with the impression that the prophecy says that one of them will have to kill the other, meaning that he will have to pursue Lord Voldemort himself to bring the war to an end, the prophecy actually indicates that both will have to die so that one can live. As long as both exist, they can "survive", but there is no assurance that either will live even after the other dies since after the other dies, the first still "survives."

With deep sorrow, Harry seeks out Nearly Headless Nick in hopes of reaching Sirius. In Harry's discussion with Nearly Headless Nick, J.K. Rowling gives us her understanding of what happens at death, and who can be ghosts. She very clearly says that only wizards can return as ghosts, meaning that only wizards have an ethereal element to them since they would have achieved either mastery over the five elements or a relationship with Christ/ Professor Dumbledore and have their name in his book. It is interesting that she has people divided between those who choose to stay around to help the living (because they were too afraid of Heaven or too attached to others sill on earth) and those who continue on to Heaven and never return, giving her own partial explanation to the concept of "guardian angels" versus those that exist in Heaven full time.

In the conclusion, we see that as Harry returns to his life with the Dursleys, the members of the Order attempt to explain to the Dursleys how much Harry means to them and see if the Dursleys might treat him any better. Unfortunately, the Dursleys will never treat Harry any better than they have because they see what they want to see, and not what is in front of them. The Order's stand against the Dursleys shows their solidarity with Harry, and indicates that Harry is a significant member of their community, elevating his spot in the wizarding world from what it was before it was lost at the end of last year.

Chapter NINE

The Guide to *The Half-Blood Prince*

Plot summary: Half-Blood Prince begins with an insight into how the two community leaders, the Prime Minister and the Minister of Magic, relate to one another – as two worlds that try to pretend the other doesn't exist. Furthermore, Professor Snape makes a secret vow to help Draco Malfoy with two well-known followers of Lord Voldemort. Back at Privet Drive, Harry is expecting Professor Dumbledore's arrival to personally lead him away to Hogwarts as Lord Voldemort begins his reign of terror in earnest. As doubts remain about the arrival, Harry forgets to tell the Dursley family about the late visitor, which results in a very one-sided discussion between Professor Dumbledore and Mr. and Mrs. Dursley. While Harry finishes his packing, Professor Dumbledore explains that Harry must be allowed to return one last time before his seventeenth birthday in order to keep everyone safe. Professor Dumbledore then has Harry help him procure a professor for Hogwarts, a Horace Slughorn, en route to The Burrow, which has been given every security measure available to ensure Harry's safety. As The Chosen One from The Prophecy, Harry is now the favorite in the magical community to destroy Lord Voldemort.

Once back at Hogwarts, Harry is given a few personal instructional sessions with Dumbledore, where they explore Lord Voldemort's past and search for clues about what his plans are. They learn about Tom Riddle's mother, father, and grandfather, how he came to Hogwarts, and other exchanges Tom had with Professor Dumbledore during which we see Tom's changing physique from a handsome man to a snake-like corpse. Meanwhile, having received all the OWLs required to continue classes to become an auror, Harry serendipitously comes into possession of an ancient book of "Advanced Potions", the previous owner being "The Half Blood Prince." After initial disgust at the state of the book, Harry realizes that the book had many helpful corrections and other notations in the margins that if followed, gave him better results in Potions class as well as new spells to use.

The mystery Harry tries to decipher this year is what Draco Malfoy is doing, since Draco has given up Quidditch and seems to be missing from Hogwarts much of the time. To add to the mystery, some students become victims of misdirected curses, and Professor Dumbledore has a very dead-looking hand. One of the new spells Harry tries out puts Draco Malfoy in the infirmary, and Harry goes from being Quidditch captain to having to quit the Quidditch team to serve detention for his actions. One of Harry's challenges during the year is the acquisition of a memory from Professor Slughorn that could be the key to understanding Lord Voldemort's plan for overtaking the world, and the key to his undoing.

In the end, Harry is able to get the memory, which holds the clue to Lord Voldemort's immortality – the creation of seven Horcruxes. Having already discovered two of them by accident (the diary and the ring that caused Dumbledore's hand to wither), Harry is allowed to travel with Professor Dumbledore to obtain a third Horcrux from its hiding spot. It is this event that brings about the death of Professor Dumbledore – weakened by the act of obtaining the locket, Professor Dumbledore is unable to defend himself against Draco Malfoy who disarms him, but is unable to kill him. Other Death Eaters arrive, having a secret entrance that Draco opens for them, but Professor Snape joins them and kills

Professor Dumbledore. A short battle ensues, Harry discovers that The Half-Blood Prince is no other than Professor Snape, the Death Eaters and Draco escape Hogwarts through the gate while the rest of the school mourns the loss of Professor Dumbledore then returns home, heavy hearted.

Chapter One: The Other Minster

Without knowing the truth, the Prime Minister and others keep trying to make sense of the random violence and destruction that is going on around them. Their explanations get somewhat outrageous as they try to create anything that might be logical rather than accept the fact that there might be other elements at work. In this case, it is the occurrence of evil things through Lord Voldemort, but we tend to do the same for miracles – we search for a logical explanation rather than accept God's benevolence towards us.

Once the Prime Minister understands why there is so much violence and destruction in the world, he calms down a bit but is outraged that he cannot tell the world the truth. Logically, a world that won't accept benevolence of God won't accept the evil of Satan either, so declaring either one would not be allowed through the social and political rules of our time.

More historically, we see a juxtaposition between the Prime Minster and the Minister of Magic similar to the working relationship between the Roman Emperor and the Pope in both the early years of the church as well as nowadays. Each one rules a distinct group; some people are ruled by both rulers, but many from each distinct group don't acknowledge the sovereignty of the other.

Chapter Two: Spinner's End

In this interesting insight into the other side of Severus Snape, we see the doubt and faith that exists amongst the Death Eaters themselves about Snape's loyalties. Ultimately, it is Lord Voldemort's decision whether to trust him or not, but having Wormtail at his house somewhat indicates that there is a little doubt since we know that Wormtail is a good spy. Also, although Severus Snape professes that Lord Voldemort trusts him completely and has told him of "the plan", this is not very likely, since Lord Voldemort trusts no one and is immune to others reading his mind. More likely, S. Snape says this to convey his higher status with Lord

Voldemort than the two women and either deduces it from what he knows about Lord Voldemort, or through his conversations with Professor Dumbledore. The confidence he gives by declaring the Oath solidifies his position as a Death Eater for the reader as well as the women here.

Chapter Three: Will and Won't

Only a few weeks after the discovery that Harry was telling the truth and Lord Voldemort was truly back, the masses jump on the bandwagon to declare Harry Potter "The Chosen One", just days after he was still the laughing stock of the magical community. This is very much a parallelism of Christ's triumphant entry into Jerusalem – after a dubious career where some believed in him and others didn't, they all feel that Christ's return to Jerusalem is the beginning of his leading them against The Evil One, which they felt was the Roman Empire, not Satan. Although very much a Christ-like reference, many prophets, saints, martyrs had similar experiences with fickle communities, making it clear that Harry has not become the Christ figure in the story.

Another turnaround in this chapter is the Ministry's stand against Lord Voldemort. In the last book, they were convincing everyone that there was nothing to fear. Now, they have put out every effort to protect everyone as evidenced by the Ministry of Magic pamphlet's seven magical steps to protecting themselves, the perfect number of protective measures. The protective measures begin with rules about a person alone, move onto people together, then about other people, then other dead people. With this progression, we see a parallel with the 10 commandments, which begin with four rules about God himself, then things individuals should not do, then progressing to things within the community and neighbors. (Exodus 20:3-17). In view of the fact that the Ten Commandments were meant as a guide to help people live together in harmony and with God from which all 613 Rabbinical laws were created to keep people safe from breaking the laws, these seven protective measures are meant to keep people safe from Lord Voldemort. By staying safe and not breaking the Laws or rules, the people do not worry about falling into sin or into the grasp of Lord Voldemort, the persona of Satan.

Although one of the steps mentions that it is better to avoid travelling by night, since that is when Lord Voldemort has the most power, Professor Dumbledore collects Harry at night without fear for two reasons. First of all, since Albus Dumbledore is the Christ figure, we are reminded of John 1:4-5: “In Him was life, and that life was the light of all mankind. The light shines in the darkness, and the darkness has not overcome it.” (NIV) Professor Dumbledore’s deluminator makes him the ultimate source and master of the light, and Lord Voldemort cannot overcome him. Secondly, Professor Dumbledore has no fear of Lord Voldemort since he is superior to his own student, and is thus protected from having to follow magical rules that apply to Lord Voldemort.

After the initial surprise that the professor actually came when he said he would, Professor Dumbledore gets to hold an audience with the Dursleys. In their discussion, Professor Dumbledore brings up the fact that Harry will be “of age” when he’s seventeen, and the Dursleys refute it, saying that Harry won’t be of age until he’s eighteen. In Jewish and Christian tradition, the person is considered to be an “adult” in that religion once he has completed bat mitzvah or confirmation, which are usually completed at 13 or sometimes a little older in some Christian traditions. As an adult in the religion, they have a voice in any decision made by that body of worshippers. This view of an adult is very different than the secular understanding of an adult, which is not driven by accomplishment but by age alone. Another item of interest during their conversation is the word “evoke” as used by Professor Dumbledore. The word “evoke” is very different than what a sorcerer or magician would more likely use – “conjure.” The main difference is that to evoke is to call forth to be visible, something not of substance in itself, whereas conjuring is bringing something from another place or world and enslaving into action, usually a spirit or something of substance. This significance shows that J.K. Rowling was very aware of other connotations and was careful to use those that conveyed to the Christian world.

Chapter Four: Horace Slughorn

Professor Dumbledore, true to his word, personally brings Harry to The Burrow after a side trip to visit a Horace Slughorn. While Harry is walking with Professor Dumbledore to places unknown, he is not afraid of any evil, living proof of Psalm 23: "Yea, though I walk through the valley of the shadow of death, I will fear no evil. Thy rod and thy staff, they comfort me." (KJV) Since Harry is walking with the Christ figure by night (the shadow of death), he has no fear. Perhaps that is the reason that Harry didn't ask any proof of Professor Dumbledore to prove who he was, since there is no proof required of Christ (although Harry tends to be overly trusting, despite his foolishness leading to Sirius Black's demise.)

Upon arriving at Slughorn's temporary dwelling, it appears that there has been a break-in, and possibly a scuffle. Despite the appearances however, the lack of a Dark Mark hanging over the house tells us that there is no death awaiting at that house. After their entrance, they find Professor Slughorn, and discuss his use of Dragon's Blood. Knowing that Professor Dumbledore wrote a thesis on the twelve uses of Dragon's Blood, Professor Dumbledore was verifying that it was indeed Dragon's Blood, since Horace was utilizing it in an interesting way – the Dragon's Blood was taking the place of Horace's own blood as a form of protection. In this sense, we see a parallel in the sacrificial element of Christ's immortal blood for our own. Horace Slughorn is hopeful that it can be reused, although its thicker consistency might not allow it be used again, just as any substitutionary sacrificial protection can only be done once – one sacrifice for all.

Chapter Five: An Excess of Phlegm

Finally safe back at the Burrow, Professor Dumbledore departs with the short comment about him being Molly's servant. This comment to his disciple, Molly, is a kickback to Jesus' declaration of servant-hood to his own disciples in the book of John. Jesus first washes their feet, then tells them all that he served them first, they will need to do the same for others if they wish to follow him (John 13:12-16).

Molly's comment about her clock being the only one in existence raises questions again about their singularity within the wizarding world. The Weasleys are also the only "blood traitors" that we ever hear of or meet and yet they are "purebloods" with ancient wizarding artifacts. Biblically, a family that was "pure" and yet considered a traitor to their people could indicate a reference to the Samaritans. The Samaritans, who likewise were considered "untouchable" by the Jews of Jesus' time, were those left behind in the Northern Kingdom after the Assyrian conquest in 722 B.C.[91] Left behind after centuries of interrupted devotion to God, the Mosaic Law changed very slightly to allow for a second temple not in Jerusalem and other small differences. Because they were left behind and did not fight, there was speculation that they had made prior arrangements with the fierce Assyrians and the Jews from the Southern Kingdom (the tribes of Judah and Benjamin) determined that the Samaritans were no longer part of their race. However, Jesus makes amends with the Samaritans during his lifetime, first by asking for water from the woman at the well, then by speaking to her fellow villagers where many converted and became disciples. (John 4:1-42.) Since we get to know Molly in book two, the alchemical water book, she is a likely candidate for that role especially since The Burrow is another key meeting place for the Order of the Phoenix, just like the Woman at the Well and the Good Samaritan were helping others, regardless of their pasts.

After a good night's sleep, Harry is finally able to get caught up on the gossip within the Weasley household. The big news is Fleur's announcement of her wedding to Bill. From Granger's analysis, this is the alchemical wedding – the red king to the white queen, meaning that the end of the alchemy is in sight and resolution of the series is nearing (with the final book).[92] Surprisingly, George and Fred have set up their joke shop, which is thriving in the midst of all the anxiety about Lord Voldemort. This lighter side to the wizarding world from the two representatives of saints and martyrs recall a bit of the early Christian

---

[91] "Samaritan," *Encyclopaedia Britannica [Online],*Encyclopaedia Britannia, Inc.: 2012.

[92] Granger, J, 2010, *The Deathly Hallows Lectures*, p. 54.

attitude of happiness despite the obstacles and horrors they faced. Like the typical martyrs and saints of old, Fred and George stay steadfast in their faith of others, using humor and magic to keep others from despair in the face of Lord Voldemort's reign of terror.

On a side note, we finally get the full number of classes offered at Hogwarts with the delivery of the trio's OWL results. From Hermione's list of eleven OWL scores, we see that there are twelve classes taught at Hogwarts (since she dropped Divinations), the Judeo-Christian number of completion. Thus, the classes are Ancient Runes, Astronomy, Arithmancy, Care of Magical Creatures, Charms, Defense against the Dark Arts, Divination, Herbology, History of Magic, Muggle Studies, Potions, and Transfiguration.

Chapter Six: Draco's Detour

Since Harry is now in the white stage of the alchemical work, Harry is now in a heightened awareness stage called illumination. In this stage, he makes connections with everything he's learning, he learns everything he can, everything makes sense to him, and he makes connections that others are not able to make. He is also highlighted as the "Chosen One", the white lamb, being prepared to fight off evil as part of this illumination stage, or the white stage. In this heightened awareness state, while Harry and his friends are at Diagon Alley, he senses that Draco is up to something. Despite their reservations about Harry's hunches (since they are usually wrong), his supportive friends accompany him to see if there is any truth to his claims.

From their visit to Diagon Alley on the whole, we see how things have changed in Diagon Alley from the happy, loud place they visited in years past. Now, many of the stores carry popular amulets and other protective devices that can protect a wizard against evil forces. However, although there is comfort in these placebo trinkets, they either do not do everything they propose to do or they are fakes. Similarly, there is a large enterprise in the real world. Many people wear rosaries, pieces of relics, crosses, crucifixes, scapulars, etc. to protect them again Satan or other evil forces. Unfortunately, many of these items are not real, and even if they were, it is not the physical realm that Christ taught us to master, but the spiritual one - one that we cannot protect physically with objects. Essentially, our souls must transform in order to skirt death spiritually. Nothing physical will outlast eternity.

Chapter Seven: The Slug Club

As Draco subtly explains to his friends on the Hogwarts Express, he is on to better things than a Hogwarts education – he already has a job lined up that has already started for him. In his discussion, Draco shows a surprisingly clear insight and true understanding of Lord Voldemort's desires: a high level of devotion and service, without regard to the people at all. For Lord Voldemort, who has no love or trust of anyone, it's all about him and what he can get from others. Once he has everything he needs from someone, then that person has outlived his/her usefulness, and that person is expendable. This is a key difference between Lord Voldemort and Albus Dumbledore. Whereas a person's worth for Lord Voldemort depends on what he can get from the person without forgiveness for any mistakes or attitudes, a person's worth for Albus Dumbledore is determined only by whether the person is alive or not. Even if the person is a muggle, Albus Dumbledore still treats that person with respect, kindness, and offers every form of protection he can. For wizards, he allows all of them to train at Hogwarts, even if he disapproves of their attitudes, because he believes that everyone should have a second chance to prove himself.

Chapter Eight: Snape Victorious

Thankfully, Tonks is at the train station and is able to rescue Harry from a return trip to London. Using her patronus to give an advanced note of their coming highlights the change in her patronus' form. Tonk's change of heart changing her patronus gives us a glimpse of her change in understanding the celestial mysteries, a more personal connection to understanding the passions and sacrifices of Christ. Similarly, Harry's patronus is a stag, because he loves his parents even more for their sacrifices.

Chapter Nine: The Half-Blood Prince

As Professor Slughorn introduces his class to the more advanced potion concepts, he shows one concoction of Amortensia, a very powerful love potion. Here we have another theme, although less significant to the plot – that of obsessive love. In all aspects of the world and magic, love is not something you can truly force upon someone. Professor Slughorn seems to know a lot about obsessive love, even though there is never any mention of his personal life, but he is well aware of its power as he tries to explain it to his class. However, he is careful to explain the difference between an obsessive love and true love, another key theme in this book. Obsessive love does not let the beloved do what he/she wishes to do – the beloved must do everything the lover wants the beloved to do. However, in true love, the lover and beloved are seen more as equals, and each is allowed to make decisions, even if the decision is to leave. This love is the same love shown by God to the Israelites throughout the Old Testament and throughout history. In St. Augustine's explanation of the trinity, God is considered the lover, Jesus is the beloved, and the Holy Spirit is the love that passes between them.[93] With this understanding, God gives us free will to show that he considers us somewhat as equals, and not as something to be controlled – free to love or despise Him as we choose.

Another potion that resurfaces in this first potion's class of Professor Slughorn's is The Draught of the Living Death. This potion is mentioned first in Professor Snape's Potions class, but is spoken of throughout history and used in Romeo and Juliet to help bring about the union between two opposing forces. The Draught makes someone appear to be dead for three days – a clear reference to the three days Christ was in the tomb - and a Gnostic explanation for his revival/ resurrection. The fact

---

[93] Simmons, B, 2002, "Perhaps Augustine's most difficult work," retrieved from http://www.amazon.com/Trinity-Saint-Augustine/dp/0911782966.

that Harry is the only one able to create this potion, albeit with help from the mysterious "Half Blood Prince", again reinforces that Harry is the Chosen One to denounce Lord Voldemort and reunite the magical community. Furthermore, in creating the Draught, Harry realizes that he can't create it alone and takes the risk of using the suggestion from the book. The seven stirs counterclockwise then one stir clockwise works immediately, with no surprise – seven is the number of perfection, with an eight turn in a different direction (the number of a new creation) and a resting period to allow everything to settle.

After his win, Harry begins discussing his find with his friends, and we get a clue about Harry's true love. The "flowery smell" that Harry remembers from the dungeon turns out to be Ginny Weasley. This is the first indicator that Harry is falling in love with Ginny Weasley – the love potion smells like elements of the Burrow, and Ginny is the only one there that could attract Harry. The connection is also inevitable, given their names – Harry meaning King, and Ginny referring to Guinevere from King Arthur.[94]

Chapter Ten: The House of Gaunt

Harry finally has his first private lesson with Professor Dumbledore in his office, where they explore the past using the pensieve. Within the memory, Professor Dumbledore recognizes the Parseltongue, acknowledges that Harry can understand it, but never asks him to translate what is said. This indicates that Professor Dumbledore probably understands Parseltongue as well, even though he is not an heir of Slytherin, or understands it enough to get the gist without a literal translation. Along with the fact that he speaks Mermish and so many other languages, these elements help promote Professor Dumbledore's omniscience and again highlight his role of the Christ figure of the saga.

---

[94] Harry Potter Lexicon, "Ginerva "Ginny" Molly Weasley," retrieved from http://www.hp-lexicon.org /wizards/ginny.html.

Within the memory are a couple of interesting notes. One of the more subtle elements is in the names for this last of the Slytherin line – Marvolo, Morfin, and Merope Gaunt – are symbolic of the family tree's transformation. Marvolo, like the seven marvels of the world, is the father who represents the proud and brilliant past of the Slytherin family. Morfin, like the morphine his names comes from, is the son who does nothing for anyone or himself, and only lies around causing trouble and putting people to sleep (attacking them and making them unconscious). Merope, named after the seventh and most faded star in the Pleiades constellation, is the physically deformed daughter who similarly fades from view after producing Tom Riddle. Thus, we see yet another triangle of people Ms. Rowling created. A little more obvious, the names in this last remaining house of Slytherin blood show us both lunacy and family pride in this small family's doings. Proud of their heritage, the three are willing to forego everything else - wealth, work, love, etc. – as long as they stay pure and untainted by muggles.

The most striking symbolic element in the chapter is the withered snake on the door. This snake is an echo of the bronze snake that Moses puts on a pole to keep the Israelites from dying from snakebites (Numbers 21:7-10). The snake on the pole reminds the people that snakes will do them no harm, just as those who speak Parseltongue have nothing to fear from snakes. More telling, Marvolo Gaunt tells Ogden that he has no use for owls. Symbolically, since owls represent the wisdom of God, Marvolo is saying that he has no use for God or for wisdom, preferring rather to trust in his bloodline – perhaps a touch of pre-destination prejudice. Secondly, it could mean that he can't read and thus doesn't need the owls, or that he feels there is no one outside his family worth speaking to.

At last, we have the only reference to blood traitors outside the Weasley family – Marvolo Gaunt calls Merope a "blood traitor" for looking at a muggle, not because she has red hair. If being a blood traitor means not only being interested in, but also associating with, muggles, this again points to the Samaritan group as the allegorical group for "blood traitors" since the Samaritans (Israelites from the Northern Kingdom) in Jesus' time were a mixed-blood race of repatriated Israelites with other gentile nations in Israelite territory.[95]

Chapter Eleven: Hermione's Helping Hand

After dropping Care of Magical Creatures, Harry, Hermione, and Ron have a difficult time reconciling with Hagrid, but they all settle their differences once they understand that Hagrid is just upset about Aragog's declining health. Hagrid tends to introduce Harry to the creatures that will lead to his mastery of the phase or element, and even though Harry met Aragog in *The Chamber of Secrets*, this is Hagrid's introduction between the two. In the end, it is Aragog who creates the situation that helps Harry master his understanding of Lord Voldemort.

Chapter Twelve: Silver and Opals

A mystery arises about why Headmaster Dumbledore leaves Hogwarts for days at a time. Although in the past years we do have a day by day account of Albus Dumbledore's whereabouts, we do know that he goes to other places occasionally. Now that Harry is solidly within the white stage of his transformation, he is finally aware of how often the Professor leaves the premises. The Mormons have used the fact that Christ's history is not accounted for on a day to day basis in the Bible to suggest that He was making trips either around the world or around the solar system, going everywhere he could to help bring salvation to all souls. Knowing that Albus Dumbledore has a withered hand, we know that the times that he is not accounted for at Hogwarts is time that he is busy working on solving Lord Voldemort's past, to help with what he can and make Harry's life easier.

With Katie Bell in the infirmary, the trio is questioned by many people about what happened, and we see that Harry is quick to accuse Draco Malfoy of treachery, as part of a long line of other treacherous acts. As

---

[95] "Hatred between Jews and Samaritans," 2012, bible.org, retrieved from <http://bible.org/illustration/hatred-between-jews-and-samaritans> on June 12, 2012.

Professors McGonagall and Snape quickly squash his accusations, we see that Harry's illumination stage only applies to him. While in the sixth book, we are constantly reminded of Harry's white stage, but there is also a reference here to silver with the cursed necklace. There are seven alchemical metals in the transformation from lead to gold, and the sixth alchemical is silver. This is one of the few places where we are given such an obvious hint that Harry is in the sixth/ silver stage of alchemical transformation, showing his tarnishing as he is exposed to the Slytherins (water).

Chapter Thirteen: The Secret Riddle

Harry is surprised that Professor Dumbledore is back for their lessons since he was gone for so long, and is worried about Dumbledore's haggard and tired appearance. However, he still has time to meet with Harry and hear his thoughts, with patience. This is yet another attribute of God and Christ – they are never too tired to hear someone's prayers. Moreover, there are countless accounts in the Bible of Christ coming to the disciples in the middle of the night and healing long lines of invalids without ever complaining of being tired.

During their discussion, Harry tells Professor Dumbledore about what Mundungus has been stealing. From Dumbledore's response, we see that Mundungus' interaction with both Harry and Professor Dumbledore shows how much Mundungus obsesses about money and lacks morals about stealing things from his own friends. Biblically, J.K. Rowling is setting Mundungus Fletcher up as the Judas of the disciples –he is not concerned with what selling out on his friends will mean to the future of the world.

Once they finish with their catching up on what has been happening at Hogwarts, Professor Dumbledore shows Harry another memory of Tom Riddle's past. In the memory, we see how Tom Riddle grew up, and how similar it was to Harry's life – both were orphans, only had grey clothing to wear, both could do things that set them apart and made them feel alone. However, the differences are dramatic. Tom Riddle enjoyed being solitary, using his powers to coerce and enslave others, showing no love for others, and even demanding that Professor Dumbledore tell him the truth (showing no respect of authority or age). On the opposite end of the spectrum, Harry has never used his powers for anything but protection or in reaction to how he was treated, and he had love for anyone that showed him any kindness. He also never tried to hurt anyone, and despite his sudden wealth, he cherished friendship above all else and only used his wealth to help those who don't have it, knowing what it's like to not have any money. At the end of the chapter, Professor Dumbledore makes sure that Harry understands how different he is from Tom Riddle, but also indicates that the key elements that will help decipher what Lord Voldemort's plans are revolve around his lack of trust and friends, and love of hoarding.

Even as a young boy, we see that Tom Riddle's demands for the truth are very similar to the requests from Professors Snape and Dumbledore. Tom's requests are also surprisingly rude, especially in light of it being Professor Dumbledore's first encounter. However, these similarities seem to indicate that Tom can already read minds. An able mind-reader himself, Professor Dumbledore was able to block Tom's attempts and require Tom's attitude and behavior changes to remain with others of the magical community. For this invitation, Tom is indebted to Professor Dumbledore for naming and claiming him as part of the wizarding world, and thus Tom can never be greater than Professor Dumbledore.

One key insight into Tom Riddle that helps explain what drives Lord Voldemort is Tom's obsession and misunderstanding of death. For some reason, Tom equates being magical with being immortal. Although immortality with Christ is something that Christians do claim, the claim is not in the physical sense on this side of the grave – only in the spiritual sense on the other side.[96] With this common misconception and utter misunderstanding of the concept of "immortality," the conflict begins

[96] Miller, Dave, "Afterlife and the Bible," Apologetics Press, Inc, 2005, retrieved from http://www.apologeticspress.org/apcontent.aspx?category=11&article=1478 on 4 Jun 2012.

within Lord Voldemort. His failure to embrace love and community will prevent him from any spiritual transformation towards an immortal soul, so he will have to resort to physical means to create immortality.

The burning wardrobe that Professor Dumbledore chooses to demonstrate his power to Tom is also symbolic of the future hell that God creates for Lucifer. Since Tom Riddle is an allegory for Lucifer within the series, this is a bit of foreshadowing as well as the first warning from Christ. In another light, Dumbledore's requirement that the objects within the burning closet be returned to their owners reminds us of the burning bush through which God speaks to his servant and the baptism by fire that burns away Tom's old sins. However, without love or remorse for his actions, once the fear of retribution is gone, the person has not moved forward in his walk with God, since without remorse there is no path that leads to righteousness.

Chapter Fourteen: Felix Felicis

The placebo effect, where someone thinks he/she is getting a medicine that is actually nothing, is a very strong influence on the psyche. Many people feel that spirituality is a placebo effect, and the atheists would have you believe that humans created God to help us feel better about ourselves, explain our successes, and generate reason for guilt. However, since no one else has created anything else that has the same effect, either the reality of Christ and God exists, or the placebo is a special brand of sugar no one else can imitate. There are many religious placebos on the market, from people preying on faithful people, selling false icons, etc. However, the items themselves are not what generates the healing or other act – it is God who acts on the faith of the person using the object, whether the object is a placebo or not.

In this same vein, Ron's abilities as goalkeeper swing wildly, indicating that he is able to achieve greatness with time and confidence. These situations warrant a placebo – they give the person a reason to believe in themselves without fear of failure, and usually they succeed. Unfortunately, Ron's success is Hermione's failure. With Ron's success, he gets together with Lavender Brown, and Hermione is left out. This separation, however, is a key part of the transformational process, so Harry will get the full force of Hermione's thoughts for the next while.

Chapter Fifteen: The Unbreakable Vow

With the new arrangement of Ron with Lavender Brown and Hermione by herself, Harry tries to hide himself in his books to avoid taking any sides. The book he was supposed to read for Charms class, *Quintessence, A Quest,* is a bit of a paradox. From *Order of the Phoenix,* we learn that Quintessence is that element between the physical and spiritual plane, that place where Angels and dreams lie and why so many times we hear stories of people getting visions from angels in their dreams. However, as we also saw in the last book, it is very difficult to control what you dream about. With the symbol of the veil, we see further evidence of how difficult it would be to search for that element, since the physical tangibility of a veil is so thin. All of that aside, charms classes are about learning how to focus faith into the wand (God) and letting God work through us. Spiritually, we can put this together. A Quest for quintessence means working toward living constantly in the in between state –in constant communion with both the physical and the spiritual realms. Paul suggests we do this exact quest in Colossians 3:1-2 "Therefore if you have been raised up with Christ, keep seeking the things above, where Christ is, seated at the right hand of God. Set your mind on the things above, not on the things that are on earth" (NASB) and Thessalonians 5:17 "Pray without ceasing", (NASB) both of which indicate a life where we live above the purely physical realm although still existing within it.

After avoiding Professor Slughorn's parties for as long as he could, Harry ends up going to the Christmas party with Luna Lovegood. Running into Professor Trewlaney, Harry hears her insistence that Harry of all people should want to know the future, since he's supposed to be the "chosen one." On one hand, this echoes of Christ knowing what the Old Testament says of him (which he knows full well) and the fates prescribed for every man who would follow Him. (Matthew 5:10-11 (Sermon on the

Mount), Revelations 6:9 (Fifth Seal revealing those killed for the Word of God) and Luke 12:51-53 (family members divided against each other because of Christ)). On the other hand, reading into the prophecies denies both a person's free will and the concept that it is not for us to read the future for ourselves, since only God knows the future ("[Jesus] said to them: "It is not for you to know the times or dates the Father has set by his own authority, Acts 1:7, NIV).

Interrupting the party, Draco is dragged in as a party crasher. In the discussion that follows at the party, Harry notices that Professor Snape looks both sad and a bit afraid of Draco. Knowing that Draco is somehow behind the attacks, Snape is most likely saddened by Draco's lack of choice for his future since his father's failure required his service as retribution. On the other side, Snape is afraid of what Draco is trying to do, the ways in which Draco is failing and the collateral damage, and what Draco is turning into. It is possible that Snape sees a bit of himself in Draco – another person trapped in Lord Voldemort's world against his will. As such, he fears that Draco is entrenched in the dark arts deeper than Draco himself knows, but Snape is unable to help since Draco is also now an Occlumens.

Chapter Sixteen: A Very Frosty Christmas

After overhearing Professor Snape's conversation with Draco, Harry tells the Order his suspicions once he arrives at the Burrow for Christmas. Remus Lupin restates one of the main themes of the last half of this series - if you trust Professor Dumbledore, then you have to trust his judgment, meaning here that they have to trust that Professor Snape has good intentions. This can be a serious philosophical question – when we decide to follow Christ and trust in His judgments, can we trust every leader in the church? If we find someone who is rather dubious, do we give up hope on the whole church, or just that one person? Within the series, Ms. Rowling has made the point that although we cannot know the whole story, we have to trust that God has plans for all of us and will protect us in ways we cannot understand. Biblically, the verse is "And we know that for those who love God all things work together for good, for those who are called according to his purpose." (Romans 8:28, ASV)

Under false pretenses, Percy Weasley returns with Rufus Scrimgeour to The Burrow to allow Minister Scrimgeour to meet with Harry Potter. Rufus Scrimgeour's discussion with Harry shows the general opinion of the people: they want to believe that they are safe and will cling to anything that confirms their safety. I propose that Ms. Rowling's supposition here is that people innately want to believe that all is good in the world, especially if they are wizards. If that fails, then they hope all is good enough that they don't have to do anything extensive themselves.

To try and convince Harry to make people feel that the Ministry is doing everything it can, Rufus Scrimgeour tells Harry that he is a hero, whether or not he actually is one. This leads to a serious philosophical/ theological question: is being declared a hero just a placebo for the masses – a symbol of hope for everyone else, or is there a spark of reality? Despite the multiple references in the Bible to the wondrous acts of the prophets, Christ, and the disciples, through the years the masses have denounced many miracles, preferring social comfort and conformity to truth. This is a warning about what Christianity might become – a symbol of hope, that even with some failures, is only enough to keep hope alive but without any action behind the rhetoric. Again, this is a recurring theme in the series – Christianity is to be lived and practiced, not studied in the theoretical sense.

This conversation between Harry and Minister Scrimgeour is also representative of the early Christians' bitter relationship with the Sanhedrin. The Sanhedrin wanted Jesus's disciples to work with them and keep quiet about Jesus (Acts 4:1-22,) but the disciples disagreed with the Sanhedrin's direction, which eventually caused a complete separation between the Jews and Christians. In the series, both Professor Dumbledore and Harry have avoided agreeing with the Ministry, which leads to multiple confrontations and an obvious split in leadership. From Professor Dumbledore and Harry's perspectives, the Ministry is not interested in the truth, but rather the appearance of truth and righteousness.

As one last analysis of the interview, we see that J.K. Rowling is also poking fun a bit at those who have religion, but not spirituality. Those who have a true relationship with Professor Dumbledore have spirituality, a true relationship with Christ. In direct opposition, those who just follow the rules of the ministry have religion. In Jesus' time, he saw many people who were careful to abide by the law, but miss the message within the law as pointed out in The Good Samaritan parable. While the Jewish authorities were more interested in pursuing the religious aspects of Judaism, Jesus stepped to the side of the law to help anyone who would listen about warming their hearts for God and creating that relationship that fosters spirituality. As we saw at the beginning of *Half-Blood Prince,* as long as Harry is with Professor Dumbledore, he has no fear of anything. He knows he is safe (Psalm 23).

Chapter Seventeen: A Sluggish Memory

At the next lesson with Professor Dumbledore, we are reminded that Professor Dumbledore forgave Tom Riddle's past and allowed him to have a clean slate going into Hogwarts, a favor Tom probably never forgets. This also shows a truth of Christianity – with or without remorse, people are always given a second chance to turn over a new leaf first through baptism, then through confession. Although others might not fully trust someone who betrayed their trust, they are still given a chance to prove themselves as are all at Hogwarts. Further descriptions of Tom Riddle's life at Hogwarts bring up a key element about being Christian – attending church and jumping through the right hoops does not give someone physical immortality. Rather, being a true Christian shields the truly transformed soul from hell in the spiritual world beyond.

In the last memory Professor Dumbledore shares with Harry through the pensieve, we see Tom Riddle getting information from Professor Slughorn through sleek politics. First of all, Tom gives the Professor his favorite candy – candied pineapple, a symbol of hospitality. His affinity for the pineapple also reiterates his obsession with appearances and the material aspects of life. Secondly, the fact that Tom Riddle knows things even before Horace Slughorn and seems more knowledgeable than most of the Hogwarts staff shows that his legilmens abilities are already fully honed and being used to Tom's advantage.

Chapter Eighteen: Birthday Surprises

Ron's confusion on his birthday leads to his eating Harry's love-potioned sweets. Through the antidote and following celebration, Ron's life hangs in the balance as yet another life is accidentally threatened by an unknown attacker. Harry is able to save his life, but Harry has now saved three Weasleys from death. Three being one of the complete numbers, most likely this is the end of what Harry can do in the lifesaving arena for the Weasley family.

Chapter Nineteen: Elf Tails

Harry's suspicions and worries about the "big picture" outside of Hogwarts almost make him forget about his favorite game – quidditch. Although Quidditch was an important element for both Harry and Draco in the first three books, now that Lord Voldemort is in the picture, there are more important things than the small-sided games with only momentary gains like Quidditch. From Paul's first letter to the Corinthians, we are reminded: "When I was a child, I talked like a child, I thought like a child, I reasoned like a child. When I became a man, I put childish ways behind me" (1 Corinthians 13:11, NIV), exemplified here as the two of them have moved on to the worries of the adult world.

Chapter Twenty: Lord Voldemort's Request

As Harry meets again with Professor Dumbledore, we see a bit of the history of Tom Riddle as an older person. Within the memories and discussion, there are a couple of interesting tidbits and parallels. First of all, the previous headmaster, Armando Dippet, had the same initials as Albus Dumbledore – AD, again a reference to a Christ figure as the shepherd leading the sheep at Hogwarts, even though the headmasters before that had other initials, just as prophets and judges came before Christ.

Secondly, if Professor Dumbledore is a fabulous legilmens, we have to ask why he doesn't obtain the memory from Horace Slughorn himself. My suspicion is that although Professor Dumbledore could use both his persuasion and his legilimens to obtain the needed memory from Horace Slughorn, he allows Harry to fight that battle for a couple of reasons: 1) Professor Dumbledore respects his relationship with Slughorn and does not want to force anyone to do something he doesn't want to do, even if it is for the best for all concerned; 2) Professor Dumbledore needs Harry to learn how to win information from people so that he's prepared for when he's by himself; and 3) Professor Dumbledore knows that information freely given is better than information extracted from someone.

Throughout this exchange between Harry and Dumbledore, we see a couple of smaller instances of input from house-elves. Dobby helped Harry discover the inner workings of the Room of Requirement, a room that Professor Dumbledore never truly understood for what it was. Since Professor Dumbledore was always a brilliant student who did the right thing, and as an adult his wand always did everything he needed it to, there was no need to hide a mistake and thus he never discovered the Room of Requirement. The second house-elf relationship, the relationship between Hepzibah Smith and her house-elf, showcases the differences between the masters who demonstrate the Biblical understanding of how to treat slaves (Colossians 4:1, "Masters, provide your slaves with what is right and fair ", "Do not threaten them, since you know that he who is both their Master and yours is in heaven, and there is no favoritism with him (Ephesians 6:9) and Leviticus 24:53 "Do not rule over them ruthlessly, but fear your God.") and the dominating relationship that the Malfoys showed to Dobby. One thing to note – only the oldest families have house-elves. Perhaps this is a suggestion that having servants is an old fashioned idea, especially in a magical household where magic can do most of the work for them.

In the discussion that results between Professor Dumbledore and Tom Riddle, we are reminded that an important theme in the Bible is the importance of a name, and who gives the name. The fact that Professor Dumbledore refuses again to give in to Tom Riddle's requests and acknowledge his new name shows that Professor Dumbledore does not acknowledge any new powers, status, or following beyond his own. Biblically, this follows God's abolition of Lucifer from Heaven: Lucifer was one of God's three arch angels, just as Tom Riddle was a top student at Hogwarts (Head Boy, Award for Service to the School). However, Lucifer felt he was an equal to God, and thus should be allowed to split the Kingdom or take it over, and he had one-third of the angels on his side, ready to lead a revolution. As a parallel, Tom Riddle explores the Dark Arts and learns about elements that only Dumbledore knows about, and with this knowledge, Tom begins to plant a new regime leading one-third of the students of Hogwarts to his side. Lastly, with Professor Dumbledore's dismissal of Tom when he comes looking for a job to begin his takeover, Tom's group of Death Eaters are permanently evicted from Hogwarts' business.

The main reason Professor Dumbledore refuses to allow Lord Voldemort to teach at his school is because the re-made Tom Riddle doesn't understand the key to all magic: it is the amount of love, faith, and hope in the wizard that determines the strength of the wizard, and the wand responds to that power of faith. Lord Voldemort might have gone beyond the realms of normal dark magic, but only because most other wizards have morals that prevent them from crossing completely over to the dark side. Even Lord Voldemort's insistence that he is there for Professor Dumbledore to command is only a cover, since he says beforehand that he is mostly interested in sharing his knowledge with the students.

Chapter Twenty-one: The Unknowable Room

As Harry continues to put the pieces together that shows that Draco is up to something, we can sense Harry's frustration that no one else can understand what he can sense going on around him. What's the point of illumination if you can't share it or no one else understands? This is one of the reasons why there are communities of faith – so that each person has other people to share insights and experiences with that might understand them. I suspect that this is the same frustration that Jesus felt during his life when he would tell the disciples something and they didn't seem to understand what he was saying at all.

Chapter Twenty-two: After the Burial

Harry's success from giving in to the simple but unknown solution of using Felix Felicis and not trusting to his own devices is what happens when we finally give over a problem to God – everything goes right. Harry had already tried many times to get the memory from Professor Slughorn, and Professor Dumbledore knew that Harry had the Felix Felicis (a "liquid luck" potion) when he asked Harry to obtain the memory. This request could have been a test to see how long it would take Harry to understand that he needed to trust in God's direction, especially since Dumbledore likes to have Harry work things out for himself. The lesson Harry learns here is that God can see things that we can't see, and when we trust in God, He will lead us in the right direction even if it seems insane at the time.

Chapter Twenty-three: Horcruxes

With the memory fresh in hand, Harry goes to see Professor Dumbledore and learns about Horcruxes. Through the memory, we finally get to see what Tom Riddle's game plan is for immortality without love. His inability to love is perhaps the result of his father not truly being in love with his mother when Tom was conceived, but it could also have been that Tom sees love as the element that destroyed his mother, since she would rather have loved and lived poorly than possess something and lived well. Whatever the reason, Tom cannot move beyond the physical realm and thus is poised to do whatever possible to use the magic that he knows to create the immortality he's always felt belonged to all magical people.

Once he discovered that magical people could die physically (the only type of existence he ever acknowledged), he researched everything he could find, using all means necessary (asking the librarian questions then reading her mind if she wouldn't answer them directly) to derive a plan for immortality. The Horcrux idea he discovered is literally *"the golden cross,"* translated from the French words *"or"* meaning "gold," and *"crux"* meaning "cross." Just as the wooden cross, with all of its imperfections, meant death for Jesus Christ, the "golden cross" would provide protection from death through its cold imperviousness to decay of any kind and by extension, protect the person that controls it. Understanding Lord Voldemort's obsession with all forms of protection from death, the Horcrux is a natural obsession for Lord Voldemort and his ultimate plan for eternal life in the physical realm.

Knowing the significance, perfection, and magic of the number seven, Tom decides to put all of his trust in the combination of the number of perfection joined with the darkest magical force, the Horcrux. Metaphorically, since Tom refuses to achieve the spiritual transformation that requires love as Dumbledore professes and through which "rules" the magical community, Tom had to go a different route to take control. It's hard to tell if his plan at this time is to rule, just become immortal, or become immortal so that he can rule the magical community without impunity.

Dumbledore's description of how Tom Riddle has changed over the years, especially in the eyes is the concept from *The Picture of Dorian Grey* that the soul is mirrored in one's appearance. Also, remembering that the eyes are the mirror of the soul, Tom Riddle's slow transformation and decent into evil shows in his eyes as he transforms/ transfigures from a handsome boy into an albino snake. In this transformation, his eyes become snakelike, which mirrors his soul's transformation from mortality to a loss of mortality, without immortality. In folklore, there are tales of dragons becoming immortal by removing their hearts and placing them under guard in a secluded place – in other words, they create a horcrux.

Once again, Professor Dumbledore reminds Harry of his differences from Lord Voldemort. In his discussion about why Harry has a desire to thwart Lord Voldemort, he brings up that whenever someone defeats another, the "winner" knows the defeated will want revenge for the actions until death of either party. Similarly, if the snake had never spoken to Eve in the garden and she and Adam had never eaten of the apple, then there would never be any enmity in the world. However, as it is, Eve and Adam were tricked by the serpent, and we are thus constantly on the watch for Satan to show himself or any opportunity to return ourselves to God's graces and restore harmony to humankind.

A second element that Lord Voldemort underestimates is Harry's purity, as described by Dumbledore. After Harry's neglected and abusive childhood, his sole desire is to be part of a wider community and family that love him. His love for others and desire for love in return makes him a sponge for all that is good, and a talisman from absorbing anything evil, the absence of love. However, since evil is the absence of love, it absorbs love too readily. just as warmth is fire to someone extremely cold. In truth, love burns that which is all evil, making love undesirable to those who chose evil. In conflict, heat will always thaw the cold, following the second law of thermal dynamics: heat always flows from a warmer to a cooler body. From this idea, we could also theorize that if God is love, then if everyone is collected unto God when they die, the fires that the evil ones feel are the fires of warmth to an extremely cold soul.

By the end of the conversation with Professor Dumbledore, Harry finally comes to realize the difference between fate and free will, which is both an important theme in the series and an important distinction in Christianity. Primarily, we serve others, love others, and fight evil because we choose to, not because we are required to. Secondly, Christians serve God not for revenge against Lucifer for all the past doings, but to help and protect those around us from any future harm from evil. Thus, we are not dragged to church, but we go willingly to learn how to defend ourselves and others against Lucifer. This is also why Kingsley Shacklebolt suggests later in *Deathly Hallows* that everyone put protections on muggle houses nearby: Christians can and should protect others, not just their own community. In doing so, Christians will help lessen Lucifer's power on the world as a whole and bring about peace.

Chapter Twenty-four: Sectumsempra

After weeks of wondering what *sectumsempra* does, Harry finally gets the chance to use it. Unfortunately, the curse creates more damage than he could possibly imagine. When used, the mark of this curse is a cross shape which horrifies Harry for a few reasons: 1) something he did hurt someone else, regardless of who it was; 2) the cross is a mark of sacrifice and death, not something he would wish for anyone other than himself; and 3) everything the Half Blood Prince had shown him so far were good spells that helped him, and this is the first one that showed a darker side to his unknown benefactor.

On a deeper level, this interaction between Draco and Harry is the crux of Draco's reformation. Through this scene of Draco talking to himself and Moaning Myrtle in the mirror, we see how far Draco has come in his understanding of which Lord Voldemort is, and how much he wants out of his bondage. Overcome with anxiety about the consequences of what will happen when he fails Lord Voldemort, Draco attacks Harry when Harry discovers him in the bathroom. In defense, Harry uses an unknown curse, supposedly "for enemies" that almost destroys Draco. The words "sectumsempra" means "supreme cut" in Latin, meaning the ultimate, transformational act and takes the shape of a cross. Draco survives through Snape's help and concern, and Harry puts away his most recent source of insights and information forever. Although not an overt change, Draco is definitely a changed man after this event. After recovery, Draco has a very bold cross emblazoned on his chest, a constant reminder of the death he avoided just as Harry has the musical cross burned on his forehead as a constant reminder of his own escape. Rather than trying to take Harry down, Draco seems worried about saving his own skin and not doing any more damage around him. With Christ's permanent mark now on Draco, Draco's mindset changes quietly and he is no longer able to raise his wand against Harry or anyone else in the series.

On a different note, we see a more symbolic element of Snape through this scene. Harry has gotten to know the "Half-Blood Prince" pretty well, and they all agree that his little spells and charms are very handy. As Harry goes through the book, however, he notices that the thoughts get darker, ending with "Sectumsempra." After using the curse, Harry feels much remorse, and so hides the book that caused the pain. This relationship between Harry and the book parallels Snape's relationship with Lord Voldemort. At first, the Dark Arts and Lord Voldemort's vision might have seemed benign, and Snape idolized Lord Voldemort for his insights and abilities. However, as Lord Voldemort drew Snape into ever darker events and thoughts, Snape eventually caused the one unforgiveable pain (death), so he changed his mind about Lord Voldemort's intentions and turned against him.

Chapter Twenty five: The Seer Overheard

In a hurry to see Professor Dumbledore, Harry runs into Professor Trelawney muttering to herself in the hallway outside the Room of Requirement. From her mutterings, Harry finally figures out which room Draco is using and figures out his plan. Professor Trewlaney's repeated prediction about the lighting-struck tower (the Astronomy Tower), calamity, and disaster is one of the few predictions that is correct. In a way, Professor Trelawney represents all of the past prophets, where many predictions are questionable or for another time, but some of them do speak to the present time accurately.

Professor Trewlaney gives Harry another insight about his particular prophecy that reminds us of the other side of the Good Shepherd story – that of the separation of the sheep and the goats (Matthew 25:31-45 (NIV)). Albus Dumbledore only says that he is friendly with the barman, never telling Harry that the barman is his own younger brother. Despite the unacknowledged connection between Albus and his brother

Aberforth, Aberforth still does what he can to protect his brother and tells him about Severus Snape's snooping. Perhaps Aberforth (the goat herder) only interfered because he needed to protect his brother from Lord Voldemort, but here we hear that Aberforth is a bartender. As such, he can theoretically serve food and drink to all, although we have seen that his bar is not very hospitable.

In a last ditch effort to protect his friends from the plan he is sure Draco is carrying out soon, Harry hastily gives them the Felix Felicis to share. Professor Dumbledore won't be around, and Harry won't need the potion since he'll be with the professor. Similarly, when Christ departs from this world, he sends the Holy Spirit to protect his followers (the paraclete), and those who walk with Christ have nothing to fear (Psalm 23). Although unasked for, the friends accept the Felix Felicis willingly when given, just as we should accept the Holy Spirit, regardless of how unprepared we might be when offered.

Chapter Twenty-six: The Cave

As with all the books, as Harry leaves Hogwarts with Professor Dumbledore, Harry is becoming separated from everything – magical community, friends, Hogwarts, and now even the Invisibility cloak which Professor Dumbledore says he does not need. However, whereas in all the previous books Harry's rescue is through a Christ symbol, here Harry is with the Christ figure himself, Professor Dumbledore, so Harry has more protection than he's ever had before. The remainder of this chapter and the events following parallel the passion narrative, with other mythological references to add symbolism to the events as they unfold.

As soon as the duet enters the cave, we begin to collect more information about Lord Voldemort. As they enter the cave through raging waters and sharp rocks, we see Lord Voldemort's modus operandus – intimidation of others. As Dumbledore reminds Harry, for muggles without knowledge of Christ or something beyond this life this scene would have cowed them into obedience to anything Lord Voldemort wanted them to do. Lord Voldemort knew that if a person were frightened enough, he/she would do anything requested, leading that person into despair and destroying their hope in any relief from their fear.

However, the omniscient, Christ-like Professor Dumbledore can sense that magic has occurred in the cave (a talent few people have, if any beyond Dumbledore). Knowing that Lord Voldemort has used this cave in the past alerts them to the secrets and symbols of death hidden within the cave. For instance, before they can access the inner chambers, Dumbledore remarks about the simplicity of the payment required for entrance, meaning that the payment is one of an ancient style (a blood sacrifice) and not a more modern understanding of payment. This requirement of a blood sacrifice for entrance to the cave is both a reference to the pre-Canaanite demands for blood sacrifices as well as the beginning of Christ's total blood payment for the final sacrifice through his passion and suffering to come.

Although many of the characters take on different Biblical roles throughout the series, Harry finally takes on a very distinctive discipleship role at the cave – that of St. John the Evangelist. Through the years, Harry's relationship with Professor Dumbledore has grown ever stronger, and everyone recognizes Harry as "Dumbledore's favorite/ beloved student." Secondly, beyond being the beloved student, he is now the only student to travel with Professor Dumbledore through the remaining elements of the passion, just as St John was the only disciple that was with Christ through his torture and subsequent death on the cross. (John 15:18; John 19:26). As St. John, Harry's future becomes a bit clearer with the upcoming events.

As we follow Harry and Professor Dumbledore into the inner chamber of the cave, we see the parallels to Christ's prayers in the garden and discussions with Pontius Pilate. Just as those scenes give us insight into Christ's mission and reasons for his suffering death, here we gain insight into the two main reasons why Dumbledore shares this horcrux-finding experience with Harry. First, Dumbledore alone is able to understand the depth to which Lord Voldemort goes with his enchantments. Since this is the first horcrux we readers are allowed to help find, it is hard to determine whether all of the horcruxes are as well protected or this is a unique situation, and we would side with Harry in our angst that the other horcruxes might be as well protected. Thus, Harry has to learn all he can about debunking Voldemort's dark magic so he can succeed in future endeavors to obtain horcruxes. Secondly, because of Dumbledore's skill and knowledge of his upcoming death, he is singular in his ability to act sacrificially in the cave and beyond for Harry and the rest of the wizarding world. The number of enchantments around this one horcrux seems on a much grander scale than the protection around any of the other horcruxes we've seen to date. Perhaps that is why Professor Dumbledore chose this opportunity to not only get the horcrux but fulfill the sacrificial requirements to protect Harry from the worst of the enchantments. Knowing to what depths Professor Dumbledore goes to help Harry on his quest to defeat Lord Voldemort imbues Harry with strength, courage, and steadfastness to continue when all seems lost.

One of the themes we are reminded of at the water's edge is also one of the biggest challenges for many Christians: to believe in the invisible. However, it is the belief that makes some elements visible, or if not completely visible, it might at least be tangible as shown here with Harry and Professor Dumbledore's ability to find the guide for the boat that will take them to the island and the unknown. In believing it was there, they were thus able to find it. In response to Harry's question about why the professor knew to look for an invisible object, Professor Dumbledore explains to Harry that since Dumbledore molded Tom's magical ability, he knows how Tom does things. Similarly, God knows us because he knit us together in the womb (Psalm 139:13: "For you created my inmost being; you knit me together in my mother's womb" (NIV)).

As a continuation of the symbolism of death surrounding the cave, J.K. Rowling has included this boat scene in the cave that rings of the Greek's underworld and Arthurian legend. In Greek mythology, a boat crosses the river of the dead (Styx), which is full of the dead souls, eager to exchange their lost soul for one that still has a connection to the physical world. The ghostly boat ride over a ghostly lake is also a very Arthurian concept, although King Arthur only sailed to the land of Avalon after his demise. In another reference to mythology, the souls of those aboard in Egyptian mythology are weighed, and only those of fully grown hearts are counted. Likewise, Lord Voldemort's boat only registers a full wizard's magical ability, as if a full wizard were the only soul that would be worth counting. In addition to the repetition of the "cave of death", this adds to Lord Voldemort's prejudices and is also a reference to the age theme that it's not the age that matters. Rather, wizards/ people can make significant change to the world around them no matter what their age (or magical race), and Harry and his friends prove this again and again.

As Dumbledore drinks the potion, we begin to see the Passion Narrative more clearly as references to other myths and legends fade. The potion here not only echoes of the drink of the underworld that makes one forget the physical realm, but it also has significant implications for the passion of Christ. First, when Christ goes to the Garden of Gethsemane, he prays that God not make him drink this cup, but "not my will, but Thine be done." Secondly, although Harry might be younger, only Dumbledore can drink the cup to save everyone, just as Christ was the only one equipped to drink the Cup of Salvation for all humankind. In this, Harry plays St. John, who is the only disciple to watch Christ suffer, but he also plays humankind's part in requiring Christ's passion for our sins and separation from God. Third, Professor Dumbledore has to drink twelve cups to empty the basin – one for each son of Israel, and thus sacrificing himself for all the children of God. After drinking the cup, in essence, completing Dumbledore's torture, Dumbledore is no longer able to stand by himself and needs help, just as Christ needed help with the cross after his floggings. As much as Harry loves the Professor, he is unable to prevent the suffering that only Professor Dumbledore could endure.

As further analogy to the Passion, Harry's inability to fight off the inferi (dead people who have been brought back to life with Dark Magic) while Professor Dumbledore is in his delirious/ weakened state amplifies our inability to fight off death without Christ's help, but it also echoes of the dead walking around after Christ died on the cross. In Jewish thought, all souls went to Sheol, and it wasn't until the last judgment that the good were separated from evil. Here, the inferi souls belong to Lucifer, and are thus afraid of love, warmth, and light, especially that which comes from God/Christ/ Dumbledore. In true form, Harry has just fought with Lord Voldemort again in an underground structure, and Christ has saved him from death.

In the Passion narrative, Christ is battered, bruised, and forced to walk quite a ways to Golgotha. In this parallel, after their return to Hogsmeade, Professor Dumbledore is obviously "battered and bruised" from his ordeal in the cave, and whereas Dumbledore has always provided the protection, here it is now Harry who must carry that burden, just as it was Simon the Cyrene who had to carry Christ's cross for a while on the way to Golgotha.

Chapter Twenty-seven: The Lightning Struck Tower

Continuing the parallel, Harry leads Professor Dumbledore to Hogwarts, where they see the Dark Mark over the "Lightning Tower." The Dark Mark over the Tower is a symbol of Golgotha, literally "the Place of the Skull", where Dumbledore knows his death awaits, and a death has not yet occurred. Just as Golgotha is at the top of a hill, the Astronomy Tower (where lightning struck it years ago) is one of the top points at Hogwarts and Hogsmeade. Similarly, along the way to the tower, just as many disciples watched Jesus as he walked the slow road to Golgotha ready to help him if he stumbled or fell, Harry stands guard near Professor Dumbledore, ready to help him if he needs it until they reach the tower.

Once in the lightning tower, Draco Malfoy shows everyone what he's been up to, secretively bringing Professor Dumbledore's enemies to his sanctum. Thus, Draco plays an unwilling Judas – not eager for the death of Albus Dumbledore, but feeling pressured with the fear of death upon himself if he fails to turn Christ over to Death and the Death Eaters. It is an interesting depiction of Judas, with remorse for everything he's done, and Christ with love and vision beyond the physical realm of what Draco is. At the end of Draco and Professor Dumbledore's discussion, we see the ultimate turn of events as Professor Dumbledore says "No, Draco, ... it is my mercy, and not yours, that matters now." (HBP, p. 592). Truly, it is Christ's mercy on Judas' soul that will determine whether or not Judas' soul is saved or not, not Christ's physical body that depends on Judas's physical compassion.

After Draco's apparent submission to Dumbledore, the Death Eaters arrive to complete the Passion Narrative with their taunts and jeers at Dumbledore, who takes it all as meek as a lamb led to the slaughter. Severus Snape appears, and just as Christ speaks then gives up his spirit, Professor Dumbledore speaks to Snape, who then unwillingly takes Dumbledore's spirit using the Killing Curse. Through all these harrowing events, Harry Potter, invisibly frozen to the spot, is thus helpless to act in the ensuing demise of Professor Dumbledore. He watches, horrified, just as St. John the Evangelist did at the foot of the cross as the executioners disarm Christ, jeered at him, then killed him and as we all do whenever we retell the story in the church on Palm Sunday.

Chapter Twenty-eight: The Flight of the Prince

Understandably, Harry is both angry and frustrated with Professor Snape, since it is obvious to everyone now that Severus was showing his allegiance with evil and Lord Voldemort, having killed the best defender and wizard of the magical community. With the clarification that Severus Snape is the Half-Blood Prince, Harry becomes confused as he had seen and defended this man against many others, and yet it turns out to be the man Harry despises most in the world. As for Severus Snape, his bravery at the moment is tremendous – not only did he have to kill a great friend, Professor Dumbledore, but he now has no one to confide in except his mortal enemy, Lord Voldemort, and thus the game of trust and lies begins.

Secondly, we can understand Harry's frustration again with the discovering that the locket they retrieved from the cave is not the true horcrux but a fake, leaving more questions than answers. However, it also symbolizes the disciples' frustration with the death of Christ. At the moment of Christ's death, everything Christ had ever tried to achieve with them and the community seemed lost. In following Christ, these disciples had defied the Jewish authorities, left their families, and have suffered losses in the businesses they left before following Christ, and now it was all for naught. In the series, this same loss is felt not only by Harry, but acutely by the Order of the Phoenix, who had placed their trust in both Dumbledore and Snape and now one was dead and the other found to be a turncoat.

Chapter Twenty-nine: The Phoenix Lament

Kneeling next to Dumbledore's body, Harry is unwilling to move away from the one man who meant everything to him. In a symbolic gesture, we see the Arthurian connection between Harry and Ginny, as Ginny is the only one who can move Harry from his immobility and disbelief at the loss of Dumbledore.

Although everyone's sadness exhibits itself in different ways, the song of Fawkes, the Phoenix, mourning the death of Professor Dumbledore is an echo of the song of Creation, just as in the Narnian chronicles Aslan's song creates Narnia and the Song of Creation sings everything into being. Now, with the loss of Dumbledore, his spirit is carried away through Fawkes' flight, singing its song until its ascension into Heaven. Just as Christ's spirit was with us for forty days after his resurrection and then he was gone forever, Fawkes sings for forty minutes, then all is quiet. Harry feels abandoned, as I'm sure the disciples did first after Christ's death and then again by the ascension into Heaven. Despite his loss, Harry has all the training Professor Dumbledore could give him, and he is alchemically and spiritually ready for the final battle on his own.

Alchemically, with the death of Albus Dumbledore, we have the beginning of the end of the white stage, especially since Albus means "white" in Latin. The red stage, as we saw with the beginning of the black and white stages, won't begin until there is another juxtaposition of opposites (Harry and Lord Voldemort joining together in some fashion) and a short golden phase. Whereas the black stage was finished with a single death (Sirius Black), the white phase will include three "white" deaths, as will the red stage since 1+3+3=7. In this "limbo" at the end of the *albedo* (white stage), we will also see echoes of the Passion that end the white stage, just as the illumination of Christ's life seemed to end with Christ's death.

Chapter Thirty: The White Tomb

Throughout the series, we have been journeying with Harry as he masters the five elements and completes the three stages needed alchemically to achieve immortality. These have been the seven steps guiding him forward, but with the introduction of the Horcruxes, Harry also needs to sever the bonds that are connecting him to the physical earth through Lord Voldemort – the seven horcruxes. The horcruxes, one for each house (representing the four elements) and the three additional horcruxes that represent Slytherin will have to be destroyed in order to achieve a true bridge for humanity to connect with Christ and sever the bonds of death.

As Harry thinks about the path that Professor Dumbledore put him on, he realizes that it will be a lonely path, and one he does alone, ultimately. Similarly, in life, we are alone on our path – the narrow path that God and Christ put us on to follow with only a few signposts, and not much else. Many times, we do not realize how few directions there are until we have to forge ahead alone, just as Harry is beginning to realize at the funeral.

At the funeral, we hear two clear opinions from J.K. Rowling. The first is a chiding that J.K. Rowling makes about the fickle public. She notes through Harry that when things were tough, there weren't that many that defended Professor Dumbledore to the public, just as the fickle public changes its attitude towards every famous person based on the news. Alternately, when an event is popular or something big happens, then many people suddenly are good friends, and making a show of support, just as the Ministry of Magic pretends to be a Dumbledore supporter, even though everyone knew the Ministry didn't get along with Professor Dumbledore. The other opinion is more a call to arms: "It [is] very important, ... to fight, and fight again, and keep fighting, for only then could evil be kept at bay, though never quite eradicated..." (*Half-Blood Prince*, p. 644.) It is difficult to fight a known, losing battle, but just like the squeaky wheel that gets oiled, eventually it gets attention. It is also easy to exhaust oneself in a fight if fighting alone. However, if we fight as a community, as in a relay, victory is more easily accomplished. When one person ends a turn, the others can fight and eventually as a community, they can win the fight. Fighting regardless of the opinions of others was something that Dumbledore was able to do well, and sets an example for all of us.

At the end of this book, we see that Harry thinks he has a clear vision of what he needs to do to accomplish the mission set before him from Dumbledore: collect the Horcruxes and finish what Professor Dumbledore started. Harry remembers something that Dumbledore said to him - that Professor Dumbledore will only be truly gone when everyone has forgotten him. Remembering this, Harry devotes himself to carrying on Dumbledore's mission while going away from the flock to fight the battle in safety.

Chapter TEN

The Guide to *The Deathly Hallows*

Plot Summary: This concluding book in the series begins with a meeting of the Death Eaters at the Malfoy Manor. The twelve Death Eaters and Lord Voldemort sit around the dining room table discussing how disgusted they are by the interbreeding of the pureblood wizards with muggle-borns, wizards cursed with being a werewolf, and how wizards should be taught that muggles were to be loathed and controlled with Lord Voldemort at the helm. Meanwhile, Charity Babbage, the wizard who taught Muggle Studies at Hogwarts, hangs in midair as a tortured centerpiece. Concerned about the twin cores of his wand with Harry's, Lord Voldemort demands the use of Lucius Malfoy's wand, leaving Lucius empty handed. At the conclusion of their meeting, Lord Voldemort kills Charity Babbage and allows Nagini to feast on her.

Back at Privet Drive, Harry Potter reads the obituary about Albus Dumbledore while the Dursley family packs to leave and go into hiding. Only through Dudley's insistence do they finally leave with a couple of wizard guards for points unknown. Shortly thereafter, thirteen wizards arrive to help Harry escape from Privet Drive through the only means not monitored by the Ministry – the air. Six of Harry's closest friends drink

Polyjuice potion to become Harry's twins, and they all depart in pairs into the air to various heavily secured points around London. Each of these points in turn has a portkey to transport them finally to The Burrow and safety. During the escape Mundungus gets scared and disapparates, leaving Mad-Eye Moody behind to face Lord Voldemort alone. Harry, with Hagrid, is able to fend off a few Death Eaters, but Hedwig is killed and Lord Voldemort finds him right before he gets to safety. Magically, Harry's wand performs its own magic back at Lord Voldemort, again repelling the Killing Curse and destroying Lord Voldemort's wand. Back at the Burrow, twelve wizards return in pairs, and Lupin reports that Severus Snape cursed off George's ear, leaving an irreparable hole. The last pair, Bill and Fleur, report that after Mundungus panicked when he saw Lord Voldemort, the Dark Lord killed Mad-Eye Moody right away.

The next day, preparations ensue for Fleur and Bill's wedding, set for the first part of August. During that time, Harry celebrates his seventeenth birthday, which marks his ascendance to majority and the right to perform magic without punishment. The Minister Scrimgeour appears with the gifts from Albus Dumbledore's will to the three friends: to Ron, the deluminator; to Hermione, the *Tales of Beedle the Bard*; and to Harry, both the Sword of Gryffindor (which he is not allowed to keep) and the first snitch he ever caught. Later, at the wedding, Harry meets many older wizards who have unfavorable reports of Albus Dumbledore's life and he begins to doubt his friendship with the Professor.

At the conclusion of the wedding, Kingsley's patronus appears, announcing the fall of the ministry to Lord Voldemort and warning them that the Death Eaters will be arriving at the wedding momentarily. Harry, Ron, and Hermione disapparate to Tottenham Court Road, where they attempt to figure out where to hide. They finally decide to stay at 12 Grimmauld Place, and after ensuring that Death Eaters were not in the place, they set up camp at the old headquarters.

While at Grimmauld Place, the trio tries to determine the location of the real locket horcrux after figuring out that Sirius's brother, Regulus, took the original locket. After much persuasion, Kreacher tells them the story of his involvement in placing the locket in the cave, and he brings back Mundungus Fletcher who took the locket from Grimmauld Place when Sirius died. The trio eventually made friends with Kreacher, while they planned how to get the locket away from Delores Umbridge at the Ministry. After school began again September first, they made their attempt.

At the ministry, the trio is split up unwillingly. Harry goes to Umbridge's office where he finds Mad Eye Moody's magical eye and removes it; Ron tries to end a weather spell in someone's office, and Hermione ends up taking notes for the court proceedings with Delores Umbridge. All three eventually meet at the courtroom, where Harry comes out of hiding. Now exposed, they grab the locket from Umbridge, and parade the rescued muggle-born wizards out of the court halls. However, as they try to escape, Yaxley grabs hold of Hermione's ankle. With the protective spell broken, the three leave Yaxley at Grimmauld Place and they continue on to an empty campground. Ron was splinched (part of him was left behind) during the disapparition, so Hermione tends to Ron then places all the protective enchantments around the campsite while Harry sets up the tent.

Harry, Ron, and Hermione camp for a few weeks, always moving from place to place, doing what they could for food, and taking turns with the locket, since the presence in the locket seemed to have a negative impact on the bearer. After a while, Ron is tired of being hungry and cold, and he leaves Harry and Hermione to return to the wizarding community.

While Ron is gone, Harry and Hermione try to find other possible locations of the remaining horcruxes with no success. They finally decide there must be something in Godric's Hollow, which they visit on Christmas Eve. At Godric's Hollow, they find the Dumbledore family graves, the Potters' graves, and the symbol for the Deathly Hallows on the grave of Ignotius Peverell. Once they leave the graveyard, they notice that they are being followed by Bathilda Bagshot, an old friend of Albus Dumbledore, who invites them to her house. Warned by ill omens at her house, they discover that Bathilda Bagshot was actually Nagini in a dead body. Hermione rescues Harry from Nagini's clutches by using a blasting curse that allows them to disapparate right as Lord Voldemort arrives to the house. Harry's wand is broken in the process, so he uses Hermione's wand for his watch that evening.

During Harry's turn at the night watch, he sees a doe patronus just outside the borders of their protective charms. Curious about who might be nearby, he follows it to a frozen pond where he finds the real Sword of Gryffindor. Diving in after it, the locket begins to strangle Harry. Just as Harry was convinced he was going to drown, Ron saves Harry and is able to free the sword as well. Harry finally figured out that he needed to use Parseltongue to open the locket, so he opened the locket, and Ron then uses the sword to destroy the locket. Although it is a happy reunion for Harry and Ron, Hermione is not happily reunited, despite Ron's story that the light from the Deluminator went inside of him and took him to their tent when he heard their voices.

Reunited, Ron, Hermione, and Harry pursue the horcruxes with new vigor and decide that perhaps the strange symbol in Hermione's book is a clue they must follow. The clue leads them to Xenophilius Lovegood, who explains to them the history of the Deathly Hallows and the significance and uniqueness of the elements. However, Mr. Lovegood is no longer a strong supporter of Harry Potter now that his daughter, Luna, has been abducted from him, but the trio is able to escape just as the Death Eaters come to capture Harry and his friends.

After more camping and Horcrux searching, Harry accidentally uses Lord Voldemort's name, a taboo, which brings the snatchers to their tent and breaks through all the protective enchantments. They are taken to the Malfoy Manor where Hermione is tortured for being a mudblood, but Harry is disguised enough that Draco surprisingly doesn't tell the Death Eaters who Harry is. Harry and Ron are then put in the dungeon where they find Mr. Ollivander, Griphook the goblin, Luna Lovegood, and Dean Thomas held hostage. In despair, Harry pulls out his small mirror for comfort and seeing an eye, asks for help. Suddenly, Dobby appears, and Harry is able to convince Dobby to take Dean, Luna, and Mr. Ollivander to

Bill and Fleur's Shell Cottage. Hearing the noise, Peter Pettigrew is sent to investigate, but when his silver hand realizes that Peter was intending to kill Harry, the silver hand acts of its own accord and strangles Peter, despite everyone's efforts to release the grip. Once Dobby returns to the Manor, Harry, Ron, and Dobby then walk out of the dungeon, battle with Draco and Bellatrix (winning their wands), and Dobby then takes Harry, Ron, Hermione and Griphook to Shell Cottage. Bellatrix threw a dagger at them as they disapparated, killing Dobby.

At Shell Cottage, Harry buries Dobby, then together with Hermione, Ron, and Griphook devise a plan to break into Gringotts for horcruxes after Harry discovers more about wand allegiance from Mr. Ollivander. During their stay at Shell Cottage, Remus Lupin arrives to announce the birth of their baby, Ted, and after Fleur's careful attention, the Manor hostages' wounds are healed.

The trio and Griphook then disguise themselves (Harry using the cloak with Griphook on his back), get into Gringotts, and are able to break into Bellatrix LaStrange's vault where they are sure another horcrux exists. Although they find the Hufflepuff Horcrux, Griphook takes the sword and turns against them, so the trio resorts to releasing the guard dragon and escaping on it. Once free of Gringott's, the trio race against Lord Voldemort to Hogwarts for the final horcrux.

Upon their arrival at Hogsmeade, they set off a curfew charm but are rescued by Albus Dumbledore's brother, Aberforth, who shows them a secret entrance to Hogwarts through a painting at Hogshead. The pathway leads them to the Room of Requirement, where many students are hiding from Lord Voldemort and his followers at Hogwarts. Many other former students and members of the Order come through Hogsmeade to help Harry, assuming that he has returned for a fight. Harry, Ron, and Hermione enlist their help to determine what the horcrux from Ravenclaw might be, and while Harry is looking for it, Ron and Hermione destroy Hufflepuff's cup with a basilisk fang.

While looking for the final Ravenclaw horcrux, Harry and Luna alert McGonagall and the rest of Hogwarts that Lord Voldemort is coming. With the reinforcements coming from the Room of Requirement (via Hogsmeade), the underage wizards are returned to Hogsmeade to safety and everyone else takes up defensive positions around the castle, mobilizing every object in the castle.

Lord Voldemort and all of his allies position themselves around the castle and after a call for Harry Potter as a truce, begins an all-out attack. Meanwhile, Harry discovers that the Ravenclaw horcrux is the diadem that he remembers from when he last used the Room of Requirement, and Ron and Hermione visit the sewer to use a Basilisk fang to destroy the Hufflepuff horcrux. Reunited, the trio searches the old Room of Requirement for the diadem, but just as they find it, Malfoy, Crabbe, and Goyle arrive to relieve them of it. During the ensuing battle, Crabbe creates “Fiendfyre”, an enchanted and extremely dangerous form of fire that consumes everything as if it were alive. Crabbe and the horcrux die in the fire, but Harry, Ron, and Hermione are able to rescue Malfoy and Goyle from certain death. On their way downstairs, a huge blast destroys a major section of the castle, and Fred is killed.

Nagini is the last horcrux, so the trio goes in search of Lord Voldemort to find his location. Interestingly, Severus Snape is with Lord Voldemort, discussing the Elder Wand. Lord Voldemort, not understanding the true nature of the wand, kills Snape to ensure the allegiance moves to Lord Voldemort. With the wand in hand, Lord Voldemort leaves to return to the castle and kill Harry. Harry goes to Snape to see what he can do, but Snape only insists that Harry take his memories and go to the pensieve before dying.

In the pensieve, Harry discovers that Snape has always been in love with his mother, Lily, and did everything he could to save her from Lord Voldemort’s planned execution of her once he realized Lord Voldemort’s true nature. When Lord Voldemort killed her, Snape, full of remorse, became Dumbledore’ s strongest ally in keeping Harry safe and protecting him from Lord Voldemort. Harry also hears the discussion and reasons behind why Snape had to kill Dumbledore, and everything Snape endured in his dual nature of trying to protect Harry and Dumbledore's students while pretending to be a Death Eater. Lastly, Harry hears Dumbledore tell Snape that when the time is right, Harry has to let Lord Voldemort kill him, since Harry is the last horcrux, and this alone will finally remove Lord Voldemort's ties to immortality.

Numbed and enlightened by this exchange, Harry dons the invisibility cloak and goes to the forest to face Lord Voldemort and certain death. As he enters the forest, he speaks to the snitch from Dumbledore, and the snitch opens to reveal the Resurrection Stone. With the stone, Harry is reunited with his parents, Sirius, and Lupin, who walk with him, promising never to leave him. Once they reach the Death Eater's encampment, Harry finds that Hagrid has been taken hostage, but he removes the invisibility cloak, dropping the stone at the same time. Lord Voldemort speaks the Killing Curse, and Harry apparently dies.

Harry finds himself in a white station, alone, naked, with the only sound being moans from an unidentifiable, mangled baby-like creature. Things begin to take shape, Harry is suddenly clothed, and Albus Dumbledore appears. Harry and Dumbledore talk, and Dumbledore tells Harry he can choose to go on or return. Harry decides to return, and finds himself in the forest again, and everyone is worried about what happened to Lord Voldemort.

Unsure of what transpired, Lord Voldemort calls to Narcissa Malfoy to determine whether Harry is dead or not. She feels his beating heart, but rather than give him away, asks if Malfoy is still alive. Harry tells her he is, and she declares that Harry Potter is dead. Hagrid is made to carry Harry out of the forest, where Lord Voldemort announces to the castle that he killed Harry as Harry was trying to escape.

Neville speaks against Lord Voldemort, who tries to make an example of him by placing the sorting hat on his head and setting it on fire. Instead, the Sorting Hat delivers the Sword of Gryffindor, extinguishes the flames, and Neville uses the sword to kill Nagini. The house-elves come out of the castle armed to do battle, and the centaurs come out of the forest, bows drawn to fire on Lord Voldemort's followers. Amidst the chaos, Harry jumps up and dons the invisibility cloak.

The battle continues into the Great Hall, where eventually Bellatrix is killed and Harry and Lord Voldemort circle around in a discussion. Harry points out that the Elder Wand now has allegiance to Harry, and that Lord Voldemort's magic through that wand is not binding. Harry also tries to get Lord Voldemort to show some remorse for his actions, since that is what would return Lord Voldemort to a human state, but Lord Voldemort renews the attack instead. As Lord Voldemort issues a Killing Curse, Harry speaks a disarming charm, so Voldemort's curse rebounds on himself and his wand leaves his hand and goes to Harry. Lord Voldemort is dead.

In the epilogue, we see the resolution of many of the relationships. Harry and Ginny Weasley have married, and they are sending their middle child to Hogwarts for the first time. Ron and Hermione have also married, and are also sending their daughter to Hogwarts. Harry remarks that there has been no trouble since that last Battle, since his scar hasn't hurt in a long time.

END OF SERIES

Author's Note of Explanation: As the seventh book of this series, *Harry Potter and the Death Hallows* reminds us of Easter during the Early Christian years. With Jesus' death and ascension fresh in their minds, and the dangers of persecution from all sides ever around them, the Early Christians worked in secret, trusting no one, but doing what they could to collect followers. Because of Jesus' resurrection, they also believed that they shared in that resurrection since the bond to death had been broken. This is still what is celebrated today on Easter morning – since Christ rose from the dead, we too shall rise. (Romans 8:11: "And if the Spirit of him who raised Jesus from the dead is living in you, he who raised Christ from the dead will also give life to your mortal bodies through his Spirit, who lives in you.") Throughout the book, we see the various persecutions and trials of the early Christians, including martyrdom, but it concludes with the resurrection of the everyday Christian, just as Christ has promised to those who follow him and believe.

Prologue:

The two thoughts presented in the prologue of *The Deathly Hallows* are reflections on how the physical death of Albus Dumbledore does not require an end to his existence. From the two parts of the prologue, J.K. Rowling seems to be supporting the "spiritual" resurrection argument for Christ, which states that Christ's death was necessary to enable him to dwell within each of us spiritually and commune with us, thus immortalizing him. Essentially, this is a retelling of Professor Dumbledore's line that he will only truly be gone when no one is loyal to him anymore: "help will always be given at Hogwarts to those who ask for it" (*Chamber of Secrets*, p. 266).

Chapter One: The Dark Lord Ascending

As the final book begins at the Malfoy Manor, JK Rowling uses subtle symbolism to drive home that the white stage has not quite yet ended and that Lord Voldemort's evil has strengthened his hold on humanity and the wizarding world. As we follow Snape onto the grounds of Malfoy Manor, we see the white peacock, reminding us of the white stage of the alchemical process, but we also see the yew hedge, symbolizing the Malfoys' fears of death. The yew is said to be resistant to death since it is impervious to rot, and so it is used to stand guard in graveyards all over England. Here, it is used both in defiance of death and symbolic of their home being a graveyard, a foreshadowing and nod to the symbolic death to come through Lord Voldemort soon.

Following Snape into the Malfoy's dining room, we are again reminded of the alchemical colors as Snape's eyes meet Lord Voldemort's, perhaps as a non-verbal exchange takes place. The three occlumens together represent the three different colors and ideologies represented in the alchemical process: 1) the black eyes of Professor Snape who divides his time between Professor Dumbledore and Lord Voldemort and renounces the evil he embraced before; 2) the red eyes of Lord Voldemort representing his ideologies of purification and battle, and 3) the white/blue eyes of Professor Albus Dumbledore, representing illumination. Although these three people are never in the same room, their abilities to read others' minds centralize them to the alchemical story and forward the plot's action.

As the Death Eaters mock the werewolves, Lord Voldemort and the Death Eaters show their true natures. Although Lord Voldemort is doing all he can to encourage and bribe the werewolves, giants, and dementors to join him in his efforts to take over the wizarding world, the Death Eaters have no desire to share any equity with them. Although there isn't any discussion about the relationship between the two races, this show of disgust about the werewolf's interaction with wizards indicates that the other races are being used only for the purpose of keeping them from siding with Harry Potter, not out of any true interest in their future. Adding to the insults, in discussing the husbandry of the wizarding stock, Lord Voldemort twists Jesus' statement about God's people being his branches, and how as the gardener, God will cut off any branches that don't produce fruit and prune those that do (John 15:1-4). Lord

Voldemort acts as if he were God, responsible for trimming the tree of the branches that don't produce "pure-blooded" fruit. With Albus Dumbledore gone and the reign of evil in both wizarding and muggle worlds, it is as if Lord Voldemort has apparently taken over as the modern day anti-Christ figure.

A more subtle event at the table is the change in the Malfoy family's attitude towards Lord Voldemort and their realization of the realities of serving the Dark Lord. First, Lord Voldemort demands Lucius's wand, saying that Lucius won't need it anymore. Symbolically, the wand represents the wizard's connection to the tree of Christ and the power of God (John 15:5). Thus, Lord Voldemort's statement subtly tells the Malfoys that they are being cut from the "pure-blood" tree, even as Lord Voldemort uses them as hosts. Secondly, the Malfoys only seem to communicate with each other and not with the other Death Eaters, another signal that they are separating themselves from the rest. Lastly, with Draco's terror at Lord Voldemort's questioning him, Draco shows that he is truly remorseful for his family's involvement in the Dark Arts, a continuation of his parallel as Judas' reincarnation.

As the chapter closes, we witness the gruesome and heartless murder of Charity Babbage. John Granger points out here that Charity Babbage's name aptly describes the situation at the Malfoy manor as per the old hymn – "where charity and love prevail, then I am in the midst." Without charity, there is no love or God, as there is no love within Lord Voldemort or his followers.[97] Again, this points to the feeling of the anti-Christ running the wizarding and muggle world.

Ms. Rowling also uses this obscure connection of charity representing God to echo the passion of Christ, but from a different point of view. There are three key disciples that had a significant interaction with Christ during His passion and death. In *Half Blood Prince,* we see the passion and death from St. John's point of view, through the eyes of Harry Potter. In this scene, we see Severus Snape in his role as St. Peter during the

[97] Granger, J, 2010, *The Deathly Hallows Lectures*, p. 14.

passion of Christ – that of denial. As Charity revolves slowly, she calls to Severus twice to help her, and both times he turns his head as if she wasn't there. The third time, she is only able to look at Snape, and again, he averts his eyes. This threefold denial echoes the words of Christ: "before the rooster crows twice, you will deny Me three times." (Mark 14:30, NKJV). To further the analogy, Snape is sitting with the Death Eaters, just as St. Peter was outside the gates with others who denied Christ during his questioning. The third disciple, Judas, also had a significant role, but that is yet to come in the novel. In this chapter, Ms. Rowling is giving a bit of foreshadowing that Severus Snape is St. Peter, meaning that he is not the one that betrayed Jesus to the Sanhedrin, but is/was a good friend who is there to lead the followers in safety.

Chapter Two: In Memorium

In the article that Harry reads about Albus Dumbledore's life, he discovers that Aberforth, Albus' brother, had a proclivity for goats. Up until now, we have heard very little about Albus Dumbledore's brother, since the two do not have much to do with each other. This reference to goats is another hint that Albus Dumbledore is the Great Shepherd and that Hogwarts is the sheepfold for Christ's followers. In the Biblical book of Matthew, Christ gives a parable about the division of the sheep from the goats, the sheep being those who helped Christ, and the goats being those that never saw him to help him. (Matthew 25: 31-46) As events unfold, we learn more about Aberforth, his relationship to Albus, and their paths toward their respective callings: Albus to the education of the new generations to come, and Aberforth to the feeding and watering of all of come to Hogsmeade.

Chapter Three: The Dursley's Departing

In this final chapter with the Dursleys, it is interesting to note that the Dursleys, after all of their not believing in magic, have finally come around to at least an agnostic point of view of God. At a minimum, they are acting very Pascalian by at least taking measures to assure their safety regardless of what they feel the truth is. Whereas an atheist believes that no God exists, and thus there is no reason to worry about the afterlife, an agnostic is unsure. To help these unbelievers, Blaise Pascal created Pascal's Wager to try to convince both of these groups to at least act as if there were a God to "hedge their bets." According to the wager, if one acts as if there is a God and he is right, then all is well and the person is rewarded with heaven. If he is wrong, then nothing happens. However, if one acts as if there were no God and there is a God, then the person will suffer eternal damnation, and if there is no God, then nothing happens. Either way, it is better to believe in God and act accordingly so as to avoid the eternal fires. Having finally sensed what that type of eternity might be with the help of the dementors' attack two years before, Dudley understands the importance of moving as if there was magic, and thankfully his parents follow en suite.

Chapter Four: The Seven Potters

John Granger points out that Harry's Polyjuice potion turning gold tells everyone that Harry has mostly transformed his inner metal,[98] although he has not fully completed the transformation since it does not produce an elixir of life. Harry has now mastered the four base elements and the astral plane (the fifth element), and the mercury and sulfur that are both corroding and healing his inner metal are almost congealed as one.

Multiplying Harry into seven Harrys is another means of both showing the oppositional nature of Harry and Lord Voldemort. Whereas Lord Voldemort divided his soul into seven pieces to solidify his bodily survival on the physical earth, Harry's body is multiplied to protect his soul from death. Furthermore, whereas Lord Voldemort's division of his soul has transformed him into only a fragment of a man and mostly a symbol of evil, Harry's multiplication has transformed his soul into gold, as shown by the Polyjuice potion. Again, the Bible verse: "For whoever wants to save his life will lose it, but whoever loses his life for me will find it." (Matthew 16:25)

---

[98] Granger, J, 2010, *The Deathly Hallows Lectures,* p. 56.

The escape from Privet Drive resembles the scattering of the disciples after Christ's death, each member representing apostles while also completing the white phase of Harry's transformation. Within Harry's own flight are three significant elements that give important insights into the storyline, the opposition, and themes of the series. Alchemically, Hedwig's unfortunate death during the escape from Privet Drive is alchemically the second white object to die in the closure of the white stage. Far from feeling that he understands everything (white stage), Harry is beginning to battle his own feelings as he loses hope and faith in everything around him (red stage).

With Albus Dumbledore gone, Harry is now the key player to oppose Lord Voldemort and as the Dark Lord appears next to Harry, we see how the two measure up against each other. Lord Voldemort's ability to fly shows that he has mastery over the physical air, and his thoughts about his talents show his understanding about two of the other three elements: earth (using unicorn blood and snake venom to create an "elixir of life" of sorts while he waited for his "rebirth"), and water (control over the basilisk), but no mastery over fire. The opposition between the two is heightened by their similar abilities, but Harry has a spiritually transformational understanding of the elements, whereas Lord Voldemort only has an understanding of power and the physical transformation of elements.

The last piece reiterated here and throughout this last book is the power of the wands, a major theme throughout the series. As Lord Voldemort and Harry's wands meet, their connection makes a gold bond, showing the completion of the white stage. The fact that Harry's wand moves of its own accord shows that the wand has its own "mind" and abilities, above and beyond Harry's. As a recall to Ollivander's words when Harry received his wand, the wand chooses the wizard, symbolic of God choosing us as his own. As such, God will defend his people and do what is necessary to protect them. This important theme within the series - God looking out for his people - is a critical element of Christian belief today.

Chapter Five: Fallen Warrior

After the detour through the Tonks' house, Harry and Hagrid arrive at the Burrow and await everyone else's safe arrival. Despite claims that J.K. Rowling never mentions God in the series, she makes mention and references to Christian aspects many times in this book, much as the early Christians became more overt amongst themselves to profess Christ's providence and love for each other. Seeing George return hurt but alive, Harry acknowledges God's providence by giving Him thanks directly. Although the Christian themes have been very covert throughout the series, this is the first overt mention of God in the series.

Making light of the loss of his ear in his flight from Privet Drive, George alludes to his stand-in for Saint George, a martyr after declaring his allegiance to Christ and the patron saint of England.[99] As such, we begin to see the twins as the representatives of all saints and martyrs of the church. The loss of the ear from Snape's wand work also shows us how the mass escape from Privet Drive is also reminiscent of the short skirmish at the Mount of Olives. Judas betrayed Jesus with a kiss, and Peter cut off the slave Malchus' ear in an attempt to prevent Malchus and the soldiers from taking his master, Jesus. (We find out later that Severus Snape is indeed the Peter figure in the series – the rock that holds the keys to Hogwarts once Christ/ Albus Dumbledore is gone, and the one who slices off George's ear to prevent the Death Eaters from killing the Harry-twin flying on the broomstick.)

As the complete story of the escape from Privet Drive unfolds from the various reports upon each group's arrival, we see the third significant role during the passion – that of Judas during the passion. This third replay of Christ's passion is a reflection of the reactions of the apostles after Christ died, just as the first replay was the individual's reaction and the second was from the opposition's point of view. The Early Christians and disciples were persecuted for following Him and the flight from Privet

---

[99] Catholic Online, "St. George," Saints and Angels, retrieved from http://www.catholic.org/saints/saint.php? saint_id=280.

Drive shows their dispersal and reunion after his death. In the escape, we see that Mundungus plays the role of Judas, the thief who betrays all of them and causes the death of an important figure, Mad-Eye Moody. During their escape, Harry shows himself as St. John again, and Severus Snape is again playing the part of Peter, cutting off an ear of someone at the Mount of Olives.

With the passing of Alastor Moody, the third and last of the symbols signaling the end of the white stage (Alastor being similar to alabaster, a white substance), Harry's emotionally painful transformation through the white stage is complete. In typical stage transformational fashion, the gold connection between Lord Voldemort's and Harry's wands symbolizes completion and commencement as well. Knowing the significance of numbers, we know that if there were two deaths already (Albus Dumbledore and Hedwig), and we are subsequently not surprised to hear about Alastor Moody's death. Whereas in the white stage everything is very clear and the path easy to follow, Harry's new stage is punctuated with doubt about who he is, who Albus Dumbledore is, and what he should do. Nevertheless, with the closing of the white stage and the return of Harry's scar pain, we realize that Lord Voldemort stayed out of Harry's mind during the white stage completely – allowing Harry to think clearly while he was training and learning everything he could.

As the remaining twelve now stand at The Burrow toasting Mad Eye Moody, we see the new central core of the Order of the Phoenix members: Harry, Hermione, Ron, Bill, Molly, Arthur, Lupin, Tonks, Kingsley, Fred, George, and Hagrid. Similarly, the original twelve had to keep redefining themselves to keep the mission moving forward as some were martyred or died for other reasons. Fleur is there and shares in the experience, but is never truly a member of the Order. These twelve go on to continue the original Order's work: thwarting Lord Voldemort, wielding the only weapon they can – Harry Potter.

With the chapter's closure, J.K. Rowling begins the red stage of Harry's transformation in the series, but she also initiates the black stage of this book. Alchemically, we see the signs of the renunciation: Harry is beginning to withdraw from his friends and family in order to keep them safe as he attempts to leave and complete his mission alone. As the black stage begins and the red stage of purification/ reunification and battle begin, Harry also begins to lose faith in Albus Dumbledore since he is no longer available to communicate directly and answer his questions. Rather, he finds, unwillingly, that his enemies might have some answers he needs for his own survival.

Chapter Six: The Ghoul in Pajamas

The discussions that surround the safety of the headquarters of the Order of the Phoenix bring to light an interesting point about the spells that were cast by previous wizards. Whereas Mad-Eye Moody's spells did not die when he died, many other spells disappear as soon as the person who cast them dies. Similarly, there are many churches that arise based on the interpretations of one particular person, or that person's charisma. These churches are very strong as long as the pastor is around to preach and visit, but as soon as the pastor leaves or takes a vacation, the attendance drops tremendously. Just as the spells that focused on the safety of others are able to live on once the casting wizard has deceased, churches or organizations that are based on a generalized attitude or strong belief are able to survive from one pastor to the next, forming a never ending bond.

Up until now, Harry keeps focusing on how much his fight with Lord Voldemort only involves himself and his own sufferings. He only vaguely recognizes the sufferings and ordeals others go through to side with him against Lord Voldemort. He finally understands the bigger picture in Ron's bedroom, where Hermione and Ron set Harry straight once again by showing him the extent they have gone to help him in his quest against evil. Resigned to having his friends by his side until the end, Harry finally agrees and they move on to discussing how to destroy the horcruxes.

As the three discuss the horcruxes, Hermione's explanation of how a person loses any connection to the horcrux after it's made (from information she obtained from Dumbledore's office) brings to light how similar the horcruxes are to past sins. Just as remorse is required for forgiveness from sins, horcruxes can only be "unmade" by having remorse for having created it. Both of these actions will reunite the soul, leading the person to a true reconciliation with God. Some might scoff at the concept of confession and the subsequent reconciliation and what it might appear to be for unremorseful souls, just as the Death Eaters scoff at the concept of remorse for their actions - even Dietrich Bonhoeffer agreed that confession was a necessity for the soul.[100] This concept is initiated by 1 John 1:9: "If we confess our sins, he who is faithful and just will forgive us our sins and cleanse us from all unrighteousness." False remorse actually indemnifies the soul more than lack of remorse, but both of them will result in the same torn soul. For Lord Voldemort, who personifies the connection between mortality and humanness, this ability to feel emotion no longer exists, and thus he has very little hope of reuniting his soul to itself (let alone God) when the time comes.

One last point that arises within the conversation in Ron's bedroom continues with Hermione's explanation of how horcruxes work and how Ginny was possessed by the diary horcrux. Since possession is caused by getting too emotionally close to a horcrux, this points to an interesting metaphysical viewpoint of J.K. Rowling's about "form" and "matter". The "matter" is the vessel in which the soul's form takes, a concept Rowling explores in her third book with the Animagi and the converse concept taught in the Catholic Church with transubstantiation. (The animagi are a transfiguration – change in matter, not form, whereas the transubstantiation is a change in form, not matter.) In truth, anytime someone spends more time with an object than with other people, that object will become ever more sacred to that person until it is as if his soul were carried within it. As it is written in Luke 12:34: "Where your treasure is, there your heart will be also."

---

[100] Bonhoeffer, D, 1966, *The Cost of Discipleship*, p. 284.

Chapter Seven: The Will of Albus Dumbledore

Harry's seventeenth birthday is a significant event in many ways. Beyond the normal magical allowances made to the wizard who has finally made the age of majority (and his freedom from the "trace") are many Christian symbolic elements. To begin with, as Ron gives Harry his birthday present, we see two important symbols joining Christianity and alchemy together – the number twelve, and gold - both representatives of the end state of Harry's white stage of illumination. The continual gold and purple references also point to the beginning of the red stage – the reunification, purification, and battle stage.

Secondly, the objects Minister Scrimgeour gives to the trio from Dumbledore's will provide additional symbolism for Harry's birthday. Despite the mistrust the Order members have for the Ministry, again paralleling the Early Christian mistrust of the Sanhedrin, Rufus Scrimgeour delivers the objects from the will to their proper owners. The three gifts willed to the trio are symbolic of Christ deputizing the trio into their representational parts of Christ. To Hermione, who represents the mind of Christ, the book represents knowledge or the mind of Christ. For Ron, the deluminator represents the spirit and light of God, given with the hope that Ron will remember Dumbledore when he uses it. In a way, this is a foreshadowing that Ron might forget about the mission Dumbledore gave to him, but if someone is lost and loses his or her way, that person must remember Christ who will again show them the way. (John 14:16 "I am the way, the truth, and the life.") As Minister Scrimgeour hands Ron the deluminator willed to him from Professor Dumbledore, Ms. Rowling also reminds readers that Professor Dumbledore was the Christ figure in a different way – Christ was the only one to have been able to create a light in the darkness and have power over who is allowed to see the light. As the deluminator is passed on to a devoted follower, it symbolizes taking the light into the world, and is both a blessing and a light to see Christ's path by: Matthew 5:14: "You are the light of the world." The third gift, the snitch, given to Harry as the embodiment of the body of Christ, represents the physical search for God and doing His will. The challenge to the trio from these gifts is figuring out how to use each of the three together on their journey to defeat Lord Voldemort.

Lastly, Harry's heated argument with the Minister echoes various events that occurred after Christ's death. Primarily, we see the differences of opinion that stood between the disciples and the Sanhedrin after Christ's death. On a more distant thought, although not exactly fifty days after Dumbledore's death, the gifts given that send the trio out into the world come far enough after Dumbledore's death that they echo the Holy Spirit descending upon the disciples in the Upper Room on Pentecost. Hereafter, their journey is upon them as they use their given gifts to help carry out God's plan of Salvation without the help of the Ministry.

Chapter Eight: The Wedding

Normally in a story, a wedding signifies the ending of a long drawn out plot. However, the wedding between Bill and Fleur is both an ending and a beginning. In *The Deathly Hallows Lectures,* John Granger points out that this wedding is the alchemical wedding between the red king (red hair) and the white queen (Fleur's white Veela hair). Thus, their wedding symbolizes the ultimate end of the white stage and the beginning of the great battle between good and evil. [101] However, on a Christian level, there is first the Biblical concept of a marriage presented during the ceremony: "the two shall cleave and become flesh" and "what God has joined together, let no man put asunder." (Mark 10:6-9) as the couple are married. On a more philosophical level, on the Christian's walk, this wedding shows the doubts that arise for every Christian at the ending of their conversion as two separate people, but the beginning of their journey together.

Beginning Harry's descent into wondering what truth is, Viktor Krum tells Harry what he knows of the history of the "Dark Symbol" that Xenophilius Lovegood is wearing. We see that Xeno Lovegood is wearing

---

[101] Granger, J, *The Deathly Hallows Lectures*, p. 55.

the Deathly Hallows, but Viktor Krum is convinced it is a symbol of dark magic since the dark wizard Grindelwald burned it onto the walls of Durmstrang. During their conversation, Viktor brings up Gregorovich, the wand maker who had foolishly advertised that he had the Elder Wand. The name points to St. Gregory, a saint revered in the Catholic and Orthodox churches who was one of the Cappadocian Fathers that finalized the church's understanding of the trinity as one nature with three essences after proving the oneness of God.[102]

At the wedding reception, Harry meets with many older wizards who have very different opinions of Albus Dumbledore and further Harry's questioning of who the man really was. Ms. Rowling writes "Did Doge really think it was that easy, that Harry could simply *choose* not to believe?"[103] This is one of those deeper questions that the various theologians have tried to answer: how does someone believe in something without already having all of the answers; and how does someone continue believing when the answers given do not paint a picture of perfection? This is another theme in the later books – does accepting Christ mean everything is so perfect we avoid death altogether? J.K. Rowling clearly answers "no" to this question, both in the fact that Tom Riddle's mother died despite her magical status, and in the fact that even martyrs have bad days that might make someone question their beliefs. Perhaps it is the tarnished version that is a better picture, since finding another scar or scratch then doesn't make someone lose their faith in the overall community and purpose. Assuming that something is perfect and has to be either perfect or nothing sets a costly stage. For many people, this implies that Christ can't still exist as soon as they find a flaw in the plan. Having only had the perfect, pure version his whole life, Harry is now struggling with viewpoints that show more humanness in

---

[102] "Cappadocian Father," *Encyclopedia Britannia*, Encyclopedia Britannia, Inc, 2012, retrieved from http://www.britannica.com/EBchecked/topic/94102/Cappadocian-Father 4 Jun 2012.

[103] Rowling, J, 2007, *Harry Potter and the Deathly Hallows*, p. 153.

Dumbledore that he never thought existed. Can he still believe in the overall plan despite the small problems he sees?

In contrast, after Professor Dumbledore's death, Rita Skeeter is trying to publish the "truth" as she sees his life, pursuing other angles to highlight Albus Dumbledore's humanness rather than his divinity. From Rita Skeeter's quick write on his life, she focuses on the mistakes to excuse her from having had a good relationship with him or Harry Potter. On the flip side, the apostles had the opposite issue after Christ ascended to heaven. They needed to write their memories and a plan for other Christians to follow when they themselves passed on. What exactly should be passed on to future generations took centuries to compile, and many outsiders were suspicious that the disciples only put in their own perspectives to make Christ more divine than what he was, leading to much external controversy about the New Testament.

Chapter Nine: A Place to Hide

Harry, Ron, and Hermione's run from Lord Voldemort and the Death Eaters seem to echo early Christians' attempts to stay hidden from Rome and their persecutors. As Harry watches Lord Voldemort's reactions to their escape through his mind, Harry has begun to understand Draco Malfoy and senses Draco's conversion. Now that Draco has seen Lord Voldemort for what he truly is, Draco is not emotionally a Death Eater anymore. Draco seems to value life in everyone now, regardless of their parentage, and is terrified by the lack of compassion he witnesses in Lord Voldemort.

Chapter Ten: Kreacher's Tale

Back at Sirius' home, the trio has a bit of breathing room to try and figure out a game plan by themselves. During that time, they find that Sirius' room is decorated with Gryffindor colors, signifying his conversion to Gryffindor from Slytherin. In the bigger picture, it also represents the family's alchemical transformation: Phineas Nigellus (the first Black in the lineage) begins as lead through his initials (PB), and by the time Sirius and his brother Regulus grow up, they see the truth and shun Lord Voldemort and all those who think along similar lines. Sirius is the juxtaposition, joined with James Potter, that begins the final transformation to create gold, and since Harry is Sirius's foster child, Harry then completes the transformation to gold.

As Harry and Hermione discuss Albus Dumbledore's life while at Grimmauld Place, the parallel of Harry representing St. John comes into play once more. Having been with Jesus as a young man (about 20 years old), John had a very different relationship with Jesus than the other disciples did. As St. John grew older, he probably heard many other stories about Jesus that were probably false that would have made Jesus seem more human and not be the same person St. John thought him to be. Again, Rowling brings up her theme of "choose what to believe", which is a very difficult thing to do.

After some time, the trio finally finds a clue in the house that helps them along their journey. Examining the house in detail led the trio to find the name Regulus A Black on one of the bedroom doors, and this answers their question of who RAB was and what happened to the locket. At the end of Kreacher's tale about the locket, Hermione explains both how house-elves think, and the trio come to understand and sympathize with the house-elf. From the explanation, we realize that the name Kreacher, is a re-spelling of the word "creature", who represents all of God's creatures. Whereas the wizards of the magical community has wands and some magical abilities, house-elves and other magical creatures have different rules. Since they can perform a different form of magic they are able to perform magic that wizards are not allowed to do, such as apparate into an unplottable house. Their loyalties are to those who show them kindness, and not to their masters' goodness. Similarly, although God created all the other animals, there is no record of their Plan for Salvation, and perhaps there is little need of one since they did not violate God's rules in the Garden of Eden. Thus, they are not judged by what they do and do not worry about their fate as humans do.

Chapter Eleven: The Bribe

In the short excerpt the Daily Prophet publishes from the new memoirs of Albus Dumbledore, we hear what happens when non-magical people are born into wizarding families. Rita Skeeter reports the shame magical families would share when one of their members was born without magic and how the squibb (a non-magical person) would be hidden or sent into the muggle world to try to learn how to live without the magical community. In our Christian world today, a child of Christian parents who decided to scorn God and live without his Christian community would probably not face the same type of ridicule. Rather, many would continue to try to help him see the light. Moreover, the fault would most likely be found with the parents and not the child himself.

Chapter Twelve: Magic is Might

With the advent of the beginning of September, we see connections on different fronts. First off, now that it is September 1st, the action of the year is about to begin with Harry, Ron, and Hermione embarking on their infiltration of the Ministry. As with all seven books of the series, the day the train leaves for Hogwarts brings in the question or situation whose resolution brings about the end of the conflict of that year at the end of the school year (usually around Pentecost). Here, the infiltration highlights many different issues that show the status of events in the magical world, all of which will have to resolve to truly complete the story by the end of the book.

The next observation is the significance that Harry places on his wand versus his own abilities. As Harry and Hermione recount the incidence with Harry's wand fighting off Lord Voldemort on its own accord, Harry is very careful to give credit where it is due – to the wand, which symbolizes the power of God. Hence, Harry is testifying that his wand/God has taken care of him when he could not take care of himself, subjecting himself to God's power. This is a very important tenet in Christianity: all miracles come from God, and not from us.

One last observation notes that the black "Magic is Might" statue is in strong contrast to the golden statue that used to exist in that same spot near the fireplaces. The new statue is black for the darkness of evil, and appropriately placed near the fires (of hell). The golden statues were destroyed at the end of Harry's black transformational stage, and although he is now in the red stage, the black "Magic is Might" statue stays to show Lord Voldemort's permanent, black renunciation state throughout the series.

Chapter Thirteen: The Muggle-born Registration Commission

In the depths of the ministry itself, Hermione finds herself with Ms. Umbridge and many dementors. Although Delores Umbridge is not actually a Death Eater, she definitely seems to have the same ideas and agrees with how Lord Voldemort runs things. In many ways, the Muggle-Born Registry smacks of the registry of Jews during World War II in Germany, where each Jew was questioned about the depth of their faith but was more about their lineage than any feelings they had. Furthermore, any indication that they converted to Christianity was not believed unless it went past their grandmother's generation.

From a historical Christian perspective, we can see this Muggle-born Commission as a reflection on the early Christian debate about the gentiles. Originally, they thought that only the people related to the chosen people of God were supposed to receive the gift of the Holy Spirit (Acts 10:45), so other races were not included in the initial disciple's celebrations of the Eucharist . However, the book of Acts records that many gentiles upon hearing the gospel converted to following Christ (eventually Christianity), requiring the "chosen people" to expand their sphere of inclusion to those not born into the chosen race. There were divisions about whether the non-Jews should be given the gospel, but after their conversion, the early Christians felt they had no choice to deny what God has given the gift of the Holy Spirit to already (Act 11:17-18): "So if God gave them the same gift as he gave us, who believed in the Lord Jesus Christ, who was I to think that I could oppose God? When they heard this, they had no further objections saying, 'So then, God has granted even the Gentiles repentance unto life.'") Again, it echoes that the wand chooses the wizard, and God is free to choose anyone to have faith.

Chapter Fourteen: The Thief

Although Harry, Ron, and Hermione are able to escape the Ministry of Magic, they end up sacrificing their comfort and are not allowed to return to Grimmauld Place in safety. This is the same recurring "hide-and-seek" event the apostles lived in the New Testament as well as throughout the early years of the church on a physical level. On a spiritual level, rather than live within the temptations of the every day, many third century Christians would go out to the desert to clear their minds for Christ, following St. Anthony's example.[104] The theory is that in any spiritual journey, the person must eventually go "to the desert" – an allusion to Jesus' forty days in the desert and the Israelites' forty years in the desert - away from temptations and any comforts of this world to help focus on what is important in life. Here, Harry, Hermione, and Ron are essentially going "to the desert", or at least, as desert-like as one can get in England – a forest. In the forest, especially with the locket on their chests in turn, they are reliving Christ's temptations of thirst, hunger, cold, and despair as they try to focus on what they can do to continue following Dumbledore's Plan.

Chapter Fifteen: The Goblin's Revenge

Visitors to the area brought news with them of happenings around the magical community, but more importantly, about the friends back at Hogwarts. With the knowledge from the wanderers about the Sword of Gryffindor being a fake, Harry and Hermione change strategies and begin their search for the true Sword of Gryffindor rather than the Horcruxes themselves. Logically, without a means to destroy the evil, it makes no sense to look for more evil objects that might be able to possess the user/

---

[104] Passionist Nuns, "Saint Anthony, Desert Father," retrieved from http://www.passionistnuns.org/Saints /StAnthonyDesert/index.htm.

wearer, but hopefully by looking for that which can destroy all horcruxes, they might find the other horcruxes in the process.

Chapter Sixteen: Godric's Hollow

With Ron's departure around Halloween time, losing Ron shows the trio their vulnerability to the enemy, this time from division within their ranks. Ron's parting remarks haunt Harry, because Harry feels he has no direction, no clear understanding of where to go, or what he is to do – definite elements of the black or renunciation stage. Likewise, for the original eleven disciples, their only directive upon Christ's departure was to stay in the Upper Room until the Holy Spirit appeared and gave them direction. Although only a few of the twelve disciples were learned people as a whole (meaning they could read and write in Greek), they were given a difficult job: to go out and make disciples of all nations, baptizing in the name of the Trinity, and to love and forgive as Christ loved and forgave them. None of these directives are any more specific than Dumbledore's directive to find the remaining horcruxes, wherever they may be, and destroy them. Ultimately, with the loss of Ron and the deluminator, Harry and Hermione are destined to wander thoughtfully until Ron's passion brings them some direction.

To help them decipher what Professor Dumbledore wanted them to do, Harry and Hermione attempt to analyze the book from Dumbledore for hints and clues to follow. As Hermione re-reads the story of the Three Brothers, she finds the Deathly Hallows symbol and begins a true analysis with the syllabary (another name for a sound/ symbol translation dictionary). Ms. Rowling then uses Harry and Hermione's analysis of Grindelwald to show that Grindelwald's use of the Deathly Hallows is a key example of how many symbols that were originally meant for good were taken out of context. Misunderstood and used for ill-driven purposes, people made these symbols themselves seem to be representatives of evil. However, if people read the original language and use a dictionary, they will find the original meaning of the words or symbols and come to understand the beauty of the symbol rather than see it as a tool of the Devil. As with the Bible, the more a reader reads it, uses the commentary, and returns to the original version in Hebrew and/or Greek, the more insights the reader has, thus deepening his faith. One major clue within Hermione's analysis here is that the mark was not something that the Minister or Ministry recognized, and they were experts in the dark magic symbols. Thus, the Deathly Hallows is not a dark magic symbol, but a symbol taken by Grindelwald and used for ill purposes. Similarly, many symbols and sacraments were vilified because of what a few people in high places did, not acknowledging God's original purpose for the church or the symbols. Hence, many symbols outside the cross are not used in the church nowadays, and many people are wary of their use in everyday life.

In desperation, Harry and Hermione turn to Godric's Hollow to find more clues and possibly the Sword of Gryffindor after finding nothing in any of the other places Lord Voldemort might hold sacred. Their decision to go to Godric's Hollow is pivotal in their desert quest: Godric's Hollow itself is a symbol of a pit, or more specifically, the hollow of God's hand. Although God's hand is where life began through Adam and Eve, we again find beginnings as well as endings here.

One of the beginnings and endings occurs as Harry and Hermione approach the church. As they approach, Ms. Rowling makes a clear connection between the singing at church and the singing at Hogwarts – the church is the continuation of a movement that began at Hogwarts, which Harry is no longer a part of. Continuing the parallel, Harry sees a clerical hat in church that reminds him of the vulture hat/ bonnet in Professor Snape's Christmas cracker a few years ago. In a way, Ms. Rowling is poking a little fun of the hats worn at church by the bishops, and Ron's maroon sweater is a head nod to the Catholic cardinals' capes. The last connection between Hogwarts and the Christmas church service is the remembrance of the twelve Christmas trees that Hagrid would bring in every year, symbolic of the twelve apostles of the church.

As they roam about Godric's Hollow, Harry and Hermione visit the graveyard at the church. Visiting the graves of Albus Dumbledore's family, they stumble upon the verse Luke 12:34: "Where your treasure is, there will your heart be also." Although this is rather an odd verse to have on a tombstone, it does give a bigger clue about one of Ms. Rowling's big themes of the series that was first mentioned in the first book. This closes the circle of beginnings and endings: that our love is always bound up into what we treasure, physically and spiritually. From the first book, the mirror of Erised showed you what your heart truly desires or treasures physically, as if the treasure resides in the heart itself and the mirror is able to look within the heart. At the other end in this seventh book, we see Lord Voldemort's literal mistranslation of this same verse as he places his soul into his treasured objects to keep himself alive: the horcruxes. Through these varied interpretations, we see how closely knit Ms. Rowling sees treasure, heaven, and love bound together physically and spiritually.

Further on in the graveyard, Hermione finds the grave of Ignotus Peverell, who has the symbol found in Hermione's book on his tombstone. Ignotus is a facsimile of Saint Ignatius of Antioch, who is one of the early Church Fathers and a disciple of St. John the Evangelist. Ms. Rowling uses St. Ignatius' ideas throughout her work, especially the concept of the Eucharist being the food and drink of immortality: "breaking one bread, which is the medicine of immortality and the antidote that we should not die but live forever in Jesus Christ."[105] From this quote, we begin to see the foundations of Christian alchemy – the transformation of the soul that allows a person to participate fully in the Eucharist and thus ingest the elixir of life to live forever in Christ. In relation to the symbol on the rock, Ignatius himself was not aware that he was defining a doctrine that others would follow, he was more focused on other elements of the Church that would ensure its survival in the centuries to come.

Their last stop in the graveyard is at James and Lily's gravesites. As Harry and Hermione discuss the Bible verse on the Potters' tombstones (1

---

[105] Lightfoot and Hammer, Early Christian Writings, "Ignatius of Antioch to the Ephesians," Chapter 20:2, retrieved from http://www.earlychristianwritings.com/text/ignatius-ephesians-lightfoot.html.

Corinthians 15:26: "the last enemy that shall be destroyed is death"), Harry is surprised that his parents would have a comment in league with the Death Eaters. Hermione explains that it is a spiritual explanation, not a physical one, giving us the main difference between the Death Eaters and the Order of the Phoenix. Death Eaters seem to imply that a command over physical death allows them to control who is worthy enough of a physical life. In contrast, the Order members look more to a spiritual life that sustains them beyond a physical death. At that moment, Harry doesn't understand very much about the spiritual element of death, he only sees the physical death of his parents even though he has seen and interacted with them in their ghost forms in the past. In tribute to them, Hermione places the white rose wreath on their tombstone, symbolizing their purity and innocence on Christmas Eve.

Chapter Seventeen: Bathilda's Secret

Harry has run into many people or animals within the magical world that can see through the invisibility cloak, but all of them have magical abilities beyond normal wizards. Not even Lord Voldemort can see beyond the physical boundary of the cloak. Thus, the fact that Bathilda can sense Harry and Hermione under the cloak should warn Harry that there's something wrong. However, Harry's character "flaw" is his trust of everyone around him, and so doesn't see anything wrong yet. However, as the events unfold, Harry's trust in Bathilda leads him to keeping his mind open, which provides many insights into Lord Voldemort's history and motives.

Once Harry realizes that Bathilda must be dead and Nagini has taken over her body, he finally sees things for how they truly are, and once again his mind is connected to Lord Voldemort and Nagini's. As the images blur between Harry's thoughts, Nagini's thoughts, and Lord Voldemort's thoughts, their differences become indistinguishable, reminding us that the two are intertwined physically with Harry's blood existing in Lord Voldemort, and a piece of Lord Voldemort's soul resides within Harry (and Nagini). This constant intermingling is what keeps the two from truly living their own lives, only surviving as a physical object until one of them obtains purity of soul and mind from the other.

During Lord Voldemort's reminiscence, we see the entirety of the events of the night he killed Harry's parents for the first time, in a small way indicating that Harry is now in the white stage of this book. Lord Voldemort reveals to us that he sees the natural ability to withstand or avoid death puts people in a pecking order. Accordingly, the muggle girl isn't even worth notice, and Lord Voldemort degrades James for not having his wand, since it is their wands that give them power over death or at least give them a defense. In further reflection, Lord Voldemort reveals for us the reason why Lily's death was more sacrificial than James' death. Lord Voldemort had truly planned to spare Lily from death, but since she offered herself in Harry's stead, she was killed. James had no choice in the matter, but since Lily did, that free will offering was able to protect Harry through their blood connection.

Thankfully, Hermione was able to come to Harry's aid, and through the blasting curse, freed Harry from Nagini's clutches. On the down side, the blasting curse broke Harry's wand in symbolic fashion – the logic blasts away the physical attachment to God. If we come to understand that the wand is representative of the power of God the Father, Harry's broken wand represents his broken faith in Dumbledore,[106] bringing Harry to the depths of despair as illumination and truth/ reality overcome his belief. As a last note here, Ron, the representative of passion and will, has been away for quite a while and the breaking of the wand is the last piece of will that he had. Without Ron, Harry has nothing to recharge his emotional battery, and he wallows in his own despair.

Chapter Eighteen: The Life and Lies of Albus Dumbledore

One of the facets of Christianity that many Christians struggle with is the attainment of faith for "cradle Christians" (those who have grown up with the tenets of faith but never experienced them from a novice's

---

[106] Granger, J, *The Deathly Hallows Lectures,* p. 104.

perspective). As cradle Christians, faith in God eventually becomes part of who we are, and we don't realize what we have until it's gone. With a true faith, there is a special connection between God and his creation that gives the person direction and a sense of purpose. If that faith is shattered for whatever reason, the person suddenly feels empty, aimless, and vulnerable just as Harry feels without Ron, his wand, and Albus Dumbledore. As Harry begins the white stage of this last book, he is learning everything he can to help him through the final battle that he knows must follow with Lord Voldemort. In accepting that Dumbledore did not give them very much to follow and all trails they did have are now cold, Harry must forge a new plan that will help him defeat Lord Voldemort while still following the vague guidelines he was given.

As Harry reminisces about their experience at Godric's Hollow, his frustration at not getting what he wanted overwhelms him. However, what we get from an experience or sacred place usually is not what we expect, especially when many rumors exist about the place and what others received there. However, what someone takes from the place might be important, just not what was expected, so it isn't valued until later. Harry's analysis of the events helps him understand Lord Voldemort better, and allows him to understand Lord Voldemort's true motivations and lack of love, an element Harry will need to include in his final plan to save the wizarding world.

In his search for understanding Albus Dumbledore, even from a source as unverifiable as Rita Skeeter, Harry reads the book Hermione was able to take from Bathilda's house, *The Life and Lies of Albus Dumbledore*. In the letter from Albus Dumbledore to Gellert Grindelwald reprinted within the book, Albus discusses the concept of stewardship – if people were given abilities from God, are they given to protect others or dominate others? Protection and domination are very closely linked, and protection for some might be considered domination by those around them. Albus sees their abilities as a means to protect others, and sees their position above those without abilities so that they can be protected. Contrary to this, Gellert seems to feel that their powers were given to them to enable them to exert any force necessary to help others see their natural superiority This same debate has existed for years about the meaning of God's statement granting humankind dominion over the earth in Genesis 1:26: "Then God said, 'Let us make man in our image, in our likeness, and let them rule over the fish of the sea and the birds of the air, over the livestock, over all the earth, and over all the creatures that move along the ground.'"(NIV) Does this statement entitle humankind to do with animals as they desire (domination), or grant them permission to do whatever acts necessary to keep them protected from annihilation? As with many of the divisions within the wizarding world, they debate over the same verses or literature, but have different points of view causing division within the wizarding world (and Christian world as well).

As Harry finishes reading about Albus Dumbledore, he feels the depths of his losses – Ron is gone, Dumbledore is gone and has left him with very little to go on, his phoenix wand is broken, and they have been camping for four months. Harry's reference to everything being ashes is both a reference to the phoenix (both the symbol and the feather in his wand), and a foreshadowing of the rebirth of his faith and purpose, just as the phoenix is reborn from the ashes. As part of the enlightenment of the white stage that will bring him out of the depths, Hermione points out to Harry that despite Dumbledore's past, Dumbledore fought Grindelwald in the end and took the wand that Grindelwald was misusing for his own purposes. Why did it take Dumbledore so long to fight Gridelwald? Perhaps Dumbledore, as the Christ figure, was determining which of the predictive songs of Isaiah he was truly there to fulfill – the conquering hero, the suffering servant, the brilliant rabbi, or the light to the nations as the pure nation that has a direct link to God and should rule the earth. In the end, Dumbledore is the brilliant Headmaster who never uses his wand to kill anyone. Rather, he only uses the wand for good, and with the Phoenix, Fawkes, as a pet, Dumbledore must have chosen to be the brilliant rabbi/ servant. As such, he first teaches others about the love of God; but in the end, he accepts his necessary sacrifice for the good of others, trusting in the resurrection that God promises to everyone after him.

At the end of Harry and Hermione's discussion, Hermione reminds Harry that Dumbledore loved him, and implies that Dumbledore loved Harry (platonically) more than he loved anyone else. Similarly, Jesus loved John, the son of Zebedee, and they had the same relationship of rabbi and student that Dumbledore shared with Harry. Both Harry and John are the "beloved disciples", both are the youngest of their twelve closest friends, and both of them were witnesses of the entire passion of Christ. With this connection, Ms. Rowling indicates to her readers that Harry will pull out of his despair and move forward, leading his friends in battle against Lord Voldemort soon just as St. John became a leader in Christianity in his own time.

Chapter Nineteen: The Silver Doe

As this chapter opens, Harry's white stage begins in earnest, with references to snow, light, and the silver doe.[107] This continues the themes of white and light that began with Harry and Hermione's visit to the graveyard on Christmas Eve. The reference to the silver doe is also a reference to the alchemy of the moon, of which silver is the alchemical metal. Silver is known for its antibiotic/ purification abilities, which returns people to their state of innocence and purity.[108] Here the doe helps Harry return to his original purpose after losing his faith in Dumbledore.

In Christian thought, we are reminded of the light shining in the darkness (John 1:5) here again on the 25th of December, referring to the light of Christ shining through the darkness of the world on Christmas Eve. As the concept developed in Christianity, this was actually unintentional symbolism, stated in a time that they did not acknowledge Christ's birth at all. However, subsequent followers tried to establish dates for the new converts and began to research the date of his birth. John Chrysostom, a fourth century bishop, used the date of the Jewish New Year in mid-

---

[107] Granger, J, *The Deathly Hallows Lectures,* pp. 105-110.

[108] International Alchemy Guild, 2011, retrieved from http://www.alchemylab.com/dictionary.htm#top.

September, from which we get the conception date of John. Since John was six months in the womb when Mary went to visit her cousin Elizabeth (John's mother), we know that Jesus was conceived mid-March. From March, nine months makes a birth date in December. Since December contains the shortest days of the year, they set the date for December 25th, one of the shortest days of the year to remind people of the symbolism of the light of Christ shining in the darkness.[109]

As the silver doe leads Harry away from the camp and to the edge of the water, the dreamlike sequence connects Harry to the astral plane again – the silver patronus, the moonlight, and the snow at night – a moment of reflection that will lead to purification and restoration. Furthermore, the doe patronus, as a combination of a Christ symbol and the wizard's projection of hope, joy, and happiness, is protection against the despair that Harry felt before. Unbeknownst to Harry or anyone else, the wizard behind it has also vowed to protect Harry from Lord Voldemort.

Continuing with the Christian symbolism of the white stage, we are reminded of the historical process of baptism as Harry goes into the water and Ron pulls him out. Before Christianity became a national religion in the Roman Empire, candidates for baptism would undergo months of instruction, and although they were invited to the first half of the Eucharistic / worship service, they were dismissed before the Eucharistic prayers. When they were ready to be baptized, they would wear a black robe to the conversion service at the Easter Vigil. They would face west, then descend a step walking backwards three times, each time in response to a renunciation of evil. At the bottom, they would be dunked under the water and turned around, literally "converted." They would then ascend three steps, each step corresponding to their acceptance of God, Jesus, and the Holy Spirit. They were then brought out of the water, and given their white robes to wear as they then continued in their training of Christian ways.[110]

---

[109] Bennett, D, 2009, *Why is Christmas celebrated on December 25th?* Retreived from http://www.ancient-future.net/christmasdate.html.

In a similar vein, we see this exact transformation in this chapter: we have all of the symbols of baptism: water, light, submersion, conversion, salvation. Ron saves Harry from a near-death experience under water, and removes the locket, a symbol of the spirit of evil, from Harry's chest.[111] Symbolically, Christ led Harry to the water's edge, where Harry saw the cross (the hilt of the sword of Gryffindor) – both a symbol of death and faith – with the ruby stone in the hilt as a reminder of the blood of Christ spilt on that cross. The waters of baptism themselves symbolize both rebirth and death, close to the reality for the early Christians and Jews who were both afraid of the water and non-swimmers. Alchemically, submersing while coming to terms with one's emotions is called ablution, and that restoration leads Harry closer to gold and the Philosopher's Stone.

As the baptizer, Ron has taken on a much stronger role within the trio – the re-energized, passionate leader. However, he was not able to return on his own devices, even though he always had the ability to return with him. In Ron's explanation to Harry and Hermione about how the deluminator was able to bring him to their location, we see the power within a name, not just thoughts of the person. Hermione and Harry had thought of Ron many times, but never really spoke of him, but once they used his name, Ron was able to return. Names are always significant, since they both define a person and create a handle for others to use. In some denominations, as people are confirmed, they choose a Christian name for themselves, one that will identify who they are in their new life, the name that God will call them by. In the reverse, God is ever there for his people, but only interferes when He is called upon to help (2 Chronicles 7:14). This same type of event occurs in the Old Testament – the Israelites stray from God, they are punished, then they call to God for help, and God provides for them and their safety. We experience this in our own lives as well – people suffer, but until they call someone to help them, many times we are not aware of their suffering. Although

---

[110] Fr. Himes, M, lecture notes, University of Notre Dame, Spring, 1992: "Sacrementality."

[111] Granger, *The Deathly Hallows Lectures,* p. 108.

Hermione and Harry weren't calling to Ron for help and Ron is in no way a God figure, using his name granted him access to them and created a mental connection that allowed him to find them and save Harry from death.

Beyond being an amplifier for Ron's name and a symbol of the light of Christ, the deluminator has another purpose – a physical representation of John 14:16: "I am the way, the truth and the life," meaning that as long as a person follows Christ, he is on the right path and Christ will lead him where he needs to go. When the Christ figure, Dumbledore, goes away, he left a guide for those that he felt might get lost along the way and need a light to help them back on the right path. Here, Ron has the deluminator, as the light of Christ, and by following that light and letting that light lead him, Ron found the right path and was led back to his mission to destroy the horcruxes and the embodiment of evil.

Chapter Twenty: Xenophilius Lovegood

Although Xenophilius Lovegood himself is rather eccentric and thus many would disregard the symbol he wore to the wedding, the fact that it appears in connection with other less eccentric people gives the symbol a bit more credence. Harry's response that questions whether Dumbledore left them hidden signs and clues speaks to the Gnostics, who believed that there were many hidden things in the legacy left behind by Christ that only those "in the know" could ever understand (amongst other, heretical ideas). It could also be the beginnings of the illumination of the books written by John in the Bible, books that seem to be written in code, still misunderstood, and full of alchemical references. However, Ms. Rowling speaks through Hermione to explain herself on two different levels. Within Christianity, there are many ways of understanding the Bible and each denomination has its own interpretation of what the words mean. Similarly, although Ms. Rowling has been criticized for not coming forward to explain what she truly intended to the smallest detail, she is allowing for interpretation, understanding that it is the quest that brings people to illumination more than being given the answers. Hermione's statement "maybe it's something you need to find out for yourself" explains that every person has an individual path to follow to find one's spiritual beliefs and connections to Christ and the world/ hereafter.

As the trio begins a physical search for the Lovegood's place, Ron admits that he couldn't return home after leaving his friends and tell his family he had left Harry and Hermione, so he went to Bill's cottage. The Shell Cottage is another reference to baptism, since in the Anglican churches, the shell represent the waters of baptism and usually either uses a shell to hold the baptismal water or a shell to scoop the water to baptize the candidate. Furthermore, since baptism is also a time of washing all previous sins, the shell cottage symbolically helps Ron's reconciliation to the community, providing a pathway back to Harry and Hermione and their mutual quest.

Upon arriving at the Lovegood's house, there is a short discussion about its appearance. The Lovegood's house looks like a castle, but when Ron mentioned that it looked like a rook, Hermione immediately thought of a bird. Ron corrected her to say he meant the rook from chess, but it is an important connection. The bird rook, a member of the crow family, many times symbolizes death or the coming of death,[112] encouraged by the blackness of the building. Ron's correction introduces the symbolism of the rook from chess: a hidden treasure or knowledge.[113] This symbolism completely fits with what the Lovegood family stands for: Mr. Lovegood is the editor of a fantastical magazine that speaks of many hidden, unknowable, or impossible subjects always in pursuit of the truth, and Luna loves in a fantasy world in the astral plane in search of a hidden truth.

Chapter Twenty-one: The Tale of the Three Brothers

At the Lovegood's house, while they wait for Luna to return from her outing, the trio continues its quest for knowledge by questioning Mr.

---

[112] The Blue Roebuck, 2008, "Rook," retrieved from http://www.blueroebuck.com/rook.html.

[113] Chess-poster.com, 2000, "Chesmayne: The History of Chess," retrieved from http://www.chess-poster.com/english/chesmayne/the_rook.htm.

Lovegood about the symbol. As Hermione finishes reading about the three brothers, Mr. Lovegood explains that she just read all about The Deathly Hallows, even though the word combination never appeared in the story itself. Similarly, the word trinity is not in the Bible, but many would say that the New Testament is all about the trinity. In truth, the Deathly Hallows represents the trinity: 1) the elder wand represents the power of God; 2) the Resurrection Stone represents the resurrection of Christ, and 3) the Invisibility Cloak represents the Holy Spirit. The Resurrection Stone's representation is an easy connection since Christ's three days of death are represented by the three turns of the Resurrection Stone. The invisibility cloak is a bit more subtle. As the representative of the Holy Spirit, they have many elements in common: 1) they are both invisible; 2) they can both be shared between two-three people; 3) they are both passed down from generation to generation; and 4) they both protect the wearer from a physical or spiritual death (the Invisibility cloak repels all charms, and the Holy Spirit gives the bearer eternal life).

The wand has a complicated theology all of its own. Beginning with John 15:5, "I am the vine, you are the branches", the wand is a branch of God's vine. Secondly, the wand is the instrument used to implement the prayers and wishes of God's people, and the wand does the magic, not the people, just as God is responsible for miracles, not the people themselves. Historically, just as the Elder Wand's possession is easily traced from wizard to wizard, so is the power of God through the Ark of the Covenant. Wherever the Ark was, the Israelites triumphed; but when it was stolen, the raiders were persecuted. Through time, the wood of the Ark was transformed to a more general meaning of wood and in the New Testament, we see that Jesus was a carpenter and spent lots of time around wood - shaping it, forming it, and dying on it. With this important link to Christ, those woods that he worked with are imbued with a spiritual connection between people and God, and show that Jesus himself felt that working with wood was an important element of life. Lastly, the three cores used in Ollivander's wands have Christian connections. Thus, the wand becomes the power of God, answering to the prayers and needs of the wizard God chose as his instrument.

Just as the trinity is a concept passed along through tradition, the Deathly Hallows is also a concept handed down by tradition. After persecutions and other issues, the wizarding world had to go into secrecy, so the knowledge of the Deathly Hallows was not passed to everyone that it could have been. Coincidentally, there were many people at the Council of Nicaea that were not entirely convinced of the trinity, and it took many years to confirm the concept amongst the whole Christian community. Unfortunately for the wizarding community, there were many who felt the Deathly Hallows was a secret to mastering death which over time was first ridiculed then misinterpreted as a means to conquer physical death. For this reason, the concept was not handed down for fear of either ridicule or that others might think them part of the Dark Arts.

Beyond the trinity concept, Mr. Lovegood explains to Hermione that the story is for children, meant to amuse not to teach even though those who see the symbolism see it for more than just an amusing story. Perhaps Ms. Rowling speaks through Mr. Lovegood a little about the Bible stories, as many of them are used almost as entertainment for younger children. Once these same children mature and become adults, then the stories are suddenly explained a bit more in depth and the hidden mysteries are put forward to discuss and debate. As Paul said in 1 Corinthians 13:11: "When I was a child, I talked like a child, I thought like a child, I reasoned like a child. When I became a man, I put childish ways behind me." Unfortunately, many children forget these stories when they become adults so they never see the symbolism and morals beyond the surface of the stories.

As an ending note about the references within the story itself, the names of the three brothers that are credited with furthering the concept of the Deathly Hallows: Antioch, Cadmus, and Ignotus, refer to two different elements: Ignatius of Antioch, and Cadmus from the Greek myth. Cadmus is a Greek hero known as the founder of Thebes, but eventually is transformed into a snake with his wife, Hermonia.[114] Similarly, Cadmus is the second brother that had the Resurrection Stone that eventually fell to the Slytherin line, represented by the snake. The other two elements, the Elder Wand and the Invisibility Cloak, went to Antioch and Ignotus, respectively. Antioch, representing the power and descendency of God, is now the See of the Orthodox church (the seat of power), and Ignatius of Antioch, a disciple of St. John, was one of the early church Fathers who was instrumental in developing the theology of the church and laying the foundations for the development of the trinity concept.[115] In essence, Ignatius, as a bishop of Antioch, was able to bestow the Holy Spirit on many new believers, just as the bishops in the early church and today bestow the Holy Spirit through the laying on of hands on the confirmands (those being confirmed into the church.

Chapter Twenty-two: The Deathly Hallows

Just as different people react differently to the same Bible stories, after the discussion about the Deathly Hallows, Harry believes in the Deathly Hallows, but Hermione and Ron feel it is all only a story to make people feel better. The elements of the trinity are meant to comfort others, even if that comfort comes from the individual elements at different times in one's life. As Hermione, Harry and Ron discuss the three elements and which would be the most important one, they all claim a different element. For Harry, it is the Stone, because he wishes to be reacquainted with those that he has lost. For Ron, it is the Wand, because he feels powerless always in the shadow of five other brothers and now Harry or Hermione. Hermione's choice of the Cloak acknowledges her understanding that she has neither known true loss nor ever had to compete with others, and the Invisibility Cloak would grant

---

[114]V.E.K. Sandels, 2010, "Cadmus," retrieved from http://www.in2greece.com/english/historymyth/mythology /names/cadmus.htm.

[115] Myth Index, 2007, Greek Mythology Index, "Cadmus," retrieved from http://www.mythindex.com/greek-mythology/C/Cadmus.html.

[115] Peck, J, 2012, Preacher's Institute, "The Trinity in the Writings of St Ignatius," retrieved from http://preachersinstitute.com/2010/10/17/the-trinity-in-the-writings-of-ignatius-of-antioch/.

her access to things she is otherwise unable to obtain. The reality, however, is that the trinity, being three entities but one God, are equal and one is not more important that the others.

Unfortunately, many people who attend church do so for their children, so that they will have friends, learn morals, and hear comforting stories about how God will always be there for them without truly believing those stories themselves or in the God behind the history. In essence, people feel that as we grow older we put our faith only in what we can verify through our five senses. Hermione, in all of her wisdom, has the hardest time accepting that there might be something beyond the physical realm that interferes with history. In essence, she is personifying all of those who feel that there is always a reasonable explanation for everything. Case in point, Hermione is convinced that the wand is only as powerful as the wizard behind it. However, from Harry's experience, the wand is more about the faith of the wizard, and since the wand represents the power of God, the wand responds to the prayers and needs of the wizard, in accordance to that wizard's faith.

Hermione's disbelief in the Tale of the Three Brothers is echoed by many people who believe that the Bible is just a collection of stories, not to be believed, but interpreted as mythology, folklore, or historical fiction, regardless of the history that proves its accuracy. Her response to Harry's interest in the Resurrection Stone, however, shows that Hermione's concept of the Resurrection Stone is that of necromancy, the art of raising dead physical bodies to do one's will. To the contrary, Harry's concept of the Resurrection is one of a spiritual return, where the spirit communicates with the currently living and all is at peace. It is difficult to tell whether Ms. Rowling advocates for a bodily resurrection of Christ and a spiritual resurrection of everyone else, or a spiritual resurrection for all, including Christ. In the Jewish faith, the belief is in a bodily resurrection, and thus they do not advocate for cremation or anything less than a full body burial.[116] In the Christian faith, they believe in only an immediate spiritual resurrection with a physical resurrection once Christ returns.

---

[116] Religious Facts, 2004, *Jewish Death and Funeral Rites.* Retreived from

Convinced of the truth of the tale, Harry tries to convince Hermione and Ron that the pieces of the Deathly Hallows are real objects because he sees how they fit together and thinks he has two of the three items. However, Hermione takes the opposite view, that the objects are fictional and any coincidences are accidental, just as many nonbelievers believe. All things work and fit together well when God is involved ("All things work together for good, for them that love the Lord," (Romans 8:28, NIV), not forced to fit together. Ron finally agrees with Harry that Harry might have the pieces of the Hallows that allows him to master death and thus give him the ability to live through his match against Lord Voldemort. However, Harry has to learn what it means to truly master death. Lord Voldemort tries to master death by avoiding it and ensuring physical existence, but is a master of death afraid of death or accepting of death? Through Harry's thought process, Ms. Rowling sets up the oppositional crux of the entire series: Lord Voldemort's division of his soul into seven pieces, showing a physical, man-made attempt at eternal life versus Harry's belief in the Deathly Hallows (and thus the trinity) and the spiritual life beyond the grave. This is God's plan for our salvation – acceptance of Christ as one's Lord and Savior, believing in the power of God, and being a dwelling place for the Holy Spirit. As an obvious set up between man's plan and God's plan, Ms. Rowling defines who the winner has to be in the final fight – Harry.

An important piece here that Harry deliberates about for the next few pages (and chapters...) is what it means to "possess" the Deathly Hallows. As Harry begins to figure out the Deathly Hallows, he initially has the wrong idea that the Deathly Hallows will protect him from death, which is what Albus Dumbledore thought as well and why he had to give up his pursuit of the Deathly Hallows. Harry's concept that it is possession alone that provides protection isn't quite right – it is the acceptance and belief in the objects (or the Triune God) that gives a person mastery over death, since true belief in the three means accepting death as believing that these three elements will be there to sustain you spiritually in the end.

---

http://www.religionfacts.com /judaism/cycle/death.htm.

Even though Harry struggles with the Deathly Hallows, he at least has a concept that they represent more than merely tangible objects. This is not true for Lord Voldemort, who has never been able to see anything beyond its physical state. As Harry ponders whether or not Lord Voldemort knew about the Hallows, he figures that the answer was "no," since if Lord Voldemort did know, he would have done everything he could to possess them. Blaise Pascal had the same idea – that if someone knew that he were running off a high cliff to certain doom and knew a method of preventing it, he would do everything to obtain it.[117] However, the Old Testament is full of examples of what happened when the Philistines tried to keep the Ark, thinking that possession of the Ark would protect them from death and help them defeat others. The Philistines endured many hardships while the Ark was with them, so it was returned. (1 Samuel Chapters 5, 6). It is a true understanding of what the power of God is, what the Resurrection of Christ represents, and what the indwelling of the Holy Spirit does that helps a person see life around them in a way that leads them to accept and thus master death.

Finally understanding how the Deathly Hallows can help him defeat Lord Voldemort, Harry now has to determine which direction Albus Dumbledore wanted Harry to go first – establish his own insurance against the death he knows will happen when he meets Lord Voldemort, or trust in Albus Dumbledore's plan that destroying the Horcruxes (Lord Voldemort's life-lines) will be sufficient for all, even if death is a consequence. Harry shares this debate with Hermione, and brings up the concept of the quest – Dumbledore left the clues for him to follow and find the answers himself. In truth, this is the reality of faith – people are much stronger in their faith if they discover it for themselves rather than receiving one handed to them by someone else and just accepting it.

Accepting that Dumbledore truly did love him and provide for him by giving him the Cloak, the Resurrection Stone, and knowledge of where the wand is, Harry finally feels the love of Christ within him. As John Wesley

---

[117] Pascal, B, 1660, translated by Trotter, W. *Pensees, 168, 183*. Retrieved from http://oregonstate.edu/instruct /phl302/texts/pascal/pensees-a.html.

would say, "my heart was strangely warmed."[118] As a newborn Christian, Harry is fully fixated on the Trinity and what it means for him, and can't think of anything else. For his friends who aren't sharing this same experience, Harry is difficult to be around, somewhat as expected. This is a common experience for many newborn Christians who have many friends who haven't had that same experience, but after a couple weeks as they learn how to live their lives renewed. In the end, Ron rouses Harry from the Deathly Hallows obsession in the same way that Harry had to be rescued from his obsession of the Mirror of Erised from Book 1. The main difference here is that with the first obsession, Harry was obsessed with things from the past and in this last book, Harry is obsessed with the future.[119] Furthermore, whereas the Mirror made Harry long for death, the obsession with the Deathly Hallows prompts Harry to think of life, showing his full transformation.

With the Deathly Hallows understood, we now see the differences between Lord Voldemort's concept of eternity versus Albus Dumbledore's concept of "eternity". Under the Lord Voldemort plan, eternity includes the very un-Christian concept of building up a physical connection to the world for one's soul to remain in the physical realm. This is a man's plan for immortality. In direct opposition to this, we see the Deathly Hallows as God's plan of Salvation – the concept of the Trinity. With Lord Voldemort's plan, its success depends completely on the physical abilities of the individual. Conversely, God's Plan of Salvation requires an individual's trust in the spiritual connection to God's Trinity. The two oppositional plans present a dilemma that Harry will have to solve to determine which path he takes.

At the conclusion of this chapter, Ron finally gets the right codeword for "Potterwatch", and the three friends enjoy reconnecting with the wizarding world. First, we have another baptismal reference in keeping

---

[118] Christian Classics Ethereal Library, 2005, *Journal of John Wesley,* retrieved from http://www.ccel.org/ccel/wesley/journal.vi.ii.xvi.html.

[119] Granger, J, ed. Prinzi, *Harry Potter for Nerds,* "On Turtleback Tales and Asterisks," p. 61.

with the white stage: Lee Jordan's nickname of "River" refers to the River Jordan, the original baptismal stage for Christ. Secondly, as part of the Potterwatch, Kingsley Shacklebolt appeals to the magical community to protect their muggle neighbors by putting protective charms on their homes and persons to help them avoid being a victim. Essentially, this is asking for all Christians to bless their non-Christian neighbors and pray for their safety without their knowledge, to help in the overall picture of defeating death and Satan. From a historical point of view, we see now that Kingsley Shacklebolt is analogous to Paul, extending the love of God to the gentiles/ muggles. As the radio program closes out, their parting statements outline the purpose of a Christian community – supporting the community in the quest for truth, avoiding evil, and protecting others from death.

Chapter Twenty-three: Malfoy Manor

Forgetting the taboo on Lord Voldemort's name, the three are taken hostage and taken to the Malfoy's Manor. At the manor, we see the true status of Lord Voldemort's followers, and the trio uses their weaknesses to their advantage. For starters, standing in the Malfoy Manor to be judged by the Malfoys and Bellatrix LaStrange, Harry begins to understand that it is the depth of one's emotion that blocks out evil thoughts, or at least helps him separate himself from Lord Voldemort's possessive thoughts. Additionally, Harry has accepted the truth of the Deathly Hallows, which has begun to help him understand that although death and evil are inevitable, they are not impossible to overcome. With this knowledge, Harry no longer fears the Death Eaters as he used to, and he continues to reason through their situation as events occur.

Interestingly, Draco does not behave the way Harry though he would. Asked to identify Harry Potter, Draco resists, despite the pleadings of his parents to end Lord Voldemort's battle soon by identifying Harry. This resistance is a continuation of Draco's conversion that began with his "sectumseptra" curse. Having finally realized what Lord Voldemort's true desire is, Draco passively resists any additional conquests the Death Eaters pursue and accepts the love, direction, and protection that

Professor Dumbledore offered to him shortly before he died. These pieces are new pieces for Harry to digest, but they will help him see another possibility for those who seem destined for evil futures.

Bellatrix acts on the only solid evidence she has – the Sword of Gryffindor. She throws Harry and Ron into the basement of Malfoy's Manor, and tortures Hermione for information because she is a mudblood, echoing the early Christians' fates at the Coliseum outside Rome. As some Christians were randomly kept to enter the arena, the others could only stay downstairs to pray for help while hearing the cries of those above them. Sometimes their prayers for help were heard, just as Peter was thrown into prison and rescued by an angel who releases them from their bonds and brings a bright light (Acts 12:5-19). In the basement, Harry's cries for help are answered when the unknown person through the mirror shard sends Dobby to them, like an angel, who releases all the prisoners from their bonds. Furthermore, the dark dungeon of Malfoy Manor poses as the tomb of Easter, and Dobby's arrival acts as Christ's saving grace.

Before Harry and Ron are able to leave the dungeon, there is one inevitable surprise – Peter Pettigrew's checking on their status in the dungeon. Again, we see the surprise of self-incrimination when Peter Pettigrew/ Wormtail tries to bring Harry to the torture arena. Harry reminds him of how he spared Wormtail's life earlier, and this debt is repaid by the silver hand, which suffocates Wormtail. Coincidentally, Silver and Wormwood both have medicinal properties that are helpful in small quantities but lethal in larger quantities. Together, they represent the end of the poisoning of the world – the Death Eaters have expanded their realm as far as it will go, and with the removal of the wormwood from the world, the world can begin healing. Alchemically, this removal is the end of the distillation process – the silver (and wormwood) is now permanently removed from Harry's past, where Lord Voldemort can't use it against him anymore.

Just as with any early Christian martyrdom at an arena, there are casualties from their Malfoy Manor visit. As a representative of St. John,

Harry sees his first "disciple" Dobby die at the hands of his enemies, just as St. John mourned all of those that died around him in the early years of the church. As a side point, St. John had two important disciples that died martyr's deaths shortly after he died – St. Ignatius of Antioch and Polycarp, both of whom helped shape the early church. Dobby was loyal to Albus Dumbledore after Harry introduced them, and truly understood the Christian concepts of others over self, helping others see their bondage to help set them free, and the continual conquest against evil in their lives.

Chapter Twenty-four: The Wand-maker

Arriving safely at Shell Cottage, Harry and his friends grieve over Dobby's death. While the friends recollect themselves to heal, bond, and plan their next move, Harry transitions alchemically from the white stage of illumination within this book to that of purification/ battle – the red stage. Harry's first victory comes shortly after Dobby's death. The depth of love Harry feels for Dobby helps him sense Lord Voldemort's rage without being absorbed into the emotions of anger and hatred that Lord Voldemort feels. In times past, Harry was not thinking of how much he loved someone who had died, he thought only of how much he missed them and what his own losses were. With this final death of someone that didn't owe Harry anything, Harry finally feels true grief. However, since grief and love are oppositional emotions to Lord Voldemort's abilities, Harry can find safety from the pain of Lord Voldemort's rage through this love.

Ultimately, Dobby's freedom came from his belief that Harry Potter was the champion against Lord Voldemort, and it drove him to move beyond the typical house-elf trait of being loyal only to those who are kind to them. Dobby's death is the first sacrificial House-elf death – Dobby took a stand to fight evil rather than just serve a master and follow the rules. Similarly, many early Jews were bound to the rules of the Old Testament, and by accepting Christ, they were freed from those bonds to go out and make disciples of all nations. No matter which faith we choose, the goal is the same – to fight evil as the world sees it, not only as our "master" sees it, because we might be showing blind loyalty to something we do not truly understand. "Masters" can come in many disguises – trunks of gold, dogmas, ideologies, traditions, or vices. A truly freed person is the one who follows his "master" because he believes his master has chosen wisely, not because of the way a "master" treats us.

Harry's second victory is his understanding that although the Deathly Hallows will help him safe his own life, unless the horcruxes have been eliminated, Lord Voldemort will keep returning. In choosing to visit Griphook rather than Mr. Ollivander first, Harry makes the conscious decision to pursue the destruction of the Horcruxes first. However, he thinks only of the sequential nature of the two – if he conquers the Horcruxes first, then the Hallows will enable him to stay master of death. As part of this decision, Harry debates between which set of elements to pursue – Hallows or Horcruxes – and realizes that the horcruxes only help prevent death without enabling the person to master death. Mastering death is about not fearing it. With this clarity, Harry makes the right decision to follow what Albus Dumbledore told him to do – find the horcruxes and destroy them. With his recent experiences, he is now more certain of where the horcruxes are and he formulates a plan.

Harry's third victory at Shell Cottage is his ability to win over the trust of a goblin and master wand lore as if he were a master wand maker himself. Although Griphook, the goblin, thinks that Harry is unusual, his unusualness stems from his trust of everyone and everything, regardless of race. Unlike many people, when Harry finally accepted that he was a wizard and accepted that the magical world existed, he accepted it in its entirety, giving equal respect to every race and creed it contained. This respect for all elements of the wizarding world convinces Griphook that Harry is someone he can trust. In speaking to the wand maker, Mr. Ollivander, Harry asks him about wand lore and wand allegiance, especially of the extra wands he has in his hand. Mr. Ollivander reveals that Draco's wand has unicorn hair, not a dragon heartstring, even though his name means dragon and most of the Death Eaters have dragon heartstring in their wands. This is another example of Draco's severance from the Death Eater community. Mr. Ollivander also restates to Harry that the wand chooses the wizard, explaining how and why wands change owner allegiance. In the same way, God chooses us to follow him, but can decide not to continue with us if we do not continue doing as God commanded, as happened with King Saul (1 Samuel 5:26). After the discussion, Harry suspects that he is now the true master of the Elder Wand, since Draco's wand has claimed allegiance to Harry, and Draco was the master of Dumbledore's wand, the Elder Wand. Thus, Harry now knows that he is the rightful owner of the Deathly Hallows, assuming that Albus Dumbledore has put the Resurrection Stone inside the snitch. Thus, the true challenge now lies in finding the horcruxes and destroying them before Lord Voldemort destroys too much more of the wizarding world. With these two allies, Harry feels more confident in his plan against Lord Voldemort.

Having asked all the questions in his interrogation of the goblin and wand maker, Harry fills Ron and Hermione in on what he's discovered about the Horcruxes and the Hallows. First, he painfully admits that he realizes that Albus Dumbledore wanted Harry to destroy the Horcruxes and never possess the Hallows. In truth, the Hallows / trinity is more powerful as a quest and a belief than in a physical possession: when someone possesses something, he tends to take that object/idea for granted and forget to continue in the quest. This is the baptismal resolution – first renounce evil, then obtain continual relationships with the triune God. Similarly, St. John had a similar requirement from Christ – eliminate evil's clutches on humanity so that the Christian community would have a chance at true life with Christ.

Through Harry's mind, we see Lord Voldemort pursuing a victory of his own – taking the Elder Wand from Albus Dumbledore's tomb. Lord Voldemort's sacrilege in opening Dumbledore's tomb shows to what depths he will go to overcome death, even symbolically entering the realm of the dead to take something back. It is very much a replay of Christ's three days of lying in the tomb, where we can imagine that Satan felt rewarded and victorious obtaining Christ's soul, anticipating being able to destroy humankind's connection to immortality once and for all. In the series, it seems to be symbolic of taking away a wizard's faith in God, but since Dumbledore had already passed his faith on to the community, Lord Voldemort's stolen article reaped him no rewards.

Interestingly enough, the fact that Professor Dumbledore's body hasn't decomposed after a full year of being in a tomb is odd for someone that never ate the preservatives eaten nowadays. This phenomenon is called "incorruptible", occurs with some devout Christians,[120] and has never been answered by science. As the Christ figure, Professor Dumbledore would of course become an incorruptible body in the afterlife, another hint that even though Dumbledore is no longer walking on the earth, memories of his life live on.

Chapter Twenty-five: Shell Cottage

Once Harry's mind is made up, we sense him devising a plan, even if it is not all completely thought out, or he is unwilling to share critical pieces with his friends. As the trio discusses the issues around the incomplete Deathly Hallows elements, Ron agrees that they need to destroy the Horcruxes. However, he also voices all of Harry's doubts and plays out his part as the will/heart of Christ's debate in the desert – how was he going to conquer Satan/Lord Voldemort in the end? Without Horcruxes to save Lord Voldemort and Hallows to protect Harry, the scale seems still tipped in Lord Voldemort's favor. Harry mentioned the ace he has in Philosopher's Stone (p 287) – since he was able to avoid death once, he could get lucky again, but he doesn't mention it again here so as not to worry his friends.

As a last piece of the alchemy of the series, John Granger points out that Ted Lupin is the future alchemical orphan that finalizes the white stage,[121] and according to the ring composition, concludes that the Lupin/Harry Potter stand-off resolves the conflict from the mirrored

---

[120] Overcomeproblems.com, 2004, "Incorruptibles," retrieved from http://www.overcomeproblems.com /incorruptables.htm.

[121] Granger, *Deathly Hallows,* p. 22.

chapter in which Harry dismissed Remus Lupin at 12 Grimmauld Place.[122] The next morning, the trio leaves for Gringotts, and they begin the red stage in earnest as they seek to purify Lord Voldemort's essence and go to battle to purify the world against evil.

Chapter Twenty-six: Gringott's

Every year within the series is situated around the Christian calendar. At Halloween (All Hallow's Eve), we are introduced to the challenge of the year, and reminded of their vulnerability to the enemy. At Christmas time, Harry is given a gift that will help him along in his quest toward becoming the alchemical gold, and at Easter, we see new evidence that completes the picture of what the enemy is seeking. With these pieces, they work together to finish the puzzle as they devise a plan that will help them defeat the enemy. In this last book, the trio was at Lovegood's house during Spring Break, and at the Malfoy's Manor right around Easter time. Breaking into Gringott's is a few weeks past Easter, making it just about the time of Pentecost, the time of the coming of the Holy Spirit. Once it is Pentecost, all three elements – Father, Son, and Holy Spirit – come together symbolically in the Trinity to save Harry ultimately from death.

As a subtle reminder to us of the baptismal references throughout the white stage that they are leaving behind, Harry takes a moment to reminisce about the sea and how he will miss the sound of the moving water. The reference also reminds us of how the baptismal waters move us toward Christ as we sink, convert, and finally rise again in Christ. With this renewed fervor, Harry, Hermione, Ron, and Griphook depart the safety of Shell Cottage and begin their battle first at Gringott's.

Gringott's Bank is itself a representation of where the treasures in heaven are stored, from Matthew 6:19-20 ("Do not lay up for yourselves treasures on earth, where moth and rust destroy and where thieves break

---

[122] Granger, J, ed. Prinzi, 2011, *Harry Potter for Nerds,* "On Turtleback Tales and Asterisks," p. 62.

in and steal; but lay up for yourselves treasures in heaven, where neither moth nor rust destroys and where thieves do not break in and steal. (NIV)). The name itself uses the German name for God – "Gott", juxtaposed with a respelling of the word "green" to "grin." Just as many people misinterpret the meaning of what's valuable, we see the various wizards have stored different types of wealth in their vaults. In the past, we have seen the Weasley's vault with very little in it, but every time they empty it, they are suddenly given money through a windfall of some sort. Vault 713 only carried the Philosopher's Stone in its walls, since the only element of value was Christ, the true Philosopher's Stone. Harry's vault contained metals of all sorts (mostly gold, silver, and bronze) which represents his alchemical journey and the inheritance of faith he's been given to help him on this journey. Lastly, we see Bellatrix LaStrange's vault which is cluttered with things of all sorts – household items, jewels, and other riches, representing what most people would put in a vault, but as the verse says, have no business in heaven. Within this vault, symbolic of what man values as opposed to what God values, Lord Voldemort has placed one of his horcruxes – "where one's treasure is, there lies his heart also" (Matthew 6:21). We see here how much value Lord Voldemort places on worldly possessions and faith in their endurance over the ravages of time.

Knowing that they only had Griphook's loyalty as long as they held the Sword of Gryffindor, there was little surprise when Griphook turned on them although they had hoped it would be later than while still in Gringott's. In desperation, they turn to the white dragon to rescue them – again, a Christian symbol rescuing them from the depths of the earth and certain death.

Chapter Twenty-seven: The Final Hiding Place

As Harry, Ron, Hermione and the dragon escape the prison of Gringotts, Lord Voldemort's lack of forgiveness, compassion, and love has made him feel he is alone in the world – creating his own prison in his mind. Alchemically, as Harry and the Dragon emerge from Gringott's, the two alchemical elements depart as well: Harry represents the

Philosopher's Stone almost complete, and the dragon represents the completed Philosopher's Stone and immortality. The departure of the white dragon is one last whisper that it is the end of the white stage - time to move on to the final battle at Hogwarts. With only the alchemical metals still in the vaults and no immortal elements left, Gringott's is temporarily destroyed through Lord Voldemort's wrath, but will be rebuilt and reopened soon.

Chapter Twenty-eight: The Missing Mirror

It is interesting to note how many people know about Harry's invisibility cloak, but despite its abilities, they never try to steal it from him. Professor Snape used it once, but it was returned to Harry soon after. The other Death Eaters also know about Harry's cloak, but they do not recognize it as THE Cloak from the Deathly Hallows or its uniqueness, so they never make a move to keep it. Others claim that they don't need a cloak to make themselves invisible (Dumbledore in book 1 and Lord Voldemort in book 7). However, Dumbledore recognized the importance and significance of the cloak, but he returned it to the rightful owner once he knew that Harry was the rightful owner of the cloak.

Rescued from their unexpected tangle with the Death Eaters, the trio seeks refuge in The Hogshead from Aberforth Dumbledore, Albus' brother. In support of Albus being the Good Shepherd at Hogwarts, Aberforth is the goat-tender as seen by his patronus and history, a reflection on Jesus' parable about the separation of the sheep and the goats. True to form, Aberforth doesn't like to help others or want Harry to pursue Lord Voldemort. Instead, he simply accepts that evil will rule the world because the fight will be difficult and Harry might die. Perhaps this is why the Hogshead is not known for its hospitality, food, or drink, since the goats of the parable are those who did not offer any food, drink, or help to those who needed it.

Since Harry has already decided that he will trust Albus Dumbledore, Harry challenges Aberforth as he rants about the perils of fighting evil. As Aberforth's glasses flash in the firelight and Harry is reminded of the blind spider, Aragog, Ms. Rowling reminds us of Jesus' saying that he came to make the blind see, and the seeing, blind (John 9:39). Here, Aberforth is blind to the mission and the big picture rather than just the safety of his own neck. We are also reminded through Aberforth's insistence that Harry "save himself" of the robber next to Christ on the cross, telling Christ to save himself since he has that ability.

One interesting argument that Aberforth makes against following Albus's directions is that there seem to be a lot of secrets and lies imbedded in those directions. Similarly, many atheists condemn the Christian faith for not being upfront about everything that is required or expected of their followers, and that each denomination or sect seems to interpret the same words from the Bible differently. For those who are not part of the "in crowd" or those who do not seek to understand the deeper meaning of things, everything can seem to be lies and secrets. This was a key frustration for the Early Christian who did not have anything but the Hebrew (in Greek) scriptures and the letters they received as a community from the Apostle Paul for verification of their belief system. Outside of these writings were the established traditions, ceremonies, and understandings handed down from the disciples to the converts as they travelled through the towns.[123]

In defending Albus Dumbledore, Harry reminisces about having made his decision when he buried Dobby to follow the path Dumbledore set out for him. We can see this as a short autobiographical sketch and admission – it is Ms. Rowling's (subconscious) renewal of her commitment to Christ despite her anger and grief over the death of her mother. Furthermore, it is Harry's personal declaration and affirmation of John 14:16 "I am the way, the truth, and the life." As Harry decides to simply trust and "continue along the winding, dangerous path indicated for him by Albus Dumbledore" (*Deathly Hallows,* p. 563), he is finally embodying that verse. In another symbolic walk, Harry's return to Hogwarts mirrors Christ's return to Jerusalem and the early disciples' eventual entry to Rome – their final destination before death. In life, everyone has a

---

[123] Kirby, Peter, 2012, "Didache." *Early Christian Writings*.

Jerusalem to go to, a place where they have to face their enemies in an ultimate battle - be it physical, emotional, or metaphysical - that might claim their lives.

Chapter Twenty-nine: The Lost Diadem

Neville's arrival at the Hogshead and his apparent relationship with Aberforth is beginning to loosen Aberforth's stinginess. This arrival also comes with the news that the original seven openings have all been closed, but when the students needed a means by which to access the outside world, this new opening made itself. As such, the Ariana photo is the eighth opening to Hogwarts. The number eight is the symbol of a new creation from the story of David, the eighth son of Jesse and the new King of Israel. Here, we see the eight as a new beginning to Hogwarts from the crumbling of the old building and regime that operated in constant fear of Slytherin and his heirs.

Just as the return to Hogwarts echoes the historic return of the early Christians to Rome, the Room of Requirement in book seven duplicates the catacombs of Rome or other places just outside Rome where early Christians would hide from persecution.[124] Just on the outskirts of Rome, the catacombs were a safe hiding place (although not the only one) for the early Christian Eucharistic services and a place for their burials. In hiding, they were sustained by others, given room, food, and water enough for everyone just as the Room of Requirement sensed their needs and provided for the student wizards in hiding as their needs arise.

The Jews were hoping that the Christ would lead them to overthrow the Romans.[125] However, Christ ascended into heaven and his idea of overthrowing the powers that exist was of the source of sin, not just the current government of Rome (John 6:15, John 18:36). In later times, the Jews continued to hope for the coming of a Messiah that would lead them

---

[124] White, M, 1998, "In the Catecombs," retrieved from http://www.pbs.org/wgbh/pages/frontline/shows/religion /first/catacombs.html.

[125] Lendering, J, retrieved from http://www.livius.org/men-mh/messiah/messiah_07.html.

against the Romans, so there were many thoughts of revolution. Ultimately, in 70 AD, the Romans moved into Jerusalem and decimated the town to near rubble and eliminating the revolt.[126] From that time forward, the Jewish Christians in that area spread out all over the Roman Empire in more earnest (carrying out the Great Commission of Matthew 28:16-20). The Christians were also hoping for freedom of religion, being persecuted by both the Romans and the Jews, although their thoughts of revolution were mostly just about breaking free of their physical prisons and getting to a safer place, as Luna, Dean, and the others are hoping Harry has led them to do. Again, just as many times the disciples came only to give courage and words of hope and not conquest, the trio is there for another purpose beyond conquest.

Chapter Thirty: The Sacking of Severus Snape

After seven years, we finally learn something about Ravenclaw's tower and the way they think. The questions asked at the end of the last chapter and here posed to Professor McGonagall are pointedly reminiscent of the opening passages of this book. The first question, asking which came first – the phoenix or the flame – refers to the first passage, in which there is acknowledgement of the existence of a resurrection from within the creature that dies, not from outside (*Deathly Hallows, p. xi)*. Luna's answer, "that a circle has no beginning" refers to this mythological resurrection from within which brings forth a physical resurrection, but not true immortality. Professor McGonagall answers the second question - "Where do vanished objects go?" - and we are reminded of the second passage in the prologue which speaks of how memories of love and friendship immortalizes others. In her answer: "into nonbeing, which is to say, everything", we see how this immortality means omnipresence. This is also an answer to where people go when they die as well as how that person is always with us, and perhaps more so. More theologically, this implies that if God is invisible, then he

---

126 Eyewitness to History, 2005, "The Romans Destroy the Temple at Jerusalem, 70 AD," retrieved from www.eyewitnesstohistory.com.

appears to have "vanished" but is thus omnipresent – everywhere at once.

Chapter Thirty-one: The Battle of Hogwarts

Dragged into a conquest by Lord Voldemort's attack on Hogwarts, Harry, Ron, and Hermione reunite to try and sever all bonds that connect Lord Voldemort to life. The last horcrux before Nagini is the Diadem (a tiara), which Harry remembers seeing in the Room of Requirement. In the Room of Requirement, the trio is sidetracked by Malfoy and his two friends, Crabbe and Goyle, and Malfoy and Harry get into a short discussion about their wands: Draco acknowledges that Harry has his wand, and states that his mother lent him her wand. That means that neither Lucius nor Narcissa have wands for the final battle. This has several meanings. First of all, Lucius, meaning light, finally comes to live up to his name, having seen the light of truth whereas Narcissa, meaning self-absorbed, has become sacrificial in her protection and love for her son and thus has grown out of her namesake. Secondly, since both of them somewhat willingly gave up their wands, they have renounced their wicked ways and will no longer be participants in the destruction of others, even if Lord Voldemort has not yet grasped that change and still holds them hostage by living in their home. Lastly, the similarities between Harry and Draco have grown. Besides the mutual abhorrence of causing pain and death, both have parents that are sacrificing for their only sons but now can only standby while they watch their sons undergo horrible tests of inner strength against an evil, unforgiving master.

The Room of Requirement becomes a different place depending on what people seek, and as a place for lost items, it is symbolically Sheol, or a holding place of the dead (as seen by the number of skeletons of past mistakes).[127] In Lord Voldemort's case, it is a holding place for his soul, a place he hopes will keep it safe for eternity. As with the locket, Lord

---

[127] Rose, O., 2012, retrieved from http://www.myjewishlearning.com/beliefs/Theology/Afterlife_and_Messiah/Life_After_Death/Heaven_and_Hell.shtml.

Voldemort's soul fragments are protected by death symbolism to ward others away from seeking it. Undeterred, Harry, Ron, and Hermione look for the lost Diadem in the Room of Requirement and encounter the unquenchable fire that consumes Crabbe. Although they snatch Draco Malfoy and Gregory Goyle from certain death, they lose the Diadem horcrux. This seems to echo Matthew 3:12: "His winnowing fork is in his hand, and he will clear his threshing floor, gathering his wheat into the barn and burning up the chaff with unquenchable fire." After Draco and Gregory are rescued from the fire, it does seem that their chaff of Dark Arts (their sins) is burned off because neither of them joins into the action afterwards. Furthermore, with the destruction of the Diadem, the black soul of Lord Voldemort is destroyed in the fire as prescribed in the Bible for the devil: "Then he will say to those on his left, 'Depart from me, you who are cursed, into the eternal fire prepared for the devil and his angels." (Matthew 25:41, NIV) Appropriately named Fiendfyre in the series, God must have a special fire that can destroy souls if souls are a metaphysical element and not something tangible, explaining the destruction of the Diadem's soul fragment without complete loss of the Diadem itself.

Alchemically, with the deaths of Vincent Crabbe (a red animal if male) and Fred, we know the end of the red stage is coming.[128] Since there was one death heralding the beginning of the end of the black stage, three for the beginning of the end of the white stage, there is one more death to signal the end of the red stage, making seven alchemical deaths total. From a Christian standpoint, we see that the trio has again emerged from a "baptism", a literal baptism by fire. As such, we are reminded of the other baptisms they have gone through in this book: 1) baptism by earth, when the trio emerges from Ministry of Magic; 2) baptism by water, where Ron rescues Harry from the icy waters; 3) baptism by air, where the trio is rescued by the dragon and flown out of Gringotts; baptism by fire – the trio emerges from the Room of Requirement which has been consumed by the Fiendfyre. After these four baptisms, we can see that

[128] Granger, J, *The Deathly Hallows Lectures*, p. 82.

the gold stage is coming soon, since all four of the physical elements are now mastered. There is only the quintessential element baptism to complete the work.

Chapter Thirty-two: The Elder Wand

Exemplifying the purpose of community, the trio runs into trouble with the dementors as they leave Hogwarts. As they cross towards the Shrieking Shack, the dementors begin to remove the last remnants of hope from Harry, already low after the loss of Fred. With Hermione and Ron's hope as low as his own, the three friends have a hard time producing patronuses. Their friends, Luna, Ernie, and Seamus protect them with their own patronuses and do so without asking them where they are going or judging them in any way. With their encouragement, Harry was able to refocus and find his happiness in his memories of his parents (and in Christ). Similarly, the Christian community needs to stay together to support one another, especially when they are in doubt or despair. Essentially, the patronuses are the embodiment of Nehemiah 8:10 "The joy of the Lord is your strength" and using them to support your friends: 1 Thessalonians 5:11 "Therefore encourage one another and build each other up, just as in fact you are doing. "

Listening to Lord Voldemort explain his reasoning for why the Elder Wand isn't working for him very well shows us that he assumes that the last owner of the wand had to be the one who killed the previous owner, not the one who took the wand. For Lord Voldemort who is fixated on death, he always assumes death is the answer to everything and can think of nothing less that might achieve the same objective. This is a very familiar theme in evil characters and people – they tend to take everything to the extremes and are incapable of seeing anything in less than black and white terms. Thus, Lord Voldemort does not acknowledge Draco's possession of the Elder Wand since Draco only disarmed Professor Dumbledore, and again, since Draco is an under-aged wizard, he doesn't quite rank in Lord Voldemort's mind as anywhere near his equal. (Draco doesn't realize he's the owner either, though, since most wizards regard wands as possessions, not wood that has any power of its own). Lastly, in working with the Deathly Hallows elements, since Lord Voldemort dreads the cloak for its community expectations and the stone for its association with the dead, he does not understand that to master death is to accept all three elements and what they represent: 1)the power of God (the Elder Wand) establishes or helps those that are not our equals yet; 2) the Invisibility Cloak binds those together that are our equal so they can work together; and 3) the Resurrection Stone helps people work with those beyond their physical reach. It is only with all three levels working together that one can succeed – in union, not alone. With this understanding, Lord Voldemort can never truly master death.

Snape's death results from Lord Voldemort's misunderstanding of a person's worth, but gives Harry a legacy. Lord Voldemort attacks Snape, but Snape sensed that the end was near, which is why he wanted to find Harry himself – to give him the message/ memory from Dumbledore. At the end, Professor Snape's dying wish, to have Harry look at him, is to look into Lily's eyes once again, and remember his love for her through Harry. Secondly, with Snape's death, five members of the Order have died – Alastor Moody, Remus Lupin, Tonks Lupin, Sirius Black, and Severus Snape. This leaves seven members of the Order – the number of perfection. Although a bit of a stretch, Severus Snape can also be seen as a red symbol – the SS, the dreaded German group during World War II wore red arm bands. Again, the number seven points toward the end of the battle, and this is the third red death. The purification process is mostly complete, and the red stage is almost at its end as Harry moves toward the gold stage of completion.

Chapter Thirty-three: The Prince's Tale

Returning to the castle, Harry enters an almost dream-like state where he feels more distant and removed from the action around him. First, Harry notices that the dead look like they are only sleeping beneath the enchanted ceiling. This is a reminder of the time that Jesus went to Jarius's house to bring his daughter back to life, noting that she was only "asleep" (Mark 5:37), as well as Daniel's reference to the dead as "those who sleep in the dust of the earth" (Daniel 5:12). Once by himself, Harry goes to Dumbledore's Office to see Snape's memories. As if from a dream, Professor Snape's password of "Dumbledore" shows his true allegiance was to the Order to the end as well. However, the lack of people in the portraits means that Harry doesn't even have people from the past to speak to as he discovers the secrets Snape needs him to see.

Entering into Snape's mind and memories helps Harry understand not only who Severus Snape was, but also helps him understand what is to come. Through these memories, we also come to realize that some issues have not changed over time. As we see in Snape's memories, Lily was worried about her status of not having been born into a wizarding family, and Snape assured her that her blood status doesn't determine the amount of magic she will have. Similarly, whether a person was born into a Christian family or not doesn't have any effect on the amount of faith that person has. On the flip side, we also discover that Petunia wrote to Hogwarts to gain entrance, and was rejected. It is difficult to determine whether this is making any statements about people seeking faith and not obtaining it, or if this is making a statement that faith is not something one seeks but just has. Knowing Petunia's personality later on, it is more likely that she did not seek entrance to Hogwarts because she believed in magic (or God), but rather because she wanted to be part of something exclusive.

More revealing about Severus himself are the scenes that show more about his remorse at what he said about Lily and did that caused her demise. As Snape returns to Professor Dumbledore, contrite and broken about Lily's death and his part in it, Ms. Rowling begins her last theme of remorse in earnest. Snape's remorse leads him to take on the toughest job he's ever had to do – save and protect the son of the man he hated most, but that remorse repairs and renews his soul and leads Snape down the right path of returning love for hate, just as Hermione had explained earlier at The Burrow.

Another issue that never seems to change with time is how someone sees something else. Dumbledore's comment to Professor Snape "you see what you expect to see, Severus" is a key element to the whole series, from Petunia always spying on her neighbors, Vernon always seeing Harry as "bad", and many Christians discrediting Harry Potter because of the title of the first book and the word "wizards." Just as the nose tells the brain what the food will taste like before it even gets to the taste buds, the brain tells the eyes what to see before the object or person has even been tried. As Shakespeare said in "Romeo and Juliet" – "A rose by any other name would smell as sweet" (Act II, Scene ii, 1-2).[129] If instead of wizards she had used another term, would the Christianity within the series be more easily swallowed?

Having lost many people that he loved, Dumbledore confesses that he succumbed to the temptation of the Resurrection Stone, forgetting about the curse that was associated with it. In the Garden of Eden, the temptation of the Tree of the Knowledge of Good and Evil carried with it the curse of separation from God, but also the curse of judgment at the end of one's life. To end the curse and separation, God had a plan of Salvation, which involved the death of his only Son, Jesus. With the full curse upon him, Professor Dumbledore is feeling the weight of his mission and the timeline growing shorter. Thus, he makes his decisions about what needs to be done before he dies and what the important messages are that need to be passed on.

Regardless of his trust and confidence in Snape, Professor Dumbledore doesn't seem to have shared with him the knowledge of the Deathly Hallows. As a wizarding child, Snape would have heard the stories and perhaps did not realize the significance or known that two of the three were within Hogwarts. However, since Snape was thereafter very close to Dumbledore and Dumbledore himself didn't use either the stone or the cloak for any purpose, Snape didn't see their use either even though both he and Dumbledore had remorse for the loss of their loved ones. Despite this, Dumbledore does tell Snape that he wants Snape be the rock of Hogwarts once he is gone, to ensure that the students are safe from the Death Eaters (*Deathly Hallows, p. 682)*. For the community as a whole, Albus Dumbledore does everything he can to reunite the wizarding

[129] Shakespeare, W, 1597, "Romeo and Juliet," Act II, Scene ii, 1-2.

world by giving each person his or her piece of the puzzle to figure out or fight according to his or her own abilities.

In the discussions we see between Professors Dumbledore and Snape, we see more and more of a similarity of their relationship to that of Jesus and Peter according to the book of John. In addition to the above mention of Snape being the next headmaster at Hogwarts to protect the future of the wizarding world – becoming "the rock" as Peter was, we also see Snape's denials when Dumbledore predicts his own death. Knowing exactly how his own death is supposed to be carried out (even if he doesn't know the exact details), Dumbledore asks Snape to intercede (*Deathly Hallows, p 682,685)*. Next, we see Snape jealous of Dumbledore's relationship with Harry, thinking that Harry has more secrets than Snape himself does, just as Peter felt jealous of John's relationship with Jesus and asked for more information (John 21:22).

However, Dumbledore does attempt to give Snape a better picture of what the Plan is and asks Snape to follow his lead, continuing the biblical parallel from John 21:22 "Jesus answered.... You must follow me." In that picture, Dumbledore tries to explain to Severus about Harry and Lord Voldemort, showing that they are the two opposite minds united into one soul, because of the soul fragment that attached itself to Harry when Lord Voldemort "disappeared." Even with this explanation, giving everything he has to protect Harry makes no sense to Snape if Harry still has to die, especially if there doesn't seem to be a reason for it. However, for Harry's sake, Dumbledore doesn't tell Snape about the resurrection part since it is probably better if the person going to his/her death seeks only for an afterlife as a ghost and not protection from death, since then the death is not truly a sacrifice. For this matter, Jesus doesn't tell Peter and the disciples that he will be resurrected in the book of John, even though he does in the other gospels. In John, Jesus only tells the disciples that he is going somewhere where they cannot follow, but they will follow eventually. (John chapters 13, 17, and 21). From the other interactions Snape has with Dumbledore's portrait, Harry sees how much Snape truly loved Dumbledore, still loved him, and still worked against Lord

Voldemort, even as he pretended otherwise. Peter carries out Jesus' declarations to the end, becoming the rock of the church until his death in Rome in 64 AD.[130] One last parallel between Snape and St Peter comes with Snape's account of how George lost his ear. Harry sees that Snape actually saved Lupin that night from a killing curse intended for Remus Lupin (p. 688). Again, this demonstrates the echo of the high priest's servant, Malchus, who lost his ear when Peter sliced it with his sword.

At the conclusion of the memories, Harry finally realizes that Snape has been much braver than he thought, but the memories also connect him to his mother and to a different side of Severus Snape, essentially giving Harry his own time in the Garden of Gethsemane to pray and embolden him for what is to come – his own final hour, just as every early Christian faced death.

Chapter Thirty-four: The Forest Again

Harry walks towards his death, realizing that knowing death is coming takes far more courage than having death catch you unawares. Perhaps the truth behind how the Peverell Brothers mastered death was that they went to death themselves expecting death and found a way around it, rather than letting death catch them unawares. To reclaim his victory, Death had to give them things that would give them a false sense of protection so that he could catch them unawares later on. With this understanding, the resurrection has a different promise, as Ms. Rowling depicts with the Resurrection Stone hidden in the snitch. The snitch is the symbol of truth, and once Harry accepts death regardless of what lies beyond, he can then accept the truth of the Resurrection. This is J.K. Rowling's way of telling us that if we accept the truth that Christ has given us, and we accept our mortality, we are then given the power of resurrection – the truth IS the resurrection we share with Christ once we believe.

---

130 Catholic Saints, 2008, "Saint Peter," retrieved from http://www.catholic-saints.info/patron-saints/saint-peter.htm.

Christians, especially the early martyrs, have historically gone to their deaths willingly knowing that there is a resurrection beyond death that brings them spiritual immortality. Those who fight for life in fear of death have not accepted the resurrection beyond, making it easy for Death to catch them unawares. Harry is an odd mix – he understands the concept of resurrection as a spiritual one, but he does not think about whether that resurrection applies to him or not. Rather, Harry dwells on Dumbledore's part and apparent betrayal to him and begins to feel abandoned by everyone. This is reminiscent of Jesus' cry on the cross "Eli, eli, lambathani" ("My God, my God, why have you forsaken me?"), which is the last thing Christ said on the cross before he died. Christians also have to take up their cross and follow Christ (Luke 5:23). The following verse, however, is the key to Harry's survival and a major theme in the series: "For whoever wants to save their life will lose it, but whoever loses their life for me will save it" (Luke 5:24, NIV). This is the exact stand of Lord Voldemort versus Harry –Lord Voldemort wants to save his own life, and Harry is willing to lose his life to save everyone else.

In essence, this renunciation of life itself is the black stage at the end of the series – a fractal set of stages at the end of the alchemical process. As Harry thinks of the trio of abandoned boys, Lord Voldemort, Professor Snape, and himself, we see yet another threesome of conversion: Lord Voldemort was all Slytherin, Professor Snape began as a Slytherin but became a member of the Order; and Harry, who was a part of the Order from the beginning. This reminder of the transformation that has occurred through the three generations points us to this final burst through the three stages yet again and one that we see at Easter. The black, easily seen at Black Friday as we see Christ renounce his life, the white of the illumination that Christ was indeed the Son of God (Matthew 27:54, Mark 15:39), and the red stage of Christ's battle for the life and purification of the world before his return to our world.

Contrary to many people's beliefs, Harry is not the Christ figure in the series, he only represents the common Christian on his walk towards Christ. In this last book of the series, Ms. Rowling brings in the more complex understanding of Easter. In this advanced understanding, Easter reminds us that Christ rose from the dead, but in that celebration is the knowledge that because of Christ's Resurrection, we are allowed that same gift from God (more on this next section). As the possessor of the Resurrection Stone, Harry can turn the stone three times, representing the three days of Christ's entombment. In accepting his own mortality, Harry turns to those key figures from his life who are now beyond the grave to help bring him to the other side. With all of those that Harry loved surrounding him, Ms. Rowling shows us the power of past friends and angels that protect God's people. This also mirrors the transfiguration scene in which Jesus spoke to near-solid figures of Moses and Elijah on the mountain shortly before his passion (Mark 9:2).

Lord Voldemort symbolically chooses Aragog's lair for his final snare of Harry, representing his cunning and thorough weaving of death all around him. From this, we see why the chapter is entitled "Into the Forest Again." This is the second time that Harry has gone into the Forbidden Forest willingly to help someone else. In *Chamber of Secrets*, Harry and Ron entered the forest in hopes of stopping the Monster from the Chamber of Secrets but they run into Aragog. In return for answers, Aragog declares Harry and Ron to be "food" and they are rescued by the Ford Anglia (one of the angel representations of the series). Furthermore, this sticky lair is in keeping with Lord Voldemort's style – he enjoys being in places that make others uncomfortable, as in the cave. These places help put him in a position of advantage, much as a spider does in its web, as it inflicts a slow and painful death to all who enter. The surrounding scene, with the many jeering Death Eaters seated around an open fire, is also reminiscent of the many "trials" the early Christians endured in defense of their faith.

As an echo of Christ's passion, Harry goes as a willing lamb to meet with Lord Voldemort, alone, without his wand or any means of defense. He drops the stone, and the cloak is tucked away in his robes in an effort to remove any temptation to fight for life. Similarly, all of the Early Christians considered it an honor to die for Christ, and the height of honor to die in a similar manner. As Christ said himself, "There is no greater love than to lay down one's life for one's friends," (John 15:16).

In alchemy, the final "Great Work" must die in order to be reborn into the new element – the new Philosopher's Stone.[131] Thus, Harry is now the new Philosopher's Stone, having been reborn as well as united with the Divine Mind of Albus Dumbledore/ Christ. As a final alchemical note, John Granger points out that this is chapter thirty-four, and 3+4 = 7.[132] This is therefore the final act, the act of perfection, and is also the end of the series' red stage since now Lord Voldemort and Harry are finally purified from each other.

Chapter Thirty-five: King's Cross

Having fully to experience pain or still be in the same area in which he died, Harry is surprised to find himself with a physical existence where he thinks and feels. Not needing glasses anymore, Harry's new perfect body reminds us of the verse from Hebrews 12:23: "to the spirits of righteous men made perfect" (NIV). From this verse, we see that in Heaven, God perfects us, just as Harry is now perfected – not feeling pain, not needing glasses, having no scars of recent battles. Realizing the perfect nature of his surroundings, Harry glances about the place that he is at, and he sees the first horrible element: a small, abandoned child-like thing whimpering. It is hard to decide which is more surprising – that something could be sad in this place of perfection, or that something could be so horrible that is was not able to become perfect in this perfect place, as Harry was. Ms. Rowling tells us that this horrible child is the horcrux piece of Lord Voldemort that has finally been separated from Harry's mind and body,[133] which then explains why he cannot be happy in

---

[131] Dooling, D., "What is Alchemy?," retrieved from http://www.alchemylab.com/what_is_alchemy.htm.

[132] Granger,J, Nov 5th, 2010, Lecture notes: "Unlocking Potter-Mania: The Christian Content Behind the World's Best Selling Books," Vienna, VA.

[133] The Leaky Cauldron, 2007, "Interview with J.K. Rowling," retrieved from http://www.the-leaky-cauldron.org/2007/11/19/new-interview-with-j-k-rowling-

both death and perfection. As the final piece of information about where Harry is, Albus Dumbledore approaches Harry with midnight blue robes, the color blue representing heaven.

Albus Dumbledore is a welcome comfort to Harry, and in addition to the all white surroundings, this subtly tells us that Harry is now in the white stage at the end of this alchemical work. As part of this stage, we understand that all the answers to the multitude of questions are coming, beginning with the most fundamental question: is Harry alive or dead? As Albus Dumbledore explains, Lord Voldemort was able to stay alive because of the fragment of soul placed in Harry (amongst other things), but Harry was able to stay alive because his blood was within Lord Voldemort. With the "death" of Harry, Lord Voldemort now has no connections to him at all, so Harry has regained his original protection from his mother and Voldemort has lost his horcrux through Harry. Overall, the theme is that through death, we have life since in dying to self, we rise in Christ, and in sharing His death, we rise again (Romans 6:4).

Knowing now that Harry is not dead, there is an important distinction to make here. Although many people believe that Harry's "resurrection" makes him the Christ figure, there are two important differences. First, as Ms. Rowling ensured that Harry did not die, his return is not a true resurrection as Jesus' was. Secondly, Albus Dumbledore is the Christ figure of the series, even though he does not have a physical resurrection. The phoenix song and departure parallel Christ's visits to his disciples after his death and his ascension, but I suspect that Ms. Rowling had to simplify Albus Dumbledore's death in support of the requirement to have Dumbledore meet with Harry and support others after he was gone. Harry didn't die but was knocked unconscious, continuing Harry's representation of St. John in the Early Church. St. John was sentenced to death twice, but was able to endure the process and stay alive before dying as an old man.[134]

---

for-release-of-dutch-edition-of-deathly-hallows.

134 Eternal Word Television Network, St. John the Evangelist, retrieved from

Understanding that Harry is a beloved disciple, he and Dumbledore share a special bond in which they understand each other's deepest secrets without malice. In rabbinical style, Harry and Albus Dumbledore try to figure out where exactly the place is. Harry decides that it looks like King's Cross, an apt name for the crossroads between life and death, and the place of Christ's crucifixion. Most of all, the entire scene parallels our own encounter with Christ at the cross, as Harry meets Dumbledore upon his near-death. Christ's decision at the cross to give up his spirit so he could restore humankind to God's grace intones Harry's choice to continue on or return to life but also reminds us that the cross is where we all have decisions to make. Lastly, the reiteration of the concept of King's Cross station reminds us of the crossing paths between the muggle and the magical world as this makes a new crossing – between the physical and the spiritual realm. In this state of dreams, or the in-between place where angels dwell, we see Harry's last proof of mastery over this fifth element, where he is "baptized" through immersion in the element, the last baptism required of our existence.

The theology behind the Deathly Hallows is extremely philosophical. Albus Dumbledore's insistence that the Deathly Hallows are a lure for fools is more a warning that the trinity and its promise of mastery over death isn't something a person obtains through desire or physical conquest. Rather, this mastery over death occurs through acceptance of death, through understanding and transformation of the heart. Are the Hallows any better than the Horcruxes as an object that defeats death? In truth, yes, since they don't involve the maiming of anyone for its creation, but it is in the symbolic and transformational nature of the three objects that they have power, not through possession alone. As Mr. Ollivander points out with the wands – the wand chooses the wizard, and the wand won't work as well for someone else since the way it was given is as important as the wand and wizard's mutual desire for knowledge. Possession of the Elder Wand did not give every owner the power it supposedly possessed, as Lord Voldemort discovered himself. The cloak,

---

http://www.ewtn.com/library/mary/johnevan.htm.

as Albus Dumbledore points out, has power through its ability to protect others as well as the owner. Ultimately, the trinity itself is not something Christians pursue to possess as a threesome talisman. Rather, we internalize the elements of the trinity by not putting one's faith in physical objects but keeping one's faith alive through daily intercession and community, thus mastering the power of death.

Interestingly enough, as the resurrection element of the trinity, was Christ himself in need of the trinity? As Albus Dumbledore explains the limits under which he accepted ownership of the Elder Wand, we see a glimpse of a vision of Christ in the desert, deciding how he was to carry out God's mission. From the four songs of Isaiah (and the four houses of Hogwarts), we see four possibilities, and Christ himself took on many of the roles at different times (as did Dumbledore). He was first and foremost Jewish, from a pure bloodline, upholding the traditions of the Jewish world and thus was the light at the top of the mountain to guide others to righteousness. Later, he was the brilliant scholar, both at his bar mitzvah in Jerusalem with the rabbis around him, and with the disciples and other followers when he was older. Primarily, he was the suffering servant allowing his disciples to carry on the brave leadership against evil while still in the world. It is evident that he chose the role of the knowing servant to help others but not lead them into battle, knowing that he died a sacrificial death so that others may continue on, and he could protect them from Satan and evil from beyond the grave.

Each of the individual elements of the Deathly Hallows has its own transformation once Albus Dumbledore inspects and uses them. Albus Dumbledore transformed the power of God in the wand from an instrument of death to one of compassion and goodness in reflection of Christ's own transformative power on our understanding of God. Once Harry receives the Cloak, we see that the Cloak will only work if the person who uses it truly needs or believes in its power to conceal that person and assist him. Since Dumbledore had other means of invisibility, he had no need of the cloak so his possession of the cloak while Harry was at the Durseleys destroyed its seductive power. We notice that no one desires the cloak, and after its use by others, the cloak is always returned to Harry Potter, the rightful owner despite its ability to repel all charms and jinxes. The last element, the Resurrection Stone, the symbol of Christ, reminds us of Christ's self-sacrifice, and that we have to be willing to sacrifice ourselves and not seek immortality itself.

After Albus Dumbledore finds the stone and tries to use it to bring his family back to this side of the grave, the curse of the ring reminds him that the channel to bring a physical life back from death must be destroyed to break the curse. By putting on the ring, Dumbledore takes the curse of death from the ring/ Resurrection Stone to himself and fixes the method of his death. In John 10:17-18, we see this same idea: "... because I lay down my life... . no one takes it from me, but I lay it down of my own accord." Even though Albus Dumbledore passes along these three elements to Harry, they have been transformed and do not hold the original understanding or use as they had when they were created. Similarly, God's might, Christ's resurrection, and the Holy Spirit take on a different meaning through Christ's life, death, Resurrection, and translation to his disciples as they take up the fight against evil in this world.

Whereas Dumbledore understood that he was separate from the Elder Wand, working with it to accomplish good without possessing it, he explains about Lord Voldemort's discovery of the Elder Wand. In this story, Ms. Rowling shows us that Lord Voldemort doesn't understand the true power of God's love for his people and that the people of God, those chosen by God, have a bond of love that defeats all others. In the Bible, the Philistines tried to obtain this power by stealing the Ark, but they realized too late that the power wasn't just about possessing the Ark itself. God's instrument, the Ark, only protected the people he had chosen to be his people and pursue a common goal. In Lord Voldemort's denial of anything beyond the tangible world, including love, we again see one of Ms. Rowling's main themes - that the true master of death not only accepts death, but "understands that there are far, far worse things in the living world than dying," a concept Lord Voldemort never seems to understand.

As this chapter concludes, there are two side notes. In concluding his conversation with Harry, Albus Dumbledore tells Harry not to pity the dead, a ring of Luke 23:28 "Do not weep for me, but weep for yourselves and your children", Jesus' words to the women of Jerusalem when he stops because of their tears on his way to the cross. Secondly, Harry's clarifying question about whether his encounter had actually occurred or was only in his head could unleash many discussions. John Granger points to this line in an earlier book, in which he states that alchemy is all about the subject-object relationship,[135] and the fact that Harry asks about whether it is real or not or if it's just in his head is the critical line, since it is both.

Chapter Thirty-six: The Flaw in the Plan

As Harry returns to his earthly surroundings, Lord Voldemort and his Death Eaters enjoy only a partial victory with Harry's "death." First of all, Lord Voldemort's fall to the ground after he cursed Harry symbolizes the force of a total separation from Harry now that he has lost the blood bond with Harry. Secondly, Lord Voldemort is wary to approach Harry to discover for himself whether or not the Killing Curse worked, and with good reason – this is the fourth time that Lord Voldemort has tried the Killing Curse and each time, it was Lord Voldemort that suffered more of a defeat than Harry did. First, as a baby in *Philosopher's Stone*, Harry Potter was protected by his mother's love, and Lord Voldemort lost his body. Three years later, at the end of *Goblet of Fire*, Lord Voldemort tried to kill Harry and their wands united, allowing Harry to get away. Harry's witnessing brought a resistance movement Lord Voldemort was hoping to avoid. A little more than two years later, Lord Voldemort tried the Killing Curse on Harry during the escape from Number Four Privet Drive at the beginning of *Deathly Hallows*, but Harry's wand destroyed the wand in

---

[135] Granger, J, *Unlocking Harry Potter,* "Chapter & Key Two: Literary Alchemy," pp. 51-53.

Lord Voldemort's hand. Here in the forest, Lord Voldemort tried to kill Harry again, and Lord Voldemort was knocked unconscious by the effort. Because Lord Voldemort refuses to see the power of love, he does not understand that no matter what he does, he can't kill love completely – that quality that Harry has in such abundance and the ultimate moral of Christianity. The last insight before someone else knows that Harry is still alive is that within the series, Harry Potter's symbolic battle over evil at the end of each book is a different length of time. In *Philosopher's Stone*, Harry lies almost dead for three days, the time of transformation echoing Christ's return. Here at the end, Harry's almost-death is only about three minutes long; again, an echo of Christ's three-day battle against evil and his resurrection.

Lord Voldemort finally sends Narcissa Malfoy to determine whether Harry is indeed dead. Blind to her love for her family, Lord Voldemort again does not see how forcing people to turn against the people they love only turns them against himself. Sure that Lord Voldemort will curse him again as soon as his return is announced, Harry hopes for a miracle when Narcissa comes to inspect him and discovers Narcissa's love has conquered her disdain for those different from herself. As John Granger suggests that Narcissa Malfoy's nails represent the nails that pierced Christ's flesh and put him on the cross,[136] but it also echoes the nails that pierced all of those early Christians as they were hung on crosses in persecution for their faith. Narcissa then makes a more obvious statement of her conversion by declaring Harry Potter dead when he is otherwise and lying to Lord Voldemort, risking death in her mutiny. In her mind, if death is required to assure life for others, she is willing to make that sacrifice.

In this "Mastery of Death" standoff between Lord Voldemort's horcurxes and Harry's Deathly Hallows, we see more clearly how little Lord Voldemort understands of things that he cannot see physically. John Granger points out that since Harry Potter has returned from the Lord Voldemort's Killing Curse issued from the Elder Wand, Lord Voldemort's

---

[136] Granger, J, *The Deathly Hallows Lectures*, p. 124.

commands no longer hold any weight with Harry or others.[137] This ineffectiveness points back to the wand choosing the wizard, and the mutual conquest required of the wizard and wand owner. After Dumbledore's time spent with the wand, the Elder Wand no longer chooses to pursue evil or punish others making its true possession by an evil wizard impossible. It is only because of Harry's constant physical presence despite every effort to the contrary that Lord Voldemort feels that Harry is the only one that might threaten him.

There are some other warnings from Ms Rowling to others from the battle. Departing from the forest, Hagrid's wrath at the centaurs for their lack of assistance is a call out to all those who feel a fight between good and evil is never theirs to fight. The reality is that either outcome affects their future, and if they do not participate, then eventually they will have to fight evil alone, unaided. Firenze is the exception to the centaurs – he did fight, and as his name implies, he is a centaur with new ideas, as enlightened as those in the Renaissance.

Beyond the forest, Harry has now faced death and survived, so there is nothing left to fear to attract the dementors. Harry realizes that he now has a talisman – all those elements of Christ that protect him now from evil and despair – both the stag and the resurrection. Harry speaks of his father's stag, just as we are all sons and daughters of God, and God protects us through Christ's resurrection and the Holy Spirit. As Christians, those who truly accept Christ also put this talisman upon their hearts, protecting them from evil, spiritual death, and despair. The ensuing dawn as they depart the forest grounds echoes both of the time that the women discovered Christ's resurrection and the dawning of a new era – one where evil no longer has any hold on life.

In Harry's absence, Neville always takes the lead against Lord Voldemort, and thus he leads the charge when everyone still thinks Harry is dead. Neville Longbottom's valiant efforts rouse others to stand against the Death Eaters, and a combination of Harry's resurrection and their own

---

[137] Granger, J, *the Deathly Hallows Lectures,* p. 124.

will to overpower the Death Eaters (as was shown in *Goblet of Fire* in Defense Against the Dark Arts class) have overwhelmed Lord Voldemort's cursing abilities, so none of his curses hold anymore.[138] Thankfully, this means that the Sorting Hat's fiery end extinguishes quickly as it produces the Sword of Gryffindor – again, a protection against death for another disciple of Christ.

With this renewal, Neville kills Nagini and destroys the last horcrux that attaches Lord Voldemort to life. Now completely mortal, Lord Voldemort and Harry are now and physically whole once again, although Lord Voldemort only has a portion of the soul he began with while Harry has all of his intact. This signals the end of the red stage – the unification of the races in a final battle and stand against evil, and the purification of Harry and Lord Voldemort. Alchemically, this is the distillation process – the final removal of all impurities for a pure substance.

Renewed by Dumbledore's comments about the Deathly Hallows and the strength of the cloak, Harry transforms its previous use to a more active one. With its ability to protect others, he now uses it to defend others more fiercely, not just to shield himself and those closest to him showing a new growth in understanding. This renewal from Dumbledore's words parallels the outpouring of the Holy Spirit on the early disciples during Pentecost, reminding us that it is Pentecost at Hogwarts since this battle takes place a few weeks after Easter. This is the new direction that the disciples of Christ take as they interpret Jesus' direction from Matthew 28:19 (NIV): " Go and make disciples of all nations, baptizing them in the name of the Father and of the Son and of the Holy Spirit," as an inclusion of any being resisting evil, regardless of their race. Ms Rowling suggests a protection of others against evil regardless of their understanding of God as well, as demonstrated by the Malfoy family here and echoed in Kingsley Shacklebolt's declaration that those brave enough should put protégé charms on muggle houses as well as their own since regardless of their ability, they still did not want Lord Voldemort to cause unnecessary deaths.

---

[138] Granger, J, *The Deathly Hallows Lectures,* p. 122.

As further declaration of a change in the world order now that Christ's disciples are able to resist death, we see a definite change in the house elves at Hogwarts. As the house-elves join the fray in the Great Hall, the only magical creatures not represented in the conflict are dragons and the goblins that are perhaps too entrenched in their accumulation of the alchemical metals to worry about what might be beyond. In a complete defiance to the magical code, the house-elves have taken their own stand against evil, making their own decisions, and are not making decisions based on loyalty to any master but to an idea – freedom from the oppression of evil.

In the Great Hall, Harry finally turns the tables on Lord Voldemort and declares the battle with Lord Voldemort for his own. Trying to buy time and get Lord Voldemort to see where he has been wrong, Harry tries to help him understand how his own choices have isolated him. First, rather than explain to Lord Voldemort who truly owns the Elder Wand, Harry moves to discuss remorse. Remorse is a new topic in *Deathly Hallows*, but its recurrence is significant in this book about immortality, the substance of souls, and pathways to immortality. In a clear way, Ms. Rowling explains how true remorse is the only way to heal a broken soul, which will be a significant event for Lord Voldemort, since he has many things to be remorseful about.

The actually substance of the soul is a topic that does not arise in most religious discussions, but in philosophy, there are many debates about its necessary existence and tangibility. In Ms. Rowling's explanation, the soul is a substance that can be torn, placed into another object, destroyed, and restored with the power of remorse. Severus Snape's soul was made whole through his remorse about having chosen the wrong side and the deeds he had committed, even though he had not directly killed anyone. In the Christian community, Christians are called on to ask forgiveness, and make restitution for sins they commit, restoring the relationship between the two people. However, a physical restitution does not necessitate a feeling of sadness for the emotional and physical hurt caused, the recklessness of the decision, and the act of violence. It is this emotional understanding that creates the spiritual "glue" that reconnects the soul fragments and reunites the person with his or her community.

The concept of remorse, however, is not a feeling that Lord Voldemort has ever felt before, having always been distant from others in mind, body, and soul. If Lord Voldemort chooses to feel remorse, he has a chance to reunite his soul and become something more than a fractured soul. Remorse and the rebuilding of a soul can be painful for someone who has never felt any emotions other than anger and hate in life, and for them, perhaps death seemed sweeter.

Secondly, Harry has changed the name from Lord Voldemort to Tom Riddle, another risk Harry takes to help Lord Voldemort understand his own isolation. This "renaming" echoes a few changes: 1) a change in their relationship from one of child-master to equal masters; 2) Professor Dumbledore used to call Lord Voldemort Tom Riddle, and since Harry is in Professor Dumbledore's footsteps, he feels he is stepping into those shoes; and 3) since Tom Riddle is now mortal, the name Voldemort doesn't fit – he can no longer "flee death." As two mortals, the line is now drawn between equal measures of good and evil.

The last element of Harry's speck is the symbolism at the end of Harry's statement. As the sun peers over the window ledges, the red-gold glow symbolizes the red elixir of life's glow created from the gold of the Philosopher's Stone. Just as a new dawn brings about a new beginning, the red glow of gold indicates that Harry's declaration of ownership over the Elder's Wand has completed his own metamorphosis to the Philosopher's Stone.

As a physical representation of the conclusion, Ms. Rowling depicts this closure through concentric circles surrounding Harry after the death of Lord Voldemort. The order in which the characters from the series come to hug Harry creates the concentric circles of his relationships – those in the inner circle are Ron and Hermione, then Neville, Ginny, and Luna, followed by the Order of the Phoenix, then all others. In a similar conclusion, we see the ending of the split between Order of the Phoenix and the Death Eaters in the phrases used to describe the aftermath of the battle scenes: "teachers and pupils, ghosts and parents, centaurs and house-elves" sitting together without regard to class, race, or belief. From Galatians 3:28, in which Paul speaks about breaking down the divisions within the world: "There is neither Jew nor Greek, slave nor free, male nor female, for you are all one in Christ Jesus" – they are all one at Hogwarts, the Christian community, just as the early Christian church was one community.

To remind everyone that above all, Christ is the beginning and the end, Harry, Hermione, and Ron go to speak to Albus Dumbledore to tie up the final loose ends – the elements of the Deathly Hallows. As Harry speaks to Professor Dumbledore about the elements of the Deathly Hallows, Harry essentially asks for permission to allow the Elder Wand to return to its hiding place, and the Resurrection Stone return to the earth (from dust to dust). In many ways, the Resurrection Stone returning to the earth recalls John 12:24: "I tell you the truth, unless a kernel of wheat falls to the ground and dies, it remains only a single seed. But if it dies, it produces many seeds." Harry was the first fruit to return to life from the stone, but now that it is planted, many more can rise from the ashes as well.

Before its final resting place, Harry uses the Elder Wand to renew his phoenix wand, demonstrating a restored faith in God and Christ.[139] However, Harry returns the Elder Wand to its resting place with Dumbledore in the tomb. Drawing this act into a more global element, the essence of this symbolism in modern day is that Christians no longer use the Ark as their symbolic power of God. Rather, they only carry wooden representatives that remind them of Christ: crosses, etc. On the other hand, Harry keeps the Invisibility Cloak, since by representing the Holy Spirit, it is something shared, passed on, and kept close to one's heart, keeping the love for all others alive.

---

139 Granger, J, 2007, *Deathly Hallows* pp. 104, 124.

More than anything else, the final message with the Deathly Hallows seems to be that it is not catastrophic if the three elements are scattered. Perhaps, they are only reunited for a particularly important cause (as in the apocalypse). Otherwise, a mental assurance of their existence should be enough to encourage others to make the quest for God's knowledge, Christ's love, and the indwelling of the Holy Spirit, and from their quest, form their own faith in Christ.

Appendix:
Misunderstood Christianity

Have you ever said something that someone else completely took the wrong way, and what was meant as a compliment was taken as a disparaging remark? As much as we try to think about how to make a statement very clear and positive, there will always be some people who misunderstand the intention or reference and take the statement the wrong way. As our world becomes more internationally linked, cultural connotations and traditions play into our understanding and interpretation of what we heard, and something that might have been a regular statement in one country is taken as a curse in another, setting up negativities that didn't need to exist. In many ways, J.K. Rowling has had the same misfortune – she wrote a children's collection, meant to be Christian in intent, with traditional symbolism and themes, but due to some unfortunate circumstances (such as the change of the first book's name from *Harry Potter and the Philosopher's Stone* to *Harry Potter and the Sorcerer's Stone*), her intended audience of Christians banned her books, saying they were anything <u>but</u> Christian.[140]

A Matter of Religious Interpretation

To help us understand where the debate and division arise around J.K. Rowling's work, we first need to look into the role of religious interpretation in the world today. Each world religion is unique not only compared to other world religions, but also compared to the various cultures within the religion itself. For instance, Christianity in England has very different traditions than Christianity in the United States – the English have many remembrance services in which military personnel come in uniform with poppies in their lapels, a custom that has never been held in the United States. Also, although the modern age of communication and open exchange has diminished the number of

---

[140] Elliott, B, 2007, "Harry Potter: Harmless Christian Novel or Doorway to the Occult?" retrieved from http://www.cbn.com/spirituallife/OnlineDiscipleship/HarryPotterControversy/elliott_RichardAbanes.aspx.

mysteries between religions, each is still not fully understood until there is a personal cultural exchange. To use an old First Nations adage: "don't judge someone until you've walked a mile in his moccasins." Unfortunately, when there is a new understanding or interpretation brought to a united religious community, these new interpretations are seen as a challenge to who God is. The challenge to the status quo worries many people and causes them unease as they try to understand God in the new context, but this causes enmity between brothers as they all discern for themselves where they stand. On a more global scale, these religious differences bring strife to the world when these new interpretations or insights are misunderstood, but they could also bring variety, creativity, and new clarity to more rigid concepts that re-energize the world.

With each religion having its own interpretation of the world, each religion having different sects or denominations, and each denomination having cultural interpretations of the creeds, it is no wonder that people within even the same religion feel misunderstood. For example, if the word "red" in China shows happiness, but in Spain "red" is an invitation to anger, then even the simple word "red" will conjure different emotions and images for two different people. Translations of important manuscripts from one language to another tend to change the original meaning as well, leading to further division even within the same religion. Lastly, throughout history, religions have incorporated ideas from other countries that are compatible with their religion, which also helps that country accept the truths of the new religion. Sometimes, a debate around an unclear concept will finally bring new understandings for everyone. One major debate in the first millennium of Christianity revolved around icons, a standard practice nowadays in many Christian denominations. Although the Jews are careful not to depict God in their art, the early converted Christians drew pictures of Christ on their tombs in the catacombs, and other such early images of saints emerged throughout the first seven centuries A.D.[141] With the Islamic iconoclast

[141] Religious Facts, 2012, "Orthodox Icons: History of Icons," retrieved from

influence in previously Christian lands, Christian leaders began turning away from icons, with Emperor Leo III declaring them "idolatry" in 731, a declaration carried through by his son, Constantine V.[142] After a couple centuries of the tide turning one way then the other, icons were finally allowed again in all forms of art as long as the icon focused on showing the way to heaven and not becoming heaven itself, since it shows humanity and not divinity itself. From this example, we can see that although new interpretations and cultural understandings take time, through a willingness to discuss points of view and an open mind to the truths that might be hidden in the new interpretation, we can possibly find common ground and a new perspective that help us grow within our own religious understanding.

Who is J. K. Rowling?

Perhaps a short introduction as to who J.K. Rowling is will help us see how her writing the Harry Potter series could be seen as a Christian undertaking. J.K. Rowling is first a Christian with a cultural upbringing from the British Isles; and with her classical training and deep study of traditions,[143] she has brought a different perspective of Christianity to the world through her creative *Harry Potter* series. J. K. Rowling did not intend for the magical elements within her story to be taken literally, as an "introduction to magic" book.[144] Rather, she was struggling with her faith after her mother died, found comfort in the resurrection of Christ, and wrote a story in which her main character depicts that struggle.[145] Choosing to place her characters in a magical world was more a matter of developing a little surrealism or a means of escape from the real world,

---

http://www.religionfacts.com/christianity/things/icons.htm.

142 Religious Facts, 2012, "Orthodox Icons: History of Icons," http://www.religionfacts.com/christianity/things/icons.htm.

143British Council, 2011," J.K. Rowling," retrieved from http://literature.britishcouncil.org/j-k-rowling.

144 J.K. Rowling Interview, Mugglenet, 2012, "J.K. Rowling Q&A," retrieved from http://www.mugglenet.com/jkr-royalalbert.shtml.

145145 J.K. Rowling Interview, Mugglenet, 2012, "J.K. Rowling Q&A," retrieved from http://www.mugglenet.com/jkr-royalalbert.shtml.

and not an attempt to generate a rebirth of witchcraft. However, whereas in Scotland mythical creatures and wizards are an accepted part of their culture,[146] many American Christians have denounced the series for these cultural inclusions perhaps because they are not part of the American Christian cultural identity. Could we perhaps put this cultural difference aside, and look for Christ in the series, just as Christ would have us do?

Historical Misinterpretations of the Christian Message

As part of the decision, we are reminded of some key Christian events throughout history of how Christians were either misunderstood or persecuted for their beliefs or deeds, or how Christians themselves misunderstood others of the same faith and persecuted them for their own interpretation of God's direction. First of all, Mary, the Mother of Jesus, was a very young, unmarried girl when she was visited by the Holy Spirit, and conceived a child out of wedlock (Luke 1:26-45). From both the Jewish and gentile perspective, Mary should have been severely punished. From the insider's point of view, Mary would have been punished for listening and believing in God's direction for her life. Thankfully, her husband to be, Joseph, was visited by an angel and told to accept Mary and her interpretation of what happened to her (Matthew 1: 18-25). By accepting her interpretation of events, Jesus was born and Christianity began. Thus, we see that a potential disaster was avoided by discussion and agreement, just as the disagreements about Harry Potter could be resolved through listening and the acceptance of another interpretation.

A second example of a man that helped shed new light about Christ for others is John the Baptist. As one of the last prophets pointing the way to Christ, John the Baptist had many converts that reformed themselves in the hopes of Christ's eminent coming (Matthew 3:1-6). However, in the same vein as the other prophets, he also had not-so-friendly encounters with both the Pharisees and King Herod. For the

[146] Mysterious Britain and Ireland, "Dragon," retrieved from http://www.mysteriousbritain.co.uk/ legends/dragons.html.

Pharisees and Sadducees, John offered the comforting words "you brood of vipers, who warned you to flee from the coming wrath?" (Matthew 3:7). Rather than try to incorporate them and convert them to the truth of Christ's coming, John alienates them, permanently seeming to set the Pharisees and Jesus (and his future followers) against himself and Jesus. The Pharisees came forward to understand who John was and what he was doing, but John's antagonism created division among the Jews of the time and denied them the waters of baptism and repentance. John's interaction with King Herod was also very oppositional – rather than bring King Herod kindly to a discussion about his marital problems and disobedience, John publicly denounces King Herod's affair with his brother's wife (Mark 6: 16-18). King Herod, in full knowledge and fear of John the Baptist's spirituality and vocation as prophet, was too cowardly to admit his own wrongdoings and threw John the Baptist in prison for declaring the truth (Luke 3:20).

Because John was only focused on proving everyone around him wrong, his prejudices against the Pharisees and rulers of his time clouded his ability to see them as individuals who also need God's love and forgiveness. Unfortunately, this prejudice set in motion a division among the Jews in Israel that continued into Jesus' ministry and beyond. This division resulted in wars, various acts and attempts of genocide, and mistrust between the two religions for centuries[147] that could have been avoided had John been open minded and forgiving of his fellow Jews. Christians are called to help each other return to the faith when they have turned away, but there must also be a listening element to hear the potential in the other point of view first. Similarly, within the Harry Potter conflict are many emotional issues and the reflex might be to judge the series based on the first title, but if we first listen and accept some of the surrealism despite its faults, we might be able to salvage much of what is good in the series and help defuse the religious conflict that exists.

---

[147] Sloyan, G, "Christian Persecution of Jews over the Centuries," retrieved from http://www.ushmm.org/research/center/church/persecution/persecution.pdf.

Jesus himself had similar conflicts during his lifetime with various groups of people and Jews. Although Jesus could read others' hearts and knew what they were thinking, he intentionally did not make himself clear to many people. By using parables, Jesus confused the Pharisees and only explained their true meanings to his closest disciples. To many, Jesus' words were just a simple story, but to many of the Jewish leaders, his words were blasphemous, as when Jesus said "I and the Father are one" (John 10:30, NIV). In response, the people were going to stone Jesus, but he escaped (John 10:33-38). Here we see how Jesus' words were misunderstood, but only because the people didn't understand the deeper meaning of what Jesus had said. Since the people did not understand Jesus, they persecuted him for his interpretation.

For his own disciples, Jesus has more instructional advice. Once the disciples were instructed about the parables' meaning and who Jesus was, they saw that Jesus was not being blasphemous or just a good storyteller – he was leading them to a closer relationship to God. Secondly, Jesus performed many miracles during his lifetime – healing, exorcising demons, resuscitating the dead – and many times the Pharisees accused Jesus of using magic from the Devil himself (Matthew 12:24) for doing these miracles. Jesus' explanations for his actions only incensed the Pharisees so they persecuted Jesus for being blasphemous (Mark 2:7, John 10:33-36; Mark 14:63-65). In the end, because Jesus knew the hearts of the Pharisees and Sadducees were closed to seeing the truth, Jesus did not bother to explain his actions or words very much to them. However, since those with closed hearts were in power, Jesus was denounced and put to death (Matthew 26:57-68, 27:11-50).

The Mission of Christianity

On the surface, it would seem that the Harry Potter series is just a long epic tale of good conquering evil. For some of the more zealous religious people, the entire epic is blasphemous since it talks about "magic" and "witches," and uses wands and spells.[148] However, for those

---

[148] Roper, J, "Harry Potter: the Hero for Modern Witchcraft," retrieved from

who look deeper into the series, there are more subtle Christian meanings behind the obvious magic. As readers, we follow a pilgrim, Harry Potter, along his path of challenges and rewards towards the goal of union with Christ within a world in which those with faith (magical people and creatures) live in secrecy.

One key Christian that we should mention here is Paul, since he was a fundamental element in the beginnings of Christianity who helped interpret the biblical text of the time for the early Christians. As background, Paul was a Roman citizen from Tarsus, where he was raised in the Jewish faith and began his studies to become a rabbi.[149] Zealous in the Jewish faith, Paul took it upon himself to help exterminate the Christian cult, since Paul saw the Christians changing the faith of the Jews in Jerusalem and threatening to spread their blasphemous interpretation of God around the world (Acts 8:1-3). Paul was on his way to Damascus to carry out the extermination of Christians in that city when he was suddenly surrounded by a bright light and heard Jesus' voice speaking to him (Acts Chapter 9, NIV). Now blinded, Paul continued on to Damascus, where he learned the truth behind who Jesus was and eventually came to fully comprehend the mission of Christianity. Paul finally saw a new dimension to the Jewish laws he knew and became the Apostle to the Gentiles, carrying the good news of Jesus' message to Rome and many other regions in the Roman Empire (Acts Chapters 13-28). Similarly, there have been many articles from devout Christians who were against J.K Rowling's works because of its mystical dimension. However, after they read through the series intending to find the blasphemous connections, they found mostly Christian connections (John Granger, Connie Neal and others), but in a newer, brighter light than before, just as Paul did many years ago.

---

http://www.cbn.com/spirituallife/onlinediscipleship/harrypottercontroversy/harrypotterheromodernwitchcraft.aspx.

[149] Bible Encyclopedia [Online], "Paul," retrieved from http://www.christiananswers.net/dictionary/paul.html.

One other prime battle the early Christians fought was with those who only heard pieces of what the truth was or only parts of their service, which then became false rumors that worked against them. During the Last Supper/ Passover's Seder Meal, Jesus instituted the Eucharist (communion) by declaring the matzah to be his body, and the fourth glass of wine to be his blood (Luke 22: 15-19). From John 6:51 and 53, Jesus declares himself to be the living bread and drink for humanity: "I am the living bread that came down from heaven. If anyone eats of this bread, he will live forever. This bread is my flesh, which I will give for the life of the world... Jesus said to them, "I tell you the truth, unless you eat the flesh of the Son of Man and drink his blood, you have no life in you." From these lines that were quoted from one Christian to another to help them understand the importance and new interpretation of the Passover Meal, eavesdroppers spread the rumors that the Christians were a cult that used human sacrifice in their celebrations.[150] This began a panic that spread throughout the Roman Empire, resulting in Christians being routinely executed for their beliefs.[151] Christians who understood that the Eucharist/communion was only bread and wine and not a human sacrifice had a difficult time explaining their understanding to those in power, resulting in centuries of persecutions. Even in the present day, the Eucharist is a tangible remembrance of Christ's past sacrifice and a way of keeping ourselves connected to Christ, not a sacrifice itself. However, for new Christians, this sacrament is a concept that takes time to fully understand and accept.

Within the Harry Potter fandom, there are many fans that are not Christian, and some of these followers do revel a bit in the games of Quidditch, the healing processes of herbology and potions, and the forecasting of the divination class. However, these people are still seeking for the whole truth, but without a guide, they will have a difficult time seeing the whole truth of God, just as Philip needed to help the Eunuch

---

[150] Walton, "Why were the early Christians persecuted?" *The Theologian,* retrieved from http://www.theologian.org.uk/churchhistory/persecution.html.
[151] Walton, 2005, "Why were the early Christians persecuted?" *The Theologian,* retrieved from http://www.theologian.org.uk/churchhistory/persecution.html.

understand the writings of Isaiah (Act 8:30-38). Those who do truly understand the truth within the Harry Potter series can only explain part of it at a time, and an eavesdropper would hear only part of the Biblical connection. For instance, the Deathly Hallows symbol seems to represent the trinity and not the occult.[152] However, if the eavesdropper only hears that the group is creating Deathly Hallows jewelry and doesn't listen to the Biblical connection, then the eavesdropper might go away believing his brothers and sisters in Christ were lost in witchcraft and sorcery. As demonstrated, it is important that people hear the whole truth, and not only part of it, since it is the whole picture that shows Christ. Parts of the whole have only led to misinformation and a continuity of the divide amongst Christians about the Harry Potter material.

New Traditions Discovered

Lastly, throughout the course of Christian history, as Christians spread the good news around the known world, they found that the people had discovered some truth of who God was on their own. Many times, these ideas were incorporated into the cultural understanding since it provided some common ground for those indigenous people to accept the concepts in order to help the masses convert to Christianity (i.e. The Lady of Guadalupe story). This contributed to the cultural diversity of the religion, but it helped the local people establish a relationship with Christ much sooner. Through the years, many of these traditions have become mainstays of the Christian tradition, even if they were initially denounced. For instance, when those in authority were trying to help the druids understand who Christ was, they incorporated the pagan evergreen trees into the Christmas celebration despite earlier criticism from Tertullian in the early fourth century that suggests he felt it was a pagan custom not to be found in his home.[153] Nowadays, most people's first thought of

---

[152] WordPress.com, 2010, "The Deeper Meaning of the Quest for the Deathly Hallows," retrieved from http://phoenixweasley.wordpress.com/2010/09/26/the-deeper-meaning-of-the-quest-for-the-deathly-hallows/.

[153]Tait, E. and J., 2008, "Why do we have Christmas Trees?" *Christianity Today,* retrieved from http://www.christianitytoday.com/ch/thepastinthepresent/storybehind/whychristma

Christmas is the tree itself, with its evergreens representing the everlasting love of God. Many other traditions, such as the clerical robes, stemmed from the local Roman customs and the color schemes were converted into Christian symbols as well,[154] giving the Christian churches many examples of how one element can be understood in many different ways.

Common Faith, Uncommon Traditions

Within this multidimensional context of meaning, J.K. Rowling's concept of who Christ is and what "church" means is probably very different from someone in America who has never been to a church more than fifty years old, in a land where any whisper of witchcraft near a church resulted in death. Of course there is conflict here between the cultural differences of their common Christian heritage! However, conflict can help both sides see that there might be another side to the interpretation, helping both sides grow in their faith. Because of the differences in interpretation and culture passed down through history, the various denominations of Christianity reflect these differences in their practices, art, and decorum. Some explanations are rooted in history, some in faith, and some in tradition. However, despite the differences, Christians of all denominations have at its core the love, sacrifice, and resurrection of Jesus the Christ, Son of God, as described in the Apostles' Creed. Just as Christians need to embrace each other across the denominations, we should also first forego our own cultural and religious differences with J.K. Rowling, then embrace her as a Christian with a Scottish cultural understanding of Christian history, traditions, and faith and seek to find the truth within her interpretation before condemning her work.

To further clarify her background, we must realize that in Scotland and England, fewer than 10% of the people attend church each week.[155]

---

strees.html.

[154] Smith, Roger, "The History and Use of Vestments in the Church," 1997, retrieved from http://www.awakentoprayer.org/vestments.htm.

[155] News.scotsman.com, 2008, "Catholic Church moves into Pole Position,"

J.K. Rowling herself was raised in a rather atheist household (only her mother went to services mostly at Christmas and Easter), but when a neighbor invited her to come to church for the first time when she was twelve, she attended church and came to know God.[156] As an Anglican, she would have seen many white-washed walls inside very ornate but old buildings, but she would also have seen many of the older Catholic churches from around Europe that still have the soot on the walls from centuries in the past. She portrays this image and feeling in her depiction of the magical realm as old, dark, and sooty. In churches that still carry centuries of history, the windows tell stories for those who cannot read. This symbolic reflection of the past helped shape J.K. Rowling's understanding of who God is and who we are called to be as Christians.

The symbols incorporated within the church building remind people of the spiritual realm of God, and other symbols within the pictures speak to their God-given strengths or attributes impossible to draw – divinity, courage, love, faith, and/or wisdom. These symbols – halos, unicorns, phoenixes, and owls – are used extensively to carry these same ideas to the reader and were a key element in story telling during the iconoclast period. Within the culture of the British Isles there also lies an unswerving devotion to fantasy beginning with the legends around King Arthur. The stories that were passed down speak of mythical creatures that were created not only to capture the imagination, but also to remind us of those qualities sought by God – innocence, purity, and faith - in addition to the legends of King Arthur's pursuit for the Holy Grail.[157] There is an early history of a less God-centered past – piracy, druidism, paganism –

---

retrieved from http://www.scotsman.com/news/catholic_church_moves_into_pole_position_1_1433537.

[156] Klimek, D, 2010, Ministry Values, "J.K. Rowling: "I believe in God, not Magic" and the Unknown Faith of the Famous," retrieved from http://ministryvalues.com/index.php?option=com_content&task=view&id=1203&Itemid=318.

[157] "Holy Grail and King Arthur," retrieved from http://www.legendofkingarthur.co.uk/holy-grail.htm.

but many of those histories gave the Scots newer understandings and counterpoint to Christianity before being forgotten. As echoes of the past, these mythical creatures have made their way into stories throughout English Christian literature, and J.K. Rowling's works, subliminally tuning people towards the majesty and mystery of God.

For many Christians, converting to Christianity was not something they remember choosing – their parents raised them in that faith, and they stuck with it. However, there are many who did not begin their lives in faith, but came to faith at a later age. Not too many people know that in *Harry Potter and the Philosopher's Stone,* we see much of J.K. Rowling's own beginnings in Harry's beginnings. She came to faith at twelve after a neighbor's church invitation, and her atheistic family did not want to hear anything about God – the subject was tabooed from her house, much as magic is tabooed from the Dursley's house.

A Matter of What We Choose to Believe

To come to an even fuller appreciation of Rowling's world of Harry Potter, we should also imagine the magical community to be a Christian community that has had to go into secrecy within a secular society that no longer acknowledges God's existence. Harry Potter's magical world, much like the early Christian world, has its own money system, its own holidays, and its own benchmarks that establish adulthood, and its own laws and enforcement agency. Many of these traditions still hold true today – the bar mitzvah defines an adult in the Jewish faith, just as confirmation determines adulthood in the Christian faith, despite the fact that these ages are much younger than the typical secular age of majority, 18. Since people tend to choose to see what they want to see, the non-magical people within Harry Potter never see magic (God) at work around them – they chose to believe anything except the truth about magic (God). This ultimate truth is still here today – given the same tree, some will see God in the making of the tree, and others will just see a random act of nature. Much of how we interpret things is what we allow ourselves to believe, a theme carried to the fullest throughout the Harry Potter series in brilliant detail.

Amidst all of the details that J.K. Rowling put into the Harry Potter series, we can interpret these details in two different ways. We could take elements out of context and at face value, and take the series to be one of witchcraft and magic, just as the Romans misinterpreted the early Christian rituals. We could also take elements that have both pagan and Christian ideas and choose to believe that J.K. Rowling was indeed endorsing only those pagan ideas that were in antithesis to Christianity. I will admit that in my research, I found an equal number of references to druidism or ancient beliefs as I did Christian references and beliefs, but it is what we believe something is that makes it what it is. For instance, when we use the Advent wreath to help count down the Sundays to Christmas, we could see it as the ancient wreath celebrating pagan holidays, or we could see it as the everlasting love of God with the increasing light of Christ. Since Christians believe the advent wreath to symbolize God and Christ, they have established that as their eternal interpretation, and handed down the belief from generation to generation. In parallel, J.K. Rowling's wands can be seen as something that wizards use and thus must necessarily be evil, or we could remember John 5:15 "I am the vine, you are the branches", and see that the wands are more likely symbolic of the power of God, the "branch" of Christ in the world.

Nowadays, rather than help others explain our traditions when we come under scrutiny, we tend to go into hiding and retreat more into ourselves rather than being out in the world to comfort others and help them see the love of God. Similarly, although J.K. Rowling's use of symbolism, bestiality, and alchemy have traditionally been considered a lesser connected form of seeking God, she was able to find the truth within these elements and bring them into a Christian context in a brilliant manner. However, rather than explain them when Christians attack her for her use of these elements, she withdraws and says little. She has declared openly that she is Christian, attends church weekly, and has had her children baptized in the church.[158] Her ability to see God within these

---

158 Klimek, David, "J.K. Rowling: 'I Believe in God, not Magic' and the Unknown

other elements is a true testament of her faith since Christians are called upon to see Christ in everyone and everything they do (Matthew 25:31-46). All in all, we should first ask questions lovingly in order to understand the other point of view, and then if they are of similar faith to ourselves, we should give them the benefit of a doubt and seek the truth they feel they have presented.

Unfortunately, most of those who spoke out against the Harry Potter series did so before J.K. Rowling was able to tell the entire story, setting up feelings of distrust and premature renunciation for both parties. Since the end of the series was available, J.K. Rowling has attempted to explain the Christian elements within the series with limited success. The rumors of witchcraft persist, echoed by those who choose to see that element out of context. Over time, we hope that both sides will begin to trust each other again as they come to understand the contexts of Rowling's writings and she continues to be open to meetings and discussions with others.

Faith of the Famous," *Ministry Values*, 2010, <http://ministryvalues.com/index.php?option=com_content&task=view&id=1203&Itemid=318>.

Works Cited

"A Brief Introduction to Alchemy." Magical Path. 2011. Web. 30 Aug. 2011. <http://magicalpath.net/a-brief-introduction-to-alchemy/>.

Adler. Shawn. "J.K. Rowling Opens Up about Books' Christian Imagery." 2007. Web. 4 Apr. 2012. <http://www.mtv.com/>.

"Alchemy Electronic Dictionary." International Alchemy Guild. 2011. Web. 15 Aug. 2011. <http://www.alchemylab.com/dictionary.htm#sectQ

Alchin, Linda. "Middle Ages Religion." *The Middle Ages.* 20 Sep. 2006. Web. 30 Aug 2011. <http://www.middle-ages.org.uk/middle-ages-religion.htm>.

Anonymous. "Catholic Church moves into Pole Position." *The Scotsman.* 24 May 2008. Web. 30 May 2012. <http://www.scotsman.com/news/catholic_church_moves_into_pole_position_1_1433537>.

Anonymous. "Dragon." *Mysterious Britain and Ireland.* N.d. Web. 30 May 2012. <http://www.mysteriousbritain.co.uk/legends/dragons.html>.

Anonymous. "Incorruptibles." Overcomeproblems.com. 2004. Web. 30 Aug. 2011. <http://www.overcomeproblems.com/incorruptables.htm>.

Anonymous. "J.K. Rowling." British Council. 2011. Web. 30 Apr. 2012. <http://literature.britishcouncil.org/j-k-rowling>.

Anonymous. *Jewish Death and Funeral Rites.* "Religious Facts." 2004. Web. 4 Apr. 2012. <http://www.religionfacts.com/judaism/cycle/death.htm>.

Anonymous. "Orthodox Icons: History of Icons." Religion Facts. 8 February 2007. Web. 30 May 2012. <http://www.religionfacts.com/christianity/things/icons.htm>.

Anonymous. "Saint Peter." *Catholic Saints.* 2008. Web. 4 Apr. 2012. <http://www.catholic-saints.info/patron-saints/saint-peter.htm>.

Anonymous. "The Romans Destroy the Temple at Jerusalem. 70 AD." *Eyewitness to History.* 2005. Web. 2 Apr. 2012. <www.eyewitnesstohistory.com>.

"A visual interpretation of the Table of Elements." Visual Elements. 2005. Web. 2 Apr. 2012. <http://www.rsc.org/chemsoc/ visualelements/pages/alchemist/alc_antimony.html>.

Baez. John. "Puzzle 17." n.d. Web. 30 May 2012. <http://math.ucr.edu/home/baez /puzzles/17.html>.

Bennett, David. "Why is Christmas Celebrated on December 25th?" *Ancient and Future Catholics.* 2009. Web. 4 Apr. 2012. <http://www.ancient-future.net/christmasdate.html>. Bodnick, Marc. "In Harry Potter, what does "in essence divided" mean?" *Quora*. 2009. Web. 15 Aug. 2011. <http://www.quora.com/In-Harry-Potter-what-does-in-essence-divided-mean>.

"Passage Look-up." *Biblegateway.com*. 2012. Web. Multiple dates of access. <biblegateway.com>.

Bonhoeffer, Dietrich. *The Cost of Discipleship.* United States: Touchstone, 1995. Print.

Broome, Fiona. "Yule history – Pagan and early Christianity." *Celtic Art and History.* 2008. 15 Aug. 2011. <http://celticarthistory.com/yule-history-pagan/>.

Buckwalter, Eleanor. "The Twelfth House." *House of the Month.* 2000. Web. 15 Aug. 2011. <http://www.astrologyclub.org/ articles/planets_signs_houses/pisces/twelfth.htm>.

Butler, Alban, Rev. "St. John, Apostle and Evangelist." *Eternal Word Television Network.* N.d. Web. 4 Apr. 2012. <http://www.ewtn.com/ library/mary/johnevan.htm>.

Caldon, Alex. "Find The Grail." 2012. Web. 4 Apr. 2012. <http://www.theholygrail.org.uk /find_who_found_grail.html>.

"Cappadocian Father." *Encyclopedia Britannia [Online].* Encyclopedia Britannia, Inc.: 2012. Web. 4 Jun 2012. <http://www.britannica.com /EBchecked/topic/94102/Cappadocian-Father>

Charlton, Bruce. "Heart. Mind and Body - Harry. Hermione and Ron." 2011. Web. 4 Apr. 2012. <http://charltonteaching.blogspot.com/ 2011/03/heart-mind-and-body-harry-hermione-and.html>.

Chattaway, Peter. "Giants in the Bible." Religion 303. 2001. Web. May 30, 2012. < http://peter.chattaway.com/articles/giants.htm>.

Chess-poster.com. "The Rook." *Chesmayne: The History of Chess.* 2000. Web. 15 Aug. 2011. <http://www.chess-poster.com/ english/ chesmayne/the_rook.htm>.Colbert. D... *The Magical Worlds of Harry Potter.* New York: Berkley Press, 2002. Print.

Cockren, Archibald. "History of Alchemy from Ancient Egypt to Modern Times." n.d. Web. 2 Apr. 2012. <http://www.alchemylab.com /history_of_alchemy.htm>.

Dooling, D. M. "What is Alchemy?" n.d. Web. 15 Aug. 2011. <http://www.alchemylab.com/what_is_alchemy.htm>.

Dulle, Jason. "The God-Gene: Is Religious Faith and Experience a Biological Misunderstanding?" *Institute for Religious Studies.* 2000. Web. 15 Aug. 2011. <http://www.onenesspentecostal.com/godgene.htm>.

Elliott, Belinda. "Harry Potter: Harmless Christian Novel or Doorway to the Occult?" the Christian Broadcasting Network. 2007. Web. 30 May 2012. <http://www.cbn.com/spirituallife/OnlineDiscipleship/HarryPotterControversy/elliott_RichardAbanes.aspx>.

"Flower Meanings." *Clare Florist.* FlowerDot Ltd. 2010. Web. 15 Aug. 2011. <http://www.clareflorist.co.uk/meanings.asp>.

Fr. Himes, Michael. "Sacramentality." University of Notre Dame. Spring, 1992: Lecture notes.

"Ginerva 'Ginny' Weasley." Harry Potter Lexicon. 2011. Web. 4 Apr 2012. <http://www.hp-lexicon.org/wizards/ginny.html>.

Granger, John. "Dumbledore a Christ Figure in Half-Blood Prince?" *Hogwarts Professor.* 2009. Web. 2 Apr. 2012. <http://www.hogwartsprofessor.com/is-dumbledore-a-christ-figure-in-half-blood-prince/>.

Granger, John. *How Harry Cast His Spell.* United States: SaltRiver, 2008. Print.

Granger, John. *The Deathly Hallows Lectures.* United States: Zossima Press, 2008. Print.

Granger, John. *The Hidden Key to Harry Potter.* United States: Zossima Press, 2002. Print.

Granger, John. "On Turtleback Tales and Asterisks." *Harry Potter for Nerds.* ed. Travis Prinzi. United States: Unlocking Press, 2011. Print.

Granger, John. *Unlocking Harry Potter, Five Keys for the Serious Reader.* United States: Zossima Press, 2007. Print.

Granger, John. Lecture notes: "Unlocking Potter-Mania: The Christian Content Behind the World's Best Selling Books." Nov 5th. 2010. Vienna. VA.

Harry Potter Wiki. "12 Grimmauld Place." n.d. Web. 30 May 2012. <http://harrypotter.wikia.com/wiki/12_Grimmauld_Place>.

Harry Potter Wiki. "Ginerva Weasley." n.d. Web. 4 Apr. 2012. <http://harrypotter.wikia.com/wiki/Ginevra_Weasley>.

Harry Potter Wiki. "Houses of Hogwarts." n.d. Web. 25 May 2012. <http://harrypotter.wikia.com/wiki /The_four_houses_of_Hogwarts>.

Harry Potter Wiki. "Neville Longbottom." n.d. Web. 4 Apr. 2012. <http://harrypotter.wikia.com/wiki/Neville_Longbottom>.

"Harvest Festivals." Bry-Back Manor. n.d. Web. 30 Aug. 2011. <http://www.bry-backmanor.org/holidayfun/harvestinfo.html>.

"Hedwig meaning and name origin." *Think Baby Names.* 2011. Web. 15 Aug. 2011. <http://www.thinkbabynames.com/meaning/0/Hedwig>.

"Holy Grail and King Arthur." n.d. Web. 30 May 2012. <http://www.legendofkingarthur.co.uk/holy-grail.htm>.

Jones, Terry. "The Golden Legend: The Story of St. Eustace." Saints SQPN. 2012. Web. 30 May 2012. <http://www.catholic-forum.com/saints/golden298.htm>.

Kendall, Paul. "Mythology and Folklore of the Ash." *Trees for Life*. 2011. 15 Aug 2011. <http://www.treesforlife.org.uk/forest/mythfolk/ash.html>.

Kirby, Peter. "Didache." *Early Christian Writings*. 2012. Web. 2 Apr. 2012. <http://www.earlychristianwritings.com/text/1clement-hoole.html>.

Kirby, Peter. "Historical Jesus Theories." *Early Christian Writings*. 2012. Web. 2 Apr. 2012. <http://www.earlychristianwritings.com /text/1clement-hoole.html>.

Klimek, Daniel. "J.K. Rowling: 'I Believe in God, not Magic' and the Unknown Faith of the Famous." Ministry Values. 2010. Web. 2 Apr. 2012.

<http://ministryvalues.com/index.php?option=com_content&task=view&id=1203&Itemid=318>

Lendering, Jona. "Messiah." *Livius: Articles on Ancient History.* 2012. Web. 4 Jun. 2012. <http://www.livius.org/men-mh/messiah/messiah_07.html>.

"LaVeyan Satanism." Wikipedia. 12 May 2012. Web. 4 June 2012. <http://en.wikipedia.org/wiki/LaVeyan_Satanism>.

"Lord Voldemort: Data." Harry Potter Lexicon. 2011. Web. 30 Aug. 2011. <http://www.hp-lexicon.org/wizards/voldemort.html>.

MacDonald, Scott and Norman Kretzmann. In E. Craig (Ed.), "Medieval philosophy." *Routledge Encyclopedia of Philosophy.* London: Routledge, 1998. Web. 4 Apr. 2012. <http://www.rep.routledge.com/article/B078>.

McGough, Richard. "Spoke 8 – Symbolic meaning of the number 8." *Bible Wheel Forum.* 2009. Web. 30 Dec. 2011. <http://www.biblewheel.com/wheel/spokes/chet_eight.asp>

Merton, Reginald. "A Detailed Biography of Nicholas Flamel." Flamel College. Web. 15 Aug 2011. <http://www.flamelcollege.org/flamel.htm>.

Miller, Dave. "Afterlife and the Bible." Apologetics Press, Inc.: 2005. Web. 4 Jun 2012. <http://www.apologeticspress.org/apcontent.aspx?category=11&article=1478>.

Miller, Seth. "Master Thesis: Spirit Alchemy." 2008. Web. 4 Apr 2012. <http://elements.spiritalchemy.com/t3-Ch3.html>.

Morgenstern, Kay. "Mandrake." *Sacred Earth.* 2002. Web. 15 Aug. 2011. <http://www.sacredearth.com/ethnobotany/plantprofiles/mandrake.php>.

Mursurillo, Herbert. "The Martyrdom of Saints Perpetua and Felicitas." Trans. Herbert Mursillo, 1972. Frontline. Apr 28. 1998. Web. 10 Nov. 2011. <http://www.pbs.org/wgbh/pages/frontline/shows/religion/maps /primary/perpetua.html>.

Myth Index. "Cadmus." *Greek Mythology Index.* 2007. Web. 2 Apr. 2012. <http://www.mythindex.com/greek-mythology/C/Cadmus.html>.

No Last Name, Ali. "Hornbeam - Yoke." *Tree Divination.* 2011. Web. 15 Aug. 2011. <http://www.treedivination.com/hornbeam.htm>.

Pascal. Blaise. 1660. *Pensees.* Trans. W. F. Trotter. 2003. Web. 2 Apr. 2012. <http://oregonstate.edu/instruct/phl302/texts/pascal/pensees-a.html>.

"Paul." *Bible Encyclopedia [Online].* Christian Answers Network. N.d. Web. 30 May 2012. <http://www.christiananswers.net/dictionary/paul.html>.

Peck, John. "The Trinity in the Writings of St Ignatius." *Preacher's Institute.* 2012. Web. 4 Apr. 2012. <http://preachersinstitute.com/2010/10/17/the-trinity-in-the-writings-of-ignatius-of-antioch/>.

Perrine, Ted. "Pensees." *Christian Classics Ethereal Library.* 2011. Web. 30 May 2012. <http://www.ccel.org/p/pascal/pensees/>.

Phoenixweasley. "The Deeper Meaning of the Quest for the Deathly Hallows." WordPress.com. 2010. Web. 30 May 2012. <http://phoenixweasley.wordpress.com/2010/09/26/the-deeper-meaning-of-the-quest-for-the-deathly-hallows/>.

Porter, Betsy. "Gilding, Gold Leaf over Red Bole." *Art and Iconography*. 2011. Web. 28 Dec. 2011. <http://www.betsyporter.com/gilding.html>.

Raeside, Rob. "An Overview of Pirate's Flags." Pirates. 2012. Web. 4 Apr. 2012. http://www.crwflags.com/fotw/flags/pirates.html# overview.

"Ritualized Sexual Magic." Globusz Publishing. 2012. Web. 4 June 2012. <http://www.globusz.com/ebooks/Satanism/00000014.htm>.

Roper, Jack. "Harry Potter: the Hero for Modern Witchcraft." *The Christian Broadcasting Network.* N.d. Web. 30 May 2012. <http://www.cbn.com/spirituallife/onlinediscipleship/harrypottercontroversy/harrypotterheromodernwitchcraft.aspx>.

Rose, Or N., Rabbi. "Heaven and Hell in Jewish Tradition." *My Jewish Learning.* 2012. Web. 30 May 2012. <http://www.myjewishlearning.com/beliefs/Theology/Afterlife_and_Messiah/Life_After_Death/Heaven_and_Hell.shtml>

Rowling, J. K. *Harry Potter and the Chamber of Secrets.* New York: Scholastic, 1998. Print.

Rowling, J. K. *Harry Potter and the Deathly Hallows.* New York: Scholastic, 2007. Print.

Rowling, J. K. *Harry Potter and the Goblet of Fire*. New York: Scholastic, 2000. Print.

Rowling, J. K. *Harry Potter and the Half Blood Prince*. New York: Scholastic, 2005. Print.

Rowling, J. K. *Harry Potter and the Order of the Phoenix*. New York: Scholastic, 2003. Print.

Rowling, J. K. *Harry Potter and the Prisoner of Azkaban*. New York: Scholastic, 1999. Print.

Rowling, J. K. *Harry Potter and the Sorcerer's Stone*. New York: Scholastic, 1997. Print.

Rowling, J.K. Interview with The Volkskrant. Trans. Dee. "New Interview with J.K. Rowling for Release of Dutch Edition of 'Deathly Hallows.'" *The Leaky Cauldron*. 2007. Web. 30 May 2012. <http://www.the-leaky-cauldron.org/2007/11/19/new-interview-with-j-k-rowling-for-release-of-dutch-edition-of-deathly-hallows>.

Rowling, J. K. "J.K. Rowling Q&A." Mugglenet. Web. 4 Apr. 2012. <http://www.mugglenet.com/jkr-royalalbert.shtml>.

Rowling, J. K. "J.K. Rowling Q & A Session at Royal Albert Hall." Interview with Stephen Fry. *Mugglenet*. 2012. Web. 30 May 2012. <http://www.mugglenet.com/jkr-royalalbert.shtml>.

Sandels, Victoria. "Cadmus." *History and Mythology*. 2010. Web. 2 Apr. 2012. <http://www.in2greece.com/english/historymyth/mythology /names/cadmus.htm>.

Shakespeare, William. "Romeo and Juliet." Comp. Jeremy Hylton. N.d. Web. 4 Jun. 2012. http://shakespeare.mit.edu/romeo_juliet/.

Simmons, Bowen. "Perhaps Augustine's most difficult work." *The Trinity*. 2002. Online review. 4 Apr. 2012. <http://www.amazon.com/ Trinity-Saint-Augustine/dp/0911782966>.

"Saint Anthony. Desert Father." Passionist Nuns. N.d. Web. 4 Apr. 2012. <http://www.passionistnuns.org/Saints/StAnthonyDesert/index.htm>.

"Samaritan", *Encyclopaedia Britannica [Online],* Encyclopaedia Britannia, Inc.: 2012. <http://www.britannica.com/EBchecked/topic/ 520295/Samaritan>

Sloyan, Gerard. "Christian Persecution of Jews over the Centuries." United States Holocaust Memorial Museum. n.d. Web. 30 May 2012. <http://www.ushmm.org/research/center/church/persecution/persecution.pdf>.

Smith, Roger. "The History and Use of Vestments in the Church." 1997. Web. 30 May 2012. <http://www.awakentoprayer.org/vestments.htm>.

"St. George." *Saints and Angels*. Catholic Online. N.d. Web. 30 Aug. 2011. <http://www.catholic.org/saints/saint.php?saint_id=280>.

Tait, Edwin, and Jennifer Tait. "Why Do We Have Christmas Trees?" *Christianity Today.* 2008. Web. 30 May 2012. <http://www.christianitytoday.com/ch/thepastinthepresent/storybehind/whychristmastrees.html>.

The Alchemy Dictionary. 2012. Web. 2 Apr 2012. <http://www.alchemylab.com/dictionary.htm>.

The Blue Roebuck. "Rook." *The Blue Roebuck.* 2008. Web. 14 Aug. 2011. <http://www.blueroebuck.com/rook.html>.

The Catholic Community of Northwest Wyoming. "History of Christian Initiation of Adults." 2012. Web. 30 May 2012. <http://www.stanthonycody.org/rcia-history.html>.

Troll Collectors Center. "The History of the Ny Form Troll." 2010. Web. 30 Aug. 2011. <http://www.trollsofnorway.com/>

Trueman, Chris. "Mary Queen of Scots." *History Learning Site.* 2011. Web. 15 Aug. 2011. <http://www.historylearningsite.co.uk/mary_queen_of_scots.htm>.

Tucker, Suzetta. "ChristStory Deer Page." *ChristStory Christian Bestiary*. 1997. Web. 2 Apr. 2012. <http://ww2.netnitco.net/~legend01/stag.htm>.

Tzu, Sun, "Sun Tzu Quotes (Author of "The Art of War"), Goodreads, 2012. Web. 4 Jun 2012. <http://www.goodreads.com/ author/quotes/1771.Sun_Tzu>.

Venefica, Avia. "Elemental alchemy symbols." *What's Your Sign.com.* 2011. Web. 30 Aug. 2011. <http://www.whats-your-sign.com/elemental-alchemy-symbols.html>.

Walton, Stephen. "Why Were the Early Christians Persecuted?" *The Theologian. [Online].* 2005. Web. 30 May 2012. <http://www.theologian.org.uk/churchhistory/persecution.html>.

Wesley, John. "Journal of John Wesley." *Christian Classics Ethereal Library*. Multiple editors. 2005. Web. 2 Apr. 2012. <http://www.ccel.org/ccel/wesley/journal

Wikipedia. "Astral plane." n.d. Web. 15 Aug. 2012. <http://en.wikipedia.org/wiki/Astral_plane>.

Wikipedia. "classical element." 2011. Web. 15 Aug. 2011. <http://en.wikipedia.org/wiki/Classical_element#Elements_in_Medieval_alchemy>.

Wikipedia. "Draco Malfoy." 2011. Web. 2 Aug. 2011. <http://en.wikipedia.org/wiki/Draco_Malfoy#cite_note-3>.

WiseGEEK. "What is a Death Mask?" 2011. Web. 2 Apr. 2012. <http://www.wisegeek.com/what-is-a-death-mask.htm>.

Yates, David, dir. *Order of the Phoenix*. Warner Brothers, 2007. Film.

White, Michael. "In the Catacombs." *Frontline*. 1998. Web. 10 Apr. 2012. <http://www.pbs.org/wgbh/pages/frontline/shows/religion/first/catacombs.html>.

ABOUT THE AUTHOR

Leslie Barnhart lives in the Washington, D.C. area with her husband and children, where she teaches high school math and science. She holds a Bachelor's in Science in Mathematics from the University of Notre Dame, a Master's in .Business Administration from Chapman University, and a Master's in Education From George Mason University. She enjoys music, reading, working with students, and spending time with her family.

ABOUT THE COVER

The cover design is an original design of by the author that depicts the four elements centered around Christ, as specified in Colossians 2:8. Counterclockwise from the upper right is green water, yellow grains from the earth, blue sky/ air, and red fire. The purpose of alchemy is the mastery of the four elements as a step to the gold Philosopher's Stone, which is in the center and above the four elements. However, as Christ is our Philosopher's Stone and his triumph occurred on the cross, the cross appears in the middle of the Stone. All images were taken from free public domain websites.

8486815R00199

Made in the USA
San Bernardino, CA
10 February 2014